Java Tools for Extreme Programming

Mastering Open Source Tools Including Ant, JUnit, and Cactus

Richard Hightower
Nicholas Lesiecki

Wiley Computer Publishing

John Wiley & Sons, Inc.

NEW YORK • CHICHESTER • WEINHEIM • BRISBANE • SINGAPORE • TORONTO

Publisher: Robert Ipsen
Editor: Robert M. Elliott
Managing Editor: John Atkins
Book Packaging: Ryan Publishing Group, Inc.
Copyeditor: Tiffany Taylor

This book is printed on acid-free paper. ∞

Published by John Wiley & Sons, Inc.

Published simultaneously in Canada.

Library of Congress Cataloging-in-Publication Data:

ISBN: 0-471-20708-X

Printed in the United States of America.

10 9 8 7 6 5 4 3 2 1

CONTENTS

ACKNOWLEDGMENTS

First and foremost, I'd like to thank my wife Kiley Hightower for putting up with me on this tight schedule. I spent many a night at a coffee shop with my laptop working until the coffee shop closed.

I really appreciate working with Tim Ryan at Ryan Publishing Group. He orchestrated the work of the editor, contributing authors, co-authors, technical editors, and made this a painless and smooth operation for the authors and team. In addition, Tim provided advice and asked the right questions to guide the book along from the very beginning to the very end. Tim is a true professional. Thanks!

Kudos to my co-author Nicholas Lesiecki! When I put together the outline of this book and pitched it to Tim Ryan, Wiley was excited about the project and put it on the finish-darn-quick list. I agreed to an aggressive schedule, and even considered taking time off from work to complete it, but decided not to. Nick was able to bail me out by stepping up to the plate and taking on a lot of responsibility, and eventually he became the co-author of the book. Thanks Nick.

Much thanks to Scott Fauerbach! Scott went over the pet store baseline application and simplified it a lot. Originally it was very abstract, but a little difficult to understand. Scott ripped through it and simplified it. Together we made it as simple as possible. Scott and I have been on several teams at several companies—we work well together. Scott also did an excellent job on the session bean case study for the business tier of the Pet store application. Thanks, Scott.

Erik Hatcher is a wealth of information on Ant and JUnit. I consulted him many times. It was great having the FAQ moderator for Ant in the office next to you when you are having problems with Ant. Thanks Erik for all of the support.

I'd like to thank Andy Barton for allowing me to host the Web site for the book for free, and Ron Tapia and Chris Lechner for setting up the site. Also, Ron helped me debug problems when porting the application from SQL Server to Hypersonic SQL.

Thanks to Jon Thomas and Paul Visan for stepping up to the plate and taking on case studies. I would like to thank all of the contributing authors, Paul Visan, Erik Hatcher, Jon Thomas and Douglas Albright.

I'd also like to thank Mary Hightower & Richard Hightower (Mom and Dad), Mrs. Wooten my third grade school teacher, and Whitney Hightower for understanding.

Last, but not least, I'd like to thank Avery Regier and Tiffany Taylor for editing the book. Avery was the technical editor, and in my opinion he went above and beyond the call of duty. He had great suggestions and was able to contribute ideas that were readily incorporated into the book. Thanks, Avery. Tiffany, the copyeditor, found every misplaced tab and run on sentence—any remaining mistakes I take full credit for. Let's just say Tiffany had her work cut out for her. Thanks, Tiffany.

ABOUT THE AUTHORS

Rick Hightower is the Director of Development at eBlox, where he leads the adoption of new processes like Extreme Programming, and helps implement coding standards and guidelines for development.

Rick is a software developer at heart with over a decade of development experience in creating frameworks & tools, enforcing processes, and developing enterprise applications using J2EE, XML, UML, CORBA, JDBC, SQL, and Oracle technologies.

Formerly he was the Senior Software Engineer for Java Architecture at Intel's Enterprise Architecture Lab; there he lead a team of developers, designing and implementing three tier client-server applications, introduced O-O CASE tools to his department, and later created several frameworks using a variety of Java, COM, CORBA, middleware technologies. Rick also created ICBeans and authored the patent application for this technology, which was awarded to Intel.

Rick has contributed to several Java books and written articles for the *Java Developer's Journal*. He has also taught classes on developing Enterprise JavaBeans, JDBC, CORBA, Applets as CORBA clients, and EJB.

Nicholas Lesiecki serves eBlox as a Technical Team Lead where he takes charge of team development and architects the company's vertical application framework. Hired as an intern in the middle of the dot-com boom, he has since become a Java master, boasting the 5th highest Java 1 score in the nation according to Brainbench.com. He maintains active committer status on Jakarta's Cactus project and constantly looks for ways to improve code structure through testing and vigorous refactoring.

Nick resides in the heart of Tucson Arizona where the fire-play in the sky at sunset sweeps through his mind and washes strange objects upon the shores of his memory. He lives with his wife Suzanne and their two "children"—Edgar the Dog and Juno the Wonder Cat. All three should be fairly regarded as contributors because of their generous donations of Nick's time. Nick loves his wife very much.

About the Contributors

Doug "Chakka" Albright is a software developer who wrote the Ant tag reference.

Jon Thomas is a Senior Systems Engineer for HealthTrio in Tucson AZ. Prior to HealthTrio he developed Products for eBlox, SimplySay (Voice Portal) and GroupSystems.com, in both Java and VB. Originally from Los Angeles he "escaped" to the hidden jewel of the southwest in 1995. He lives in Tucson with his family, where he writes software, prays everyday, and cheers for the Minnesota Vikings (proof that not all prayers are answered the way we want them to be.) Jon wrote the Ant API reference. In addition, Jon wrote the case study that converted the Pet store sample application to use XML/XSL for the presentation.

Erik Hatcher has more than 10 years of software development experience, most recently with J2EE. He is a Sun Certified Java Programmer, actively involved in Apache's Jakarta efforts, and is the Ant FAQ maintainer at jGuru. Erik is currently a Senior Java Architect for the University of Virginia's Darden Graduate School of Business Administration." He wrote the case study on using HttpUnit. In addition, he provided a technical support for using Ant when we ran into snags.

Paul Visan is a Technical Lead for eBlox, Inc doing exciting J2EE development. He comes from Romania, where he was a close acquaintance of Vlad 'Dracul' a.k.a. 'Dracula' in the western world." He converted the Pet store application to use Struts, and the HttpUnit code to test both the straight JSP version and the Struts version of the application. In addition, he wrote the case study explaining the struts conversion of the pet store application.

Scott Fauerbach is a principal software engineer who specializes in software frameworks and development tools in both the user interface and server side realms of Java. Scott has been developing with Java professionally since it was in Beta and authored a complete set of lightweight GUI components called Widgets, which were included with the first versions of Visual Café.

Scott currently works at FourthStage working on the next level of business-to-business software using Java, SOAP, and JSP. He worked on the Pet Store example, and wrote the case study that moves the business tier of the application to several Enterprise Session beans.

Ron Tapia, systems engineer at eBlox, helped setup the website and debug the application running on Linux.

Introduction

This book describes techniques for implementing the Extreme Programming practices of automated testing and continuous integration using open source tools.

Let's unpack that statement. Automated testing and continuous integration are 2 of the 12 core practices of the Extreme Programming (XP) software development methodology. Extreme Programming is a lightweight software development process that focuses on feedback, communication, simplicity, and courage. The full XP process is summarized in Chapter 1; suffice it to say for now that it consists of common-sense development practices practiced religiously and in concert.

Two of these common-sense practices are testing and frequent integration. Almost no software development shop would consider leaving these steps out of its process entirely—after all, a system has to be integrated to ship, and it must be tested to ensure that the customers accept the shipment. Thanks to the dot-com shakeout, most of the shops that did skip these practices are now out of business. Still, many software companies either struggle with implementing these processes, or acknowledge that they should be done but claim that "things are just too busy right now" to do them. This book explains and demonstrates the use of software tools to help put these valuable practices into place.

Why Spend So Much Time on the Tools?

We focus on tools, ironically enough, because XP is a human-centric development philosophy. It recognizes that the key challenges of writing software are human challenges—such as getting people to work together, helping programmers learn, and managing emotions. Its four core values (communication, feedback, simplicity, and courage) are human values. Most books published on XP so far have focused on the human issues: outlining the philosophy, spreading the ideology (*Extreme Programming Explained* was described by Kent Beck as a manifesto), and talking about the *feeling* of writing software. By doing so, Kent Beck and the originators of XP have followed their own philosophy: Solve the most pressing problems first. However, the current books do not cover the technical details of implementing some of their practices. That's where books like this one come in.

We will explain how to set up continuous integration and automated testing in a Java environment (specifically J2EE, although most of the tools apply generally). Technical detail will be addressed, and we will offer loads of examples to show the tools in action. Specifically, we will cover how to use JUnit, Cactus, HttpUnit, JUnitPerf, and JMeter to write automated tests and how to use Ant (along with the aforementioned tests) to achieve continuous integration.

Who Should Read this Book

Although this book speaks from an XP perspective, you need not practice XP to benefit from it. Anyone who needs help automating testing and integration can benefit from the tools and practices outlined herein. If you know nothing about Extreme Programming, you should probably read the rest of this Introduction, along with Chapter 1 to get a sense of the practices covered in this book, both alone and in their XP context. In particular, the Introduction touches on the value of automated testing and continuous integration for all developers.

This book assumes you are at least a moderately experienced Java developer. Because it covers the application of testing and integration tools to the J2EE platform, this book also expects familiarity with J2EE technologies and development practices. Those who are not interested in J2EE applications will still find plenty of worthwhile material, because most of these tools can be applied to almost any Java (or, in the case of JMeter and HttpUnit, even non-Java) software project. Developers who aren't familiar with J2EE but who want to apply these tools and techniques to a J2EE application may also want to pick up a comprehensive J2EE book like *Developing Java Enterprise Applications, 2nd edition*, by Stephen Asbury and Scott Weiner.

Why Open Source?

It is hard to miss the growing prominence of open source development in software engineering. Of course, *open source* is a buzzword of the moment, but open source development tools do offer compelling advantages over traditional tools—especially for XP development. The advantages fall into two categories. First, open source tools are practical. Second, the open source philosophy is closely aligned with XP.

Open source tools offer several practical advantages:

The price is right. Open source software can almost always be obtained for free; all the tools we cover in this book can be downloaded at no cost from the Internet. Free software means no immediate overhead for yourself or your company, which is always a benefit, but in this case not the major one. The major benefit in the case of these tools is that their adoption will not be hampered by corporate red tape or management worried about buying into the latest fad. Once you have downloaded JUnit, for example, and you've fallen in love with it and spread it to your team—speeding development and improving quality—no one will want to throw roadblocks in your way. Starting the adoption of XP by asking for $7,500 worth of whiz-bang deployment tools might invite skepticism.

The tools are high quality. Programmers use open source development tools every day. Because improving the tool means improving their immediate situation, open source development tools often receive many contributions and bug fixes. Improvement and features come fast and furious.

The tools are the standard. Especially in the case of JUnit and Ant, the tools covered in this book are the standards in their field. Countless open source projects use Ant, and JUnit (upon which several of the tools are based) was written by Kent Beck (the godfather of XP) and Erich Gamma (co-author of the OO classic *Design Patterns: Elements of Reusable Object-Oriented Software*).

Synergy Between XP and Open Source

Extreme Programming and open source development are closely aligned ideologically. Both foster an open, giving style of collaborative development—they share a certain *vibe*, if you will. Both philosophies acknowledge human weakness—no code is perfect, and the assistance of others in finding and fixing problems is gratefully acknowledged. All open source code is commonly owned (as XP would have it). Many open source projects use and benefit from automated testing, which is especially important when code from a wide variety of sources must be integrated. Both systems demand small, incremental releases. Of course, both philosophies also focus heavily on the code—open source is founded on the premise that reading code is enjoyable, educational, and helpful.

The list could continue for quite a while. By using open source tools (and by giving back to the open source community in the form of feedback, assistance, and code) you practice some of the values and processes that make XP great.

Read the Source

If you are looking for more information than this book provides on any of the tools, the best place to start is the source code. In addition to containing the Javadoc (another handy reference), the source code is the definitive authority on the tool's behavior. Open source software exists because (in addition to liking free stuff) programmers value the ability to dig into the work of fellow coders. By reading the source carefully, you can gain insight into how the program works, insight into the domain, and, if you are lucky, insight into the arcane art of programming itself. If you are unlucky enough to encounter a bug while using the tool, having the source handy can help you determine where the bug lies.

Automated Testing: A Summary

XP regards testing as central to the activity of software development. To quote Dan Rawsthorne from the afterword of *Extreme Programming Installed*, "XP works because it is validation-centric rather than product-centric." Testing software continuously validates that the software works and that it meets the customer's requirements. Automating the tests ensures that testing will in fact be continuous. Without testing, a team is just guessing that its software meets those requirements. XP cannot be done without automated testing, nor can *development* be done successfully without it. All software projects need to satisfy the intended customer and to be free of defects.

Tests and Refactoring

Another core XP practice is refactoring (changing existing code for simplicity, clarity, and/or feature addition). Refactoring cannot be accomplished without tests. If you don't practice XP, you may not be refactoring religiously. Even the most stable or difficult-to-change projects require occasional modification. To do it right, programmers will have to change the existing design. That's where automated testing comes in.

Object-oriented programming (and, to a lesser extent, other programming styles) separates interface from implementation. In theory, this means you can change the underlying logic behind a class or method, and dependent code will handle the change seamlessly. Entire books have been written about this powerful abstraction. However, if in practice the programmers are scared to change the underlying logic for fear of disturbing code that interacts with the interface, then this separation might as well not exist. Comprehensive tests (run frequently) verify how the system should work and allow the underlying behavior to change freely. Any problems introduced during a change are caught by the tests. If Design A and Design B produce equivalent results when tested, the code can be migrated from one to the other freely. With testing in place, programmers refactor with confidence, the code works, and the tests prove it.

Types of Automated Tests

Unit tests are the most talked-about test in XP; however, they are only a part of the testing picture. Unit tests cooperate with integration tests, functional tests, and auxiliary tests (performance tests, regression tests, and so on) to ensure that the system works totally.

Unit Tests: JUnit

Unit tests are the first (and perhaps the most critical) line of tests in the XP repertoire. Writing a unit test involves taking a unit of code and testing everything that could possibly break. A unit test usually exercises all the methods in the public interface of a class. Good unit tests do not necessarily test every possible permutation of class behavior, nor do they test ultra-simple methods (simple accessors come to mind); rather, they provide a common-sense verification that the code unit behaves as expected. With this verification, the public interface gains meaning. This approach makes changing unit behavior easier, and also provides a convenient (and verifiable) guide to the behavior of the unit. Developers can consult a test to discover the intended use of a class or method.

In XP, unit tests become part of the cycle of everyday coding. Ideally, programmers write tests *before* the code, and use the test as a guide to assist in implementation. The authors both work in this mode, and we find ourselves unable to live without the guidance and corrective influence of unit tests. After a unit is complete, the team adds the test to the project's test suite. This suite of unit tests runs multiple times per day, and all the tests always pass. This sounds extreme; however, a 100 percent pass rate on unit tests is far more sane than the alternative: a piece of vital production code that *does not work*. (If the code isn't vital, why is it in the project?)

Verifying each class builds a higher-quality system because it ensures that the building blocks work. Unit tests also lead the way toward clean architecture. If a developer writes a test three times for the same code in different locations, laziness and irritation will compel her to move the code to a separate location.

JUnit is a lightweight testing framework written by Erich Gamma and Kent Beck (one of the chief proponents of XP). The authors based its design on SUnit, a successful and popular unit-testing framework written by Beck for Smalltalk. The simplicity of the framework lends itself to rapid adoption and extension. All the testing tools covered in this book (with the exception of JMeter, a GUI tool) interact with or extend the JUnit frame.

Integration/In-Container Tests: Cactus

Unit testing covers Object X, but what about related Objects Y and Z, which together make up subsystem A? Unit tests are deliberately supposed to be isolated. A good unit test verifies that no matter what chaos reigns in the system, at least *this* class functions as expected. Several papers have been written (many can be found at http://www.junit.org) about strategies to avoid dependencies in unit tests (the core idea is to provide mock implementations of objects upon which the tested class depends). By all means, the unit tests should be made as independent as possible.

In their book *Extreme Programming Installed*, Jeffries et al. have an interesting observation about errors that show up only in collaborations between classes; they say, "Our own experience is that we get very few of these errors. We're guessing here, that somehow our focus on testing up front is preventing them." They go on to admit, "When they do show up, such problems are difficult to find." Good unit testing should indeed catch most errors, and the behavior of the *entire* system falls under the category of *acceptance testing* (also known as *functional testing*); however, a good test suite should verify subsystem behavior as well. *Integration testing* occupies the gray area between unit and acceptance testing, providing sanity-check testing that all the code cooperates and that subtle differences between expectation and reality are precisely localized. Integration tests may not always run at 100 percent (a dependency class may not be completed yet, for instance); however, their numbers should be quite high (in the 80 to 90 percent range).

An important variety of integration tests is the *in-container test*. The J2EE development model dictates *components* residing in a *container*. Components rely on *services* provided by the container. Interaction with those services needs to be verified. Although some interactions can be successfully mocked-up, creating mocked implementations for all the services provided by a J2EE container would consume time and verify behavior imperfectly. Some services, such as behaviors specified by deployment descriptors, could be very difficult to test, because container implementations differ.

The Cactus framework provides access to J2EE Web containers (which in turn usually provide access to other types of containers, such as EJB containers). By allowing tests to exercise code in the container, Cactus spares developers the chore of providing extensive or difficult mock-ups (they can use the real services, instead). This approach also provides an extra measure of feedback, because the code runs in an environment that is one step closer to its production habitat. In the case of single objects that just interact with container services, in-container tests serve as quick-and-dirty unit tests.

Acceptance/Functional Tests: HttpUnit

Functional testing ensures that the whole system behaves as expected. These tests are also called *acceptance tests* because they verify for the customer that the system is complete. (In other words, a Web site is not done until it can log in users, display products, and allow online ordering.) Functional tests are daunting in some ways (they are not an immediate productivity aid like unit tests), but they are crucial to measuring progress and catching any defects that slipped past the other tests or result from unimplemented/incomplete features. Acceptance tests are written by the customer (the programmers may implement them) because they are for the customer. Unit testing verifies for the programming team that the Foo class works correctly. Acceptance tests verify for the customer (who may not know a Foo from a Bar) that their whole system works correctly.

Acceptance tests are less dependent upon specific implementation: For example, during an aggressive refactoring, the team may decide they no longer need a SubCategory object. If so, the SubCategoryTest goes to execute in the Big Container in the Sky. The team modifies the integration tests (if necessary) to account for the new system structure. However, the functional tests remain unchanged, validating that the user's experience of the catalog navigation system remains unchanged.

Functional tests do not need to *always* run at 100 percent, but they should do so before the software is released. Functional tests often verify specific *stories* (an XP representation of a customer-requested feature). As such, they can track progress through a development cycle. Each test that runs represents a finished feature.

Unfortunately but understandably, no one has written a universal acceptance-testing tool. JUnit can work on just about any Java class, but an acceptance-testing tool must be tailored to the needs of a specific application. For a number-crunching program, acceptance testing could be as easy as verifying inputs versus outputs. For a data-entry application, a GUI recording and playback tool might be necessary.

We chose to cover HttpUnit, a testing API that allows programmatic calls to Web resources and inspection of the responses. The framework cooperates with JUnit and exposes the underlying structure of an HTML page to allow easy verification of structural elements. (The response to show_product.jsp returns a table with product prices.) It seemed a natural fit for the focus of this book, because J2EE is heavily concerned with Web components. Acceptance testing the deeper components of J2EE might not even require a special framework because of the low level of presentation logic involved.

Performance Tests: JUnitPerf and JMeter

Several types of testing exist besides basic verification of function parallel tests (verifies that a new system exactly like an old system), performance tests, validation tests (the system responds well to invalid input), and so on. Of these, performance testing is perhaps the most widely applicable. After all, the most functional system in the world won't be worth a dime if end users give up on the software in disgust. Client-side applications that perform poorly are trouble; server-side applications that drag are emergencies. J2EE applications are usually hosted on servers handling anywhere from hundreds to thousands (and up!) of transactions per minute, so a small section of inefficient code can bring a system to its knees. In this sort of environment, performance ranks with functional (or even unit) testing in its priority.

We will not be covering performance profiling tools (critical to solving performance issues); rather, we'll discuss the testing tools used to uncover these problems early. JUnitPerf does unit performance testing—it *decorates* existing JUnit tests so that they fail if their running times exceed expectations. Such tests support refactoring by verifying that performance-critical code remains within expected boundaries. JMeter provides functional performance testing—measuring and graphing response times to requests sent to a remote server (Web, EJB, database, and so on). With JMeter, customers can write acceptance tests like, "The Web server will maintain a three-second or better response time to requests with a 150-user simultaneous load."

Continuous Integration: A Summary

Continuous integration is another XP practice that benefits from the use of good software tools. In essence, continuous integration means building a complete copy of the system so far (and running its full test suite) several times per day. By doing this, you can be sure the system is ready to walk out the door (at least as ready as it could possibly be) at any moment. This process must be relatively automatic (a single command, perhaps on a timer, builds and tests the whole system), or no one would ever do it. There are several reasons for spending the set-up time and energy to achieve continuous integration: The customer and team can see progress on the system, integration bugs are reduced, and the tests are run frequently.

Visible Progress

Continuous integration includes something subtle that goes beyond its practical benefits. It affirms the unity of the team development effort. The built and tested system acts as a center of gravity toward which all development is pulled. As a developer, you know that as soon as you check code into the repository, it will be pulled into the main development stream. You're less likely storm off in your own direction if you know that later that day your code will be playing with the entire system. Anyone can see the state of the working system at any time; and as more acceptance tests pass and new features show up in the built system, coders sense the progress toward the goal and gain confidence in its eventual attainment. (If the built system languishes and acceptance test scores don't rise, this signals serious trouble that might have lain dormant far longer in an un-integrated system.)

Reduced Integration Pain

If class X doesn't jibe with class Y, it makes sense to know about the problem as soon as possible. The longer the X and Y go before meeting, the fuzzier the authors' memories will be on the subject when the time comes to discover the show-stopping X vs. Y bug. Continuous integration makes sure the incompatible dance partners meet within hours or minutes. Not only does it solve the immediate problem (the defect introduced by incompatible changes), but it forces the developers concerned to examine why the defect might have occurred in the first place: "Ah, I see, Sandra already refactored the CapriciousDictator class, so there's no reason for me to have added the extraEnforcement method to OppressiveRegime." A cleaner (and working!) system results.

Tests Run Frequently

Unit testing is an integral part of a continuously integrated system. The build is not complete until the unit tests have all passed at 100 percent and the functional and integration tests have run. The result is not only a system that runs but also one that is proven to run correctly. Tests lose value if they aren't run frequently. If they are run as often as the build, and the build is frequent, they provide a constant update on how the system performs.

Restart!

The first big software project I worked on was a mess...but it had continuous integration. Why? The team, who were a bunch of inexperienced Java developers, couldn't get a reliable build running on anyone's machine. Too many dependencies and libraries had to be linked in for anyone to get them straightened out with the mounting pressure of an impossible deadline. Finally, we had someone cobble together a shell-based build script that compiled all the code that currently resided on the integration server. Because no one could compile individual files locally, in order to see something work, it had to be uploaded to the integration server.

With five or six developers working simultaneously, the script was run (and the Web server restarted) about once every five minutes. The developer hoping to integrate had to shout for permission before actually restarting the server: "Anybody mind a restart?!" The result was chaos—but if anyone's changes clashed, we knew about it within seconds.

Continuous Integration and J2EE

Under the J2EE development model, applications undergo significant customization during assembly and deployment. Wrapping and packaging a full J2EE application requires in-depth knowledge of different archive formats (JARs, WARs, and EARs), deployment descriptors, and methods of deploying applications and components into existing containers. Given the complexity of a J2EE build, an automated build tool is required.

Ant to the Rescue

Unlike many of the other practices of XP, achieving continuous integration is mainly a technical feat. Once an automated process is in place, using it should be easy (and beneficial) enough that developers barely have to breathe on it to keep the monster rolling. All a shop needs to begin continuous integration is a tool set to help automate and put together a repeatable build. This book will cover Ant, the emerging standard for build automation in Java.

Ant allows developers to write tests in an XML build script that calls on Java classes to do its work. The tool is cross-platform (a critical criteria for any Java-based tool) and easy to extend and modify. Ant performs all the basic tasks of a build tool: compilation, archive creation, classpath management, and so on. It also supports test and report automation as well as a variety of miscellaneous useful tasks, such as source control interaction, FTP, and property file editing. This arsenal of predefined build tasks allows developers to automate complicated build processes with ease. After some work with Ant, a Java application can be retrieved from source control, built, customized to its intended environment (production versus integration for instance), tested, and deployed to a remote server with a single command.

How This Book Is Organized

This book is divided into three parts:

Part I: Introduction and Key Concepts. This part begins with an overview of the Extreme Programming methodology—a short course for beginners and a review for practitioners. The overview allows you to see where the practices covered in this book (automated testing and continuous integration) fit into the larger picture of XP. Chapter 2 explains the J2EE build and deployment model, highlighting the need for an automated build tool to assist in the process. The section ends with an introduction to the sample application that will be built, tested, and refactored multiple times during the course of the book.

Part II: Mastering the Tools. Each chapter in Part II tutors developers on a particular tool. Chapters 4 through 6 cover continuous integration with Ant, and each of the remaining chapters covers an automated testing tool. The tutorials use code samples to illustrate how to leverage the tools to build, test, deploy, and refactor your code. By the end of Part II, you should be able to use all the tools together.

Part III: API and Tag Reference. The reference section delves into the details of the APIs covered in this book. All the classes, variables, and methods (or tags and attributes, in the case of Chapter 12, "Ant Tag Reference") needed to use an API are covered in standard Javadoc style, along with extensive code samples illustrating their use in context.

What's on the Web Site

All the configuration scripts, build scripts, applications, and other source code in this book are available online at www.wiley.com/compbooks/hightower. Posted along with the sample code and installation instructions are errata (especially necessary for fast-moving open source APIs) and other follow-up information. Information about other books in this series is available at www.wiley.com/compbooks.

CHAPTER 1

Introduction to Extreme Programming

This chapter is an overview of the Extreme Programming (XP) methodology as it applies to developing enterprise-level software in Java. You do not have to adopt the entire XP methodology to get value out of this book and chapter. Automated testing, for example, can help you refactor code regardless of whether you are doing pair programming. Continuous integration can help you detect and fix problems early in the lifecycle of the system regardless of whether your customer is on site. However, because this book discusses XP throughout, it is useful to have a short overview of the entire methodology. If you are already familiar with XP, you may want to turn directly to Chapter 2, "J2EE Deployment Concepts."

XP Overview

XP is a lightweight methodology that focuses on coding as the main task. With XP, the code-centric activities are in every stage of the software development lifecycle. Some practitioners of more traditional methodologies (most seem to be CASE tool vendors) have criticized XP, claiming that it involves reckless coding and is not a real process.

On the contrary, XP is an extremely disciplined methodology that centers on constant code review; frequent testing; customer involvement and rapid feedback; incessant refactoring and refining the architecture; continuous integration to discover problems early in the development process; ongoing design and redesign; and constant planning. The following sections of this chapter discuss the core values, principles, and practices of XP.

Four Values of XP

Kent Beck, originator of the XP methodology, defined four key values of XP:

- Communication
- Simplicity
- Feedback
- Courage

Communication is facilitated through pair programming, task estimation, iteration planning, and more. The goal of communication is to provide a place where people can freely discuss the project without fear of reprisal.

Simplicity may seem counterintuitive because it is common in our industry to overly complicate our development projects. The aim of a project is not for the alpha developer to show his technical prowess, but to deliver value to the customer. Don't over-design algorithms. Don't create an artificial intelligence system when all you need is a few if statements. Don't use EJB or XSLT just because doing so will look nice on your résumé. Choose the simplest design, technology, algorithms, and techniques that will satisfy the customer's needs for the current iteration of the project.

Feedback is crucial and is obtained through code testing, customers' stories, small iterations/frequent deliveries, pair programming/constant code reviews, and other methods. For example, if you are unit-level testing all the code you write several times a day, you are constantly getting feedback about the quality and production worthiness of the system. If something is wrong, you will know right away, instead of being unpleasantly surprised the night before product launch.

Courage is all about being brave enough to do what is right. Have you ever worked on a project where people were afraid to throw away code? I have. The code was horrible and convoluted, and it systematically broke every style, rule, and convention. Yet management and quite a few developers were afraid to throw away the code because they weren't sure how discarding it would affect the system. If you follow the tenets of XP, you will not have this problem. Unit regression testing builds an intense sense of courage. When you know the changes you make will not break the system in some unforeseen way, then you have the confidence to refactor and re-architect code. Testing is key to courage.

If, after several iterations of a project, you find a cleaner, less expensive, more performant way of developing a system, you will have the courage to implement it. I have, and it is a blast.

> ### If the Code Smells, Refactor It
>
> **In his landmark book *Refactoring: Improving the Design of Existing Code,* Martin Fowler describes code that needs to be refactored as having a certain objectionable smell.**
>
> **We have to have the courage to throw away code. Coding, like writing, gets better with revisions.**

Five Principles of XP

Building on the four values of XP, Beck created five overriding principles for XP development:

- Provide rapid feedback
- Assume simplicity
- Make incremental changes
- Embrace change
- Do quality work

The idea behind rapid feedback is that the faster you get feedback, the more quickly you can respond to it and the more it guides the process of designing, coding, and delivering the system. This feedback does not simply focus on automated testing and continuous integration to spot problems early, but also encompasses short iterations that are given to the customer to ensure that the system they need is ultimately delivered. This constant steering and learning helps keep the cost of change low and enables the developer to assume simplicity.

Assuming simplicity means treating every problem as a simple problem until proven otherwise. This approach works well, because most problems are easy to solve. However, it is counterintuitive to common thought on reuse and software design. Assuming simplicity does not mean skipping the design step, nor does it mean simply slinging code at a problem. Assuming simplicity requires that you design *only* for the current iteration. Because you are getting rapid feedback from the customer as requirements change, you will not waste time redoing code that was designed to be thermonuclear-resistant when all that was needed was a little waterproofing. The fact is, the customer's requirements always change during the development process, so why not embrace the alterations? My feeling has always been that the true test of every design is when the rubber meets the road—that is, when you are coding.

Incremental change fits nicely with simplicity. Don't over-design a system. It is always better to do a little at a time. Let's say you have decided to redo a Web application that currently uses XSLT (a technology for transforming XML data) so that it instead uses JavaServer Pages (JSP; a technology that is commonly used to create dynamically generated Web pages), to improve performance of the system.

Instead of attacking the whole system, why not just incrementally change the pages that get the most traffic first, thus getting the biggest bang for the buck while minimizing risk? As more and more of the system is done, you may decide to leave some parts using XSLT; or, after partially finishing the JSP version, you may decide to do something else. By testing and deploying on a small scale, you can make decisions based on live feedback that you otherwise could not make. This is the rubber hitting the road. (By the way, I am making no design judgments on XSL or JSP. This is just an example for illustration.)

It has been said that a picture is worth a thousand words. Well, a working model deployed to production is worth a thousand pictures. This is the synergy among rapid feedback, incremental change, and keeping it simple. XP goes further than incrementally changing the system. XP relishes change; it embraces change.

Have you ever heard a developer or a project manager declare that once the requirements were set, the customer should not change them? I have. This requirement seemed logical, but wait—isn't the system being built for the customer?

Conversely, XP developers relish and embrace change. Change is expected, because you are delivering business value incrementally to the customer. The customer has plenty of time to give rapid feedback and request needed changes. This process improves the quality of the system by ensuring that the system being built is the one the customer really needs. Customer are happy because they can steer the next revision before the project gets too far off track from their current business needs.

One of the things that drove me to XP was the principle of quality work. I feel better about myself when I deliver quality work. Early in my career, my team was required to certify that every line of code was tested: 100 percent "go code" and 85 percent exception-handling code. At first I was shocked.

I soon realized that certifying the testing of every line of code caused us to write some extremely clean code. No one had the same three lines of code in three different places, because if they did, they would have to certify nine lines of code instead of three. This discipline led to less code to maintain and made it easier to make changes because we made the change in only one place.

From that point on, I loved testing. I liked knowing that the code I wrote worked and that I had a test to prove it. This attitude is extremely important, because we are constantly bombarded with new technology and things to learn. As I said, quality work drove me to XP. Previously I wrote my own tests using JPython, a scripting language for the JVM, which I still use for prototyping. Then, I heard about JUnit, and from JUnit I learned about XP.

Of course, the quality work principle applies to more than making you happy. You would much rather write quality code and deliver a quality solution to the customer than write sloppy code and deliver a shoddy solution that does not meet the customer's need. Customers would much rather receive quality code than something that just does not work. It has been said that customers will sometimes forget that software was delivered late, but they will never forget poor quality.

When I was initially learning about XP, it seemed to be about 90 percent common sense, 8 percent "Aha!", and 2 percent revolution. So far, we have been covering the common sense and "Aha!" The next section covers these as well as the revolution.

Twelve Practices of XP

In his landmark book on XP, Beck iterated four basic practices: coding, testing, listening, and designing. These practices are expressed further in 12 major areas of practice, as follows:

- Planning game
- Small releases
- Simple design
- Testing
- Continuous integration
- Refactoring
- Pair programming
- Collective ownership
- 40-hour week
- On-site customer
- Metaphor
- Coding standard

Planning Game

The purpose of the planning game is to determine the scope of the current iteration. This step is centered on determining the tasks that are most important to the customer and accomplishing these tasks first. The planning game encompasses the customer's determining the scope of the project, priority of features, composition of the various releases, and delivery dates. The developers assist the customer with technical feedback by estimating task duration, considering consequences and risks, organizing the team, and performing technical risk management by working on the riskiest parts of the project first. The developers and the customers act as a team.

Time is recorded against stories to further refine your estimates of future stories, making project estimation more accurate as time goes on. Customer stories are recorded on index cards. These stories explain the features of the system. The developers work with the customer to decide which stories will be implemented for that iteration.

Small Releases

The philosophy behind the small releases practice is to provide the most business value with the least amount of coding effort. The features have to be somewhat atomic. A feature must implement enough functionality for it to have business value. This step may be counterintuitive, but the idea is to get the project into production as soon as possible. Small releases get feedback from the customer and reduce risk by making sure the software is what the customer wants. In essence, this step uses the Paredo rule: 80 percent of the business value can be completed with 20 percent of the effort. Small releases go hand in hand with the planning game to decide what features will give the biggest bang for the buck, and they also work with the practice of keeping designs simple.

Simple Design

The idea behind simple design is keep the code simple. The simplest design possible does not try to solve future problems by guessing future needs. The simplest design passes the customer's acceptance test for that release of the software.

The simplest design passes all the tests, has no duplicate logic code, and is not convoluted but expresses every developer's purpose. This step goes hand in hand with small releases. If your architecture is not expressed well and is built to anticipate future needs, you will not be able to deliver it as quickly. We are developers, not fortunetellers. We don't have a crystal ball, so the best way to anticipate customers' future needs is to give them a working system and get feedback from them. Most customers don't know exactly what they need until you deliver something tangible that they can react to. Remember, a picture is worth a thousand words, and a working model is worth a thousand pictures.

Testing

The practice of testing is key to XP. How will you know if a feature works if you do not test? How will you know if a feature still works after you refactor, unless you retest? If you admit that you don't know everything, and that the code will change and evolve, then you'll realize the need for a way to test the code when you change it.

The tests should be automated so you can have the confidence and courage to change the code and refactor it without breaking the system! This approach is the opposite of waterfall development.

Code is in a liquid state, so it can be re-architected, refactored, or thrown out and completely redone. Later, the tests can show that the system still works. Testing keeps the code fluid. Because tests typically check the public interface of classes and components, the implementation of the system can change drastically while the automated tests validate that the system still fulfills the contract of the interfaces. A feature does not exist unless a test validates that it functions. Everything that can potentially break must have a test. JUnit and friends will help you automate your testing.

Continuous Integration

Continuous integration is a crucial concept. Why wait until the end of a project to see if all the pieces of the system will work? Every few hours (at least once every day) the system should be fully built and tested, including all the latest changes. By doing this often, you will know what changes broke the system, and you can make adjustments accordingly instead of waiting until modifications pile up and you forget the details of the changes.

In order to facilitate continuous integration, you need to automate the build, distribution, and deploy processes. Doing so can be quite complicated in a J2EE environment. Ant can help you integrate with source control, Java compilation, creating deployment files, and automating testing. It can even send emails to the group letting them know what files broke the build or what tests did not pass.

Using Ant to perform continuous integration changes the whole development blueprint of your project. With a little discipline and setup time, continuous integration reduces problems linked with team development—particularly time spent fixing integration bugs. Integration bugs are the most difficult to uncover because often they lie unexposed until the system is integrated and two subsystems intermingle for the first time. Suddenly the system breaks in peculiar, unpredictable ways. The longer integration bugs survive, the harder they are to exterminate. Using Ant and JUnit to implement continuous integration often makes such a bug apparent within hours after it has been introduced into the system. Furthermore, the code responsible for this bug is fresh in the mind of the developer; thus, it is easier to eradicate. As Fowler and Foemmel state, continuous integration can "slash the amount of time spent in integration hell" (see their article at www.martinfowler.com/articles/continuousIntegration.html).

Ant can be used to automate the following tasks:

- Obtaining the source from configuration management system (CVS, Perforce, VSS, or StarTeam, and so on)
- Compiling the Java code
- Creating binary deployment files (Jar, Wars, Zip)
- Automating testing (when used in conjunction with tools like JUnit)

Developers often talk about automated building and testing but seldom implement them. Ant makes automated building and testing possible and plausible. Ant and JUnit combine well to allow teams to build and test their software several times a day. Such an automated process is worth the investment of time and effort. Automated builds and tests need the following, as stated by Fowler and Foemmel:

- A single place for all the source code where developers can get the most current sources—typically, a configuration management system
- A single command to build the system from all the sources (in our case, an Ant buildfile)
- A single command to run an entire suite of tests for the system (in our case, an Ant buildfile that integrates with JUnit)
- A good set of binaries that ensures developers have the latest working components (such as JAR files that contain classes)

Refactoring

The act of refactoring enables developers to add features while keeping the code simple, thus keeping the code simple while still being able to run all the tests. The idea is to not duplicate code nor write ugly, smelly code. The act of refactoring centers on testing to validate that the code still functions. Testing and refactoring go hand in hand. Automated unit-level tests will give you the courage to refactor and keep the code simple and expressive.

Refactoring is not limited to when you need to add a feature—refactoring is different than adding a feature. However, the catalyst for refactoring is often the need to add features while keeping the code simple. XP says not to guess what future features your customer wants. You cannot design in a vacuum. As you receive feedback, you will need to add features that will cause you to bend the code in new directions. Many software project management books say that once a project matures, adding two new features will cause one existing feature to break. The books make this statement as if such an occurrence is normal and acceptable. However, this is not the nature of software development; this is the nature of using a methodology and development environment in which adding new features and refactoring are not coupled with testing. Testing makes refactoring possible.

You will know when you need to refactor, because you will hear a little voice in the back of your head nagging you: Don't take a shortcut, make it simple, make it expressive. If the code stinks, you will fix it. If you don't hear that little voice or you aren't listening, then your pair-programming partner is there to guide you in the right direction.

Pair Programming

Pair programming is probably the most revolutionary practice of XP—and it is usually the one managers have the hardest time swallowing. On the surface, their reaction is easy to understand: If our projects are behind, then how will having two programmers work on the same task help speed things up? Why have two developers with one keyboard and one monitor?

If you think it is expensive to have two developers work together, how expensive will it be when you have to replace the whole system because it is impossible to maintain and every change causes massive ripple effects? You have undoubtedly seen it happen, and it is not a pretty picture.

I know from experience that pair programming works. For one thing, it improves communication among team members. A large part of what we do depends on the work of other developers. The developer you team with one day is not necessarily the developer you will team with the next day. In fact, the developer you team with in the morning may not be the developer you will team with in the afternoon. This process breeds better communication and cross-pollination of ideas. How often does your team reinvent a piece of code that another developer worked on?

Also, if one person knows much about a particular technical subject matter (such as EJB or Oracle) or business domain (such as accounting, semiconductor equipment, or aerospace), what better way for other developers to learn than to pair-program with that person?

What about quality? Pair programming provides constant feedback and ensures that the person who is coding is refactoring, testing, and following the coding standard. As Solomon stated, "By iron, iron itself is sharpened. So one man sharpens the face of another."

And, while one developer is focusing on the coding, the other developer can be thinking about the bigger picture: how this code will fit in with the other system. Typically, the developer who is not coding at the time is taking notes so that nothing falls through the cracks.

A few careless programmers can ruin a project team. Just like one rotten apple can spoil the whole bunch, sloppy code breeds more sloppy code. Pretty soon the team is addicted to the quick fix. In addition, because more and more of the code reeks, no one wants to own it. Pair programming is in lockstep with the practice of collective ownership.

Collective Ownership

The XP practice of collective ownership states that anyone can make a change to the system. You don't have to wait. No one owns a class. Everyone contributes, and if you need to make a change or refactor something to get it to work with a new feature, you can. Besides, you have the tests to make sure your changes did not break the system, and the old version is still in source control if anyone needs to refer to it, which is rare.

In addition, because many classes have corresponding automated test code, anyone can see how the code and API of classes were supposed to work. So, collective programming goes hand in hand with automated testing. Testing is part of what makes collective ownership possible.

Some developers will know some sections better than other developers, but all take ownership and responsibility for a system. If no one knows a particular part, the unit tests exercise the API and check that you did not break the system with your changes. Thus, you do not have to wait for another team member (let's call him Jon) to fix something. If Jon is busy helping Doug, you will fix the system with Nick, your pair-programming partner. If Jon is sick, the knowledge of a particular subsystem is not lost. Because Jon was pair programming with Andy, Andy knows about the system—and, in fact, so does Paul.

In addition, if you did not practice collective ownership and you had some critical parts of the system, then everyone would need to wait until you were done.

Or, you would have to work a very long week to accomplish the task so you wouldn't hold up Paul, Doug, Andy, and Nick. Your family would like you to spend more time with them, and you want to work a 40-hour week.

40-Hour Week

The 40-hour week practice states that if you cannot do your work in a 40-hour week, then something is wrong with the project. Let's face it, burned-out developers make lots of mistakes. No one is saying that you should never put in a 90-, 80-, 70-, or 60-hour week, but such a schedule should not be the norm. An unstated reality to this practice is to make your time count by working hard and getting the most out of your time. Long meetings should be rare, as should unnecessary red tape. Any activity that gets in the way of providing the most business value into the next release of your current projects should be avoided like the plague. Make the most of your time, and 40-hour weeks will be enough most of the time. In addition, keeping normal office hours will give you more opportunity to talk about features with your 9-to-5 customers.

On-Site Customer

The on-site customer practice states that if at all possible, the customer should be available when the developers need to ask questions. And, if at all possible, the customer should be physically located with the developers.

The customer must be available to clarify feature stories. The customer is also involved in the planning game, and this process is easier if the customer is not remote. The developers work with the customer to decide which stories are implemented for that iteration. The customer also helps write and refine the stories—which typically involves ad hoc and planned discussions with the developers. The stories, which are recorded on index cards, are written in a simple dialect that both the developers and customer understand, using a common metaphor.

Metaphor

A *metaphor* is a common language and set of terms used to envision the functionality of a project. These terms can equate to objects in the physical world, such as accounts or objects. Other times, metaphors can be more abstract, like windows or cells. The idea is for the customer and developers to have the same vision of the system and be able to speak about the system in a common dialect.

Coding Standard

XPers should follow the practice of using a coding standard. You must be able to understand one another's code. Luckily for us Java developers, we have the coding standard set by Sun; you should be able to make some light adjustments and make this coding standard your coding standard.

Your coding standard should state the proper use of threads, language constructs, exception use, no duplicate code logic, and so on. The coding standard should be more than just a guide on where to put your curly brace; it should denote style and common practices and conventions that your team will follow. Java developers have tons of reference material for coding style and standards. Like many things, developers will follow the standard if they voluntarily create it and buy into it.

Adopting XP?

As we've stated before, you do not have to adopt XP to get value out of this book. For example, automated testing can help you refactor code regardless of whether you are doing pair programming.

Here's another example: If you use Unified Modeling Language (UML) use cases with a CASE tool instead of stories written on index cards, continuous integration and small release cycles will still be beneficial for getting rapid feedback. The point is, you may decide to do things in addition to the process. Or, your corporate culture may have an adverse reaction to things like pair programming.

UML and CASE Tools

Some XP advocates swear by never using CASE tools. They say that the only UML should be written with a pencil on an index card. I don't agree. As long as the CASE tool can continually keep the model in sync with the code, the tool can be very beneficial. In addition, some CASE tools can speed development by generating the necessary boilerplate code for design patterns.

Beck notes that whether you draw diagrams that generate code or write out code, it is still code.

One of the first areas to focus on when adopting XP is automated testing. Begin by writing tests for code that you are about to add functionality to, refactor, or fix. The key is to add automated tests slowly to code written before you adopted XP, and always employ automated testing with newly developed code. Do not write tests for code you are not working on. Later, when you begin doing integration tests, you will want to automate the build, test, and integration cycle.

My company has adopted XP. We adhere to the 12 XP practices. However, I am not a purist. I believe that other software processes can benefit from automated testing, simple designs, continuous integration, incremental releases, and constant refactoring.

Beck states that XP's 12 practices will not fit every project. XP also will not fit every organization's culture. Regardless, J2EE development can benefit from automated testing, simple designs, continuous integration, incremental releases, and constant refactoring. This book focuses on tools to perform automated testing and continuous integration for J2EE to enable refactoring and incremental releases.

Summary

XP is a lightweight methodology that focuses on coding as the main task. XP is based on four values: communication, simplicity, feedback, and courage. Communication is facilitated through pair programming, task estimation, iteration planning, and more. Simplicity means avoiding making things overly complicated and insisting that the basics be addressed first and foremost. Feedback is given by way of testing, customer stories, small iterations/frequent deliveries, pair programming/constant code reviews, and so on. Courage means the courage to do what is right whether you have to refactor a working system, throw code away, cancel a project, or insist on quality.

XP is based on five principles: rapid feedback, assuming simplicity, making incremental changes, embracing change, and doing quality work. In his landmark book on XP, Beck iterated four basic practices: coding, testing, listening, and designing. These practices are expressed further in 12 major areas of practice: the planning game, small releases, simple design, (automated) testing, continuous integration, refactoring, pair programming, collective ownership, a 40-hour week, an on-site customer, metaphor, and adherence to a coding standard. This book focus on two practices of XP: automated testing and continuous integration.

XP encourages full integration testing not on a weekly or monthly basis or at the end of a project, but daily. Daily integration and integration/functional testing ensure that you'll catch problems early. Such testing is hard to do with J2EE.

Thus, in order to provide continuous integration and automatic testing, you will need tools to help with the deployment of J2EE applications. To accomplish continuous integration in this complex system, you need a way to automate the integration process. You need to automate the build, test, and deployment cycle.

Up next is Chapter 2, "J2EE Deployment Concepts," which covers the J2EE component model, deployment descriptors, and the challenges of deploying and testing in a J2EE environment.

CHAPTER 2

J2EE Deployment Concepts

This chapter is an overview of several key concepts for assembling and deploying J2EE applications. In Chapter 6, "Building J2EE Applications with Ant," we use Ant to create Java ARchive (JAR) files, Web ARchive (WAR) files, and Enterprise JavaBean (EJB) JARs, so you will need to have a background in the various deployment descriptors for these modules. If you already have considerable experience with J2EE applications, you may want to skip to Chapter 3, "Example Applications."

The J2EE platform provides component models for assembling applications. J2EE lets you "divide and conquer" an application by buying and building components and wiring them together into an application. Java and J2EE support the following components:

Client Components

- JavaBeans
- Applets

Web Application Components

- Servlets
- JSPs
- TagLibs

Enterprise JavaBeans

- Session beans
- Stateless session beans
- Entity beans

Each component executes in a container. To interoperate with various containers, these components require deployment descriptor files, configuration files, property files, and/or metadata files, and other configuration files. All these files describe the components and how they will interact with other components and their container environment.

Deployment can be a complex matter. A typical deployment might involve creating an Enterprise ARchive (EAR) file that can contain JAR and WAR files. The JAR files can in turn contain enterprise beans. The WAR file can in turn contain Web components (servlets, TagLibs, JavaBeans, and JSP), HTML pages, images, Java class files, and other JAR files that contain application components (JavaBeans, client-side remote references to enterprise beans and applets). The deployment descriptor for a Web application (which we will cover later) may contain env-entry elements that are mapped to the Java Naming and Directory Interface (JNDI) names java:comp/env (the context), ejb-ref (describes enterprise beans), and resources-ref (maps Java Messaging Service, Java Database Connectivity, and mail resources so that the Web application can use them).

Figures 2.1 and 2.2 show block diagrams of the two J2EE applications that we build, test, and deploy throughout this book (see Chapter 3 for details on these applications). As you can see, several different types of components need to be deployed to multiple servers and containers.

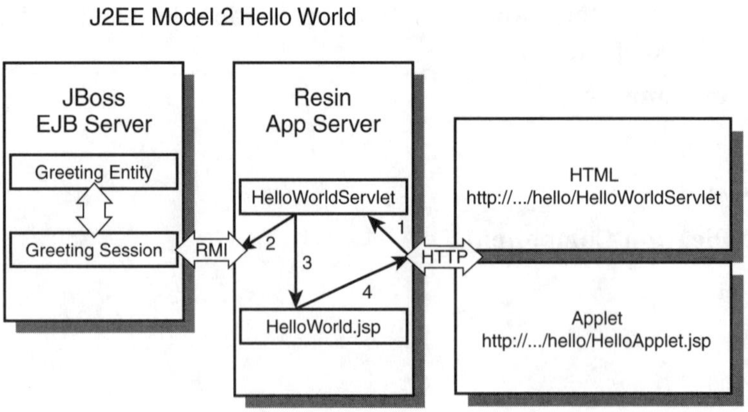

Figure 2.1 The HelloWorld application.

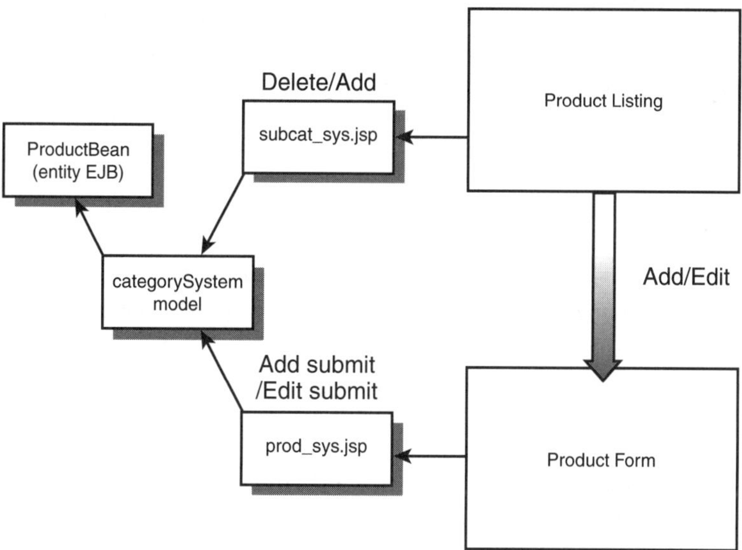

Figure 2.2 The pet store application.

To say that configuration management of a typical J2EE enterprise application is complex is an understatement. In Chapters 5 and 6 we will use Ant to help facilitate this process. Otherwise, continuous integration would be pretty tough with the complexities of the J2EE deployment environment.

The remainder of this chapter describes the basic J2EE components and how they are deployed. We also explain the JAR file format, because many components and sets of components are packaged in either a JAR file or some variation of a JAR file.

The JAR File

JAR stands for Java ARchive, although it seems to be an obvious pun on the fact that Java components are called beans ("a jar of beans"). A JAR file is a collection of other files. JAR files use the ZIP file format, which supports compression.

Many components, subsystems, and modules are deployed in JAR files or some variation of a JAR file. There are JAR files for JavaBeans and applets. Other JAR files contain libraries of Java code. There are JAR files that contain Enterprise JavaBeans. Then there are variations of JAR files that contain other JAR files and JavaServer Pages (JSPs) like the WAR files. The king of all JAR files, the EAR file, can contain other JAR files, EJB JAR files, and WAR files.

Each JAR file contains a manifest file called MANIFEST.MF, which is located in the JAR file's META-INF directory. The manifest file is a text file that consists of entries that describe the contents of the JAR file. The main section of the manifest file contains configuration information and specifies the application or extension the JAR file is associated with.

JAR files were originally developed to package Java applets and their requisite components (.class files, images, and sounds). The boon to applet development was that the applet could be downloaded to a browser in a single file, so the browser didn't have to download many files—a major boost to efficiency and speed.

JAR Files and Applets

For applets, JAR files are specified in the HTML applet tag's "archive" parameter. This parameter causes the browser to load the JAR file, which contains the applet code. For example:

```
<applet
     code= "xptoolkit.applet.HelloWorldApplet"
     archive="helloapplet.jar"
     width=200 height=200>
</applet>
```

Applet Delivery Has Complex Problems and Solutions

It's supposed to be easy to request a browser to open a JAR file. The problem is that one major Web browser vendor decided not to support Java any longer. The vendor froze its version of Java at version JDK 1.1.5. Thus, you can use the applet tag we just described if you do not use any features of Java newer than JDK 1.1.5.

Another major vendor of Web browsers supported the later versions of Java, but at the time its browser support of Java was not very robust. Thus, Sun had two choices: It could wait for the browser to catch up or write its own Java plug-in for the major browsers. The good folks at Sun decided to write their own plug-in for Java. A tag that supports both Netscape and Microsoft may look like this:

```
<object classid="clsid:8AD9C840-044E-11D1-B3E9-00805F499D93"
 codebase="http://java.sun.com/products/plugin/1.2.2/
          jinstall-1_2_2-win.cab#Version=1,2,2,0"
     height="200" width="200" align="center">
     <param name="java_code"
               value="xptoolkit.applet.HelloWorldApplet">
     <param name="java_archive" value="helloapplet.jar">
     <param name="type" value="application/x-java-applet">
```

```
        <comment>
            <embed type="application/x-java-applet"
                   codebase="http://java.sun.com/products/plugin/"
                   height="200"
                   width="200"
                   align="center"
             java_code="xptoolkit.applet.HelloWorldApplet"
             java_archive="helloapplet.jar">
        <noembed>
        </comment>
          <p> Java is cool. Get a browser that supports the plugin.
            </ br>
          </p>
        </noembed>
        </embed>
        </object>
```

The embed tag is for Netscape Navigator, and the "java_archive" parameter specifies the JAR file that contains the applet code. The object tag works with Microsoft Internet Explorer, and it uses the "java_archive" parameter to specify the JAR file.

JSP has a plug-in tag that helps simplify this issue for you. The plug-in tag specifies the JAR file that the applet needs in its "archive" parameter. It is demonstrated as follows:

```
<jsp:plugin type="applet"
            code="xptoolkit.applet.HelloWorldApplet"
            archive="helloapplet.jar"
            height="200"
            width="200"
            align="center">
     <jsp:fallback>
<!-- This fallback message will display if the plugin does not work. /-->
         <p> Java is cool. Get a browser that supports the plugin. </ br>
             Or we will hunt you down and melt your computer!
         </p>
     </jsp:fallback>
</jsp:plugin>
```

An example of using this technique to launch applets appears in Chapter 6.

Executable JAR Files

In addition to supporting applets, Java supports JAR files so that double-clicking a JAR file (or the equivalent gesture on your OS) will automatically run the application in the JAR file. In order to do this, you must specify the name of the application's startup class in the JAR manifest file. The startup class is called the *main class*.

You can run a JAR file that specifies a main class as follows:

```
C:\tmp\app\lib> java -jar greetapp.jar
```

To specify a main class for a JAR file, you specify the "Main-Class" attribute in the JAR manifest file:

```
Main-Class :  xptoolkit.HelloWorld
```

An example of how to create an executable JAR file with Ant appears in Chapter 5.

This was just a brief introduction to JAR files. Later chapters contain plenty of examples that show you how to use Ant to build the various distribution files based on the JAR format you need and use.

Web Applications and the WAR File

Web applications consist of the following components: JSPs, TagLibs, and servlets. You describe these components and their relationship with a metadata deployment filed named web.xml. The web.xml file is a deployment descriptor defined by the Servlet Specification. The deployment descriptor is stored in the root of the WEB-INF directory. The Web application deployment descriptor holds the following information for the Web application container:

- ServletContext init parameters
- Session configuration
- Servlet/JSP definitions
- Servlet/JSP URI mappings
- Mime type mappings
- Error pages
- Security
- JNDI environment
- Referenced EJBs
- Maps resources, such as JDBC connections, URL factory, JMS resources, and mail resources

The Web application is usually contained in a WAR file. A WAR file is a single archive file with the .war file extension. Like a JAR file, a WAR file uses the ZIP file format. Unlike a JAR file, a WAR file cannot be placed on the classpath. The WAR file contains all the components of a Web application, including support libraries and HTML files. The WAR file holds the HTML and JSP files in the root of the WAR file, and it holds the servlets and related classes in the WEB-INF/classes directory. Any supporting libraries (JAR files) the JSP or servlets need are held in the WEB-INF/lib directory. A WAR file can hold all the files a Web application needs for deployment.

A directory structure for a Web application may look something like this:

```
Web Application Archive file Root
|
|    index.html
|    HelloWorld.jsp
|
\--WEB-INF
     |    web.xml
     |
     +--classes
     |    \--xptoolkit
     |        |
     |        \--web
     |             HelloWorldServlet.class
     |
     \--lib
            greetmodel.jar
```

This example has index.html and HelloWorld.jsp in the root directory. It also has the servlet xptoolkit.web.HelloWorldServlet in the /WEB-INF/classes directory. In addition, the support library greetmodel.jar is in the /WEB-INF/lib directory. The greetmodel.jar file has JavaBeans and classes that are needed by HelloWorld.jsp and xptoolkit.web.HelloWorldServlet. Note that this example is based on a sample we will use in Chapters 5 and 6.

As we stated earlier, the web.xml file sets environment settings for the Web application. An example deployment descriptor for a Web application from previous WAR file may look like this:

```
<web-app>
    <error-page>
        <error-code>404</error-code>
        <location>/HelloWorldServlet</location>
    </error-page>

    <servlet>
        <servlet-name>HelloWorldServlet</servlet-name>
        <servlet-class>xptoolkit.web.HelloWorldServlet</servlet-class>
        <init-param>
          <param-name>Greeting.class</param-name>
```

```
            <param-value>xptoolkit.model.HelloWorldBean</param-value>
        </init-param>
    </servlet>

    <servlet>
        <servlet-name>HelloWorldJSP</servlet-name>
        <jsp-file>HelloWorld.jsp</jsp-file>
    </servlet>

    <servlet-mapping>
        <servlet-name>HelloWorldServlet</servlet-name>
        <url-pattern>/HelloWorldServlet</url-pattern>
    </servlet-mapping>

    <servlet-mapping>
        <servlet-name>HelloWorldJSP</servlet-name>
        <url-pattern>/HelloWorldJSP</url-pattern>
    </servlet-mapping>

</web-app>
```

This deployment descriptor creates two servlet definitions: one for HelloWorld.jsp (a JSP compiles to a servlet before use) and one for xptoolkit.web.HelloWorldServlet. The deployment descriptor then maps a few URI mappings for the servlets that were defined. A servlet mapping maps a servlet to a URI.

This was just an introduction to the Web application and WAR files. For a detailed description, refer to the Java Servlet Specification (http://java.sun.com/j2ee/), particularly the chapters "Web Applications," "Mapping Requests to Servlets," and "Deployment Descriptors." The parts of the deployment descriptor that we used here are explained as we build the sample applications deployed in Chapter 6, "Building J2EE Applications with Ant."

Enterprise Beans and the EJB JAR File

Enterprise JavaBeans use the JAR file format to package enterprise beans. The EJB JAR file is used to package un-assembled enterprise beans and to package assembled beans. *Un-assembled enterprise beans* have only generic information created by the bean developer. *Assembled enterprise beans* have information for a particular environment stored in the deployment descriptor by the application assembler. Basically, there are different roles for building and deploying enterprise beans. In this book, we are both the bean provider and the application assembler (in addition to the deployer and the administrator). However, the techniques we present can be adapted to situations in which assembling and deploying are performed by separate organizations.

Like the Web application WAR file, the EJB JAR file has a deployment descriptor. It is stored in the META-INF directory in a file called ejb-jar.xml. This deployment descriptor contains the following information:

Structural Information for an Enterprise Bean

- Name
- Class type
- Home interface
- Remote interface
- Bean type (session or entity)
- Reentrancy indication
- State management information (stateful session)
- Persistence management information (container managed persistence [CMP] entity)
- Primary key class (entity)
- Container managed fields (CMP entity)
- Environment entries (accessible via JNDI)
- Resource manager connection factory references
- References to other EJBs
- Security role references

Application Assembly Information

- Binding of enterprise bean references
- Security roles
- Method permissions
- Linking of security roles
- Transaction attributes for beans and methods

Listing 2.1 is an example of an EJB deployment descriptor; it's based on an example in Chapter 6.

```
<ejb-jar>

<description>
This ejb-jar file contains the Enterprise beans for the
model 2 Hello World application.
</description>

<ejb-client-jar>client-greet-ejbs.jar</ejb-client-jar>

<enterprise-beans>

    <entity>
        <description>
            The GreetingEntityBean is a do nothing bean to demonstrate
            how to deploy an Enterprise bean with Ant.
        </description>
        <ejb-name>GreetingEntityBean</ejb-name>
        <home>xptoolkit.ejbs.GreetingEntityHome</home>
        <remote>xptoolkit.ejbs.GreetingEntityRemote</remote>
        <ejb-class>xptoolkit.ejbs.GreetingEntityBean</ejb-class>
        <transaction-type>Container</transaction-type>
        <reentrant>True</reentrant>
        <prim-key-class>java.lang.Integer</prim-key-class>
        <persistence-type>Bean</persistence-type>
    </entity>

    <session>
        <description>
            The GreetingSessionBean is a do nothing bean to demonstrate
            how to deploy an Enterprise bean with Ant.
        </description>
        <ejb-name>GreetingSessionBean</ejb-name>
        <home>xptoolkit.ejbs.GreetingSessionHome</home>
        <remote>xptoolkit.ejbs.GreetingSessionRemote</remote>
        <ejb-class>xptoolkit.ejbs.GreetingSessionBean</ejb-class>
        <session-type>Stateful</session-type>
        <transaction-type>Container</transaction-type>

        <ejb-ref>
            <description>
                This sets up a references from the Entity bean to the
                session bean.
                Thus, the session bean can look up the Entity bean in
                its environment space.
            </description>
            <ejb-ref-name>ejb/GreetingEntityBean</ejb-ref-name>
            <ejb-ref-type>Entity</ejb-ref-type>
```

Listing 2.1 Sample EJB deployment descriptor. (continues)

```
            <home>xptoolkit.ejbs.GreetingEntityHome</home>
            <remote>xptoolkit.ejbs.GreetingEntityRemote</remote>
            <ejb-link>GreetingEntityBean</ejb-link>
        </ejb-ref>

    </session>

</enterprise-beans>

<assembly-descriptor>
    <container-transaction>
        <method>
            <ejb-name>GreetingSessionBean</ejb-name>
            <method-name>*</method-name>
        </method>
        <trans-attribute>Supports</trans-attribute>
    </container-transaction>

    <container-transaction>
        <method>
            <ejb-name>GreetingEntityBean</ejb-name>
            <method-name>*</method-name>
        </method>
        <trans-attribute>Supports</trans-attribute>
    </container-transaction>

</assembly-descriptor>
</ejb-jar>
```

Listing 2.1 Sample EJB deployment descriptor.

Listing 2.1 defines two enterprise beans: GreetingSessionBean and GreetingEntityBean. The session bean has a reference to the entity bean. We'll explain this example in more detail in Chapter 6. Notice that the enterprise-bean element defines entity and session sub-elements. The entity and session elements contain references to the remote, home, and bean classes. These classes are defined in the root of the bean class just like classes of a regular JAR file. For example, the directory structure of the EJB file described in Listing 2.1 may look like this:

```
EJB Jar File root
|
|   client-greet-ejbs.jar
|
+--META-INF
|       MANIFEST.MF
|       ejb-jar.xml
|
```

```
\--xptoolkit
    |
    \--ejbs
           GreetingEntityBean.class
           GreetingEntityHome.class
           GreetingEntityRemote.class
           GreetingSessionBean.class
           GreetingSessionRemote.class
           GreetingSessionHome.class
```

This example is based on one presented in Chapter 6. For more information about EJB JAR files and EJB deployment descriptors, refer to the official EJB specifications online at http://java.sun.com/products/ejb/ (particularly the chapters "Deployment Descriptors" and "EJB JAR File").

Enterprise Applications and the EAR File

Once you create all your components, you may want to deploy them as a single logical unit called an *enterprise application*. Doing so will ease the deployment and help ensure that the environment of the staging server is the same or at least as close as possible to the one on the production server.

An enterprise application can be contained in single JAR file with the extension .ear, called an enterprise archive (EAR) file. The EAR file contains many JAR files, EJB JAR files, and WAR files called *modules*. Following is an example of a deployment descriptor for an EAR file:

```
<application>
  <display-name>Hello World Application</display-name>
  <description>Hello World Application.</description>
  <module>
    <web>
      <web-uri>hello.war</web-uri>
      <context-root>helloworld</context-root>
    </web>
  </module>
  <module>
    <ejb>greet-ejbs.jar</ejb>
  </module>
</application>
```

This deployment descriptor would correspond to the following directory structure of an EAR file:

```
Enterprise Archive file root
|    greet-ejbs.jar
|    hello.war
|
```

```
\--META-INF
        application.xml
```

This is based on a real example that is presented in chapter 6. To find out more about EAR files and EAR deployment descriptors, refer to the J2EE Specification chapters "Application Assembly" and "Deployment."

Summary

This chapter covered the basic J2EE components and how they are deployed, and the various archive files in which J2EE components are deployed (WAR, EAR, EJB JAR, and JAR).

We talked about the many types of J2EE-supported components: JavaBeans, applets, servlets, JSP, TagLibs, session beans, stateless session beans, and entity bean. We also discussed how to create deployments that interoperate with various containers using deployment descriptor files and archive files. Deployment files make deployment easier because they describe the components, how the components interact with other components, and how the components interact with their container environment.

CHAPTER 3

Example Applications

This chapter describes the example applications used in this book. It is important that you understand the purpose and structure of these applications because we build, test, and deploy them throughout Part II of the book.

Writing example applications requires a delicate balance. If the applications are too simple, it is difficult to see how you would apply the concepts being taught to real-life projects. If the applications are too robust and full-featured, it can be difficult to follow the concepts being presented because the application's complexity gets in the way. We've tried to solve this problem by including two types of example applications in this book: simple applications and case studies.

Simple applications are used throughout the book to demonstrate a specific technique. These "applications" are very brief—sometimes only a few lines of code—so as not to get in the way of showing you how to use the underlying tools or how to deploy a component.

The case studies are stripped-down versions of a real application. They are long enough to be realistic and indicative of common Web applications, but they are not full-featured, standalone applications. The case studies are frameworks for demonstrating complex techniques with the automated testing and integration tools.

None of the case studies or simple examples do much in the way of exception-handling, in an effort to keep the code straightforward and easy to follow. If this were a book on style or object-oriented design, we would have written the samples much differently.

Where to Get the Example Applications

You can download the complete code listings and updated build instructions for all the applications in this book at www.wiley.com/compbooks/hightower.

Simple Example: Model 2 Hello World

The Model 2 Hello World example is a simple application used to demonstrate Ant and some of the basic concepts of the other tools. You can download the complete code for this example at www.wiley.com/compbooks/hightower. Model 2 Hello World involves building, deploying, and testing an applet, a servlet, a few JavaServer Pages (JSPs), an application, several Java classes, and two Enterprise JavaBeans (EJBs).

The applet is delivered to a browser using the plugin tag from a JSP. Then, the applet talks to a servlet. The servlet communicates with the EJB server, which maps a JavaBean into the session and redirects to a second JSP. The second JSP makes a call on the JavaBean, which calls an enterprise bean, which is a session bean. The session bean in turn calls an entity bean. See Figure 3.1.

All of these components must be packaged and configured so they can speak to one another. In this example, we create a JAR file, an EJB JAR file, a WAR file, and an EAR file, each with the appropriate manifest and deployment descriptors using Ant.

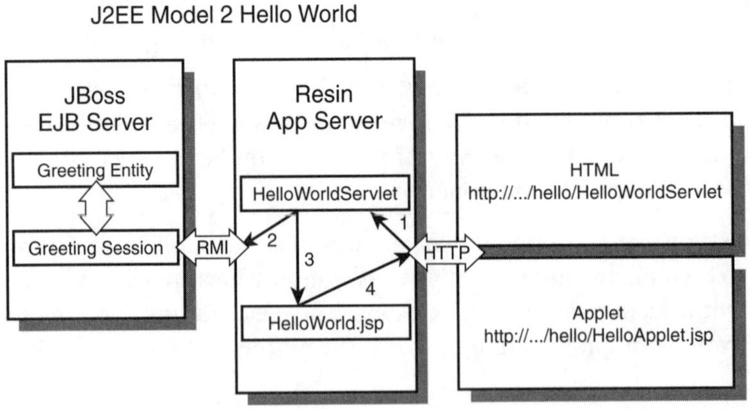

Figure 3.1 Model 2 HelloWorld.

Case Study Example: The Pet Store

The case study application is an online pet store. In this example, we have a catalog system stored in a database that is accessed by a Web application. This example can display the catalog to customers and also has a small content-management system that enables the owner of the pet store to enter catalog information (for example, new pets and new categories of pets). You can download the complete code from www.wiley.com/compbooks/hightower.

The case study application is a more complex—but more realistic—example for demonstrating how open source tools are used in a real production environment. Even so, this example is by no means a complete pet store like the J2EE Blueprint Pet Store. Sun's purpose for building the J2EE Blueprint Pet Store is to show good design and coding techniques for building an e-commerce application with J2EE. Conversely, our pet store case study is built to demonstrate good techniques for testing, building, and deploying a J2EE application with open source tools.

We'll work through several iterations of the pet store. The baseline version has no connection pooling and no EJBs. This iteration is a simple, small example. It has several JSPs, a few classes that use JDBC, and some tables in a database. We discuss the details of the baseline version in subsequent sections of this chapter.

The second iteration of the case study changes the content management piece of the system to a container managed persistence (CMP) entity bean, which implements the backend product management. This approach allows online product entry (add, delete, and edit). This iteration demonstrates how to incorporate enterprise bean deployment into your Web application and how to ensure that the unit testing of the category systems still works after the addition of the CMP entity bean support.

The third iteration of the case study uses an EJB stateless session bean to add pooling of connections and prepared statements. We use this iteration to demonstrate the use of JUnitPerf and show the time savings from pooling prepared statements when the site is hit by many users (the original, non-pooled version would most likely be a bottleneck under heavy traffic).

The fourth iteration of the case study creates a Catalog TagLib. We use Cactus to test this TagLib. This is an excellent example to show how to operate and run Cactus tests and how to integrate them in the build/deploy process.

Database

The example applications in this book use MS SQL Server, primarily because it is what a large number of developers use. Realizing the irony of writing a book about open source tools, yet using a closed source database, we ported several of the example applications to HSQL (a very fast, lightweight, open source database written in Java). These example applications are available on the book's Web site at www.wiley.com/compbooks/hightower.

The fifth iteration of the case study refactors the JSPs using the Apache Struts project. Then, it uses HttpUnit to test that the application still works. The HttpUnit test is run against the baseline and the new version to show that the new version works like the old.

The sixth and final iteration of the case study refactors the Web application to use Extensible Style Language Transformation (XSLT) instead of JSP to do the catalog view. It then compares the throughput of the two approaches using JMeter.

Baseline Version of the Pet Store

This section is an overview of the baseline version of the pet store case study, its components, the associated Ant files, and the JUnit tests (details of working with Ant files and JUnit tests are covered in Chapters 4 through 7). All other iterations of the case study in this book are based on this baseline version, so it is important that you see it laid out in one place.

In the next sections we describe the classes used, the public interface, the implementation for the baseline version, the Web interface, and the Ant buildfile structure used to build the case study. Later, we highlight an Ant buildfile that is used to create sample data for our testing. Finally, we cover some of the JUnit tests that are executed by the test. Note that a complete listing of the baseline case study appears at the end of this chapter; we don't cover the full application line by line because the focus is on the buildfiles, not the Java code.

Model Classes (Public Interface)

The online store system for the baseline consists of a navigation system. The CategorySystem class is the façade class that is mapped into the session of the Web application. Through the CategorySystem, the Web applications can access the model data (Category, Product, and Category instances) for listing views and detail views (see Figure 3.2 and Listing 3.1). The model is the public interface to the catalog system.

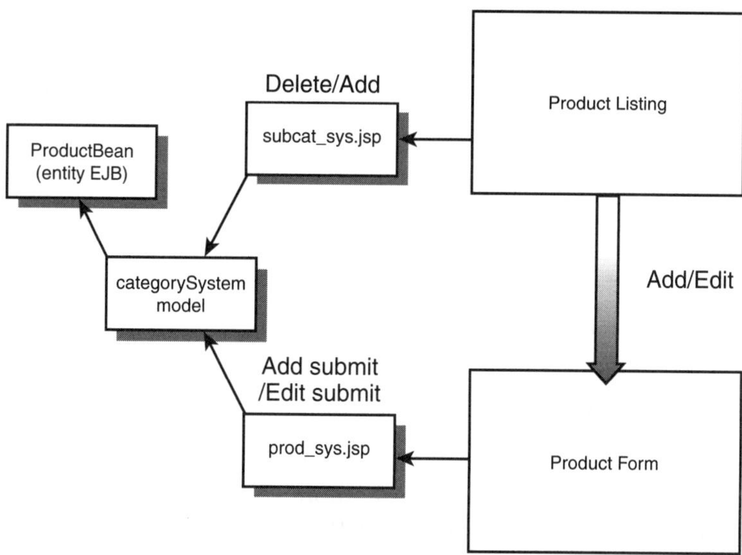

Figure 3.2 Model diagram for the baseline case study.

```
package xptoolkit.petstore.model;

public class CategorySystem {
    private Category currentCategory;
    private Subcategory currentSubcategory;
    private Product currentProduct;

    public CategorySystem() throws Exception {
        currentCategory = Category.getCategory();
        currentCategory.setId(777);
    }

    public Category getCurrentCategory() {
        return currentCategory;
    }

    public Subcategory getCurrentSubcategory() {
        return currentSubcategory;
    }

    public Product getCurrentProduct() {
        return currentProduct;
    }

    public Subcategory getSubcategory(int id) throws Exception {
        currentSubcategory = currentCategory.getSubcategory(id);
```

Listing 3.1 CategorySystem for the baseline case study. (continues)

```
        return currentSubcategory;
    }

    public Product getProduct(int id) throws Exception {
        currentProduct = currentSubcategory.getProduct(id);
        return currentProduct;
    }
}
```

Listing 3.1 CategorySystem for the baseline case study.

dbmodel Classes (Implementation)

The catalog system model only defines the public interface into our catalog system. The actual implementation is in the dbmodel package. The baseline version of the case study uses old-school JDBC with no connection pooling. In a later implementation we use EJB to provide the connection and prepared statement pooling for this application. Fortunately, we will not have to change many of our tests and JSPs, because the public interface to the system will still be the model. The implementation is hidden behind the public interface to the system. See Figure 3.3 for the dbmodel class diagram. You can find the complete dbmodel code at the end of this chapter in Listings 3.9 through 3.12.

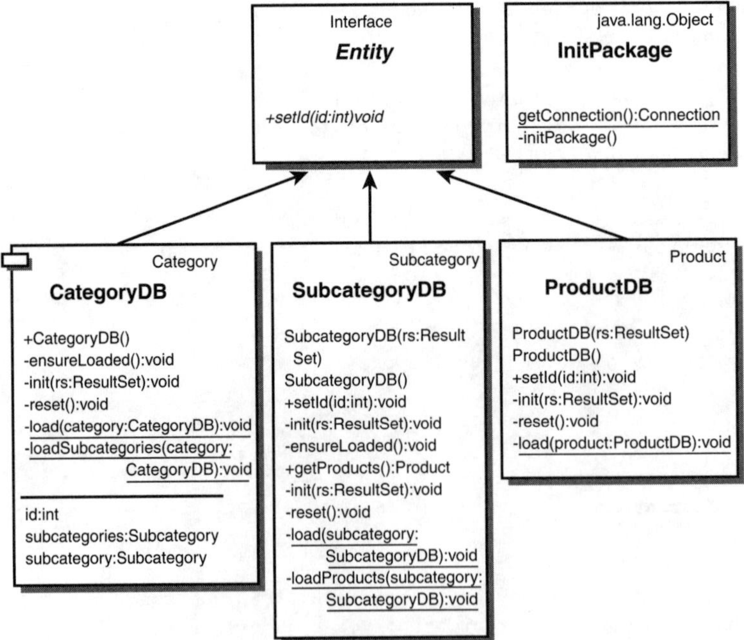

Figure 3.3 dbmodel for the baseline case study.

Database Schema

The dbmodel classes read data from a database. Again, our example endeavors to be simple, and the database schema certainly reflects this approach (see Figure 3.4 and Listing 3.2). The SQL Data definition language (DDL) for the schema in Figure 3.4 is very simple (refer back to Listing 3.1).

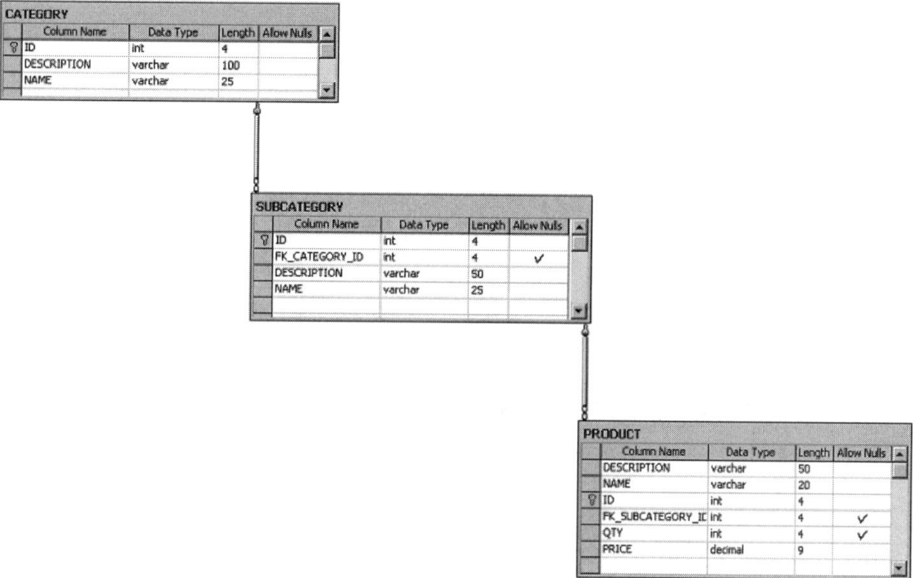

Figure 3.4 Database schema for the baseline case study.

```
CREATE TABLE CATEGORY (
    ID int PRIMARY KEY,
    DESCRIPTION varchar (100) NOT NULL ,
    NAME varchar (25)  NOT NULL
)

CREATE TABLE SUBCATEGORY (
    ID int PRIMARY KEY,
    FK_CATEGORY_ID int REFERENCES CATEGORY(ID),
    DESCRIPTION varchar (50) NOT NULL ,
    NAME varchar (25)  NOT NULL
)
```

Listing 3.2 Database schema for the baseline case study. (continues)

```
CREATE TABLE PRODUCT (
    ID int IDENTITY (1, 1) PRIMARY KEY,
    DESCRIPTION varchar (50) NOT NULL ,
    NAME varchar (20)  NOT NULL ,
    FK_SUBCATEGORY_ID int REFERENCES SUBCATEGORY(ID),
    QTY int DEFAULT (5),
    PRICE DECIMAL(10,2) NOT NULL,
```

Listing 3.2 Database schema for the baseline case study.

Web Interface

The main Web page for the case study has a side navigation that contains the subcategories. The product listing for the subcategory is in the middle of the page (see Figure 3.5). The category name and description appear in the center of the page, along with the subcategory name and description. When you click on a product, a product detail page opens (see Figure 3.6).

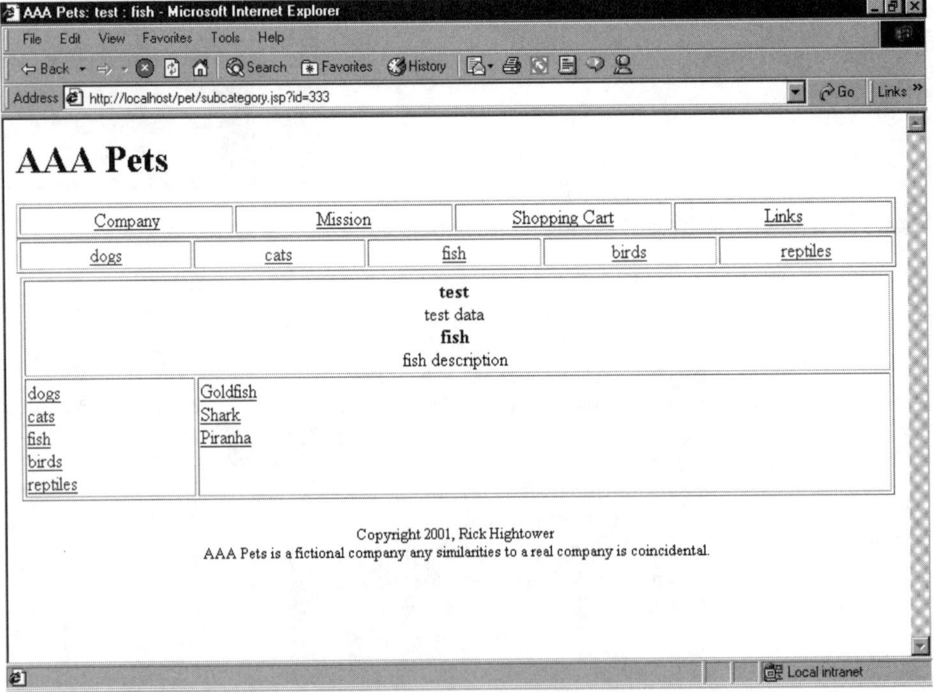

Figure 3.5 Main page and navigation for the baseline case study.

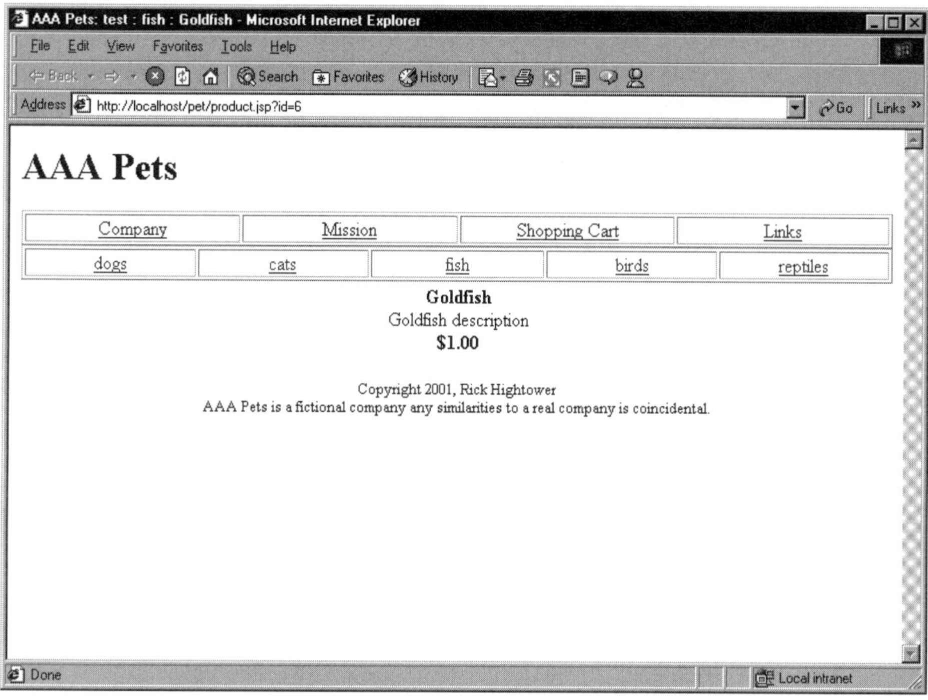

Figure 3.6 Product page for the baseline case study.

The Web interface has seven JSP pages, as follows:

- index.jsp
- category.jsp
- subcategory.jsp
- product.jsp
- category_sys.jsp
- header.jsp
- footer.jsp

The names of the JSP pages are somewhat indicative of their functionality. The product.jsp page displays product details. The subcategory.jsp page shows the subcategory details as well as the product listing for that subcategory (see Figure 3.7 for a visual representation of the JSP page structure). The code for all the JSPs appears in Listings 3.18 through 3.26 at the end of this chapter.

The JSPs use the CategorySystem to display the object model of the application. Each page includes header.jsp, which in turn includes category_sys.jsp, which uses jsp:useBean to map in a CategorySystem instance as follows:

```
<%@page import="xptoolkit.petstore.model.*" %>
<jsp:useBean id="categorySystem" class="CategorySystem" scope=
                                                    "session"/>
```

All the JSPs use the categorySystem to create and get objects. For example, here is a partial listing of the Product.jsp page:

```
...
Category category = categorySystem.getCurrentCategory();
Subcategory subcategory = categorySystem.getCurrentSubcategory();

String productId = request.getParameter("id");
Product product = subcategory
                        .getProduct( Integer.parseInt(productId) );
...
<b><%= product.getName() %></b>
                        <br>
<%= product.getDescription() %>
```

The baseline version of the application just reads data out of the database. Later versions of the application will edit, add, and delete products using an extended categorySystem.

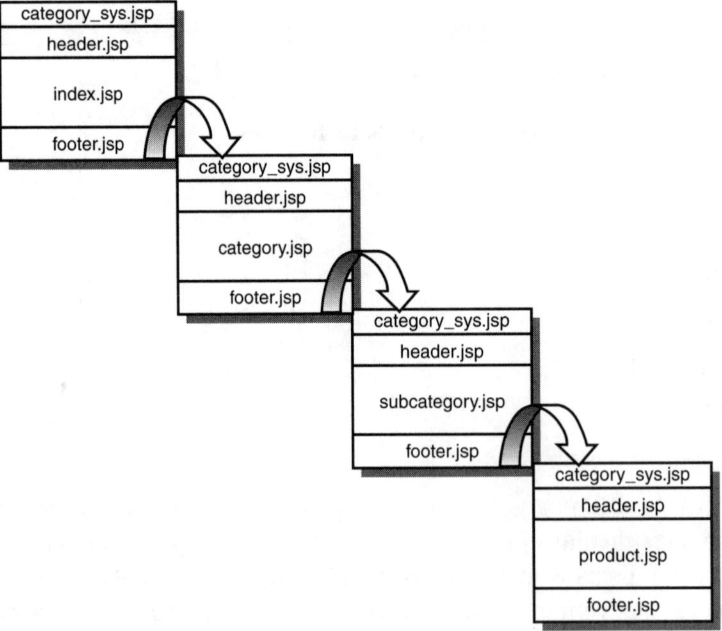

Figure 3.7 JSP block diagram for the baseline case study.

Build System

This section jumps the gun a bit. We explain how the build system is structured, but we have not yet covered Ant and JUnit. The idea is to give you a glimpse of things to come. Please read this section with the realization that the material covered in this section is explained in detail later.

The case study baseline uses five buildfiles:

- main
- model
- webapplication
- test
- setupDB

The *main* buildfile is located in the root directory of the baseline version (see Figure 3.8). The main buildfile orchestrates the execution and deployment of the other buildfiles.

The *model* buildfile builds and packages the model and dbmodel classes. The end result of the model buildfile is a JAR file (petmodel.jar) that is stored in the lib directory of the output (see Figure 3.9).

The *webapplication* buildfile compiles and builds the Web application. The end result of the webapplication buildfile is a WAR file (pet.war) that can be deployed to any J2EE-compliant servlet/JSP engine such as WebLogic, Resin, Tomcat, or Orion (see Figure 3.9 and look for pet.war).

The *test* buildfile packages and builds the test classes (JUnit) and runs the tests. The test results are stored in XML files in the reports directory (see Figure 3.9 and look for the reports directory). Then, the test buildfile transforms the XML into an HTML report (see Figures 3.10 and 3.11, which show the test results in a browser).

The *setupDB* buildfile sets up the database schema and populates the database with sample data that is used for testing. This will be covered in detail in the next section.

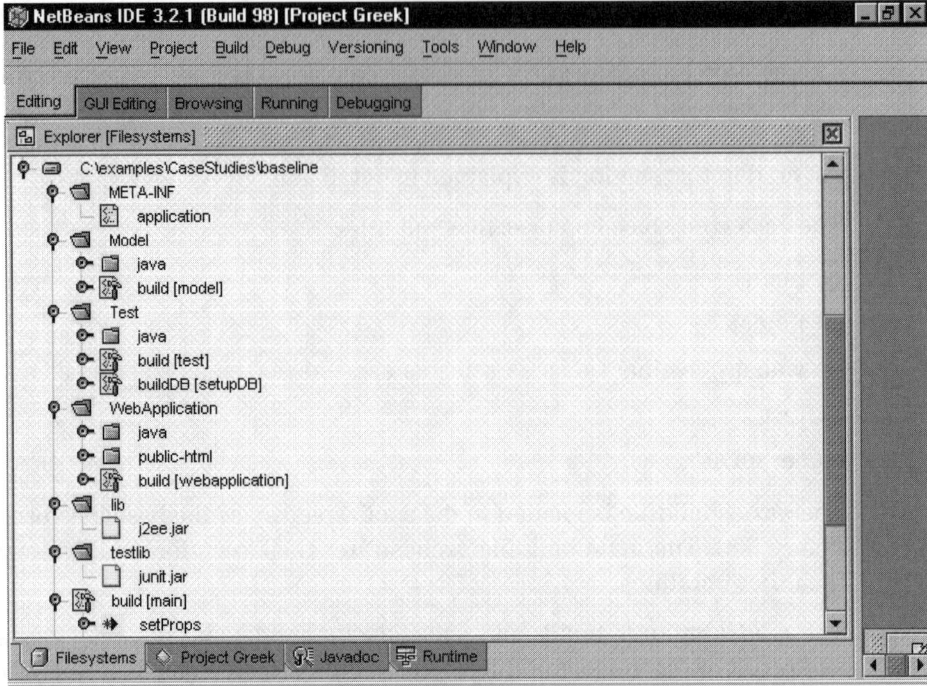

Figure 3.8 Source directory structure of the baseline.

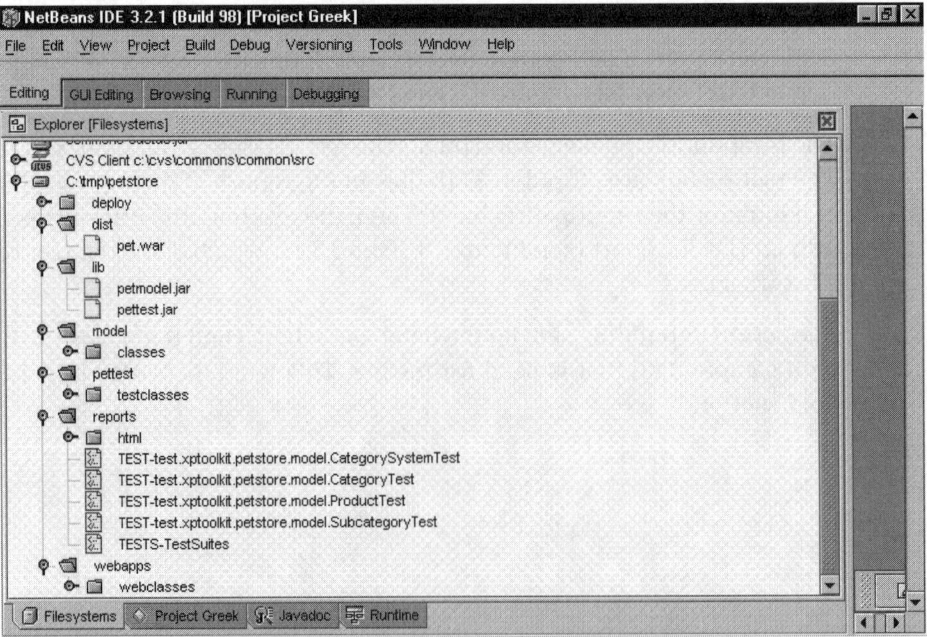

Figure 3.9 Output directory structure of the baseline.

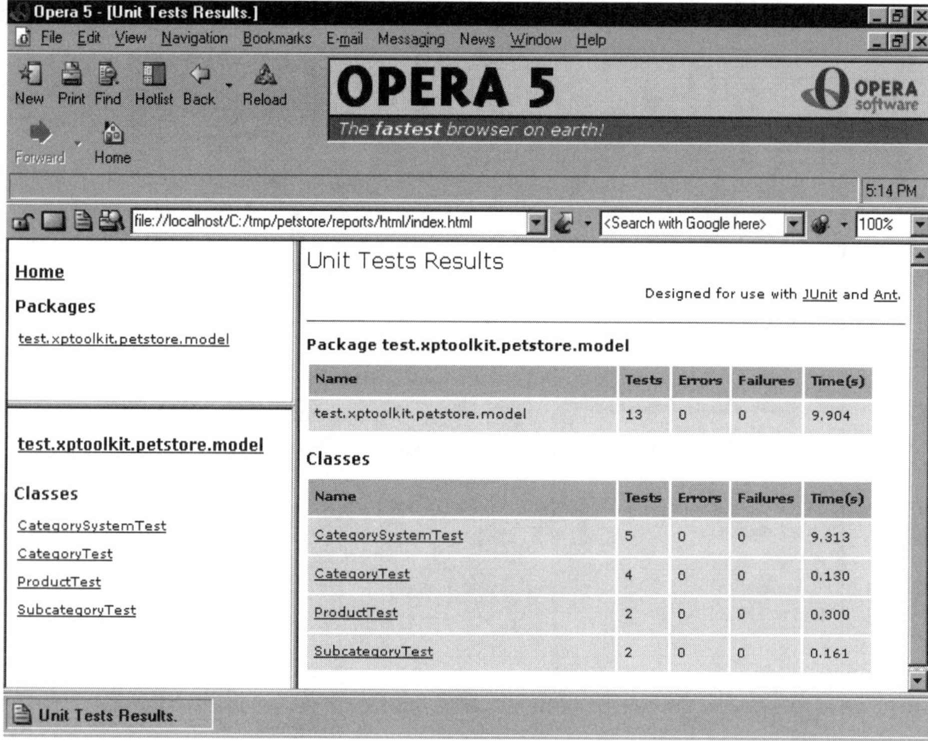

Figure 3.10 Results of all the tests.

The main buildfile has seven targets (see Figure 3.12). *Targets* are like actions that are executed. We'll explain the concept of a target in depth in Chapter 5, "Building Java Applications with Ant." We'll explore the nuances of target names in Chapters 5 through 7. By the end of those chapters, you will be able to determine what a buildfile does just by looking at the target names.

The main buildfile orchestrates the execution of other targets in the other buildfiles. For example, the main buildfile target test does the following (Figure 3.10 shows the result):

```
<target name="test" depends="clean,build"
        description="build the model and application modules.">
    <ant dir="./Test" target="cleanTest">
        <property name="outdir" value="${outdir}" />
        <property name="setProps" value="true" />
    </ant>
</target>
```

This code invokes the cleanTest target on the test buildfile. It also causes the clean and buildfile targets to be executed for main, which in turn call the clean and build targets on the model and webapplication buildfiles. For example,

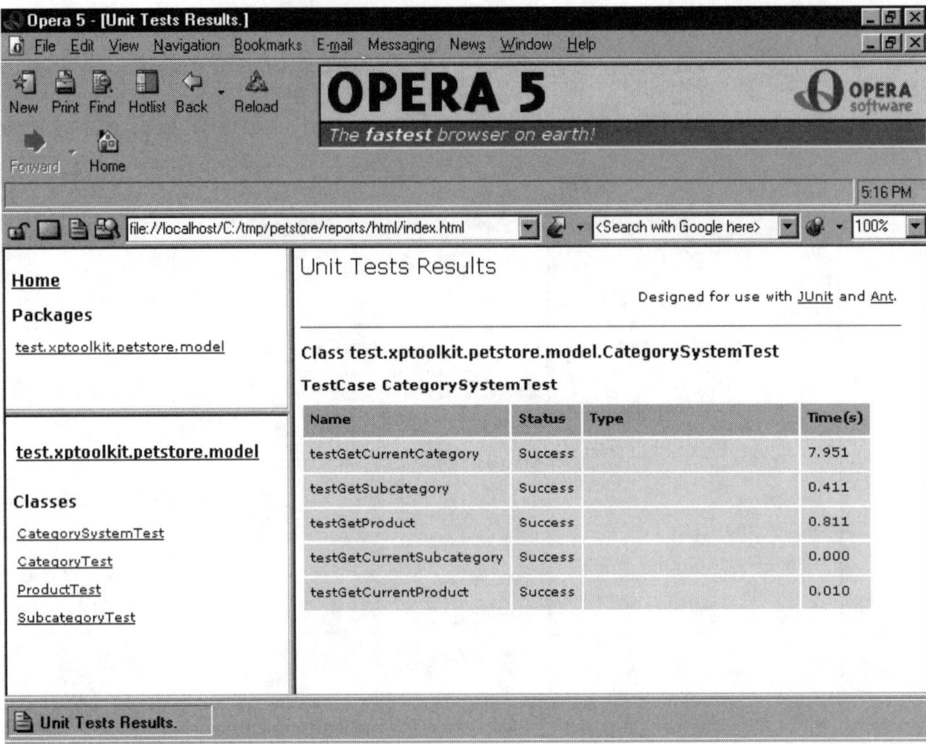

Figure 3.11 Result of CategorySystemTest.

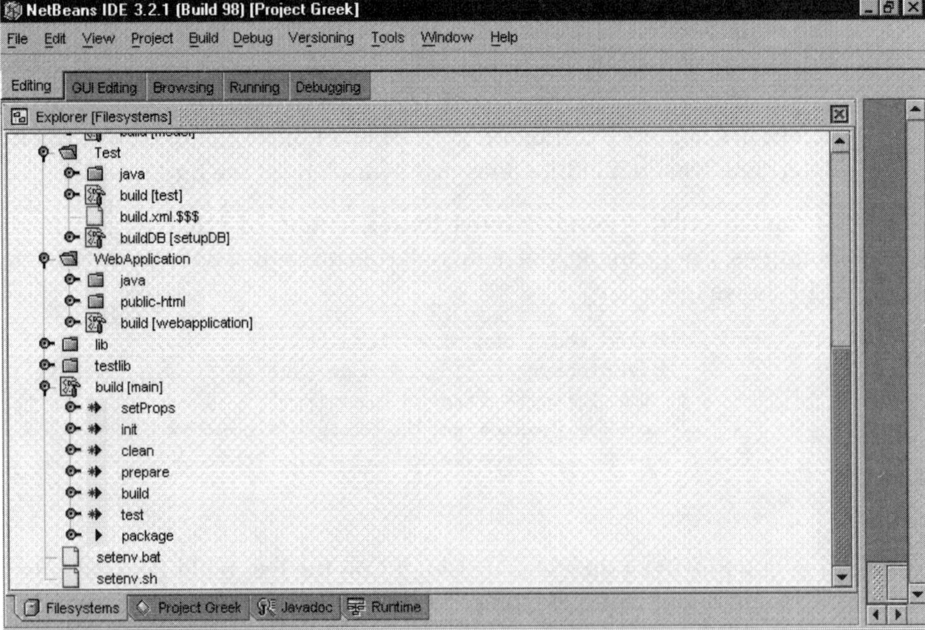

Figure 3.12 Main buildfile target structure.

here is the clean target of main that calls the clean target of model and webapplication as follows (Figure 3.11 shows the results):

```
<target name="clean" depends="init"
        description="clean up the output directories.">
    <ant dir="./Model" target="clean">
        <property name="outdir" value="${outdir}" />
        <property name="setProps" value="true" />

    </ant>


    <ant dir="./WebApplication" target="clean">
        <property name="outdir" value="${outdir}" />
        <property name="setProps" value="true" />
        <property name="ejb" value="true" />
    </ant>

    <delete dir="${outdir}" />

</target>
```

Setting Up the Database with Test Data: A Small Taste of Ant

Testing applications with database access can be tricky. One of the problems is that you need data in the database to test the application. It's a classic chicken-or-egg problem: What do you do first? Another problem with databases is realizing that the DDL for the schema is source code and should be managed in the Concurrent Versioning System (CVS) or equivalent. In this example, to solve the problem of needing data to test our model objects, we created an Ant script that can populate the database (see Listing 3.3). Although we haven't covered Ant yet, we included Listing 3.3 here because it shows the structure of the database for the sample application. We will cover Ant and buildfiles in detail throughout the next three chapters.

The fundamental problem with testing code that interacts with a database is that you cannot test database access layer code unless you have data. The data must be repeatable so that the test cases have a point of reference. The populateTables target solves the problem by populating the database with sample data that we can test for later in the unit tests.

You should also have a development and/or test database so that you can set the database back to a testable state. The code in Listing 3.3 helps you put the database into a testable state. You could connect the populateTables target to the

Ant test buildfile as a dependency. We will cover this topic further in Chapter 7 when we discuss database access layer unit testing.

```
<?xml version="1.0"?>

<project name="setupDB" basedir="." default="build">

    <property name="driver" value="sun.jdbc.odbc.JdbcOdbcDriver" />
    <property name="url" value="jdbc:odbc:petstore" />
    <property name="user" value="" />
    <property name="password" value="" />

    <target name="createTables">
        <sql    driver="${driver}" url="${url}"
                userid="${user}" password="${password}" >

            CREATE TABLE CATEGORY (
                ID int PRIMARY KEY,
                DESCRIPTION varchar (100) NOT NULL ,
                NAME varchar (25)  NOT NULL
            )

            CREATE TABLE SUBCATEGORY (
                ID int PRIMARY KEY,
                FK_CATEGORY_ID int REFERENCES CATEGORY(ID),
                DESCRIPTION varchar (50) NOT NULL ,
                NAME varchar (25)  NOT NULL
            )

            CREATE TABLE PRODUCT (
                DESCRIPTION varchar (50) NOT NULL ,
                NAME varchar (20)  NOT NULL ,
                ID int IDENTITY (1, 1) PRIMARY KEY,
                FK_SUBCATEGORY_ID int REFERENCES SUBCATEGORY(ID),
                QTY int DEFAULT (5),
                PRICE DECIMAL(10,2) not null,
            )
        </sql>
    </target>

    <target name="dropTables">
        <sql    driver="${driver}" url="${url}"
                userid="${user}" password="${password}" >

            DROP TABLE PRODUCT
            DROP TABLE SUBCATEGORY
```

Listing 3.3 Ant buildfile for creating the database (./Test/buildDB.xml). (continues)

```
            DROP TABLE CATEGORY

        </sql>
    </target>

    <target name="populateTables">
        <sql    driver="${driver}" url="${url}"
                userid="${user}" password="${password}" >

        insert into category (description, name, id)
                    values ('test data', 'test',777)

        insert into subcategory (name, description, fk_category_ID, id)
                    values ('dogs', 'dogs description', 777, 111)
        insert into subcategory (name, description, fk_category_ID, id)
                    values ('cats', 'cats description', 777, 222)
        insert into subcategory (name, description, fk_category_ID, id)
                    values ('fish', 'fish description', 777, 333)
        insert into subcategory (name, description, fk_category_ID, id)
                    values ('birds', 'birds description', 777, 444)
        insert into subcategory (name, description, fk_category_ID, id)
                    values ('reptiles', 'reptiles description', 777, 555)

        insert into Product (description, name, price, fk_subcategory_id)
                    values('Poodle description','Poodle',1,111)
        insert into Product (description, name, price, fk_subcategory_id)
                    values('Scottie description','Scottie',1,111)
        insert into Product (description, name, price, fk_subcategory_id)
                    values('Schnauzer description','Schnauzer',1,111)
        insert into Product (description, name, price, fk_subcategory_id)
                    values('Calico description','Calico',1,222)
        insert into Product (description, name, price, fk_subcategory_id)
                    values('Jaguar description','Jaguar',1,222)
        insert into Product (description, name, price, fk_subcategory_id)
                    values('Siamese description','Siamese',1,222)
        insert into Product (description, name, price, fk_subcategory_id)
                    values('Goldfish description','Goldfish',1,333)
        insert into Product (description, name, price, fk_subcategory_id)
                    values('Shark description','Shark',1,333)
        insert into Product (description, name, price, fk_subcategory_id)
                    values('Piranha description','Piranha',1,333)
        insert into Product (description, name, price, fk_subcategory_id)
                    values('Parakeet description','Parakeet',1,444)
        insert into Product (description, name, price, fk_subcategory_id)
                    values('Canary description','Canary',1,444)
        insert into Product (description, name, price, fk_subcategory_id)
```

Listing 3.3 Ant buildfile for creating the database (./Test/buildDB.xml). (continues)

```
                values('Wren description','Wren',1,444)
    insert into Product (description, name, price, fk_subcategory_id)
                values('Iguana description','Iguana',1,555)
    insert into Product (description, name, price, fk_subcategory_id)
                values('Boa description','Boa',1,555)
    insert into Product (description, name, price, fk_subcategory_id)
                values('Python description','Python',1,555)
    insert into Product (description, name, price, fk_subcategory_id)
                values('African Tree Frog description','African Tree
                                                    Frog',1,555)

    </sql>
  </target>

  <target name="build" depends="createTables,populateTables" />

</project>
```

Listing 3.3 Ant buildfile for creating the database (./Test/buildDB.xml).

Listing 3.3 uses the Ant SQL task to create the tables, populate the tables, and (later) drop the tables. In order to use the SQL task, we need to pass it the JDBC URL, user name, and password. Because we will do this three times, we define some properties to hold these values:

```
<property name="driver" value="sun.jdbc.odbc.JdbcOdbcDriver" />
<property name="url" value="jdbc:odbc:petstore" />
<property name="user" value="" />
<property name="password" value="" />
```

Each time we call the SQL task, we pass it these values. Here is the SQL task used in BuildDB:

```
<target name="createTables">
        <sql    driver="${driver}" url="${url}"
                userid="${user}" password="${password}" >
```

The first thing we do with the SQL task is create the database tables. There are only three tables, so creating them is easy:

```
<sql    driver="${driver}" url="${url}"
        userid="${user}" password="${password}" >

    CREATE TABLE CATEGORY (
        ID int PRIMARY KEY,
        DESCRIPTION varchar (100) NOT NULL ,
        NAME varchar (25)  NOT NULL
    )
```

```
        CREATE TABLE SUBCATEGORY (
            ID int PRIMARY KEY,
            FK_CATEGORY_ID int REFERENCES CATEGORY(ID),
            DESCRIPTION varchar (50) NOT NULL ,
            NAME varchar (25)  NOT NULL
        )

        CREATE TABLE PRODUCT (
            ID int IDENTITY (1, 1) PRIMARY KEY
            DESCRIPTION varchar (50) NOT NULL ,
            NAME varchar (20)  NOT NULL ,
            FK_SUBCATEGORY_ID int REFERENCES SUBCATEGORY(ID),
            QTY int DEFAULT (5),
            PRICE DECIMAL(10,2) not null,
        )
</sql>
```

IDENTITY

One problem with this example is that it uses the IDENTITY keyword to define the primary key ID of the product. The IDENTITY keyword is removed in the second iteration of our application. If you are using a database that does not support the IDENTITY keyword (such as Access or Oracle), then you will have to change this line of code to something equivalent for your RDBMS system.

After we create the tables, we need to populate them with some sample data. The tables model a hierarchial data structure, so we have to insert category rows, then subcategory rows, and then products.

First we insert the parent category:

```
insert into category (description, name, id)
                values ('test data', 'test',777)
```

Then we insert the subcategory and associate it with the parent category:

```
insert into subcategory (name, description, fk_category_ID, id)
            values ('dogs', 'dogs description', 777, 111)
  . . .
```

Finally, we add products to the subcategory:

```
        insert into Product (description, name, price,
fk_subcategory_id)
                    values('Poodle description','Poodle',1,111)
        insert into Product (description, name, price,
fk_subcategory_id)
                    values('Scottie description','Scottie',1,111)
```

```
        insert into Product (description, name, price,
                             fk_subcategory_id)
                values('Schnauzer description','Schnauzer',1,111)
    . . .
```

Sometimes we need to make additions to the tables, and we want to incorporate the additions into the build. Thus, it is very convenient to delete the tables and the test data. We add the target dropTables, defined as follows:

```
<target name="dropTables">
    <sql    driver="${driver}" url="${url}"
            userid="${user}" password="${password}" >

        DROP TABLE PRODUCT
        DROP TABLE SUBCATEGORY
        DROP TABLE CATEGORY

    </sql>
</target>
```

Notice from the DDL in the createTables target that there are primary key constraints; thus the tables must be dropped in the order specified here.

Complete Listings

The complete code for the pet store case study can be downloaded from www.wiley.com/compbooks/hightower.

Model Package Complete Listings

The model (Listings 3.4 through 3.8) is the business interface for the system. It is the façade covering the rest of the systems. Most of the tests can be run against the model classes.

```
package xptoolkit.petstore.model;

public class CategorySystem {
    private Category currentCategory;
    private Subcategory currentSubcategory;
    private Product currentProduct;

    public CategorySystem() throws Exception {
        currentCategory = Category.getCategory();
```

Listing 3.4 CategorySystem. (continues)

```
        currentCategory.setId(777);
    }

    public Category getCurrentCategory() {
        return currentCategory;
    }

    public Subcategory getCurrentSubcategory() {
        return currentSubcategory;
    }

    public Product getCurrentProduct() {
        return currentProduct;
    }

    public Subcategory getSubcategory(int id) throws Exception {
        currentSubcategory = currentCategory.getSubcategory(id);
        return currentSubcategory;
    }

    public Product getProduct(int id) throws Exception {
        currentProduct = currentSubcategory.getProduct(id);
        return currentProduct;
    }
}
```

Listing 3.4 CategorySystem.

```
package xptoolkit.petstore.model;

import java.util.*;

public abstract class Category extends CatalogItem {

    protected Subcategory[] subcategories;

    public static Category getCategory() throws ClassNotFoundException,
                                               InstantiationException,
                                               IllegalAccessException {

        String className =
            System.getProperty("xptoolkit.petstore.category.class",
                               "xptoolkit.petstore.dbmodel.CategoryDB");

        Class categoryClass = Class.forName(className);
```

Listing 3.5 Category. (continues)

```
        return (Category)categoryClass.newInstance();
    }

    public Subcategory[] getSubcategories() throws Exception {
        return subcategories;
    }

    public abstract Subcategory getSubcategory(int id) throws Exception;

    public String toString() {
        return "Category [ " +
            super.toString() +
            "]";
    }
}
```

Listing 3.5 Category.

```
package xptoolkit.petstore.model;

public abstract class CatalogItem {

    protected int id;
    protected String name;
    protected String description;

    public int getId() {
        return id;
    }

    public void setId(int id) throws Exception {
        this.id = id;
    }

    public String getName() {
        return name;
    }

    public void setName(String name) {
        this.name = name;
    }

    public String getDescription() {
        return description;
    }
```

Listing 3.6 CatalogItem. (continues)

```
    public void setDescription(String description) {
        this.description = description;
    }

    public String toString() {
        return "" + id + ", " + name + ", " + description;
    }
}
```

Listing 3.6 CatalogItem.

```
package xptoolkit.petstore.model;

public abstract class Subcategory extends CatalogItem {

    protected int fkCategoryId;

    protected Product[] products;

    public int getFkCategoryId() throws Exception {
        return fkCategoryId;
    }

    public void setFkCategoryId(int fkCategoryId) {
        this.fkCategoryId = fkCategoryId;;
    }

    public Product[] getProducts() throws Exception {
        return products;
    }

    public abstract Product getProduct(int id) throws Exception;

    public String toString() {
        return "Subcategory [ " +
            super.toString() + ", " +
            fkCategoryId +
            "]";
    }
}
```

Listing 3.7 Subcategory.

```
package xptoolkit.petstore.model;

public abstract class Product extends CatalogItem {

    protected int price;
    protected int qty;
    protected int fkSubcategoryId;

    public int getPrice() {
        return price;
    }

    public void setPrice(int price) {
        this.price = price;
    }

    public int getQty() {
        return qty;
    }

    public void setQty(int qty) {
        this.qty = qty;
    }

    public int getFkSubcategoryId() {
        return fkSubcategoryId;
    }

    public void setFkSubcategoryId(int fkSubcategoryId) {
        this.fkSubcategoryId = fkSubcategoryId;
    }

    public String toString() {
        return "Product [ " +
            super.toString() + ", " +
            price + ", " +
            qty + ", " +
            fkSubcategoryId +
            "]";
    }
}
```

Listing 3.8 Product.

dbmodel Package Complete Listings

The dbmodel package (Listings 3.9 through 3.12) is the implementation of the model. It uses JDBC to get rows out of the database and converts them to Java objects that can be manipulated by the JSPs.

```
package xptoolkit.petstore.dbmodel;

import xptoolkit.petstore.model.Category;
import xptoolkit.petstore.model.Subcategory;
import xptoolkit.petstore.model.Product;
import java.sql.*;
import java.util.ArrayList;
import java.util.HashMap;
import java.util.Map;

public class CategoryDB extends Category implements Entity {

    public static final String COLUMNS = "ID, NAME, DESCRIPTION";

    private static Connection connCategory;
    private static Connection connSubcategory;
    private static PreparedStatement prepLoadCategory;
    private static PreparedStatement prepLoadSubcategories;

    boolean loaded = false;

    static
    {
        try {
            String load = "select " + COLUMNS
                + " from CATEGORY where ID = ? ";
            connCategory = InitPackage.getConnection();
            prepLoadCategory = connCategory.prepareStatement(load);

            load = "select " + SubcategoryDB.COLUMNS
                + " from SUBCATEGORY where FK_CATEGORY_ID = ?";
            connSubcategory = InitPackage.getConnection();
            prepLoadSubcategories =
                    connSubcategory.prepareStatement(load);
        }
```

Listing 3.9 CategoryDB. (continues)

```
        catch (java.lang.Exception e) {
            System.err.println(
                "Unable to load prepared statements for CategoryDB.");
        }
    }

    public CategoryDB() {
        id = -1;
    }

    public void setId(int id) throws Exception {
        this.id = id;
        subcategories = null;
        load(this);
    }

    private void ensureLoaded() throws Exception {
        if (!loaded)
            load(this);

        if (subcategories == null)
            loadSubcategories(this);
    }

    public Subcategory[] getSubcategories() throws Exception {
        ensureLoaded();
        return subcategories;
    }

    public Subcategory getSubcategory(int id) throws Exception {
        ensureLoaded();
        if (subcategories != null) {
            for (int x = 0; x < subcategories.length; x++) {
                if (subcategories[x].getId() == id)
                    return subcategories[x];
            }
        }

        return null;
    }

    private void init(ResultSet rs) throws SQLException {
        id = rs.getInt(ID);
        name = rs.getString(NAME);
        description = rs.getString(DESCRIPTION);
    }
```

Listing 3.9 CategoryDB. (continues)

```
    private void reset() {
        name = null;
        description = null;
    }

    private static synchronized void load(CategoryDB category)
        throws SQLException {

        ResultSet resultSet = null;
        try {
            prepLoadCategory.setInt(1, category.getId());
            resultSet = prepLoadCategory.executeQuery();
            if ( resultSet.next() ) {
                category.init(resultSet);
                category.loaded = true;
            }
            else {
                category.reset();
                category.loaded = false;
            }
        }
        finally {
            if (resultSet != null)
                resultSet.close();
        }
   }

    private static synchronized void
        loadSubcategories(CategoryDB category) throws SQLException {

       ArrayList list = new ArrayList();
       ResultSet results = null;

       try {
            prepLoadSubcategories.setInt(1, category.getId());
            results = prepLoadSubcategories.executeQuery();
            while( results.next() ) {
                SubcategoryDB subcategory = new SubcategoryDB(results);
                Integer key = new Integer(subcategory.getId());
                list.add(subcategory);
            }
       }
       finally{
            if(results!=null)results.close();
       }
```

Listing 3.9 CategoryDB. (continues)

```
        category.subcategories = new SubcategoryDB[list.size()];
        category.subcategories = (Subcategory[])
                        list.toArray(category.subcategories);
    }
}
```

Listing 3.9 CategoryDB.

```
package xptoolkit.petstore.dbmodel;

import java.sql.*;
import java.util.*;
import xptoolkit.petstore.model.*;

public class SubcategoryDB extends Subcategory implements Entity {

    public static final String COLUMNS =
        "ID, NAME, DESCRIPTION, FK_CATEGORY_ID";

    private static final String FK_CATEGORY_ID = "FK_CATEGORY_ID";

    private static Connection connSubcategory;
    private static Connection connProducts;
    private static PreparedStatement prepLoadSubcategory;
    private static PreparedStatement prepLoadProducts;

    boolean loaded = false;
    Product[] products = null;

    static {
        try {
            String load = "select " + COLUMNS
                + " from SUBCATEGORY where ID = ?";
            connSubcategory = InitPackage.getConnection();
            prepLoadSubcategory = connSubcategory.prepareStatement(load);

            load = "select " + ProductDB.COLUMNS
                + " from PRODUCT where FK_SUBCATEGORY_ID = ?";
            connProducts = InitPackage.getConnection();
            prepLoadProducts = connProducts.prepareStatement(load);
        }
        catch (java.lang.Exception e){
            System.err.println(
                "Unable to load prepared statements for SubcategoryDB.");
            e.printStackTrace();
```

Listing 3.10 SubcategoryDB. (continues)

```
        }
    }

    SubcategoryDB(ResultSet rs) throws SQLException {
        init(rs);
    }

    SubcategoryDB() {
        id = -1;
    }

    public void setId(int id) throws Exception{
        this.id = id;
        load(this);
    }

    private void ensureLoaded() throws Exception {
        if (!loaded)
            load(this);

        if (products == null)
            loadProducts(this);
    }

    public Product[] getProducts() throws Exception {
        ensureLoaded();
        return products;
    }

    public Product getProduct(int id) throws Exception {
        ensureLoaded();
        if (products != null) {
            for (int x = 0; x < products.length; x++) {
                if (products[x].getId() == id)
                    return products[x];
            }
        }

        return null;
    }

    private void init(ResultSet rs) throws SQLException {
        this.id = rs.getInt(ID);
        this.name = rs.getString(NAME).trim();
        this.description = rs.getString(DESCRIPTION).trim();
        this.fkCategoryId = rs.getInt(FK_CATEGORY_ID);
```

Listing 3.10 SubcategoryDB. (continues)

```
    }

    private void reset() {
        this.name = null;
        this.description = null;
        this.fkCategoryId = -1;
    }

    private static synchronized void load(SubcategoryDB subcategory)
        throws SQLException {

        ResultSet resultSet = null;
        try {
            prepLoadSubcategory.setInt(1, subcategory.getId());
            resultSet = prepLoadSubcategory.executeQuery();
            if ( resultSet.next() ) {
                subcategory.init(resultSet);
                subcategory.loaded = true;
            }
            else {
                subcategory.reset();
                subcategory.loaded = false;
            }
        }
        finally {
            if (resultSet != null)
                resultSet.close();
        }
    }

    private static synchronized void loadProducts(
                                   SubcategoryDB subcategory)
        throws SQLException {

        ArrayList list = new ArrayList();
        ResultSet resultSet = null;

        try {
            prepLoadProducts.setInt(1, subcategory.getId());
            resultSet = prepLoadProducts.executeQuery();
            while( resultSet.next() ) {
                ProductDB product = new ProductDB(resultSet);
                Integer key = new Integer(product.getId());
                list.add(product);
            }
        }
```

Listing 3.10 SubcategoryDB. (continues)

```
        finally {
            if (resultSet != null) resultSet.close();
        }

        subcategory.products = new Product[list.size()];
        subcategory.products =
                    (Product[])list.toArray(subcategory.products);
    }
}
```

Listing 3.10 SubcategoryDB.

```
package xptoolkit.petstore.dbmodel;

import java.sql.*;

public interface Entity {

    public static final String ID = "ID";
    public static final String NAME = "NAME";
    public static final String DESCRIPTION = "DESCRIPTION";

    public void setId(int id) throws Exception;
}
```

Listing 3.11 Entity.

```
package xptoolkit.petstore.dbmodel;

import java.sql.*;

public class InitPackage extends java.lang.Object {

    private static String url;

    static {
        url = System.getProperty("petstore.jdbc.url",
                                 "jdbc:odbc:petstore");
        try {
            String driver =
                System.getProperty("petstore.jdbc.driver",
                                   "sun.jdbc.odbc.JdbcOdbcDriver");
            Class.forName(driver);
```

Listing 3.12 InitPackage. (continues)

```
        }
        catch (Exception e){
            System.err.println("unable to load driver");
        }
    }

    static Connection getConnection() throws SQLException {
       return DriverManager.getConnection(url);
    }

    private InitPackage() {}
}
```

Listing 3.12 InitPackage.

Test Package Complete Listings

The test package (Listings 3.13 through 3.17) tests each class in the model class; these classes are really implemented in the dbmodel. The concepts in these classes will be covered in detail in Chapter 7.

```
package test.xptoolkit.petstore.model;
import xptoolkit.petstore.model.CategorySystem;

import junit.framework.*;

public class CategorySystemTest extends TestCase {
    CategorySystem system;

    public CategorySystemTest(java.lang.String testName) {
        super(testName);
    }

    public static void main(java.lang.String[] args) {
        junit.textui.TestRunner.run(suite());
    }

    public static Test suite() {
        TestSuite suite = new TestSuite(CategorySystemTest.class);
```

Listing 3.13 CategorySystemTest. (continues)

```
        return suite;
    }

    protected void setUp()throws Exception {
        system = new CategorySystem();
    }


    /** Test of getCurrentCategory method, of class
        xptoolkit.petstore.model.CategorySystem. */
    public void testGetCurrentCategory() throws Exception{
        assertNotNull(system.getCurrentCategory());
    }

    /** Test of getSubcategory method, of class
        xptoolkit.petstore.model.CategorySystem. */
    public void testGetSubcategory() throws Exception{
        assertNotNull(system.getSubcategory(111));
    }

    /** Test of getProduct method, of class
        xptoolkit.petstore.model.CategorySystem. */
    public void testGetProduct() throws Exception {
        testGetSubcategory();
        assertNotNull(system.getProduct(1));
    }

        /** Test of getCurrentSubcategory method, of class
            xptoolkit.petstore.model.CategorySystem. */
    public void testGetCurrentSubcategory() throws Exception{
        testGetSubcategory();
        assertNotNull(system.getCurrentSubcategory());
    }

    /** Test of getCurrentProduct method, of class
        xptoolkit.petstore.model.CategorySystem. */
    public void testGetCurrentProduct() throws Exception{
        testGetSubcategory();
        testGetProduct();
        assertNotNull(system.getCurrentProduct());
    }

}
```

Listing 3.13 CategorySystemTest.

```
package test.xptoolkit.petstore.model;

import java.util.*;
import junit.framework.*;

import xptoolkit.petstore.model.Category;
import xptoolkit.petstore.model.Subcategory;


public class CategoryTest extends TestCase {

    Category category; //object under test

    public CategoryTest(java.lang.String testName) {
        super(testName);
    }

    public static void main(java.lang.String[] args) {
        junit.textui.TestRunner.run(suite());
    }

    public static Test suite() {
        TestSuite suite = new TestSuite(CategoryTest.class);

        return suite;
    }


    public void setUp()throws Exception{
        category = Category.getCategory();
        category.setId(777);
    }
    /** Test of getCategory method, of class
        xptoolkit.petstore.model.Category. */
    public void testGetCategory() throws Exception{
        System.out.println("testGetCategory");
        Category category = Category.getCategory();
        category.setId(777);
        this.assertNotNull("category", category);

    }

    /** Test of getSubcategories method, of class
        xptoolkit.petstore.model.Category. */
    public void testGetSubcategories() throws Exception {
        Subcategory [] categories = category.getSubcategories();
        assertNotNull("categories", categories);
```

Listing 3.14 CategoryTest. (continues)

```
        for (int index=0; index < categories.length; index++){
            assertNotNull("subcategory", categories[index]);
        }
    }

        /** Test of getSubcategory method, of class
            xptoolkit.petstore.model.Category. */
    public void testGetSubcategory() throws Exception {
        Subcategory [] categories = category.getSubcategories();
        assertNotNull("categories", categories);
        for (int index=0; index < categories.length; index++){
            Subcategory subcat=categories[index];
            int id = subcat.getId();
            assertNotNull("subcategory", category.getSubcategory(id));
        }
    }


    public void testGetters() throws Exception {
        assertNotNull("name", category.getName());
        assertNotNull("description", category.getDescription());

    }

}
```

Listing 3.14 CategoryTest.

```
package test.xptoolkit.petstore.model;
import junit.framework.*;
import xptoolkit.petstore.model.*;


public class SubcategoryTest extends TestCase {
    CategorySystem system;
    Subcategory category;

    protected void setUp()throws Exception{
        system = new CategorySystem();
        category = system.getCurrentCategory().getSubcategory(111);
    }


    public SubcategoryTest(java.lang.String testName) {
        super(testName);
```

Listing 3.15 SubcategoryTest. (continues)

```
    }

    public static void main(java.lang.String[] args) {
        junit.textui.TestRunner.run(suite());
    }

    public static Test suite() {
        TestSuite suite = new TestSuite(SubcategoryTest.class);

        return suite;
    }

    /** Test of getFkCategoryId method, of class
        xptoolkit.petstore.model.Subcategory. */
    public void testGetters() {
        assertNotNull("name", category.getName());
        assertNotNull("description", category.getDescription());
    }


    /** Test of getProducts method, of class
        xptoolkit.petstore.model.Subcategory. */
    public void testGetProducts() throws Exception{
        String [] testDataExpected = new String []
                         {"Poodle", "Scottie", "Schnauzer"};


        Product products [] = category.getProducts();
        for (int index = 0; index < products.length; index++){
            Product product = products[index];
            assertEquals("check Name", testDataExpected[index],
                         product.getName());
        }

    }


}
```

Listing 3.15 SubcategoryTest.

```
package test.xptoolkit.petstore.model;
import xptoolkit.petstore.model.*;
import junit.framework.*;
```

Listing 3.16 ProductTest. (continues)

```
public class ProductTest extends TestCase {

    CategorySystem system;
    Product product;

    protected void setUp()throws Exception{
        system = new CategorySystem();
        system.getSubcategory(111);
        product = system.getProduct(1);
    }


    public ProductTest(java.lang.String testName) {
        super(testName);
    }

    public static void main(java.lang.String[] args) {
        junit.textui.TestRunner.run(suite());
    }

    public static Test suite() {
        TestSuite suite = new TestSuite(ProductTest.class);

        return suite;
    }

    /** Test of getPrice method
        of class xptoolkit.petstore.model.Product. */
    public void testSetters() {
        product.setName("Boo");
        product.setDescription("Designer");
        product.setPrice(5);
        product.setQty(5);
    }

    /** Test of getPrice method
        of class xptoolkit.petstore.model.Product. */
    public void testGetters() {
        this.assertEquals("name", product.getName(), "Poodle");
        this.assertEquals("description",
                          product.getDescription(),
                          "Poodle description");
        testSetters();
        this.assertEquals("name", product.getName(), "Boo");
```

Listing 3.16 ProductTest. (continues)

```
        this.assertEquals("description",
                          product.getDescription(),
                          "Designer");

    }

}
```

Listing 3.16 ProductTest.

```
package xptoolkit.petstore.dbmodel;

import java.sql.*;
import junit.framework.*;

public class InitPackageTest extends TestCase {

    public InitPackageTest(java.lang.String testName) {
        super(testName);
    }

    public static void main(java.lang.String[] args) {
        junit.textui.TestRunner.run(suite());
    }

    public static Test suite() {
        TestSuite suite = new TestSuite(InitPackageTest.class);

        return suite;
    }

    /** Test of getConnection method, of class
        xptoolkit.petstore.dbmodel.InitPackage. */
    public void testGetConnection() throws SQLException{
        System.out.println("testGetConnection");
        Connection connection=InitPackage.getConnection();
        assertNotNull("connection", connection);

    }

}
```

Listing 3.17 InitPackageTest.

JSPs and Web.xml Complete Listings

The JSPs (Listings 3.18 through 3.26) don't have a corresponding test like the model. They will be added after we cover the HttpUnit in Chapter 9.

```
<%@ include file="category_sys.jsp" %>

<html>
    <head>
        <title>
            AAA Pets: <%= request.getParameter("title")%>
    </title>
</head>

<body>
    <h1>AAA Pets</h1>

    <table border="1" width="100%">
        <tr>
            <td width="20%" align="center">
                <a href="index.jsp">Company</a>
            </td>
            <td width="20%" align="center">
                <a href="under_construction.html">Mission</a>
            </td>
            <td width="20%" align="center">
                <a href="under_construction.html">Shopping Cart</a>
            </td>
            <td width="20%" align="center">
                <a href="under_construction.html">Links</a>
            </td>

    </table>

    <table border="1" width="100%">
        <tr>
        <%
            Category category = categorySystem.getCurrentCategory();
            Subcategory [] subcategories = category.getSubcategories();
            for (int index=0; index < subcategories.length; index++){
                Subcategory subcategory = subcategories[index];
        %>
```

Listing 3.18 Header.jsp. (continues)

```
            <td width="20%" align="center">
                <a href="subcategory.jsp?id=<%=subcategory.getId()%>">
                    <%=subcategory.getName()%>
                </a>
                <br />
            </td>
        <%}%>
    </table>

    <table width="100%">
```

Listing 3.18 Header.jsp.

```
        <tr>
            <td width="100%" align="left">
            </td>
        </tr>
    </table>

    <p align="center">
        <font size="-1">
            Copyright 2001, Rick Hightower<br>
            AAA Pets is a fictional company any similarities to a real
            company is coincidental.
        </font>
    </p>

    </body>
</html>
```

Listing 3.19 Footer.jsp.

```
<%@page import="xptoolkit.petstore.model.*" %>
<jsp:useBean id="categorySystem" class="CategorySystem" scope="session"/>
```

Listing 3.20 Category_sys.jsp.

```
<jsp:include page="header.jsp" flush="true">
     <jsp:param name="title" value="Welcome"/>
</jsp:include>

    <div align="center">
```

Listing 3.21 Index.jsp. (continues)

```
        <b>Welcome to AAA Pets</b>
    </div>

<jsp:include page="footer.jsp" flush="true" />
```

Listing 3.21 Index.jsp.

```
<jsp:include page="header.jsp" flush="true">
      <jsp:param name="title" value="Welcome"/>
</jsp:include>

    <div align="center">
        <b>Sorry, I could not find that page.</b>
    </div>

<jsp:include page="footer.jsp" flush="true" />
```

Listing 3.22 NotFound.jsp.

```
<%@ include file="category_sys.jsp" %>
<%
    String categoryId = request.getParameter("id");
    Category category = categorySystem.getCurrentCategory();
    category.setId( Integer.parseInt(categoryId) );
%>

<jsp:include page="header.jsp" flush="true">
      <jsp:param name="title" value="<%= category.getName() %>"/>
</jsp:include>

    <table border="1" width="100%">
        <tr>
            <td width="100%" colspan="2" align="center">
                <b>
                    <%= category.getName() %>
                </b>
                <br>
                <%= category.getDescription() %>
            </td>
        </tr>
        <tr>
            <td width="20%">
```

Listing 3.23 Category.jsp.

```
<%
    Subcategory[] subcategories = category.getSubcategories();
    for (int index = 0; index < subcategories.length; index++) {
        Subcategory subcategory = subcategories[index];
%>
<a href="subcategory.jsp?id=<%=subcategory.getId()%>">
<%=subcategory.getName()%></a>
        <br>
<%
    }
%>

            </td>
            <td> </td>
        </tr>
    </table>

<jsp:include page="footer.jsp" flush="true" />
```

Listing 3.23 Category.jsp.

```
<%@ include file="category_sys.jsp" %>
<%
    Category category = categorySystem.getCurrentCategory();
    Subcategory[] subcategories = category.getSubcategories();
    String subcategoryId = request.getParameter("id");
    int id = Integer.parseInt(subcategoryId);
    Subcategory subcategory = categorySystem.getSubcategory(id);

    String title = category.getName() + " : " + subcategory.getName();
%>

<jsp:include page="header.jsp" flush="true">
      <jsp:param name="title" value="<%= title %>"/>
</jsp:include>

    <table border="1" width="100%">
        <tr>
            <td width="100%" colspan="2" align="center">
                <b>
                    <%= category.getName() %>
```

Listing 3.24 Subcategory.jsp. (continues)

```
                </b>
                <br>
                <%= category.getDescription() %>
                <br>
                <b>
                    <%= subcategory.getName() %>
                </b>
                <br>
                <%= subcategory.getDescription() %>
            </td>
        </tr>
        <tr>
            <td width="20%" valign="top">

<%
    for (int index = 0; index < subcategories.length; index++) {
        Subcategory subcat = subcategories[index];
%>
<a href="subcategory.jsp?id=<%=subcat.getId()%>">
<%=subcat.getName()%></a>
        <br>
<%
    }
%>
            </td>
            <td valign="top">
<%
    Product[] products = subcategory.getProducts();
    for (int pindex = 0; pindex < products.length; pindex++) {
        Product product = products[pindex];
%>
        <a href="product.jsp?id=<%= product.
                getId()%>" target="_blank"><%= product.getName() %></a>
        <br>
<%
    }
%>
            </td>
        </tr>
    </table>

<jsp:include page="footer.jsp" flush="true" />
```

Listing 3.24 Subcategory.jsp.

```
<%@ page import="java.text.NumberFormat,java.util.Locale" %>
<%@ include file="category_sys.jsp" %>
<%
    Category category = categorySystem.getCurrentCategory();
    Subcategory subcategory = categorySystem.getCurrentSubcategory();

    String productId = request.getParameter("id");
    Product product = subcategory.getProduct( Integer.parseInt(productId) );

String title = category.getName() +
                   " : " + subcategory.getName() +
                   " : " + product.getName();
%>

<jsp:include page="header.jsp" flush="true">
      <jsp:param name="title" value="<%= title %>"/>
</jsp:include>


<%
    Locale locale = request.getLocale();
    NumberFormat format = NumberFormat.getCurrencyInstance(locale);
    String price = format.format(product.getPrice());
%>

    <div align="center">
        <b><%= product.getName() %></b>
        <br>

        <%= product.getDescription() %>
        <br>

        <STRONG><%= price %></STRONG>
        <br>
    </div>

<jsp:include page="footer.jsp" flush="true" />
```

Listing 3.25 Product.jsp.

```
<?xml version="1.0" encoding="ISO-8859-1"?>

<!DOCTYPE web-app
  PUBLIC "-//Sun Microsystems, Inc.//DTD Web Application 2.2//EN"
  "http://java.sun.com/j2ee/dtds/web-app_2_2.dtd">
```

Listing 3.26 Web.xml. (continues)

```
<web-app>

    <error-page>
        <error-code>404</error-code>
        <location>/notfound.jsp</location>
    </error-page>

  <!— The Usual Welcome File List —>
  <welcome-file-list>
    <welcome-file>index.jsp</welcome-file>
  </welcome-file-list>

  <servlet-mapping url-pattern='/servlet/*' servlet-name='invoker'/>

</web-app>
```

Listing 3.26 Web.xml.

Summary

This book uses two types of examples: simple examples and case studies. The simple examples demonstrate how to use the tools; they teach you the mechanics of using the tools. The case studies are more involved samples that demonstrate how the tools fit in the larger context of deploying, testing, and refactoring the application.

This chapter also highlights the structure of the pet store case study by showing you the structure of the classes, JSP files, and buildfiles. Later chapters will explain why we structure the buildfiles the way that we do. We briefly whet your appetite by showing buildfiles, test code, and test results; we'll cover them in detail in Chapters 5, 6, 7, and 8.

CHAPTER 4

Continuous Integration with Ant

This chapter is an introduction to the fundamental concepts and techniques involved in using Ant to achieve continuous integration on your projects. *Ant* is a build tool that enables you to automate the build process. In that respect, Ant is similar to the make tool; but unlike make, Ant was designed specifically for Java development. Ant is written in Java, so it works across platforms and does not rely on shell-specific commands that vary greatly in function and usage from operating system to operating system. Instead, Ant relies on the Java platform to perform file access, compilation, and other tasks you need to build your Java projects.

Where To Get Ant

Ant was developed by The Apache Software Foundation as part of their Jakarta project. Ant 1.4 is distributed with The Apache Software License, Version 1.1 and can be downloaded at:

http://jakarta.apache.org/ant/index.html

A major advantage of Ant is its extensibility. Ant is easily extensible using cross-platform Java classes. You can also extend Ant by writing custom Java tasks and using the scripting task, which works with JavaScript (Rhino), Python (JPython—my favorite), NetRexx, and others. In addition, if you must, you can call out to shell scripts, OS executables, and OS commands with the Ant exec task. Then, later, you can write a cross-platform version of the task in Java or with the Ant scripting task, which uses XML for its syntax.

The build-and-deploy cycle should be automated so you don't incorporate operator error. Writing a build script also documents the build process. Documentation becomes critical when a developer leaves your company. By using Ant, your company retains the knowledge needed to deploy the system, because the build-and-deploy process is automated by an Ant script (called a buildfile) and not locked away in the departed developer's IDE (which was set up for his local development environment). Another benefit of using Ant is that the script that automates the build-and-deploy process in effect also documents that process; unlike most IDEs' binary project configuration files, an Ant buildfile is written in human-readable text.

What Is Your Favorite IDE?

Ant complements Integrated Development Environments (IDEs); Ant does not replace IDEs, nor do IDEs replace Ant. IDEs can greatly simplify Java development, but they are not good for automating the build-and-deploy process of a complex project. Every software process needs a repeatable build system as discussed in Chapter 3, "Example Applications," and IDEs do not provide such a system.

Developers become attached to the IDE they use. At our company, we use several different IDEs, including Borland JBuilder, NetBeans, Forte CE, Visual Age for Java, JDE (Java development environment for Emacs), and Ultra Edit. Ant reduces the potential havoc by providing a standard on which to base our build-and-deploy process.

You can use Ant for the organization of deployment and for automated builds. Ant supports the concept of *continuous integration*, as described in the next section. Using Ant to perform continuous integration changes the whole development blueprint of your project. With a little discipline and setup time, continuous integration reduces problems linked with team development.

Developers often talk about automated building and testing but seldom implement it. Ant makes automated building and testing possible and plausible. Ant and JUnit combine well to allow teams to build and test their software several times a day. Such an automated process is worth the sweat. You will find out who broke what sooner—before you forget who did what. You will find integration bugs before they become strange and unpredictable.

Alternatives to Ant exist. However, Ant has become the de facto standard for automating Java builds. For example, Sun's pet store J2EE blueprint application uses Ant. The other day, we went to the Orion application server site to look at some examples, and all of them had corresponding Ant buildfiles. Of course, all the projects at Apache's Jakarta have Ant buildfiles. Ant is popular because it is easy to learn and extend. In addition, several IDEs and development tools support Ant—for example, the NetBeans IDE and Together Control Center.

The next section covers the mechanics of using Ant to create buildfiles.

Basics of Using Ant

This chapter covera the fundamentals of Ant. Chapters 5, 6, and 7 discuss automating tests with Ant and JUnit. This section is a quick tutorial covering the basics of Ant. You will learn about projects, targets, properties, tasks, filesets, pathelements, and so on. Upon completion of this chapter, you should understand Ant well enough to write your own Ant buildfiles.

Projects, Targets, and Tasks

Ant's build scripts, called *buildfiles*, are written in XML. Every buildfile contains one *project* element. A *project* element contains *target* elements. Each *target* consists of a set of *task* elements.

A task performs a function such as copying a file, compiling a project, or creating a JAR file.

A target is a collection of tasks and properties. A target can depend on other targets, meaning that a target does not execute until the targets it depends on are executed (for example, you would normally want to compile classes before you put them in a JAR). To indicate that a target depends on another target, you use the *depends* attribute. Thus, you may have something like the set of targets in Listing 4.1 (we left out the tasks associated with the targets; we'll cover them later).

The project is a group of related targets. Although you can define any target you like, a set of standard naming conventions exists, as we discuss in the section "Standard Targets."

```
<project name="myproject"   default="all" basedir=".">

      <target name="all" depends="clean,fetch,build,test,docs,deploy">
            ...
      </target>
```

Listing 4.1 Targets can depend on other targets for execution. (continues)

```
        <target name="clean" >
            ...
        </target>

        <target name="fetch" >
            ...
        </target>

        <target name="build" depends="clean" >
            ...
        </target>

        <target name="test" depends="build" >
            ...
        </target>


        <target name="docs" depends="clean" >
            ...
        </target>


        <target name="deploy" depends="build, test" >
            ...
        </target>

        <target name="publish" depends="deploy" >
            ...
        </target>

    </project>
```

Listing 4.1 Targets can depend on other targets for execution.

Listing 4.1 contains a build target that could, for example, compile the source and create JAR and WAR files. Notice that the build target depends on the execution of the tasks associated with the clean target (the tasks are not shown). The test target in turn depends on the build target. The order of the dependencies expressed with the target's "depend" attribute in this example is quite logical. For example, you can't test the code if it does not build—after the code is built, it's tested.

You can give targets any name that you like. However, people generally use common Ant names to create buildfiles, as discussed in the next section.

Standard Targets

Steve Loughran wrote an Ant guide called *Ant In Anger*. This guide explains many pitfalls and recommends ways to use Ant. Two very useful suggestions are a list of names for targets and how to divide buildfiles.

The following are some of Steve's recommended names for Ant top-level targets:

test—Run the junit tests

clean—Clean out the output directories

deploy—Ship the JARs, WARs, and so on to the execution system

publish—Output the source and binaries to any distribution site

fetch—Get the latest source from the CVS tree

docs/javadocs—Outputs the documentation

all—Perform clean, fetch, build, test, docs, and deploy

main—The default build process (usually build or build and test)

The following are some recommended names for Ant internal targets:

init—Initialize properties and perform other intialization tasks; read in per-user property files

init-debug—Initialize debug properties

init-release—Initialize release properties

compile—Perform the actual compilation

link/jar—Make the JARs or equivalent

staging—Carry out any pre-deployment process in which the output is dropped off and then tested before being moved to the production site.

We'll discuss some of the thoughts from *Ant in Anger* in this chapter and the next; however, we strongly suggest that you read this guide, because it contains excellent guidelines for using Ant. The guide is included with the Ant binary distribution under the docs directory.

Before we go any further, let's look at a simple example to cement some of the concepts of Ant. The next section presents a straightforward buildfile.

Simple Example

Let's start with a very small, straight forward example of using Ant. We will begin with the now-infamous "hello world" example. It will create an output directory and then compile a Java source file called HelloWorld.java to the output directory.

The Java source file HelloWorld.java is stored in ./src/xptoolkit as follows:

```
package xptoolkit;
public class HelloWorld{
    public static void main(String []args){
        System.out.println("Hello World!");
    }
}
```

The following ant buildfile, build.xml, compiles the source file:

```
<project name="hello" default="compile">

  <target name="prepare">
    <mkdir dir="/tmp/classes" />
  </target>

  <target name="compile" depends="prepare">
    <javac srcdir="./src" destdir="/tmp/classes" />
  </target>


</project>
```

When you run Ant from the command line, it looks for a buildfile called build.xml in the current working directory. To specify a buildfile with a different name, you must specify the buildfile name using the –buildfile command-line argument (discussed in detail later).

Notice that the hello project has targets called compile and prepare. The hello project specifies the compile target as the default target. The compile target has a task called javac, which compiles the location specified by srcdir to the directory specified by the "destdir" attribute. The built-in task javac compiles Java source. Because the default directory location for a project is the current working directory, the javac task will look for a directory called src (srcdir="./src") under the current working directory and compile the contents of the src directory to the /tmp/classes directory.

Notice that the compile target's "depends" attribute points to the prepare target (depends="prepare"). As a result, all the tasks associated with the prepare target will be executed before the tasks associated with the compile target. This is a good thing—otherwise, the javac task might try to compile the source code to a directory that did not exist.

As you can see, you can use the targets and their dependencies to logically build, deploy, and test a complex system. The next section shows you how to set up your Ant buildfiles.

Setting Up Your Environment

If you are running Unix, install Ant in ~/tools/ant; if you are running Windows, install Ant in c:\tools\ant. You can set up the environment variables in Windows by using the Control Panel. However, for your convenience, we created a Unix shell script (setenv.sh) and a Windows batch file (setenv.bat) to set up the needed environment variables.

Your Unix setenv.sh should look something like this:

```
#
# Setup build environment variables using Bourne shell
#
export USR_ROOT=~
export JAVA_HOME=${USR_ROOT}/jdk1.3
export ANT_HOME=${USR_ROOT}/tools/ant
export PATH=${PATH}:${ANT_HOME}/bin
```

Your Windows setenv.bat should look something like this:

```
:
: Setup build environment variables using DOS Batch
:
set USR_ROOT=c:
set JAVA_HOME=%USR_ROOT%\jdk1.3set
CLASSPATH=%USR_ROOT%\jdk1.3\lib\tools.jar;%CLASSPATH%
set ANT_HOME=%USR_ROOT%\tools\Ant
PATH=%PATH%;%ANT_HOME%\bin
```

Both of these setup files begin by setting JAVA_HOME to specify the location where you installed the JDK. This setting should reflect your local development environment—make adjustments accordingly. Then, the files set up the environment variable ANT_HOME, the location where you installed Ant. The examples in this book assume that you have installed Ant in c:\tools\ant on Windows and in ~/tools/ant on Unix; make adjustments if necessary. There are sample setup scripts as well the sample code at this book's Web site: http://www.wiley.com/compbooks/hightower.

Running Ant for the First Time

To run the sample Ant buildfile, go to the directory that contains the project files. On our computer, they are stored under /CVS/XPToolKit/examples/chap4. The directory structure and files looks like this:

```
/CVS/XPToolKit/examples/chap4
   setenv.bat
   setenv.sh
   build.xml
       ./src/xptoolkit
           HelloWorld.java
```

To run Ant, navigate to the examples/chap4 directory and type "ant". As stated earlier, Ant will find build.xml, which is the default name for the buildfile. For example, here is the command-line output you should expect:

```
$ ant
Buildfile: build.xml

prepare:
    [mkdir] Created dir: /tmp/classes

compile:
    [javac] Compiling 1 source file to /tmp/classes

BUILD SUCCESSFUL

Total time: 3 seconds
```

Notice that the targets and their associated tasks are displayed. That's it! We wrote our first Ant buildfile. In the next section, we describe how to use Ant properties.

Working with Properties

You'll often find it helpful to define properties. The properties in Ant are similar to the properties in java.lang.System.getProperites(). The properties can be set by the property task; so, the properties can also be set outside Ant. You can use properties for task attributes by placing the property name between "${" and "}", similar to the way environment variables are set in the Bourne shell. For example, if an "outputdir" property is set with the value "/tmp", then the "outputdir" property could be accessed in an attribute of a task: ${outputdir}/classes would be a resolved to /tmp/classes.

Thus we could change the Ant buildfile to use properties as follows:

```
<project name="hello" default="compile">

  <property name="outputdir" value="/tmp"/>

  <target name="prepare">
    <mkdir dir="${outputdir}/classes" />
  </target>

  <target name="compile" depends="prepare">
    <javac srcdir="./src" destdir="${outputdir}/classes" />
  </target>

</project>
```

This Ant buildfile defines the "outputdir" property. Then, the buildfile uses the property in the "dir" attribute of the mkdir task of the prepare target and the "destdir" attribute of the javac task of the compile target. The property is used in many attributes; then, if it has to change, you only change it once. For example, if you change the location of the output directory using properties, you only have to make the change once, in one—not two—attribute assignments. Using properties this way can make your buildfiles flexible.

Paths and Filesets

Of course, your Java source files are unlikely to be as simple as the "hello world" example. You may need to use external libraries. For example, you may need to use one or more external libraries (JAR or Zip files) with Java binaries to compile the source code of your project.

Ant can make it simple to set up the classpath for your project. You can use the path element tag, which can contain pathelement tags and filesets. There are two types of pathelements: path and location.

A location pathelement sets a single JAR or directory, and a path pathelement sets a colon- or semicolon-separated list of locations (directories and JARs) similar to the CLASSPATH environment variable. The fileset can define a group of files from one directory. This is convenient, for example, when all your library files (JAR files) are in one directory and you don't want to specify them by name. These concepts are much harder to explain than to show; so, look at the next example.

The following is a simple example that uses the Apache Log4J library file (log4j.jar) as if the HelloWorld.java source code needed it. The example shows several ways to set up the path:

```
<project name="hello" default="compile">

  <property name="lib" value="../lib"/>
  <property name="outputdir" value="/tmp"/>

  <path id="1">
    <pathelement location="." />
    <pathelement location="${lib}/log4j.jar"/>
  </path>

  <path id="2">
    <pathelement path=".;${lib}/log4j.jar"/>
  </path>

  <path id="3">
    <pathelement location="." />
    <fileset dir="${lib}">
        <include name="**/*.jar"/>
    </fileset>
  </path>

  <target name="compile">

    <javac srcdir="./src" destdir="${outputdir}/classes" >
        <classpath refid="1"/>
    </javac>

    <javac srcdir="./src" destdir="${outputdir}/classes" >
        <classpath refid="2"/>
    </javac>

    <javac srcdir="./src" destdir="${outputdir}/classes" >
        <classpath refid="3"/>
    </javac>

    <javac srcdir="./src" destdir="${outputdir}/classes" >
        <classpath id="1">
            <pathelement location="." />
            <pathelement location="${lib}/log4j.jar"/>
        </classpath>
    </javac>

  </target>
</project>
```

Notice that the three path tags define almost the same classpath, with the exception that the classpath with the id of 3 includes all JAR files that exist in ${lib}. Here the tags are repeated without the rest of the buildfile for clarity:

```
<path id="1">
  <pathelement location="." />
```

```
    <pathelement location="${lib}/log4j.jar"/>
  </path>

  <path id="2">
    <pathelement path=".;${lib}/log4j.jar"/>
  </path>

  <path id="3">
    <pathelement location="." />
    <fileset dir="${lib}">
        <include name="**/*.jar"/>
    </fileset>
  </path>
```

Also notice that to use these three path tags with the javac task, you need only set the reference of the classpath element to the reference id of the paths defined previously. Here they are, referenced respective to the last example:

```
<javac srcdir="./src" destdir="${outputdir}/classes" >
    <classpath refid="1"/>
</javac>

<javac srcdir="./src" destdir="${outputdir}/classes" >
    <classpath refid="2"/>
</javac>

<javac srcdir="./src" destdir="${outputdir}/classes" >
    <classpath refid="3"/>
</javac>
```

It's important to note that the javac task with <classpath refid="1"/> would set the classpath to the path set defined by <path id="1">. This is called referring to a classpath *by reference*. In addition, you can refer to a path in-line using the classpath subtag in the javac task, demonstrated as follows:

```
<javac srcdir="./src" destdir="${outputdir}/classes" >
    <classpath id="1">
        <pathelement location="." />
        <pathelement location="${lib}/log4j.jar"/>
    </classpath>
</javac>
```

This is a brief description of using filesets and paths to build a Java classpath. For a more detailed explanation, please refer to the Ant reference section (Chapters 12 and 13).

Conditional Targets

You don't always have to execute a target. You can write targets that are executed only when a certain property is set or when a certain property is not set.

For example, let's say we need to run a buildfile in the Windows XP (no pun intended) development environment and the Solaris production environment. Our development environment does not have the same directory structure as our production environment; thus, we may write a script that looks like this:

```
<project name="hello" default="run">

  <target name="setupProduction" if="production">

      <property name="lib" value="/usr/home/production/lib"/>
      <property name="outputdir" value="/usr/home/production/classes"/>

  </target>

  <target name="setupDevelopment" unless="production">

      <property name="lib" value="c:/hello/lib"/>
      <property name="outputdir" value="c:/hello/classes"/>

  </target>

  <target name="setup" depends="setupProduction,setupDevelopment"/>

  <target name="run" depends="setup">
     <echo message="${lib} ${outputdir}" />
  </target>


</project>
```

Notice that the setupDevelopment target uses unless="production". This means the target should be executed unless the production property is set. Also notice that the setupProduction target uses if="production". This means to execute this target only if the production property is set. Now we need to set the property (or not set it) to control the behavior of the tasks.

To set a property when you execute Ant, you need to pass the property to Ant. This technique is similar to the way you would pass a system property to the Java interpreter. When you execute Ant, you pass the argument –Dproduction=true (it does not have to equal true, it just has to be set). Following is an example of running the buildfile (build4.xml) in production mode:

```
C:\...\chap4>ant -buildfile build4.xml -Dproduction=true
Buildfile: build4.xml

setupProduction:

setupDevelopment:
```

```
setup:

run:
     [echo] /usr/home/production/lib /usr/home/production/classes

BUILD SUCCESSFUL

Total time: 0 seconds
```

From this output, we can see that run was the default target for the project. The run target depended on setup, which depended on our two conditional targets (depends="setupProduction,setupDevelopment"). Thus, because we set the production property on the command line (-Dproduction=true) the setupProduction target was executed rather than setupDevelopment. Running setupProduction sets the "outputdir" and "lib" properties to their Unix environment values. We can see this by looking at the output of the run target's echo task (<echo message="${lib} ${outputdir}" />), which displays the following:

```
run:
     [echo] /usr/home/production/lib /usr/home/production/classes
```

What happens when you have deployment descriptor files that differ between the two environments? You use filters, as discussed in the next section and Chapter 6.

Using Filters

Filters can be used to replace tokens in a file with their proper values for that particular environment. One scenario that comes to mind follows the example in the previous section. Let's say we have a production database and a development database. When deploying to production or development, we want the values in our deployment descriptor or properties file that refer to the JDBC URL of the needed database to refer to the correct database:

```
<project name="hello" default="run">

  <target name="setupProduction" if="production">

       <filter token="jdbc_url" value="jdbc::production"/>

  </target>

  <target name="setupDevelopment" unless="production">

       <filter token="jdbc_url" value="jdbc::development"/>

  </target>
```

```
    <target name="setup" depends="setupProduction,setupDevelopment"/>

    <target name="run" depends="setup">

      <copy todir="/usr/home/production/properties" filtering="true">
        <fileset dir="/cvs/src/properties"/>
      </copy>

    </target>

  </project>
```

Again, setupProduction and setupDevelopment are executed conditionally based on the production property. But this time, instead of setting properties, they set filters as follows:

```
<target name="setupProduction" if="production">

     <filter token="jdbc_url" value="jdbc::production"/>

</target>

<target name="setupDevelopment" unless="production">

     <filter token="jdbc_url" value="jdbc::development"/>

</target>
```

The filter in the setupProduction target sets jdbc_url to jdbc::production. The filter in the setupDevelopment target sets jdbc_url to jdbc::development. The copy task in the run target turns on filtering, which applies the filter to all in the fileset. Thus, the copy task will copy recursively all the files from the /cvs/src/properties directory into the /usr/home/production/properties directory, replacing all the occurrences of the string “@jdbc_url@” with “jdbc:: production” if the “production” property is set or jdbc::development if the “production” property is not set. You’ll see more examples of this technique in Chapter 6.

Nested Builds

Each project (library module, Web application, set of Enterprise JavaBeans, applet, and so on) should have its own directory with its own buildfile. A large project can depend on lots of other projects. Ant allows one Ant buildfile to call another. Thus, you may have an Ant file that calls a hierarchy of other Ant buildfiles. You can nest buildfiles using this method to build many projects and their dependent projects.

The ant task runs a specified buildfile. The ant task can be used to build subprojects and related projects. You have the option of specifying the buildfile name or just the directory (the file build.xml in the directory specified by the "dir" attribute is used). You also have the option of specifying a particular target to execute. If you do not specify a target to execute, the default target is used. Any properties that you set in the called project are available to the nested buildfile.

The following are some examples of calling another Ant buildfile from your Ant buildfile. We can call a buildfile from the current buildfile and pass a property as follows:

```
<ant antfile="./hello/build.xml">
    <property name="production" value="true"/>
</ant>
We can call a buildfile from the current buildfile. When you call the
ant task, if you don't specify an antfile attribute, then it will use
./hello/build.xml) as follows:<ant dir="./hello"/>
```

Notice above that we only specified the directory. The default buildfile is build.xml; if you only specify the directory, then build.xml is assumed.

We can call a buildfile from the current buildfile and specify that the run target should execute (if the run target was not the default target, it would execute anyway) as follows:

```
<ant antfile="./hello/build.xml"  target="run"/>
```

Summary

This chapter covered the basics of using Ant and the concepts of buildfiles, projects, targets, conditional targets, tasks, filesets, filters, nested buildfiles, and properties. Our discussion included the basics styles and naming conventions for Ant buildfiles.

The chapter also explained the importance of Ant in its relationship to continuous integration. Chapter 6 uses these basics to build sample J2EE applications. By the end of Chapters 5 and 6, you should be able to build and deploy the following: Enterprise JavaBeans, Web components (servlets and JSPs), applets, and Java applications. You should also be able to combine these elements into projects and subprojects that can be easily managed and deployed on both a production and development environment.

CHAPTER 5

Building Java Applications with Ant

This chapter explains the techniques involved in using Ant to build and deploy Java applications in an orchestrated fashion. Once you understand these fundamental techniques, you will be ready for the complexities of Chapter 6, "Building J2EE Applications with Ant," in which we build a Model 2 application complete with EJBs, servlets, and JSPs.

During the course of this chapter, we will build a "Hello World" example. Because the emphasis is on how to *build* components with Ant—and not the mechanics of implementing these various components—the example is meant to be as simple as possible. We will package the application and the common JAR, construct a buildfile that creates an applet, and construct a master buildfile that coordinates the entire build.

The source code for the Hello World example is divided into several directories. Each directory has its own Ant buildfile, which contains instructions to compile the components and package the binaries. Each directory also includes the requisite configuration files (such as manifest files). The master Ant buildfile, located in the root directory, calls the other buildfiles and coordinates the entire build.

This divide-and-conquer technique for organizing components into separate directories is quite common with Ant. It may seem like overkill on a simple project like this one, but consider building a system with 50 components. Each component has its own set of deployment descriptors and configuration files, and each component is deployed in different containers. The divide-and-conquer technique becomes necessary to mange the complexity—it also makes it easier to reuse components.

Following is the directory structure for the Hello World project. We use this same structure for the more complex example in Chapter 6:

```
Model 2 Hello World root
+--Model
+--Application
+--Applet
+--WebApplication
+--EJBeans
```

The Model directory holds the common code (in this simple project, only the application will access the common code). The Application directory holds the Java application code, including the manifest file that marks the deployment JAR as executable. The Applet directory holds the applet code. The WebApplication and EJBeans directories are discussed in Chapter 6.

Hello World Model Project

In Chapter 4 we used a Hello World example that was contained in one file. The Hello World example in this chapter is more complex because it uses several classes.

This section explains the basic structure for all the buildfiles and directories you use in this example and the rest of the book. We introduce the three Java class files: a GreetingBean class, a GreetingFactory class, and a Greeting interface. Then, we discuss how to build these files with Ant and break down the Ant buildfiles' target execution step by step. We also explain how to use the Ant command-line utility to build the files with Ant.

Overview of Model Classes

The GreetingFactory knows how to create a Greeting object. Here is the listing for the GreetingFactory:

```
package xptoolkit.model;

public class GreetingFactory {
    private GreetingFactory(){}

    public Greeting getGreeting()throws Exception {
     String clazz = System.getProperty("Greeting.class",
                          "xptoolkit.model.GreetingBean");
```

```
        return (Greeting)Class.forName(clazz).newInstance();
    }

    public static GreetingFactory getGreetingFactory(){
        return new GreetingFactory();
    }

}
```

Next we have a Greeting interface that defines the contract of a Greeting object—that is, what type of behavior it supports. The Greeting interface is as follows:

```
package xptoolkit.model;

public interface Greeting extends java.io.Serializable{
    public String getGreeting();
}
```

Finally, the GreetingBean class implements the Greeting interface. GreetingBean is defined as follows:

```
package xptoolkit.model;

public class GreetingBean implements Greeting{

    public GreetingBean(){}

    public String getGreeting(){
      return "Hello World!";
    }
}
```

The GreetingBean returns the message "Hello World!" just like the message in the Chapter 4 application. To create a Greeting instance, you use the GreetingFactory. The default implementation of the GreetingFactory gets the implementation class from a property and instantiates an instance of that class with the Class.forName().newInstance() method. It casts the created instance to the Greeting interface.

These two lines of code create the Greeting instance from the GreetingFactory's getGreeting() method:

```
        String clazz = System.getProperty("Greeting.class",
                              "xptoolkit.model.GreetingBean");
      return (Greeting)Class.forName(clazz).newInstance();
```

Thus any class that implements the Greeting interface can be substituted as the Greeting.class system property. Then, when the class is instantiated with the factory's getGreeting() method, the application uses the new implementation of the Greeting interface.

We use this technique in Chapter 6 to add support for EJBs to the Web application seamlessly. We create an Ant buildfile that can deploy the same Web application to use either enterprise beans or another bean implementation just by setting an Ant property. Later, we also map the Greeting interface with the use bean action of a JSP when we implement the Model 2 using servlets and JSP.

Creating a Project Directory Structure for Model

This part of the sample application uses the smallest buildfile. Basically, we just need to create a JAR file that acts as a common library. We don't need any special manifest file or deployment files. This is the most basic buildfile and directory structure you will see in this example. Here is the directory structure for the Model directory:

```
Root of Model
|    build.xml
|
+--src
    +--xptoolkit
        \--model
                GreetingFactory.java
                Greeting.java
                GreetingBean.java
```

Notice that there are only four files in the Model directory and subdirectories. Also notice that the name of the Ant file is build.xml. Remember from Chapter 4 that build.xml is the default buildfile; if Ant is run in this directory, it automatically finds build.xml without you having to specify it on the command line. Let's dig into the model buildfile.

Creating a Buildfile for a Shared Library

The model buildfile has six targets: setProps, init, clean, delete, prepare, compile, package, and all. The buildfiles in this example have similar targets:

- setProps sets up the output directory ("outputdir") property if it is not already set. This behavior is important so we can easily set a different output directory from the command line or from another buildfile that invokes this buildfile, and yet have a reasonable default.
- init initializes all the other properties relative to the "outputdir" property defined in the setProps target; init depends on setProps.
- clean cleans up the output directories and the output JAR file.

- prepare creates the output directories if they do not already exist.
- compile compiles the Java source files for the model into the build directory defined in the init target.
- package packages the compiled Java source into a JAR file.
- all runs all the tags. It is the default target of this build project.

Analysis of the Model Project Buildfile

Listing 5.1 shows the entire buildfile for the model project. In this section we provide a step-by-step analysis of how this buildfile executes. All the buildfiles in the Hello World example are structured in a similar fashion, so understanding the model project's buildfile is essential to understanding the others. A quick note on naming conventions: As you see from the first line of code in Listing 5.1, the project name for this buildfile is "model". Thus we refer to this buildfile as the *model project buildfile*. This naming convention becomes essential once we begin dealing with the five other buildfiles in this project.

```
<project name="model" default="all" >


    <target name="setProps" unless="setProps"
                          description="setup the properties.">
        <property name="outdir" value="/tmp/app/" />
    </target>

    <target name="init" depends="setProps"
                          description="initialize the properties.">
        <tstamp/>
        <property name="local_outdir" value="${outdir}/model" />
        <property name="build" value="${local_outdir}/classes" />
        <property name="lib" value="${outdir}/lib" />
        <property name="model_jar" value="${lib}/greetmodel.jar" />
    </target>

    <target name="clean" depends="init"
                  description="clean up the output directories and jar.">
        <delete dir="${local_outdir}" />
        <delete file="${model_jar}" />
    </target>
```

Listing 5.1 The Hello World model project buildfile. (continues)

```
    <target name="prepare" depends="init"
                           description="prepare the output directory.">
        <mkdir dir="${build}" />
        <mkdir dir="${lib}" />
    </target>

    <target name="compile" depends="prepare"
                           description="compile the Java source.">
        <javac srcdir="./src" destdir="${build}" />
    </target>

    <target name="package" depends="compile"
                    description="package the Java classes into a jar.">
        <jar jarfile="${model_jar}"
           basedir="${build}" />
    </target>

    <target name="all" depends="clean,package"
                    description="perform all targets."/>

</project>
```

Listing 5.1 The Hello World model project buildfile.

Let's go over the model project buildfile and each of its targets in the order they execute. First, the model project sets the all target as the default target, as follows:

```
<project name="model" default="all" >
```

The all target is executed by default, unless we specify another target as a command-line argument of Ant. The all target depends on the clean and package targets. The clean target depends on the init target. The init target depends on the setProps target, and thus the setProps target is executed first.

Following is the setProps target defined in build.xml:

```
    <target name="setProps" unless="setProps"
                            description="setup the properties.">
        <property name="outdir" value="/tmp/app/" />
    </target>
```

The setProps target executes only if the "setProps" property is not set (unless="setProps"). Thus, if a parent buildfile calls this buildfile, it can set the "setProps" property and override the value of outdir so that the setProps target of this file does not execute (we give an example of this later). If the setProps target executes, it sets the value of outdir to /tmp/app.

Next, the init target is executed. Following is the init target defined in build.xml:

```
<target name="init" depends="setProps"
                    description="initialize the properties.">
    <tstamp/>

    <property name="local_outdir" value="${outdir}/model" />
    <property name="build" value="${local_outdir}/classes" />
    <property name="lib" value="${outdir}/lib" />
    <property name="model_jar" value="${lib}/greetmodel.jar" />
</target>
```

The init target uses the tstamp task to get the current time, which is used by the javac task to see if a source file is out of data and needs to be compiled. The init target defines several properties that refer to directories and files needed to compile and deploy the model project. We will discuss the meaning of these properties because all the other buildfiles for this example use the same or similar properties. The init target defines the following properties:

- The "local_outdir" property defines the output directory of all the model project's intermediate files (Java class files).
- The "build" property defines the output directory of the Java class files.
- The "lib" property defines the directory that holds the common code libraries (JAR files) used for the whole Model 2 Hello World example application.
- The "model_jar" property defines the output JAR file for this project.

Using Literals

As a general rule, if you use the same literal twice, you should go ahead and define it in the init target. You don't know how many times we've shot ourselves in the foot by not following this rule. This buildfile is fairly simple, but the later ones are more complex. Please learn from our mistakes (and missing toes).

Now that all the clean target's dependencies have executed, the clean target can execute. The clean target deletes the intermediate files created by the compile and the output common JAR file, which is the output of this project. Here is the code for the clean target:

```
<target name="clean" depends="init"
        description="clean up the output directories and jar.">
```

```
        <delete dir="${local_outdir}" />
        <delete file="${model_jar}" />

    </target>
```

Remember that the all target depends on the clean and package targets. The clean branch and all its dependencies have now executed, so it is time to execute the package target branch (a *branch* is a target and all its dependencies). The package target depends on the compile target, the compile target depends on the prepare target, and the prepare target depends on the init target, which has already been executed.

Thus, the next target that executes is prepare, because all its dependencies have already executed. The prepare target creates the build output directory, which ensures that the lib directory is created. The prepare target is defined as follows:

```
<target name="prepare" depends="init"
                     description="prepare the output directory.">

    <mkdir dir="${build}" />
    <mkdir dir="${lib}" />
</target>
```

The next target in the package target branch that executes is the compile target—another dependency of the package target. The compile target compiles the code in the src directory to the build directory, which was defined by the "build" property in the init target. The compile target is defined as follows:

```
<target name="compile" depends="prepare"
                     description="compile the Java source.">

    <javac srcdir="./src" destdir="${build}"/>
</target>
```

Now that all the target dependencies of the package target have been executed, we can run the package target. Whew! The package target packages the Java classes created in the compile target into a JAR file that is created in the common lib directory. The package target is defined as follows:

```
<target name="package" depends="compile"
             description="package the Java classes into a jar.">

    <jar jarfile="${model_jar}"
       basedir="${build}" />
</target>
```

Running an Ant Buildfile

In this section, we discuss how to run the Hello World model project buildfile. There are three steps to running the Ant buildfile:

1. Set up the environment.
2. Go to the directory that contains the build.xml file for the model.
3. Run Ant.

Successfully running the buildscript gives us the following output:

```
Buildfile: build.xml

setProps:

init:

clean:

prepare:
    [mkdir] Created dir: C:\tmp\app\model\classes

compile:
    [javac] Compiling 3 source files to C:\tmp\app\model\classes

package:
      [jar] Building jar: C:\tmp\app\lib\greetmodel.jar

all:

BUILD SUCCESSFUL

Total time: 3 seconds
```

If you do not get this output, check that the properties defined in the init target make sense for your environment. If you are on a Unix platform and the buildfile is not working, make sure that the /tmp directory exists and that you have the rights to access it. Alternatively, you could run the previous script by doing the following on the command line:

```
$ ant -DsetProps=true -Doutdir=/usr/rick/tmp/app
```

Basically, you want to output to a directory that you have access to, just in case you are not the administrator of your own box. If from some reason Ant still does not run, make sure you set up the Ant environment variables (refer to Chapter 4 for details).

After successfully running Ant, the output directory for the model project will look like this:

```
Root of output directory
\--app
    +--lib
    |       greetmodel.jar
    |
    \--model
        \--classes
            \--xptoolkit
                \--model
                        GreetingFactory.class
                        Greeting.class
                        GreetingBean.class
```

Notice that all the intermediate files to build the JAR file are in the model subdirectory. The output from this project is the greetmodel.jar file, which is in ${outdir}/app/lib. The next project, the application project, needs this JAR file in order to compile. In the next section, we discuss how to build a standalone Java application with Ant that uses the JAR file (greetmodel.jar) from the model project.

Hello World Application Project

The goal of the Hello World application project is to create a standalone Java application that uses greetmodel.jar to get the greeting message. The application project buildfile is nearly identical to the model project buildfile, so we focus our discussion on the differences between the two buildfiles. We also explain how to make a JAR file an executable JAR file.

Overview of Application Java Classes

The Java source code for this application is as simple as it gets for the Hello World Model 2 examples. Here is the Java application:

```
package xptoolkit;

import xptoolkit.model.GreetingFactory;
import xptoolkit.model.Greeting;

public class HelloWorld{

    public static void main(String []args)throws Exception{
       Greeting greet = (Greeting)
```

```
            GreetingFactory.getGreetingFactory().getGreeting();

        System.out.println(greet.getGreeting());

    }
}
```

As you can see, this application imports the GreetingFactory class and the Greeting interface from the model project. It uses the GreetingFactory to get an instance of the Greeting interface, and then uses the instance of the Greeting interface to print the greeting to the console.

Creating a Project Directory Structure for the Application

The directory structure of the Hello World Java application is as follows:

```
Hello World Application root
|   build.xml
|
+--src
|   |
|   +--xptoolkit
|           HelloWorld.java
|
\--META-INF
        MANIFEST.MF
```

Notice the addition of the META-INF directory, which holds the name of the manifest file we will use to make the application's JAR file executable. The only other file that this project needs is not shown; the file is greetmodel.jar, which is created by the model project (the reason for this will become obvious in the following sections).

Creating a Manifest File for a Standalone Application

The goal of this application is for it to work as a standalone JAR file. To do this, we need to modify the manifest file that the application JAR file uses to include the main class and the dependency on greetmodel.jar. The manifest entries that this application needs look something like this:

```
Manifest-Version: 1.0
Created-By: Rick Hightower
Main-Class: xptoolkit.HelloWorld
Class-Path: greetmodel.jar
```

The Class-Path manifest entry specifies the JAR files that the JAR file that holds the Hello World Java application needs to run (in our case, greetmodel.jar). The Main-Class manifest entry specifies the main class of the JAR file—that is, the class with the main method that is run when the executable JAR file executes.

Creating an Ant Buildfile for a Standalone Application

Listing 5.2 shows the application project buildfile; you'll notice that it is very similar to the model project buildfile. It is divided into the same targets as the model project buildfile: setProps, init, clean, delete, prepare, mkdir, compile, package, and all. The application project buildfile defines the properties differently, but even the property names are almost identical (compare with the model project buildfile in Listing 5.1).

```
<project name="application" default="all" >


    <target name="setProps" unless="setProps"
                          description="setup the properties.">
<property name="outdir" value="/tmp/app" />
    </target>

    <target name="init" depends="setProps"
                          description="initialize the properties.">
      <tstamp/>
      <property name="local_outdir" value="${outdir}/java_app" />
      <property name="build" value="${local_outdir}/classes" />
      <property name="lib" value="${outdir}/lib" />
      <property name="app_jar" value="${lib}/greetapp.jar" />
    </target>

    <target name="clean" depends="init"
                          description="clean up the output directories.">
         <delete dir="${build}" />
         <delete file="${app_jar}" />
    </target>

    <target name="prepare" depends="init"
                          description="prepare the output directory.">
        <mkdir dir="${build}" />
        <mkdir dir="${lib}" />
    </target>
```

Listing 5.2 Hello World application project buildfile. (continues)

```
    <target name="compile" depends="prepare"
                      description="compile the Java source.">

        <javac srcdir="./src" destdir="${build}">
            <classpath >

                <fileset dir="${lib}">
                    <include name="**/*.jar"/>
                </fileset>

            </classpath>

        </javac>

    </target>

    <target name="package" depends="compile"
               description="package the Java classes into a jar.">
        <jar jarfile="${app_jar}"
             manifest="./META-INF/MANIFEST.MF"
           basedir="${build}" />
    </target>

    <target name="all" depends="clean,package"
                      description="perform all targets."/>

</project>
```

Listing 5.2 Hello World application project buildfile.

One of the differences in the application project buildfile is the way that it compiles the Java source:

```
<target name="compile" depends="prepare"
                  description="compile the Java source.">

    <javac srcdir="./src" destdir="${build}">
        <classpath >

            <fileset dir="${lib}">
                <include name="**/*.jar"/>
            </fileset>

        </classpath>

    </javac>

</target>
```

Notice that the compile target specifies all the JAR files in the common lib directory (<include name="**/*.jar"/>). The greetmodel.jar file is in the common lib directory, so it is included when the javac task compiles the source. Another difference is the way the application project's buildfile packages the Ant source as follows:

```
<target name="package" depends="compile"
                description="package the Java classes into a jar.">
    <jar jarfile="${app_jar}"
         manifest="./META-INF/MANIFEST.MF"
       basedir="${build}" />
</target>
```

Notice that the package target uses the jar task as before, but the jar task's manifest is set to the manifest file described earlier. This is unlike the model project buildfile, which did not specify a manifest file; the model used the default manifest file. The application project buildfile's manifest file has the entries that allow us to execute the JAR file from the command line.

In order to run the Hello World Java application, after we run the application project's buildfile, we go to the output common lib directory (tmp/app/lib) and run Java from the command line with the -jar command-line argument, as follows:

```
$ java -jar greetapp.jar
Hello World!
```

You may wonder how it loaded the Greeting interface and GreetingFactory class. This is possible because the manifest entry Class-Path causes the JVM to search for any directory or JAR file that is specified (refer to the JAR file specification included with the Java Platform documentation for more detail). The list of items (directory or JAR files) specified on the Class-Path manifest entry is a relative URI list. Because the greetmodel.jar file is in the same directory (such as /tmp/app/lib) and it is specified on the Class-Path manifest, the JVM finds the classes in greetmodel.jar.

One issue with the application project is its dependence on the model project. The model project must be executed before the application project. How can we manage this? The next section proposes one way to manage the situation with an Ant buildfile.

Hello World Main Project

The Hello World Java application depends on the existence of the Hello World model common library file. If we try to compile the application before the model, we get an error. The application requires the model, so we need a way to call the model project buildfile and the application project buildfile in the right order.

Creating a Master Buildfile

We can control the execution of two buildfiles by using a master buildfile. The master buildfile shown in Listing 5.3 is located in the root directory of the Model 2 Hello World Example of the main project. This buildfile treats the model and application buildfile as subprojects (the model and application projects are the first of many subprojects that we want to fit into a larger project).

```
<project name="main" default="build" >


    <target name="setProps" unless="setProps"
                          description="setup the properties.">
         <property name="outdir" value="/tmp/app" />
         <property name="setProps" value="true" />
    </target>


    <target name="init" depends="setProps"
                          description="initialize the properties.">
          <property name="lib" value="${outdir}/lib" />
    </target>

    <target name="clean" depends="init"
                          description="clean up the output directories.">
        <ant dir="./Model" target="clean">
            <property name="outdir" value="${outdir}" />
            <property name="setProps" value="true" />

        </ant>

        <ant dir="./Application" target="clean">
            <property name="outdir" value="${outdir}" />
            <property name="setProps" value="true" />
        </ant>

        <delete dir="${outdir}" />

    </target>
```

Listing 5.3 Hello World master buildfile. (continues)

```
    <target name="prepare" depends="init"
                      description="prepare the output directory.">
    <mkdir dir="${build}" />
    <mkdir dir="${lib}" />
  </target>


  <target name="build" depends="prepare"
         description="build the model and application modules.">

    <ant dir="./model" target="package">
       <property name="outdir" value="${outdir}" />
       <property name="setProps" value="true" />
    </ant>

    <ant dir="./application" target="package">
       <property name="outdir" value="${outdir}" />
       <property name="setProps" value="true" />
    </ant>
  </target>

</project>
```

Listing 5.3 Hello World master buildfile.

Analysis of the Master Buildfile

Notice that the main project buildfile simply delegates to the application and model subproject and ensures that the subprojects' buildfiles are called in the correct order. For example, when the clean target is executed, the main project's buildfile uses the ant task to call the model project's clean target. Then, the main project calls the application project's clean target using the ant task again. Both are demonstrated as follows:

```
    <target name="clean" depends="init"
                      description="clean up the output directories.">
        <ant dir="./Model" target="clean">
            <property name="outdir" value="${outdir}" />
            <property name="setProps" value="true" />
        </ant>

        <ant dir="./Application" target="clean">
            <property name="outdir" value="${outdir}" />
            <property name="setProps" value="true" />
        </ant>
```

```
        <delete dir="${outdir}" />

    </target>
```

A similar strategy is used with the main project's build target. The build target calls the package target on both the model and application subprojects, as follows:

```
    <target name="build" depends="prepare"
            description="build the model and application modules.">

        <ant dir="./model" target="package">
            <property name="outdir" value="${outdir}" />
            <property name="setProps" value="true" />
        </ant>

        <ant dir="./application" target="package">
            <property name="outdir" value="${outdir}" />
            <property name="setProps" value="true" />
        </ant>

    </target>
```

Thus, we can build both the application and model projects by running the main project. This may not seem like a big deal, but imagine a project with hundreds of subprojects that build thousands of components. Without a buildfile, such a project could become unmanageable. In fact, a project with just 10 to 20 components can benefit greatly from using nested buildfiles. We will use this same technique as we create the Web application in Chapter 6, the applet, and the EJB of this project. The master buildfile orchestrates the correct running order for all the subprojects. We could revisit this main project after we finish each additional subproject and update it. In the next section, we will discuss the applet buildfile.

The Applet Project

The applet project is a simple applet that reads the output of the HelloWorldServlet (defined in Chapter 6) and shows it in a JLabel. The dependency on the Web application is at runtime; there are no compile-time dependencies to the Web application. We'll discuss the applet here and the Web application in the next chapter.

Overview of the Applet Class

The meat of the applet implementation is in the init() method, as follows:

```
    public void init(){
```

```
            URL uGreeting;
            String sGreeting="Bye Bye";

            getAppletContext()
         .showStatus("Getting hello message from server.");

            try{
                uGreeting = new URL(
                       getDocumentBase(),
                       "HelloWorldServlet");

                sGreeting = getGreeting(uGreeting);
            }
            catch(Exception e){
                getAppletContext()
                 .showStatus("Unable to communicate with server.");
                e.printStackTrace();
            }
            text.setText(sGreeting);

        }
```

The init() method gets the document base (the URL from which the applet's page was loaded) URL from the applet context. Then, the init() method uses the document base and the URI identifying the HelloWorldServlet to create a URL that has the output of the HelloWorldServlet:

```
uGreeting = new URL( getDocumentBase(), "HelloWorldServlet");
```

It uses a helper method called getGreeting() to parse the output of the HelloWorldServlet, and then displays the greeting in the Applet's JLabel (text.setText(sGreeting);). The helper method is as follows:

```
    private String getGreeting(URL uGreeting)throws Exception{
         String line;
         int endTagIndex;
         BufferedReader reader=null;
        . . .

     reader = new BufferedReader(
                  new InputStreamReader (
                          uGreeting.openStream()));

            while((line=reader.readLine())!=null){
                System.out.println(line);

                if (line.startsWith("<h1>")){
                    getAppletContext().showStatus("Parsing message.");
                    endTagIndex=line.indexOf("</h1>");
```

```
                    line=line.substring(4,endTagIndex);
                    break;
                }
            }
        ...
        return line;
    }
```

Basically, the method gets the output stream from the URL (uGreeting.openStream()) and goes through the stream line by line looking for a line that begins with <h1>. Then, it pulls the text out of the <h1> tag.

The output of the HelloServlet looks like this:

```
<html>
<head>
<title>Hello World</title>
</head>
<body>
<h1>Hello World!</h1>
</body>
```

The code that the helper method retrieves appears in bold. Listing 5.4 shows the complete code for HelloWorldApplet.

```
package xptoolkit.applet;
import javax.swing.JApplet;
import javax.swing.JLabel;
import java.awt.Font;
import java.awt.BorderLayout;
import java.applet.AppletContext;
import java.net.URL;
import java.io.InputStreamReader;
import java.io.BufferedReader;

public class HelloWorldApplet extends javax.swing.JApplet {

    JLabel text;


    public HelloWorldApplet() {
        this.getContentPane().setLayout(new BorderLayout());
        text = new JLabel("Bye Bye");
        text.setAlignmentX(JLabel.CENTER_ALIGNMENT);
        text.setAlignmentY(JLabel.CENTER_ALIGNMENT);
        Font f = new Font("Arial", Font.BOLD, 20);
        text.setFont(f);
```

Listing 5.4 HelloWorldApplet that communicates with HelloWorldServlet. (continues)

```
        getContentPane().add(text,BorderLayout.CENTER);
    }


    public void init(){
        URL uGreeting;
        String sGreeting="Bye Bye";

        this.doLayout();
        getAppletContext()
.showStatus("Getting hello message from server.");

        try{
            uGreeting = new URL(
                   this.getDocumentBase(),
                   "HelloWorldServlet");

            sGreeting = getGreeting(uGreeting);
        }
        catch(Exception e){
            getAppletContext()
.showStatus("Unable to communicate with server.");
            e.printStackTrace();
        }
        text.setText(sGreeting);

    }

    private String getGreeting(URL uGreeting)throws Exception{
         String line;
         int endTagIndex;
         BufferedReader reader=null;


         try{
            reader = new BufferedReader(
                    new InputStreamReader (
                            uGreeting.openStream()));
            while((line=reader.readLine())!=null){
                System.out.println(line);
                if (line.startsWith("<h1>")){
                    getAppletContext().showStatus("Parsing message.");
                    endTagIndex=line.indexOf("</h1>");
                    line=line.substring(4,endTagIndex);
                    break;
                }
            }
```

Listing 5.4 HelloWorldApplet that communicates with HelloWorldServlet. (continues)

```
        }
        finally{
            if (reader!=null)reader.close();
        }
        return line;
    }

}
```

Listing 5.4 HelloWorldApplet that communicates with HelloWorldServlet.

Creating a Buildfile for the Applet

The applet project buildfile is quite simple (see Listing 5.5); it is structured much like the application project buildfile.

```
<project name="applet" default="all" >


    <target name="setProps" unless="setProps"
                          description="setup the properties.">
        <property name="outdir" value="/tmp/app" />
    </target>


    <target name="init" depends="setProps"
                          description="initialize the properties.">
        <tstamp/>

        <property name="local_outdir" value="${outdir}/applet" />
        <property name="build" value="${local_outdir}/classes" />
        <property name="lib" value="${outdir}/lib" />
        <property name="jar" value="${lib}/helloapplet.jar" />
    </target>

    <target name="clean" depends="init"
                          description="clean up the output directories.">
          <delete dir="${build}" />
          <delete dir="${jar}" />
    </target>


    <target name="prepare" depends="init"
                          description="prepare the output directory.">
```

Listing 5.5 Applet project's buildfile. (continues)

```
        <mkdir dir="${build}" />
        <mkdir dir="${lib}" />
    </target>

    <target name="compile" depends="prepare"
                         description="compile the Java source.">
        <javac srcdir="./src" destdir="${build}" />
    </target>

    <target name="package" depends="compile"
            description="package the Java classes into a jar.">
        <jar jarfile="${jar} "
           basedir="${build}" />
    </target>

    <target name="all" depends="clean,package"
                         description="perform all targets."/>

</project>
```

Listing 5.5 Applet project's buildfile.

Building the Applet with Ant

To build the applet, we need to navigate to the Applet directory, set up the environment, and then run Ant at the command line. To clean the output from the build, we run "ant clean" at the command line. Both building and cleaning the applet are demonstrated as follows.

First we build the applet:

```
C:\CVS\...\MVCHelloWorld\Applet>ant
Buildfile: build.xml

setProps:

init:

clean:
   [delete] Deleting directory C:\tmp\app\lib

prepare:
    [mkdir] Created dir: C:\tmp\app\applet\classes
    [mkdir] Created dir: C:\tmp\app\lib

compile:
    [javac] Compiling 1 source file to C:\tmp\app\applet\classes
```

```
package:
      [jar] Building jar: C:\tmp\app\lib\helloapplet.jar

all:

BUILD SUCCESSFUL

Total time: 4 seconds
```

Now we clean the applet:

```
C:\CVS\...\MVCHelloWorld\Applet>ant clean
Buildfile: build.xml

setProps:

init:

clean:
   [delete] Deleting directory C:\tmp\app\applet\classes
   [delete] Deleting directory C:\tmp\app\lib

BUILD SUCCESSFUL

Total time: 0 seconds
```

Hello World Recap

It's important to recap what we have done. We created a common Java library called model.jar. This model.jar file is used by a Web application and a stand-alone executable Java application in an executable JAR file. We created an applet that can communicate with the Web application we create in Chapter 6. Once the applet loads into the browser, the applet communicates over HTTP to the Web application's HelloWorldServlet, which is covered in depth in Chapter 6.

In Chapter 6 we set up the GreetingFactory so that it talks to an enterprise session bean that in turn talks to an enterprise entity bean. The Web application buildfile is set up so that with the addition of a property file, it can talk to either the enterprise beans or to the local implementation in the model library.

Summary

In this chapter, we took a very complex project with a few components and subsystems, albeit a simple implementation, and built it in an orchestrated fashion. We showed how to create a Java application in an executable JAR and a Java applet in a JAR. We also demonstrated how to package a set of classes that is shared by more than one application in a JAR.

CHAPTER 6

Building J2EE Applications with Ant

This chapter explains techniques for using Ant to build and deploy J2EE applications. The first example we use is a continuation of the Hello World application from Chapter 5. The Hello World example in this chapter includes an applet, a Web application, an application, enterprise beans, support libraries, and other components. This may be the only Hello World example that has an applet, servlet, session bean, entity bean, and JSP and attempts to be Model 2.

You're probably thinking, "Why should I implement the most complex Hello World application in the world?" This example, although a bit of overkill to say "Hello World," is as simple as possible while demonstrating how to build and deploy a J2EE application and its components with Ant. By working through this example, you will understand how to use Ant to build these different types of components and applications, and how to combine them by nesting buildfiles. In the last section of this chapter, we use these techniques to begin implementing a more realistic application: the sample pet store introduced in Chapter 3. We will build on the pet store application and refactor it at the end of every subsequent chapter in this section of the book. The remaining chapters in this part of the book will build on the pet store case study.

Hello World

The Model 2 HelloWorld example for this chapter is the simplest example of Model 2 architecture—also known as Model-View-Controller (MVC)—for JSP servlets. In this example, the applet and JSP are the view; the servlet and enterprise session bean are the controller; and the object model is a Java class and later an entity bean.

The GreetingFactory from Chapter 5 is set up so it talks to an enterprise session bean that in turn talks to an enterprise entity bean. The Web application buildfile is set up so that if we add one property file, it can talk to either the enterprise beans or to the local implementation in the original model library (common code) defined in Chapter 5.

The source code for the Model 2 Hello World example is divided into several directories for each component, and each directory has its own Ant buildfile. A master Ant buildfile in the root directory calls the other buildfiles. The directory structure is as follows:

```
Model 2 Hello World root
+--Model
+--EJBeans
+--Application
+--Applet
+--WebApplication
```

The Model directory holds the common code. The EJBeans directory holds the enterprise beans code and the deployment descriptor files. The Application directory holds the Java application code including the manifest file that marks the deployment JAR as executable. The Applet directory holds the applet code. The WebApplication directory holds HTML files, deployment descriptors, JSP files, and servlet Java source.

Because each component has its own set of deployment descriptors and configuration files, it makes sense to separate components into their own directories; this practice also makes it easier to reuse the components in other projects and applications. Each directory has its own Ant buildfile, which knows how to compile the components, package the binaries, and include the requisite configuration files (deployment descriptors and manifest files).

In the next section, we cover the Web application buildfile—the heart of this example.

Web Application Project

The Web application is another subproject of the Model 2 Hello World application; it consists of a servlet, two JSPs, an HTML file, and a deployment descriptor. This section describes how to build a WAR file with a deployment descriptor. We also explain how to map servlets and JSPs to servlet elements in the deployment descriptor and how to map the servlet elements to URLs. In addition, this section breaks down the webapplication project buildfile step by step, and shows how to use the buildfile to build and deploy the Web application.

Web Application Project Directory Structure

The following are the files that we build into a Web application:

```
Web application root directory
|   build.xml
|
+--JSP
|      HelloWorld.jsp
|      HelloApplet.jsp
|
+--src
|   \--xptoolkit
|      \--web
|             HelloWorldServlet.java
|
+--HTML
|       index.html
|
\--meta-data
       web.xml
```

Notice that the webapplication project includes only six files. There are four subdirectories: JSP, src, HTML, and meta-data, and the root directory holds the build.xml file. The JSP directory contains two JSPs: HelloWorld.jsp and HelloApplet.jsp. Under the src directory is the Java source for the servlet xptoolkit.web.HelloWorldServlet.java. The web.xml file under the meta-data directory holds the deployment file for this Web application.

HelloWorldServlet.java

The servlet is contained in the class xptoolkit.web.HelloWorldServlet (see Listing 6.1). Like the Java application, it uses the Greeting interface and the GreetingFactory class that are packaged in greetmodel.jar, the output of the model project.

```
package xptoolkit.web;
import javax.servlet.http.HttpServlet;
import javax.servlet.http.HttpServletRequest;
import javax.servlet.http.HttpServletResponse;
```

Listing 6.1 xptoolkit.web.HelloWorldServlet. (continues)

```
import javax.servlet.http.HttpSession;
import javax.servlet.ServletException;
import javax.servlet.ServletConfig;
import javax.servlet.ServletContext;
import javax.servlet.RequestDispatcher;

/* import the classes to create a greeting object or type greeting */
import xptoolkit.model.GreetingFactory;
import xptoolkit.model.Greeting;



public class HelloWorldServlet extends  HttpServlet{

    public void init(ServletConfig config) throws ServletException{
        super.init(config);
           /* Read in the greeting type that the factory should create */
        String clazz = config.getInitParameter("Greeting.class") ;
        if(clazz!=null)System.setProperty("Greeting.class",clazz);

    }


    public void doGet(HttpServletRequest request,
                              HttpServletResponse response)
                                     throws ServletException{
        RequestDispatcher dispatch;
        ServletContext context;
       /*Get the session, create a greeting bean, map the greeting
         bean in the session, and redirect to the Hello World JSP.
       */
        try {


                /* Create the greeting bean and map it to the session. */
          HttpSession session = request.getSession(true);
          Greeting greet = (Greeting)
               GreetingFactory.getGreetingFactory().getGreeting();
          session.setAttribute("greeting", greet);


                /* Redirect to the HelloWorld.jsp */
           context = getServletContext();
           dispatch = context.getRequestDispatcher("/HelloWorldJSP");
           dispatch.forward(request, response);
        }catch(Exception e){
            throw new ServletException(e);
```

Listing 6.1 xptoolkit.web.HelloWorldServlet. (continues)

```
        }
    }

     /* Just call the doGet method */
    public void doPost(HttpServletRequest request,
                                HttpServletResponse response)
                                        throws ServletException{
        doGet(request, response);
    }

}
```

Listing 6.1 xptoolkit.web.HelloWorldServlet.

Analyzing HelloWorldServlet

HelloWorldServlet is a simple servlet; it reads in the servlet initialization parameters in the init() method, as follows:

```
String clazz = config.getInitParameter("Greeting.class") ;
```

It uses the value of the initialization parameter "Greeting.class" to set the System property "Greeting.class", as follows:

```
System.setProperty("Greeting.class",clazz);
```

You will recall from Chapter 3 that the GreetingFactory uses the system property "Greeting.class" to decide which implementation of the Greeting interface to load. Now let's get to the real action: the doGet() and doPost() methods.

When the doGet() or doPost() method of the HelloWorldServlet is called, the servlet uses the GreetingFactory to create a greeting as follows:

```
Greeting greet = (Greeting)
     GreetingFactory.getGreetingFactory().getGreeting();
```

The HelloWorldServlet then maps the greeting object into the current session (javax.servlet.http.HttpSession) under the name "greeting", as follows:

```
session.setAttribute("greeting", greet);
```

Finally, the HelloWorldServlet forwards processing of this request to the JSP file HelloWorld.jsp by getting the request dispatcher for the HelloWorldServlet from the servlet's context, as follows:

```
     /* Redirect to the HelloWorld.jsp */
context = getServletContext();
dispatch = context.getRequestDispatcher("/HelloWorldJSP");
dispatch.forward(request, response);
```

You may notice that the context.getRequestDispatcher call looks a little weird. This is the case because HelloWorld.jsp is mapped to /HelloWorldJSP in the deployment descriptor for the servlet. (We will discuss the deployment descriptor later.) Next, let's examine HelloWorld.jsp.

HelloWorld.jsp

HelloWorld.jsp exists to show the world the message it gets from the Greeting reference that the HelloWorldServlet mapped into session. The HelloWorld.jsp code is as follows:

```
<jsp:useBean id="greeting" type="xptoolkit.model.Greeting"
                                               scope="session"/>
<html>
<head>
<title>Hello World</title>
</head>
<body>
<h1><%=greeting.getGreeting()%></h1>
</body>
```

If you are a Web designer at heart, we understand if you are shocked and horrified by this HTML code. But for a moment, let's focus on the following two lines of code from the JSP:

```
<jsp:useBean id="greeting" type="xptoolkit.model.Greeting"
                                               scope="session"/>

<h1><%=greeting.getGreeting()%></h1>
```

Notice that the jsp:useBean action grabs the greeting reference that we put into the session with the HelloWorldServlet. Then, we print out the greeting with the JSP scriptlet expression <%=greeting.getGreeting()%>.

This sums up what the Model 2 Hello World Web application does. We will discuss the other JSP, HelloApplet.jsp, after we examine the applet subproject. For now, the next section explains why the servlet could forward HelloWorldJSP to the JSP HelloWorld.jsp.

Deployment Descriptor for the HelloWorld Web Application

In order to configure the JSPs and servlets, we need a deployment descriptor. The following code defines a simple deployment descriptor that assigns names and mappings to the JSPs and servlet. Please note that the deployment descriptor goes in the web.xml file:

```
<?xml version="1.0" encoding="ISO-8859-1"?>
```

```
<!DOCTYPE web-app
  PUBLIC "-//Sun Microsystems, Inc.//DTD Web Application 2.2//EN"
  "http://java.sun.com/j2ee/dtds/web-app_2_2.dtd">

<web-app>
    <error-page>
        <error-code>404</error-code>
        <location>/HelloWorldServlet</location>
    </error-page>

    <servlet>
        <servlet-name>HelloWorldServlet</servlet-name>
        <servlet-class>xptoolkit.web.HelloWorldServlet</servlet-class>
        <init-param>
          <param-name>Greeting.class</param-name>
          <param-value>@Greeting.class@</param-value>
        </init-param>
    </servlet>

    <servlet>
        <servlet-name>HelloWorldJSP</servlet-name>
        <jsp-file>HelloWorld.jsp</jsp-file>
    </servlet>

    <servlet-mapping>
        <servlet-name>HelloWorldServlet</servlet-name>
        <url-pattern>/HelloWorldServlet</url-pattern>
    </servlet-mapping>

    <servlet-mapping>
        <servlet-name>HelloWorldJSP</servlet-name>
        <url-pattern>/HelloWorldJSP</url-pattern>
    </servlet-mapping>

</web-app>
```

The deployment descriptor defines two servlet elements, one for the HelloWorldServlet and one for the HelloWorldJSP. If you are wondering why there is a servlet element for the HelloWorldJSP, remember that HelloWorld.jsp is compiled to a servlet before it is used for the first time. The HelloWorldServlet servlet element maps to the servlet (<servlet-class>xptoolkit.web.HelloWorldServlet</servlet-class>). The HelloWorldJSP element maps to the JSP file HelloWorld.jsp (<jsp-file>HelloWorld.jsp</jsp-file>). Then, the servlet mapping elements map the servlet element to specific URL patterns.

Thus HelloWorldServlet maps to /HelloWorldServlet (<url-pattern>/HelloWorldServlet</url-pattern>); this is relative to the Web application location from the root of the server. And, the HelloWorldJSP servlet element is mapped to the /HelloWorldJSP URL pattern (<url-pattern>/HelloWorldJSP</url-pattern>).

The buildfile must deploy the descriptor to a place where the application server can find it. It does this by packaging the HTML files, JSP files, Java servlet, and deployment descriptor in a WAR file. The next section describes the buildfile for this project.

Buildfile for the HelloWorld Web Application

This project has many more components than the other subprojects. As you would expect, the webapplication project buildfile (Listing 6.2) is much more complex, but it builds on the foundation set by the model project—that is, the webapplication project buildfile has the same base targets with the same meanings: setProps, init, clean, delete, prepare, mkdir, compile, package, and all.

To the base targets, the webapplication project's buildfile adds the prepare_metadata and deploy targets. The prepare_metadata target sets up the Ant filtering for the deployment descriptor (we talk about this in detail towards the end of this section). The deploy target adds the ability to deploy to both Resin and Tomcat Web application servers. The remaining details of this buildfile are covered in the applet and the enterprise beans sections later in this chapter.

```
<project name="webapplication" default="all" >

    <target name="setProps" unless="setProps"
                          description="setup the properites.">
        <property name="outdir" value="/tmp/app" />

    </target>


    <target name="init" depends="setProps"
                          description="initialize the properties.">
      <tstamp/>
      <property name="local_outdir" value="${outdir}/webapps" />
      <property name="lib" value="${outdir}/lib" />
      <property name="dist" value="${outdir}/dist" />

      <property name="build" value="${local_outdir}/webclasses" />
      <property name="meta" value="${local_outdir}/meta" />

      <property name="deploy_resin" value="/resin/webapps" />
      <property name="deploy_tomcat" value="/tomcat/webapps" />

      <property name="build_lib" value="./../lib" />
```

Listing 6.2 Hello World webapplication project buildfile. (continues)

```
    <property name="jsdk_lib" value="/resin/lib" />
  </target>

  <target name="clean_deploy" >

      <delete file="${deploy_resin}/hello.war" />
      <delete dir="${deploy_resin}/hello" />
      <delete file="${deploy_tomcat}/hello.war" />
      <delete dir="${deploy_tomcat}/hello" />
  </target>

  <target name="clean" depends="init,clean_deploy"
                       description="clean up the output directories.">
      <delete dir="${local_outdir}" />
      <delete file="${dist}/hello.war" />
  </target>


  <target name="prepare" depends="init"
                       description="prepare the output directory.">
      <mkdir dir="${build}" />
      <mkdir dir="${dist}" />
      <mkdir dir="${build_lib}" />
  </target>



  <target name="compile" depends="prepare"
                       description="compile the Java source.">
      <javac srcdir="./src" destdir="${build}">
          <classpath >

              <fileset dir="${lib}">
                  <include name="**/*.jar"/>
              </fileset>

              <fileset dir="${jsdk_lib}">
                  <include name="**/*.jar"/>
              </fileset>

              <fileset dir="${build_lib}">
                  <include name="**/*.jar"/>
              </fileset>

          </classpath>
      </javac>
```

Listing 6.2 Hello World webapplication project buildfile. (continues)

```
    </target>

    <target name="prepare_meta_ejb" if="ejb">
        <filter token="Greeting.class"
               value="xptoolkit.model.GreetingShadow"/>
    </target>

    <target name="prepare_meta_noejb" unless="ejb">
        <filter token="Greeting.class"
                value="xptoolkit.model.GreetingBean"/>
    </target>

    <target name="prepare_meta"
            depends="prepare_meta_ejb, prepare_meta_noejb">
        <copy todir="${meta}" filtering="true">
            <fileset dir="./meta-data"/>
        </copy>
    </target>

    <target name="package" depends="compile">

        <mkdir dir="${meta}" />

        <antcall target="prepare_meta" />

        <war warfile="${dist}/hello.war" webxml="${meta}/web.xml">
            <!--
                Include the html and jsp files.
                Put the classes from the build into the classes directory
                of the war.
            /-->
        <fileset dir="./HTML" />
        <fileset dir="./JSP" />
          <classes dir="${build}" />

            <!-- Include the applet. /-->
          <fileset dir="${lib}" includes="helloapplet.jar" />

       <!-- Include all of the jar files except the ejbeans and applet.
            The other build files that create jars have to be run in the
            correct order. This is covered later.
       /-->
        <lib dir="${lib}" >
            <exclude name="greet-ejbs.jar"/>
            <exclude name="helloapplet.jar"/>
          </lib>
        </war>
```

Listing 6.2 Hello World webapplication project buildfile. (continues)

```
    </target>

    <target name="deploy" depends="package">
        <copy file="${dist}/hello.war" todir="${deploy_resin}" />

        <copy file="${dist}/hello.war" todir="${deploy_tomcat}" />

    </target>

    <target name="all" depends="clean,package"
                        description="perform all targets."/>

</project>
```

Listing 6.2 Hello World webapplication project buildfile.

The final output of the Web application project is a single WAR file. The WAR file is built (not surprisingly) by the package target. Here is the listing for the package target:

```
<target name="package" depends="compile">

    <mkdir dir="${meta}" />
    <antcall target="prepare_meta" />

    <war warfile="${dist}/hello.war" webxml="${meta}/web.xml">
        <!--
           Include the html and jsp files.
           Put the classes from the build into the classes directory
           of the war.
        /-->
       <fileset dir="./HTML" />
       <fileset dir="./JSP" />
       <classes dir="${build}" />

        <!-- Include the applet. /-->
        <fileset dir="${lib}" includes="helloapplet.jar" />

        <!-- Include all of the jar files except the ejbeans
         and applet.
  /-->
        <lib dir="${lib}" />
    </war>

</target>
```

As you can see, this package target is much larger than the other two we've discussed (model and application). For now we'll defer a detailed discussion of the second and third lines of code:

```
<mkdir dir="${meta}" />
<antcall target="prepare_meta" />
```

These lines do some processing on the web.xml deployment descriptor file and put the file in the directory defined by ${meta} directory (note that the "meta" property is set in the init target). We explain the processing done to the deployment descriptor in the section "Enterprise JavaBeans" found later in this chapter. Next, the package target calls the war task, which is as follows:

```
<war warfile="${dist}/hello.war" webxml="${meta}/web.xml">
   <fileset dir="./HTML" />
   <fileset dir="./JSP" />
   <classes dir="${build}" />
   <fileset dir="${lib}" includes="helloapplet.jar" />
   <lib dir="${lib}" />
</war>
```

The WAR file hello.war is put in the distribution directory (dist), which is specified by the war task's "warfile" attribute (warfile="${dist}/hello.war"). The dist directory is another common directory that is used by the main project's buildfile later to build an enterprise archive (EAR) file; the "dist" property is defined in the init target. The "webxml" attribute of the war task defines the deployment descriptor to use; it's the one we processed at the beginning of the package target. The web.xml file is put in the WAR file's WEB-INF/ directory.

In addition, the war task body specifies three file sets. One file set includes the helloapplet.jar file (which we discuss in the section "HelloWorld.jsp Applet Delivery" later in this chapter) and all the files in the HTML and JSP directories. The war task body also specifies where to locate the classes using <classes dir="${build}" />. This command puts the classes in the WEB-INF/classes directory.

The webapplication project's buildfile defines a slightly more complex compile target, as follows:

```
<target name="compile" depends="prepare"
                       description="compile the Java source.">
    <javac srcdir="./src" destdir="${build}">
        <classpath >

            <fileset dir="${lib}">
                <include name="**/*.jar"/>
            </fileset>

            <fileset dir="${build_lib}">
                <include name="**/*.jar"/>
```

```
                </fileset>

            </classpath>
        </javac>

    </target>
```

Notice that this compile target defines two file sets. One file set (<fileset dir="${build_lib}">) is used to include the classes needed for servlets (such as import javax.servlet.*). The other file set (<fileset dir="${lib}">) is used to include the Greeting interfaces and the GreetingFactory class. The only real difference from the application compile target is the inclusion of the JAR file for servlets. The "build_lib" property is defined in the webapplication project's init target, as follows:

```
<property name="build_lib" value="./../lib" />
```

The good thing about this approach is that if we need additional JAR files, we can put them in the build_lib. The second file set (<fileset dir="${build_lib}">) grabs all the JAR files in the ./../lib directory.

The webapplication project's buildfile adds a few convenience targets geared toward Web applications. The deploy target copies the WAR file that this buildfile generates to the webapps directory of Tomcat and Resin. (Tomcat is the reference implementation servlet engine of the Java specification. Resin is an easy-to-use Java application server that supports JSPs, EJBs, J2EE container specification, XSL, and so on.) Without further ado, here is the deploy target:

```
<target name="deploy" depends="package">
        <copy file="${dist}/hello.war" todir="${deploy_resin}" />
        <copy file="${dist}/hello.war" todir="${deploy_tomcat}" />
</target>
```

Both Tomcat and Resin pick up the WAR files automatically. In the interest of doing no harm and cleaning up after ourselves, the webapplication project's buildfile also adds an extra clean_deploy target that deletes the WAR file it deployed and cleans up the generated directory, as follows:

```
<target name="clean_deploy" >
    <delete file="${deploy_resin}/hello.war" />
    <delete dir="${deploy_resin}/hello" />
    <delete file="${deploy_tomcat}/hello.war" />
    <delete dir="${deploy_tomcat}/hello" />
</target>
```

"Great," you say. "But what if the application server I am deploying to is on another server that is half way around the world?" No problem; use the following FTP task (a full explanation of the task can be found in Chapter 12, "Ant Tag Reference"):

```
<ftp server="ftp.texas.austin.building7.eblox.org"
       remotedir="/deploy/resin/webapps"
       userid="kingJon"
       password="killMyLandLord"
       depends="yes"
       binary="yes"
>


     <fileset dir="${dist}">
       <include name="**/*.war"/>
     </fileset>

</ftp>
```

Building and Deploying the Web Application

This section explains how to build and deploy the Web application. The buildfile assumes that you have Resin and Tomcat installed in the root of your drive. You may need to make adjustments to the buildfile if you installed Resin or Tomcat in another directory or if you are using another J2EE-compliant Web application server.

To build the Web application, follow these steps:

1. Navigate to the WebApplication directory, set up the environment, and then do the following at the command line:

```
C:\CVS\...\MVCHelloWorld\WebApplication>ant
```

2. You will get the following output:

```
Buildfile: build.xml

setProps:

init:

clean_deploy:
   [delete] Could not find file C:\resin\webapps\hello.war to delete.
   [delete] Could not find file C:\tomcat\webapps\hello.war to delete

clean:
   [delete] Could not find file C:\tmp\app\dist\hello.war to delete.

prepare:
    [mkdir] Created dir: C:\tmp\app\webapps\webclasses
    [mkdir] Created dir: C:\tmp\app\dist
```

```
compile:
    [javac] Compiling 1 source file to C:\tmp\app\webapps\webclasses

package:
    [mkdir] Created dir: C:\tmp\app\webapps\meta

prepare_meta_ejb:

prepare_meta_noejb:

prepare_meta:
     [copy] Copying 1 file to C:\tmp\app\webapps\meta
      [war] Building war: C:\tmp\app\dist\hello.war

all:

BUILD SUCCESSFUL
```

3. Deploy the WAR files to the application server. If you install Resin and Tomcat off the root directory, then you can run the deploy target. Otherwise, modify the appropriate deploy properties defined in the init target. To deploy the application with Ant, do the following:

```
C:\CVS\?.\MVCHelloWorld\WebApplication>ant deploy
Buildfile: build.xml

...
...

deploy:
     [copy] Copying 1 file to C:\resin\webapps
     [copy] Copying 1 file to C:\tomcat\webapps

BUILD SUCCESSFUL

Total time: 0 seconds
```

4. After we run the application, we start Resin or Tomcat, and then hit the site with our browser. (More on this subject later.) We can also clean out the directories when we are ready to deploy a new version, as follows:

```
C:\CVS\...\MVCHelloWorld\WebApplication>ant clean
```

5. The output looks like the following:

```
Buildfile: build.xml

setProps:

init:

clean_deploy:
   [delete] Deleting: C:\resin\webapps\hello.war
```

```
   [delete] Deleting: C:\tomcat\webapps\hello.war

clean:
   [delete] Deleting directory C:\tmp\app\webapps
   [delete] Deleting: C:\tmp\app\dist\hello.war

BUILD SUCCESSFUL

Total time: 0 seconds
```

6. Notice that we delete the WAR files and the deployment directories. This is just good house-cleaning for when we do a build and deploy. In the next section, we will run the webapplication project.

Running the Web Application

Now that we've built and deployed the webapplication project, let's run it. We start our servlet engine and then open the site in our browser—for example, http://localhost/hello/HelloWorldServlet. (Resin's default setup is port 8080, so you may have to adjust the URL.) Refer to Figure 6.1 to see the Web application running.

You may notice a couple of things. The application URL is defined in a directory called hello (http://localhost/hello/HelloWorldServlet). By default, Tomcat and Resin unjar our WAR file in a directory called <*War file File Name*>. Later, we will use the EAR file to override this default behavior in a neutral application server way.

Figure 6.1 The Hello World Model 2 Web application in Netscape.

The HelloWorldServlet part of the application's URL is defined by a mapping in the deployment descriptor as follows:

```
<servlet>
    <servlet-name>HelloWorldServlet</servlet-name>
    <servlet-class>xptoolkit.web.HelloWorldServlet</servlet-class>
    <init-param>
      <param-name>Greeting.class</param-name>
      <param-value>@Greeting.class@</param-value>
    </init-param>
</servlet>


<servlet-mapping>
    <servlet-name>HelloWorldServlet</servlet-name>
    <url-pattern>/HelloWorldServlet</url-pattern>
</servlet-mapping>
```

The servlet tag declares the servlet and gives it a name. The servlet mapping assigns the HelloWorldServlet the URL pattern /HelloWorldServlet. We could change the URL pattern to /PeanutButter, and the URL http://localhost/hello/PeanutButter would work (see Figure 6.2).

Actually, we mapped the 404 error to HelloWorldServlet as well, so the server sends any URL it does not recognize to HelloWorldServlet to process (for the benefit of people with fumble fingers).

The next section describes a simple applet project that integrates with the webapplication project. Then, we will discuss Enterprise JavaBean deployment and enterprise archive files.

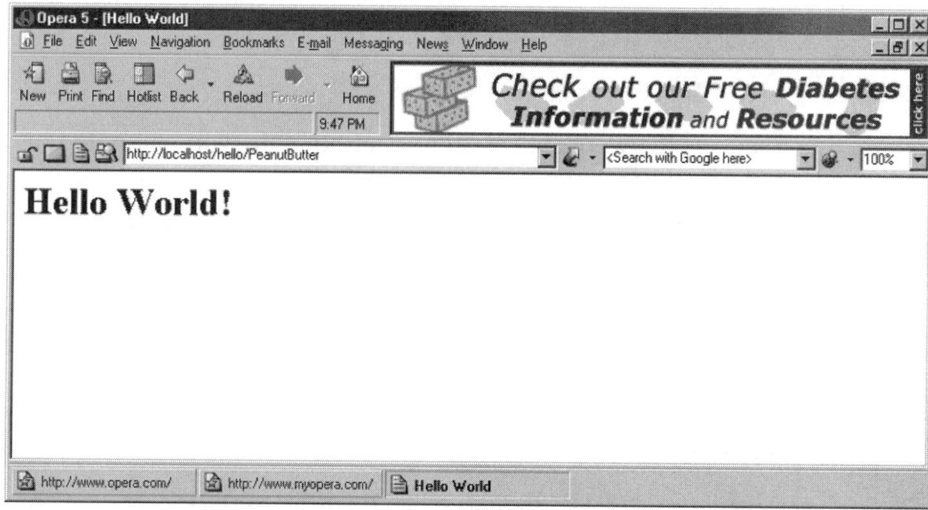

Figure 6.2 Hello peanut butter?

HelloWorld.jsp Applet Delivery

Now the applets JAR we built in Chapter 5 becomes part of the Web application. It is put in the Web application where the browser can find it. The Web application has a JSP page, HelloApplet.jsp, which has a jsp:plugin tag that delivers the applet to the browser. The HelloApplet.jsp with the jsp:plugin action is listed as follows:

```
<html>
<head><title>Hello World Applet</title></head>
<body>
<jsp:plugin type="applet"
          code="xptoolkit.applet.HelloWorldApplet"
          archive="helloapplet.jar"
          height="200"
          width="200"
          align="center">
    <jsp:fallback>
    <!-- This fallback message will display if the plugin does not work.
/-->
        <p> Java is cool. Get a browser that supports the plugin. </ br>
            Or we will hunt you down and melt your computer!
        </p>
    </jsp:fallback>
</jsp:plugin>

</body>
</html>
```

This shows how the applet is delivered to the browser. How is the applet included in the Web application's WAR file in the first place? We explain in the next section.

Including an Applet In a WAR File

If you look at the webapplication project buildfile, you will note that the war task in the package target does the following:

```
<war warfile="${dist}/hello.war" webxml="${meta}/web.xml">
      <fileset dir="./HTML" />
      <fileset dir="./JSP" />
      <classes dir="${build}" />
      <fileset dir="${lib}" includes="helloapplet.jar" />
      <lib dir="${lib}" />
</war>
```

The fileset directive

```
<fileset dir="${lib}" includes="helloapplet.jar" />
```

tells the war task to include only the helloapplet.jar file from the lib directory.

Because this file set is not a classes- or lib-type file set, helloapplet.jar goes to the root of the WAR file. In contrast, the special lib and classes file sets put their files in WEB-INF/lib and WEB-INF/classes, respectively. The end effect is that the browser is able to get the applet.

After we build the applet, we go back and rebuild the Web application and then deploy it. We run Ant in the root of both the projects' home directories (if you get a compile error, be sure you have built the model, because the Web application depends on it). After everything compiles and the appropriate JAR and WAR files are built, we deploy the webapplication project by using the deploy target of the webapplication buildfile. Then we run the applet, as demonstrated in Figure 6.3.

It's important to recap what we have done. We created a common Java library called model.jar. This model.jar is used by a Web application and a regular Java application that is a standalone executable Java application in an executable JAR file. We create an applet that is loaded with a JSP page that has the jsp:plugin action. Once the applet loads into the browser, the applet communicates over HTTP to the Web application's HelloWorldServlet. HelloWorldServlet calls the getGreeting() method on the GreetingFactory, which is contained in the model.jar file.

In the next section, we set up the GreetingFactory so that it talks to an enterprise session bean that in turn talks to an enterprise entity bean. The Web application buildfile is set up so that after we add one property file, it can talk to either the enterprise beans or to the local implementation in the model library.

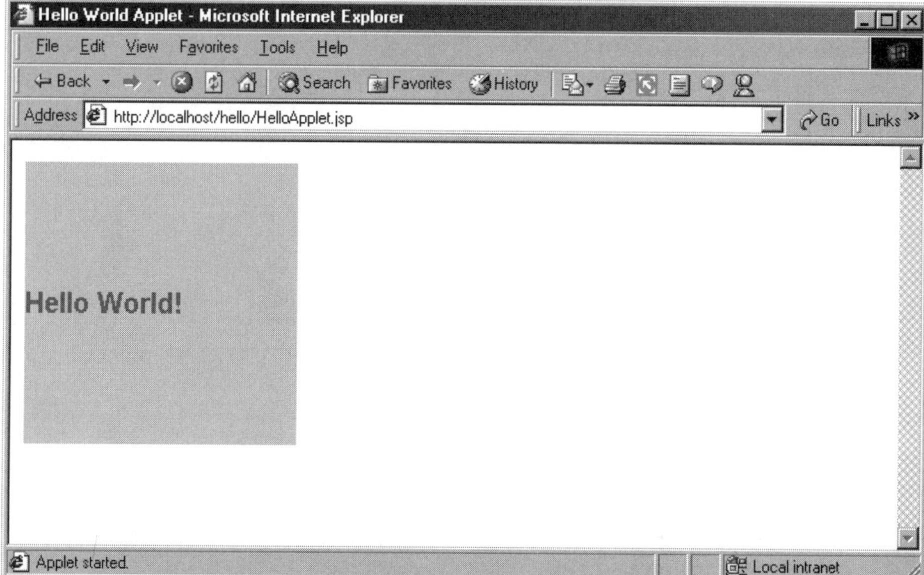

Figure 6.3 Applet talking to the Web application.

Enterprise JavaBeans

In this section, we create two simple enterprise beans and demonstrate how to build an EJB JAR file. We also create a local proxy class—the shadow bean—that knows how to speak to the enterprise beans. The shadow bean implements the Greeting interface and can be plugged-in in place of the GreetingBean from the model library. The session bean communicates with the entity bean, so its deployment descriptor entry must reference the entity bean. Let's start by examining the files in this project.

Directory Structure of the Enterprise Beans Project

This project has more files than any other project in this example:

```
Root directory of the Enterprise beans
|   build.xml
|
+--src
|   \--xptoolkit
|       |
|       |
|       +--ejbs
|       |       GreetingEntityBean.java
|       |       GreetingEntityHome.java
|       |       GreetingEntityRemote.java
|       |       GreetingSessionBean.java
|       |       GreetingSessionRemote.java
|       |       GreetingSessionHome.java
|       |
|       |
|       \--model
|               GreetingShadow.java
|
+--META-DATA
|       ejb.xml
|
|
+--jboss_clientlib
|       jnp-client.jar
|       jbosssx-client.jar
|       jboss-client.jar
|       ejb.jar
|
\--jboss_props
        jndi.properties
```

We used JBoss, an open-source implementation of Enterprise JavaBeans. For JBoss, four JAR files and one properties file are used for the client-side deployment. If you decide to use JBoss, then you have the same or similar JAR files for packaging your client (depending on the version of JBoss you're using).

There are six Java source files, which we'll discuss in depth. These six files define two Enterprise JavaBeans. In addition, one deployment descriptor describes the two Enterprise JavaBeans to the EJB container. There is nothing specific about the deployment descriptor or the Enterprise JavaBeans to JBoss; they should work on any J2EE-compliant EJB application server. Of course, build.xml is the Ant buildfile that takes all this raw material and forms it into a client-side JAR file and an EJB JAR file that can be deployed in any J2EE EJB application server. In the following parts of this section, we describe each of these files. Let's start with the entity bean.

The HelloWorld Entity Bean

Like most classes in this example, the entity bean is a simple object that returns a greeting. In fact, because the entity is generally used to represent a view of rows in a database, we had to cheat a little and define a static variable to simulate a primary key. The entity bean consists of three classes: the GreetingEntityHome interface; the GreetingEntityRemote interface; and the implementation, the GreetingEntityBean class. The Home and Remote interfaces are part of the beans contract with the EJB container. Listings 6.3, 6.4, and 6.5 show the source code for the Hello World entity bean, GreetingEntityBean.

```
package xptoolkit.ejbs;
import javax.ejb.EntityBean;
import javax.ejb.EntityContext;
import javax.ejb.EJBException;
import javax.ejb.CreateException;
import javax.ejb.FinderException;

public class GreetingEntityBean implements EntityBean{


    static int pkid;

    public Integer ejbCreate(){
       return new Integer(++pkid);

    }
    public void ejbPostCreate()throws CreateException{
    }
```

Listing 6.3 GreetingEntityBean. (continues)

```
    public Integer ejbFindByPrimaryKey(Integer i)throws FinderException{
        return new Integer(1);
    }
    public void ejbActivate(){}
    public void ejbLoad(){}
    public void ejbPassivate(){}
    public void ejbRemove(){}
    public void ejbStore(){}
    public void setEntityContext(EntityContext cotext){}
    public void unsetEntityContext(){}

    public String getGreeting(){
      return "Hello World!";
    }

}
```

Listing 6.3 GreetingEntityBean.

```
package xptoolkit.ejbs;

import javax.ejb.EJBHome;
import javax.ejb.CreateException;
import javax.ejb.FinderException;
import java.rmi.RemoteException;

public interface GreetingEntityHome extends EJBHome{

    GreetingEntityRemote create() throws RemoteException, CreateException;
    GreetingEntityRemote findByPrimaryKey(Integer i)throws RemoteException,
FinderException;
}
```

Listing 6.4 GreetingEntityHome interface.

```
package xptoolkit.ejbs;
import javax.ejb.EJBObject;
import java.rmi.RemoteException;

public interface GreetingEntityRemote extends EJBObject {

   public String getGreeting()throws RemoteException;
}
```

Listing 6.5 GreetingEntityRemote interface.

As you can probably see by looking at the implementation of GreetingEntity-Bean, it does not do much. Most of the methods are to fulfill the contract with the container. A few of the methods fake a primary key id semantic, but that is beyond the scope of this book. Instead, focus on the following method of the entity bean implementation:

```
public String getGreeting(){
  return "Hello World!";
}
```

This method returns the now-infamous greeting. The session bean connects with the entity bean and calls this method. In order to do this, the deployment descriptor must be configured properly.

The Session Bean

This session bean's sole purpose in life is to connect to the entity bean and call the entity bean's getGreeting() method. Like the entity bean, the HelloWorld session defines three source files: one for the implementation bean class, one for the remote interface, and one for the home interface. The three classes are the GreetingSessionBean class, the GreetingSessionRemote interface, and the GreetingSessionHome interface, respectively. Listings 6.6, 6.7, and 6.8 provide the full source code for the remote, home, and implementation.

```
package xptoolkit.ejbs;

import javax.rmi.PortableRemoteObject;
import javax.naming.InitialContext;

import javax.ejb.SessionBean;
import javax.ejb.SessionContext;
import javax.ejb.EJBException;
import javax.ejb.CreateException;

public class GreetingSessionBean implements SessionBean{

    public void setSessionContext(SessionContext context)
                                      throws EJBException{
    }

    public void ejbCreate() throws  CreateException{
    }

    public void ejbRemove() throws EJBException{
    }
```

Listing 6.6 GreetingSessionBean class. (continues)

```
    public void ejbActivate() throws EJBException{
    }

    public void ejbPassivate() throws EJBException{
    }

    public String getGreeting(){
        GreetingEntityHome home;
        GreetingEntityRemote remote;
        InitialContext jndiContext;
        Object ref;
        String greeting="bye bye";

        try {
         jndiContext = new InitialContext();
         ref  = jndiContext.lookup
                ("java:comp/env/ejb/GreetingEntityBean");

         home = (GreetingEntityHome)
                PortableRemoteObject.narrow (ref,
                               GreetingEntityHome.class);
         remote = home.create();
         greeting = remote.getGreeting();
         System.out.println("Greeting: " + greeting);
        }
        catch (Exception e){
            throw new EJBException(e);
        }
        return greeting;
    }

}
```

Listing 6.6 GreetingSessionBean class.

```
package xptoolkit.ejbs;

import javax.ejb.EJBHome;
import javax.ejb.CreateException;
import java.rmi.RemoteException;

public interface GreetingSessionHome extends EJBHome{
    public GreetingSessionRemote create()
                        throws CreateException, RemoteException;

}
```

Listing 6.7 GreetingSessionHome interface.

```
package xptoolkit.ejbs;

import javax.ejb.EJBObject;
import java.rmi.RemoteException;

public interface GreetingSessionRemote extends EJBObject{
        public String getGreeting()throws RemoteException;
}
```

Listing 6.8 GreetingSessionRemote interface.

Like the entity bean, the session bean's main focus is the getGreeting() method. The getGreeting() method of the session bean calls the entity bean's getGreeting() method. But first it has to look it up. Let's break down the getGreeting() method step by step, because it is important when we discuss the deployment descriptor in the next part of this section.

First the method defines five variables, as follows:

```
GreetingEntityHome home;
GreetingEntityRemote remote;
InitialContext jndiContext;
Object ref;
String greeting="bye bye";
```

The home variable creates an instance of GreetingEntityBean (a reference to its remote). The remote variable holds a reference to the remote proxy of GreetingEntityBean. The session bean never calls GreetingEntityBean directly; instead, it talks to the remote interface (a detailed discussion is beyond the scope of this book). The jndiContext looks up the GreetingEntityBean's home interface in the naming service provided by the EJB container that uses the JNDI API interface. The ref object holds a reference to the home object before it is narrowed into the home interface. (The narrow concept is similar to casting, but it could involve a CORBA narrow, which is beyond the scope of this book—please view it as a cast.) Finally, the greeting variable holds the greeting message returned from the entity bean. Now, let's look at the rest of the method step by step.

First we get the JNDI initial context. The entity beans environment is defined in the deployment descriptor, and the EJB container provides this context (environment) to the enterprise bean at runtime (more on this in the deployment descriptor part of this section) as follows:

```
jndiContext = new InitialContext();
```

Next we get the home reference from the jndiContext. Note that the home is mapped to this location by the deployment descriptor as follows:

```
ref  = jndiContext.lookup
        ("java:comp/env/ejb/GreetingEntityBean");
```

Now that we have the home interface reference, we can narrow it down to a real home interface (the PortableRemoteObject.narrow is needed for compatibility with CORBA IIOP—that is, RMI over IIOP) as follows:

```
home = (GreetingEntityHome)
       PortableRemoteObject.narrow (ref,
                               GreetingEntityHome.class);
```

Now we have a real home object proxy; thus, we can use the home to create the remote object reference to the entity bean as follows:

```
remote = home.create();
```

Once we have the remote interface, we can begin using it to call the entity bean. The first and only method we call is getGreeting(), as follows:

```
greeting = remote.getGreeting();
```

Just to prove to ourselves that we were able to call the session bean, we print out the message, which shows up in the stdout for the EJB server we are using for this book:

```
System.out.println("Greeting: " + greeting);
```

As you can see, the method for session bean just delegates the call to the entity bean. The nice thing is that the entity bean is looked up with JNDI. This approach demonstrates one enterprise bean talking to another enterprise bean. In the next section, we create a proxy bean that takes care of all the complexities of dealing with JNDI on the client side.

The Shadow Proxy Bean

The shadow bean is a proxy and an adapter for the client side. It is a proxy in that it has the same methods as the remote interface and all calls to it are delegated to the remote interface. The shadow handles all access to the JNDI interface, the home reference to create the session bean's remote interface. The shadow even handles non-compliant J2EE servlet engines, by allowing the JNDI properties to be loaded as a class resource. Note that a servlet engine can be servlet specification–compliant without being J2EE container–compliant. It is an adapter in that it adapts the remote interface of the session bean to the xptoolkit.model.Greeting interface. The code for the proxy is shown in Listing 6.9.

```
package xptoolkit.model;

import java.util.Properties;
import javax.rmi.PortableRemoteObject;
```

Listing 6.9 Shadow proxy bean. (continues)

```
import javax.naming.InitialContext;

import xptoolkit.ejbs.GreetingSessionRemote;
import xptoolkit.ejbs.GreetingSessionHome;
import xptoolkit.ejbs.GreetingEntityRemote;
import xptoolkit.ejbs.GreetingEntityHome;

import java.io.InputStream;


public class GreetingShadow implements Greeting{
    GreetingSessionRemote remote;
    static Properties env = new Properties();
    static {
        InputStream is;
        try{
            is=
            GreetingShadow.class.getResourceAsStream("/jndi.properties");
            env.load(is);
        }
        catch(Exception e){
            System.out.println(""+e);
            System.out.println();
            e.printStackTrace();
        }
    }

    public GreetingShadow() {
      GreetingSessionHome home;
      InitialContext jndiContext;
      Object ref;

      try{
         jndiContext = new InitialContext(env);
         ref  = jndiContext.lookup("GreetingSessionBean");
         home = (GreetingSessionHome)
          PortableRemoteObject.narrow (ref, GreetingSessionHome.class);
         remote = home.create();
      }
      catch(Exception e){
          System.out.println(e.getMessage());
          System.out.println();System.out.println();
          e.printStackTrace();
      }
    }
```

Listing 6.9 Shadow proxy bean. (continues)

```
    public String getGreeting() {
        String greeting="bye bye";
        try{
            greeting=remote.getGreeting();
        }
        catch(Exception e){}
        return greeting;
    }

}
```

Listing 6.9 Shadow proxy bean.

The bean tries to load the properties needed to run the JNDI naming service (that is, to create the initial context):

```
static {
    InputStream is;
    try{
       is=
       GreetingShadow.class.getResourceAsStream("/jndi.properties");
       env.load(is);
    }
    catch(Exception e){
        System.out.println(""+e);
        System.out.println();
        e.printStackTrace();
    }
}
```

As you can see, this code is not very robust. However, if you are expecting the properties for JNDI to be loaded elsewhere, the code won't complain. For example, some Web application servers allow you to set up the JNDI environment in the configuration file for the server. If you decide to use these features of the Web application server, then this code works regardless—and because it is in the static initializer block, it runs only once.

The constructor of the GreetingShadow class tries to load the initial context based on the properties loaded in the static initializer block. If those properties are not set, JNDI uses the initial context that is configured for this environment; if nothing is set or the wrong JNDI initial context is mapped, then you will not be able to look up the home object of GreetingSessionBean. Otherwise, the following code is a lot like the code for the session to talk to the entity, except now it is the shadow (client side proxy) talking to the session. Look at the following code and compare it to the session code talking to the entity code:

```
public GreetingShadow() {
  GreetingSessionHome home;
```

```
        InitialContext jndiContext;
        Object ref;

        try{
           jndiContext = new InitialContext(env);
           ref  = jndiContext.lookup("GreetingSessionBean");
           home = (GreetingSessionHome)
           PortableRemoteObject.narrow (ref, GreetingSessionHome.class);
           remote = home.create();
        }
        catch(Exception e){
            System.out.println(e.getMessage());
            System.out.println();System.out.println();
            e.printStackTrace();
        }
    }
```

Next, all methods (such as getGreeting()) are delegated to the remote interface that was create in the constructor. This is demonstrated as follows:

```
    public String getGreeting() {
        String greeting="bye bye";
        try{
            greeting=remote.getGreeting();
        }
        catch(Exception e){}
        return greeting;
    }
```

The important thing to note is that because the GreetingShadow implements the Greeting interface, it can be swapped out for GreetingBean. All we have to do is set the system property "Greeting.class" to "GreetingShadow", and the GreetingFactory will instantiate it on a call to getGreeting() instead of GreetingBean. If you recall, HelloServlet reads a "Greeting.class" servlet parameter and uses it to set the system property "Greeting.class". Thus, if we change the "Greeting.class" servlet parameter in the Web application deployment descriptor, we can swap the local GreetingBean with the remote proxy GreetingShadow. We accomplish this trick with the buildfile for the Web application at the end of this section. First, let's look at the deployment descriptor for the Enterprise JavaBeans. (Note that the jndi.properties file may need to be changed for your environment; refer to the EJB documentation of your EJ application server.)

The Enterprise JavaBeans Deployment Descriptor

As we discussed in Chapter 2, "J2EE Deployment Concepts," the Enterprise JavaBean deployment descriptor sets up the environment for the Enterprise

JavaBeans that we are going to deploy. Listing 6.10 shows the Enterprise JavaBean deployment descriptor (ejb-jar.xml) for our Hello World application.

```
<ejb-jar>

<description>
This ejb-jar files contains the Enterprise beans for the
model 2 Hello World application.
</description>
<enterprise-beans>
    <entity>
        <description>
            The GreetingEntityBean is a do nothing bean to demonstrate
            how to deploy an Enterprise bean with Ant.
        </description>
        <ejb-name>GreetingEntityBean</ejb-name>
        <home>xptoolkit.ejbs.GreetingEntityHome</home>
        <remote>xptoolkit.ejbs.GreetingEntityRemote</remote>
        <ejb-class>xptoolkit.ejbs.GreetingEntityBean</ejb-class>
        <transaction-type>Container</transaction-type>
        <reentrant>True</reentrant>
        <prim-key-class>java.lang.Integer</prim-key-class>
        <persistence-type>Bean</persistence-type>
    </entity>
    <session>
        <description>
            The GreetingSessionBean is a do nothing bean to demonstrate
            how to deploy an Enterprise bean with Ant.
        </description>
        <ejb-name>GreetingSessionBean</ejb-name>
        <home>xptoolkit.ejbs.GreetingSessionHome</home>
        <remote>xptoolkit.ejbs.GreetingSessionRemote</remote>
        <ejb-class>xptoolkit.ejbs.GreetingSessionBean</ejb-class>
        <session-type>Stateful</session-type>
        <transaction-type>Container</transaction-type>

        <ejb-ref>
            <description>
                This sets up a references from the Entity bean to the
                     session bean.
                Thus, the session bean can look up the Entity bean in
                     its environment space.
            </description>
            <ejb-ref-name>ejb/GreetingEntityBean</ejb-ref-name>
            <ejb-ref-type>Entity</ejb-ref-type>
            <home>xptoolkit.ejbs.GreetingEntityHome</home>
            <remote>xptoolkit.ejbs.GreetingEntityRemote</remote>
```

Listing 6.10 EJB JAR deployment descriptor for the Hello World Model 2 application. (continues)

```
            <ejb-link>GreetingEntityBean</ejb-link>
        </ejb-ref>
    </session>


</enterprise-beans>
<assembly-descriptor>
    <container-transaction>
        <method>
            <ejb-name>GreetingSessionBean</ejb-name>
            <method-name>*</method-name>
        </method>
        <trans-attribute>Supports</trans-attribute>
    </container-transaction>

    <container-transaction>
        <method>
            <ejb-name>GreetingEntityBean</ejb-name>
            <method-name>*</method-name>
        </method>
        <trans-attribute>Supports</trans-attribute>
    </container-transaction>

</assembly-descriptor>
</ejb-jar>
```

Listing 6.10 EJB JAR deployment descriptor for the Hello World Model 2 application.

This deployment descriptor is fairly standard. We'll point out some areas of interest. Inside the session bean's descriptor element is a sub-element to define a reference to the entity bean, as follows:

```
<ejb-ref>
    <description>
        This sets up a references from the Entity bean to the
             session bean.
        Thus, the session bean can look up the Entity bean in
             its environment space.
    </description>
    <ejb-ref-name>ejb/GreetingEntityBean</ejb-ref-name>
    <ejb-ref-type>Entity</ejb-ref-type>
    <home>xptoolkit.ejbs.GreetingEntityHome</home>
    <remote>xptoolkit.ejbs.GreetingEntityRemote</remote>
    <ejb-link>GreetingEntityBean</ejb-link>
</ejb-ref>
```

This is how the session bean can find the entity bean. The container takes care of the setting for the initial context (unlike the shadow, where we loaded the properties from jndi.properties). In addition, the container reads the ejb-ref element and maps GreetingEntityBean's home into the GreetingSessionBean's environment context. Cool!

As you can see, we have a lot of files to manage. We have JAR files and a JNDI property file that must be locatable by the client-side shadow's class loader. We also have a set of classes (remote and home) that must be packaged in the client-side shadow's JAR file. On the flip side, we have a deployment descriptor and six Java files that need to be packaged in the server-side JAR file for two the Enterprise JavaBeans.

The Ant buildfile, which is described in the next section, takes care of all these complexities. It documents the process and ensures the build is repeatable.

The Enterprise Bean Buildfile

As we stated, the output of the buildfiles is two JAR files. One JAR file is for the EJB's container; and the other file is for the server. Also, unlike the war command, there is no special command to build EJB JAR files. Frankly, you don't need a special command because EJB JAR files are very similar to regular JAR files. Look at Listing 6.11 to see the complete buildfile for the enterprise beans.

```
<project name="enterprise_beans" default="all" >

    <target name="setProps" unless="setProps"
                          description="setup the properites.">
        <property name="outdir" value="/tmp/app" />
        <property name="jboss" value="/jboss/jboss/deploy" />
    </target>

    <target name="init" depends="setProps"
                          description="initialize the properties.">
      <tstamp/>
      <property name="ejbout" value="${outdir}/ejbs" />
      <property name="build" value="${ejbout}/ejb-jar" />
      <property name="client" value="${ejbout}/ejb-jar-client" />
      <property name="dist" value="${outdir}/dist" />
      <property name="lib" value="${outdir}/lib" />
      <property name="meta-data" value="${build}/META-INF" />
      <property name="build_lib" value="./../lib" />
      <property name="ejb_lib" value="/JBoss/jboss/lib/ext" />
    </target>

    <target name="clean_jboss" if="jboss">
        <delete file="${jboss}/greetbeans.jar" />
    </target>
```

Listing 6.11 Buildfile for the enterprise bean project. (continues)

```
<target name="clean" depends="init,clean_jboss"
                     description="clean up the output directories.">
    <delete dir="${build}" />
    <delete dir="${meta-data}" />
    <delete dir="${client}" />
    <delete dir="${dist}/greet-ejbs.jar" />
</target>


<target name="prepare" depends="init"
                     description="prepare the output directory.">
    <mkdir dir="${build}" />
    <mkdir dir="${lib}" />
    <mkdir dir="${meta-data}" />
    <mkdir dir="${client}" />
    <mkdir dir="${dist}" />
</target>

<target name="compile" depends="prepare"
                     description="compile the Java source.">
    <javac srcdir="./src" destdir="${build}" >
        <classpath >
            <pathelement location="." />

            <fileset dir="${build_lib}">
                <include name="**/*.jar"/>
            </fileset>

            <fileset dir="${lib}">
                <include name="**/*.jar"/>
            </fileset>

            <fileset dir="${ejb_lib}">
                <include name="**/*.jar"/>
            </fileset>
        </classpath>
    </javac>
</target>

<target name="config_jboss_jndi" if="jboss">
    <copy todir="${client}" >
         <fileset dir="./jboss_props" />
    </copy>
</target>

<target name="config_jndi" depends="config_jboss_jndi" />
```

Listing 6.11 Buildfile for the enterprise bean project. (continues)

```
<target name="package" depends="compile,config_jndi"
          description="package the Java classes into a jar.">

 <copy todir="${client}" >

      <fileset dir="${build}" excludes="**/*Bean*"
                                 includes="**/*.class*" />

 </copy>

 <copy file="./META-DATA/ejb.xml" tofile="${meta-data}/ejb-jar.xml" />

 <jar jarfile="${dist}/greet-ejbs.jar"
       basedir="${build}" />

 <jar jarfile="${lib}/client-greet-ejbs.jar"
       basedir="${client}" />
</target>

<target name="deploy_jboss" depends="package" if="jboss">
    <copy file="${dist}/greet-ejbs.jar" todir="${jboss}" />
    <copy todir="${lib}"  >
        <fileset dir="./jboss_clientlib" />
    </copy>
</target>

<target name="deploy" depends="package,deploy_jboss"
              description="deploys the jar file to the ejb server.">
</target>


<target name="all" depends="clean,deploy"
                     description="perform all targets."/>

    </project>
```

Listing 6.11 Buildfile for the enterprise bean project.

Analyzing the Buildfile for Enterprise Beans

This buildfile is structured like the other buildfiles. It has similar targets that do similar things. One key difference is that the package target for this buildfile outputs two JAR files instead of one, as follows:

```
<target name="package" depends="compile,config_jndi"
           description="package the Java classes into a jar.">
```

```
<copy todir="${client}" >

     <fileset dir="${build}" excludes="**/*Bean*"
                                  includes="**/*.class*" />

</copy>

<copy file="./META-DATA/ejb.xml" tofile="${meta-data}/ejb-jar.xml" />

<jar jarfile="${dist}/greet-ejbs.jar"
      basedir="${build}" />

<jar jarfile="${lib}/client-greet-ejbs.jar"
      basedir="${client}" />
</target>
```

Because the client JAR file (client-greet-ejbs.jar) does not need the implementation classes (GreetingEntityBean and GreetingSessionBean), the output classes are copied to a temporary directory and a file set is defined that excludes all files with the substring *Bean* in them. This is demonstrated as follows:

```
<copy todir="${client}" >

     <fileset dir="${build}" excludes="**/*Bean*"
                                  includes="**/*.class*" />

</copy>
```

After we copy the buildfiles to the ${client} output directory, we jar them into the client file as follows:

```
<jar jarfile="${lib}/client-greet-ejbs.jar"
      basedir="${client}" />
```

The astute reader may wonder about the jndi.properties file that the shadow needs to create the initial context. Notice that the package target depended on compile and config_jndi targets. The config_jndi depends on the config_jboss_jndi target, which in turn copies the jndi.properties file located in ./jboss_props to the client directory that is jarred, as follows:

```
<target name="config_jndi" depends="config_jboss_jndi" />

<target name="config_jboss_jndi" if="jboss">
    <copy todir="${client}" >
         <fileset dir="./jboss_props" />
    </copy>

</target>
```

Notice that the config_jboss_jndi target is executed only if the jboss environment variable is set. Thus you can easily turn it off by not setting this environment variable. If you wanted to set up a similar mechanism for, for example, Orion (another J2EE application server environment that supports EJB), you could add a config_orion_jndi dependency to the config_jndi target, and then define a config_orion_jndi target that copies the jndi.properties file from the ./orion directory. Note that it is not necessary to use either if the servlet engine you are using is also a J2EE-compliant container.

That takes care of the client-side bean. What about the sever-side bean—the EJB bean for the EJB container, which needs the deployment descriptor? Remember, we said that Ant does not have a special task as it does for the WAR file. Thus, we need to build an exact replica of the directory structure needed by the EJB JAR file and then jar the directory. The prepare target prepares the output directory for the server side. Then, the package target copies the deployment descriptor to the correct location and jars the location as follows.

First we copy the deployment descriptor to the right location:

```
<copy file="./META-DATA/ejb.xml"
                    tofile="${meta-data}/ejb-jar.xml" />
```

Next we jar the location:

```
<jar jarfile="${dist}/greet-ejbs.jar"
      basedir="${build}" />
```

You may want to examine the metadata and build property settings, demonstrated as follows:

```
<target name="init" depends="setProps"
                      description="initialize the properties.">
  <tstamp/>
  <property name="ejbout" value="${outdir}/ejbs" />
  <property name="build" value="${ejbout}/ejb-jar" />
  <property name="client" value="${ejbout}/ejb-jar-client" />
  <property name="dist" value="${outdir}/dist" />
  <property name="lib" value="${outdir}/lib" />
  <property name="meta-data" value="${build}/META-INF" />
  <property name="build_lib" value="./../lib" />
</target>
```

Another difference between this buildfile and the webapplication project buildfile is that the deploy target works with JBoss instead of Resin and Tomcat like the Web application. The deploy target is set up in a similar fashion to the way the config_jndi is set up, in that it can easily be modified to support more types of application server—even remote servers using the ftp task, as we mentioned earlier in this chapter. Here is the deploy target:

```
<target name="deploy_jboss" depends="package" if="jboss">
    <copy file="${dist}/greet-ejbs.jar" todir="${jboss}" />
```

```
    <copy todir="${lib}"  >
        <fileset dir="./jboss_clientlib" />
    </copy>
</target>

<target name="deploy" depends="package,deploy_jboss"
              description="deploys the jar file to the ejb server.">
</target>
```

Notice that it copies the server-side JAR (greet-ejbs.jar) to the JBoss deployment directory, and it copies all the support libraries that the client-side JAR needs to the common directory (<copy todir="${lib}".. <fileset dir="./jboss_clientlib" ...).

The next part of this section covers a little magic that we do to the webapplication buildfile to use either the enterprise beans or the local version of the greeting bean.

Defining the ejb Property In the Web Application Buildfile

All the buildfile snippets in this part of the section are for the webapplication project. By defining the "ejb" property, the webapplication project has the option of deploying/configuring whether the Web application that is deployed uses enterprise beans. Notice that the prepare_meta target, which is a dependency of the prepare target, has two dependencies prepare_meta_ejb and prepare_meta_noejb, demonstrated as follows:

```
<target name="prepare_meta"
        depends="prepare_meta_ejb, prepare_meta_noejb">
    <copy todir="${meta}" filtering="true">
        <fileset dir="./meta-data"/>
    </copy>
</target>
```

The prepare_meta_ejb target is executed only if the "ejb" property is set as follows:

```
<target name="prepare_meta_ejb" if="ejb">
    <filter token="Greeting.class"
            value="xptoolkit.model.GreetingShadow"/>
</target>
```

If the "ejb" property is set, then the target creates a filter token called Greeting.class. Here, we set the value of Greeting.class to GreetingShadow. Conversely, the prepare_meta_ejb target is executed only if the "ejb" property is not set, as follows:

```
<target name="prepare_meta_noejb" unless="ejb">
    <filter token="Greeting.class"
             value="xptoolkit.model.GreetingBean"/>
</target>
```

Here, we set GreetingBean as "Greeting.class". But how is this used by the application? You may recall that HelloWorldServlet uses the servlet parameter "Greeting.class" to set the system property "Greeting.class" that is used by the GreetingFactory to create an instance of Greeting. We put an Ant filter key in the webapplication project deployment descriptor, as follows:

```
<servlet>
    <servlet-name>HelloWorldServlet</servlet-name>
    <servlet-class>xptoolkit.web.HelloWorldServlet</servlet-class>
    <init-param>
      <param-name>Greeting.class</param-name>
      <param-value>@Greeting.class@</param-value>
    </init-param>
</servlet>
```

If we copy this file using the filter command after the filter token Greeting.class has been set, then *@Greeting.class@* is replaced with the value of our token Greeting.class, which is set to xptoolkit.model.GreetingShadow in the prepare_meta_ejb target and to xptoolkit.model.GreetingBean in the prepare_meta_noejb target. Notice that the prepare_meta target copies the deployment descriptor with filtering turned on, as follows:

```
<copy todir="${meta}" filtering="true">
    <fileset dir="./meta-data"/>
</copy>
```

Running the Buildfiles

In order to get the webapplication project to run with the enterprise beans, we do the following.

1. Navigate to the EJBeans directory and build the EJB buildfile, as follows:

   ```
   C:\CVS\...\MVCHelloWorld\EJBeans>ant
   ```

2. For the EJB file, the deploy target is part of the all-target dependency, so it is deployed just by running it.
3. Build the webapplication project with the "ejb" property set so that the correct Greeting.class is set in the webapplication project deployment descriptor, as follows:

   ```
   C:\CVS\...\MVCHelloWorld\WebApplication>ant -Dejb=true deploy
   ```

4. Note that you may want to run both of these buildfiles with the clean option before you attempt to deploy.

5. Now that we have the application deployed, we start the EJB server (we used JBoss installed in /jboss) and the Web application server (we used Resin installed in /resin) and try the application as before. If we set up everything correctly, we get something like the following message in the stdout of our EJB container. The following is from JBoss:

```
[GreetingSessionBean] Greeting: Hello World!
```

You should have a buildfile for each major subsystem or component in your application. A medium-size application could have 50 to 100 subsystems and components with separate buildfiles. The small example that we presented in this chapter now has five buildfiles that must be executed in the correct order. Having 5 buildfiles and expecting a deployer, system admin, or fellow developer to execute them in the right order is loony; expecting a fellow developer, system admin, or deployer to build 50 buildfiles in the correct order is suicide.

Besides, human intervention defeats the purpose of automating the buildfile process (having a repeatable build). What we need is a master buildfile that manages all the complexities of this simple Hello World application. In the next section, we create such a buildfile to manage the complexities of building these five projects and perform some special deployment magic.

EAR Enterprise Application

In addition to having a master buildfile called main (we discussed the master buildfile in Chapter 5), we want to deploy all our applications into an application server that can accept them. The main buildfile serves two purposes:

- It ensures that all the subprojects are created in the correct order.
- It builds an enterprise archive (EAR) file so that the EJBs and Web applications can be easily deployed to a single application server.

The HelloWorld Main Project Buildfile

The main project's buildfile is structured (not surprisingly, we hope) very much like the other buildfiles. There are setProps, init, prepare, clean, build, and package targets. One of the key differences is that the main buildfile delegates the clean and build targets to the subproject while ensuring that they execute in the correct order. Also, the package section creates an EAR file. Refer to Listing 6.12 to see the final main buildfile.

```
<project name="main" default="package" >

    <target name="setProps" unless="setProps"
                          description="setup the properites.">
        <property name="outdir" value="/tmp/app" />
        <property name="setProps" value="true" />
    </target>

    <target name="init" depends="setProps"
                          description="initialize the properties.">
         <tstamp/>
         <property name="dist" value="${outdir}/dist" />
         <property name="deploy" value="${outdir}/deploy" />

         <property name="build" value="${outdir}/classes" />
         <property name="lib" value="${outdir}/lib" />
    </target>

    <target name="clean" depends="init"
                          description="clean up the output directories.">

           <ant dir="./Model" target="clean">
               <property name="outdir" value="${outdir}" />
               <property name="setProps" value="true" />

           </ant>

           <ant dir="./EJBeans" target="clean">
               <property name="outdir" value="${outdir}" />

               <property name="setProps" value="true" />
               <property name="jboss" value="/tools/jboss/jboss/deploy" />

           </ant>

           <ant dir="./WebApplication" target="clean">
               <property name="outdir" value="${outdir}" />

               <property name="setProps" value="true" />
               <property name="ejb" value="true" />
           </ant>

           <ant dir="./Application" target="clean">
               <property name="outdir" value="${outdir}" />
```

Listing 6.12 The enterprise application's main project buildfile. (continues)

```
            <property name="setProps" value="true" />
        </ant>

        <delete dir="${outdir}" />
</target>

<target name="prepare" depends="init"
                    description="prepare the output directory.">
      <mkdir dir="${build}" />
      <mkdir dir="${lib}" />
      <mkdir dir="${dist}" />
      <mkdir dir="${deploy}" />
      <mkdir dir="${dist}/META-INF" />
</target>

<target name="build" depends="prepare"
        description="build the model and application modules.">

      <ant dir="./Model" target="package">
           <property name="outdir" value="${outdir}" />
           <property name="setProps" value="true" />
      </ant>

      <ant dir="./EJBeans" target="deploy">
           <property name="outdir" value="${outdir}" />
           <property name="setProps" value="true" />
           <property name="jboss" value="/tools/jboss/jboss/deploy" />
      </ant>

      <ant dir="./Applet" target="package">
           <property name="outdir" value="${outdir}" />
           <property name="setProps" value="true" />
      </ant>

      <ant dir="./WebApplication" target="deploy">
           <property name="outdir" value="${outdir}" />
           <property name="setProps" value="true" />
           <property name="ejb" value="true" />
      </ant>

      <ant dir="./Application" target="package">
           <property name="outdir" value="${outdir}" />
           <property name="setProps" value="true" />
      </ant>
</target>

<target name="package" depends="build">
```

Listing 6.12 The enterprise application's main project buildfile. (continues)

```
        <copy file="./META-INF/application.xml"
                                  todir="${dist}/META-INF" />

        <jar jarfile="${deploy}/hello.ear"
                                  basedir="${dist}" />
    </target>

</project>
```

Listing 6.12 The enterprise application's main project buildfile.

Analyzing the Buildfile for the Enterprise Application

The build target uses the ant task (<ant…>) to call the other Ant buildfiles. The build target is as follows:

```
<target name="build" depends="prepare"
        description="build the model and application modules.">

      <ant dir="./Model" target="package">
           <property name="outdir" value="${outdir}" />
           <property name="setProps" value="true" />
      </ant>

      <ant dir="./EJBeans" target="deploy">
           <property name="outdir" value="${outdir}" />
           <property name="setProps" value="true" />
          <property name="jboss" value="/tools/jboss/jboss/deploy" />
      </ant>

      <ant dir="./Applet" target="package">
           <property name="outdir" value="${outdir}" />
           <property name="setProps" value="true" />
      </ant>

      <ant dir="./WebApplication" target="deploy">
           <property name="outdir" value="${outdir}" />
           <property name="setProps" value="true" />
           <property name="ejb" value="true" />
      </ant>

      <ant dir="./Application" target="package">
           <property name="outdir" value="${outdir}" />
           <property name="setProps" value="true" />
      </ant>
</target>
```

Notice that each call to invoke another buildfile sets the relative directory of the subproject's buildfile (<ant dir="./Model" target="package">) and the target of the buildfile. Because we named each buildfile of each subproject build.xml, we only need to specify the directory. In addition to specifying the target that we want to execute, the ant task passes two properties to each subproject, as follows:

```
<property name="outdir" value="${outdir}" />
<property name="setProps" value="true" />
```

The second property ensures that the subproject's setProps target is not executed, by setting the property "setProps". Remember, the "setProps" property for each project is not executed if the setProps property is set (<target name="setProps" unless="setProps">). The first property ensures that the value of the outdir of the main project is passed to the subproject. When we combine these two properties, it's easy to set a new directory for all the output of the main project and all its subprojects at the command line, demonstrated (using bash) as follows:

```
rick@CANIS_MAJOR /usr/rick/cvs/XPToolKit/examples/chap5/MVCHelloWorld

$ ant -DsetProps=no -Doutdir=/usr/rick/output
```

These lines could be used to redirect the output to a directory to which you have access, if you are developing on a Unix box.

The clean target follows many of the same concepts as the build target, so we will not discuss it in detail. The next major piece of the main project is the package target, as follows:

```
<target name="package" depends="build">
      <copy file="./META-INF/application.xml"
                              todir="${dist}/META-INF" />

      <jar jarfile="${deploy}/hello.ear"
                              basedir="${dist}" />
</target>
```

This code copies the application.xml metadata from the ./META-INF directory to the distribution directory. The distribution directory is also where the webapplication project buildfile's package target and the enterprise beans project buildfile's package target put their WAR and EJB JAR file, respectively.

The next task is for the main's package target to jar the WAR, EJ JAR, and application.xml files into a JAR file format. It does this with the jar task, as follows:

```
<jar jarfile="${deploy}/hello.ear"
                basedir="${dist}" />
```

The output of the file is hello.ear, which is put into the deployment directory. The deployment directory is defined in the init target (for example, /tmp/deploy). The application.xml file is the deployment descriptor for the EAR file.

Enterprise Application Deployment Descriptor

If our intention is to deploy the Web application and the enterprise beans as a single logical unit, it may be useful to create an EAR file as we did. In order for the J2EE container to understand what we are deploying, we have to tell it with the deployment descriptor in Listing 6.13.

```
<application>
  <display-name>Hello World Application</display-name>
  <description>Hello World Application.</description>

  <module>
    <web>
      <web-uri>hello.war</web-uri>
      <context-root>helloworld</context-root>
    </web>
  </module>

  <module>
    <ejb>greet-ejbs.jar</ejb>
  </module>

</application>
```

Listing 6.13 The enterprise application deployment descriptor.

Looking at Listing 6.13, you may wonder why we don't list the model library, the applet JAR, the enterprise bean client JAR, and so on. Remember, they were included with the WAR file. Instead, the deployment descriptor describes two modules: our Hello World Web application and our Hello World enterprise beans. First the Web application:

```
<module>
  <web>
    <web-uri>hello.war</web-uri>
    <context-root>helloworld</context-root>
  </web>
</module>
```

Notice that the URI for the Web application is set to helloworld; thus, when we deploy it, it runs under the helloworld directory (http://localhost/helloworld). Next, we defined the Enterprise JavaBean module as follows:

```
<web>
  <web-uri>hello.war</web-uri>
  <context-root>helloworld</context-root>
</web>
```

We can use it to deploy in one simple step to any J2EE container that supports both Web applications and enterprise beans.

Pushing the Envelope

Note that one of the reviewers of this book was able to get the EAR file to work with JBoss+Jetty, which can be downloaded from the JBoss site. You just need to copy it to the jboss/jboss/deploy directory. The EAR file should also work with the JBoss+Tomcat installation. As an exercise, you can add it to the deploy target of the Ant buildfile.

The Pet Store Case Study

The Web application for the pet store baseline is much like the one in the Hello World application. For simplicity and ease of development, most of the presentation tier is implemented in JSP. We added a nonsensical servlet just for demonstration purposes. Note that in the real world, we use Struts, a framework from Apache, and we have many Java classes to deploy—we use Struts in several examples later in this book.

You may recall from the last case study that the main project buildfile for its build and clean target calls the webapplication subproject buildfile's clean and deploy targets respectively. The webapplication subproject buildfile's deploy target is defined as follows:

```
<target name="deploy" depends="package">
    <copy file="${dist}/${pet_war}" todir="${deploy_resin}" />
    <copy file="${dist}/${pet_war}" todir="${deploy_tomcat}" />
</target>
```

The deploy target copies the WAR file specified by ${pet_war} to both the Resin and Tomcat deployment directories. (Resin and Tomcat are J2EE Web application servers.) The deploy target depends on the package target. The package target creates the WAR file that is deployed to Resin and Tomcat, which is defined as follows:

```
<target name="package" depends="compile">
    <mkdir dir="${meta}" />
    <war warfile="${dist}/${pet_war}" webxml="${meta}/web.xml">
        <!--
           Include the html and jsp files.
```

```
                Put the classes from the build into the classes directory
                of the war. Exclude web.xml file and WEB-INF directory.
             /-->
          <fileset dir="./public-html" >
              <exclude name="WEB-INF" />
              <exclude name="web.xml"/>
            </fileset>
            <classes dir="${build}" />
          <lib dir="${lib}"  />
          </war>
     </target>
```

As you will notice, the package target is much like the one in the Hello World Web application sample. The package target uses the war task to create a WAR file. The WAR file includes all the libraries in the lib (${lib})—namely, the pet-model.jar file created in the model subproject. It also includes the web.xml Web application deployment descriptor using the "webxml" attribute. Listing 6.14 shows the complete Web application.

```
<project name="webapplication" default="all" >
    <target name="setProps" unless="setProps"
                             description="setup the properites.">
        <property name="outdir" value="/tmp/petstore" />
    </target>

    <target name="init" depends="setProps"
                             description="initialize the properties.">
     <tstamp/>
     <property name="local_outdir" value="${outdir}/webapps" />
     <property name="lib" value="${outdir}/lib" />
     <property name="dist" value="${outdir}/dist" />
     <property name="build" value="${local_outdir}/webclasses" />
     <property name="meta" value="public-html/WEB-INF" />
     <property name="deploy_resin" value="/resin/webapps" />
     <property name="deploy_tomcat" value="/tomcat/webapps" />
     <property name="appstub" value="pet" />

     <property name="pet_war" value="${appstub}.war" />
     <property name="build_lib" value="./../lib" />
    </target>

    <target name="clean_deploy" >

        <delete file="${deploy_resin}/${pet_war}" />
        <delete dir="${deploy_resin}/${appstub}" />
        <delete file="${deploy_tomcat}/${pet_war}" />
```

Listing 6.14 Complete Web application project buildfile. (continues)

```
        <delete dir="${deploy_tomcat}/${appstub}" />
    </target>

    <target name="clean" depends="init,clean_deploy"
                        description="clean up the output directories.">
        <delete dir="${local_outdir}" />
        <delete file="${dist}/${pet_war}" />
    </target>

    <target name="prepare" depends="init"
                        description="prepare the output directory.">
        <mkdir dir="${build}" />
      <mkdir dir="${dist}" />
    </target>

    <target name="compile" depends="prepare"
                        description="compile the Java source.">
        <javac srcdir="./java" destdir="${build}">
            <classpath >
                <fileset dir="${lib}">
                    <include name="**/*.jar"/>
                </fileset>

                <fileset dir="${build_lib}">
                    <include name="**/*.jar"/>
                </fileset>
            </classpath>
        </javac>
    </target>

    <target name="package" depends="compile">
        <mkdir dir="${meta}" />
        <war warfile="${dist}/${pet_war}" webxml="${meta}/web.xml">
            <!--
                Include the html and jsp files.
                Put the classes from the build into the classes directory
                of the war. Exclude web.xml file and WEB-INF directory.
            /-->
        <fileset dir="./public-html" >
            <exclude name="WEB-INF" />
            <exclude name="web.xml"/>
        </fileset>
          <classes dir="${build}" />
        <lib dir="${lib}"  />
        </war>
    </target>
```

Listing 6.14 Complete Web application project buildfile. (continues)

```
    <target name="deploy" depends="package">
        <copy file="${dist}/${pet_war}" todir="${deploy_resin}" />
        <copy file="${dist}/${pet_war}" todir="${deploy_tomcat}" />
    </target>

    <target name="all" depends="clean,deploy"
                            description="perform all targets."/>

</project>
```

Listing 6.14 Complete Web application project buildfile.

As you can see, the standard targets are present in this buildfile as they are in the Hello World example, the model subproject, and the rest of the buildfiles in this book. This makes it easy to tell what the buildfiles are doing at a glance. You also may notice that the optional "description" attribute is set for each target. This also helps to document your targets and can be shown when running Ant.

The next case study will include the Test subproject buildfile using junit and the junitreport tasks. Then, it will add EJBeans support with a new subproject, and rerun the tests to ensure that the refactored CategorySystem still functions.

Summary

In this chapter, we took a very complex project with many components and subsystems (albeit a simple implementation) and deployed it to an enterprise application server and servlet engine, and to both at the same time with the EAR file. We demonstrated the use of three types of deployment descriptors for Web applications, enterprise bean modules, and enterprise applications. We also demonstrated how to use a similar set of tags to create consistent sets of related buildfiles. Finally, we showed how to assemble all these buildfiles into a single project using a master buildfile to coordinate the building and deploying of the application. The last part of the chapter presented a case study showing a more realistic version of an enterprise application.

CHAPTER 7

Unit Testing with JUnit

This chapter discusses unit-level testing of Java classes with JUnit. Automated unit-level testing is an essential ingredient to continuous integration and XP; accordingly, several chapters in this book cover JUnit. This chapter is primarily a tutorial that introduces the JUnit framework. Chapter 9, "Functional Testing with HttpUnit" and Chapter 11, "Load Testing with JUnitPerf" illustrate techniques for using JUnit with other tools. Chapter 14, "JUnit API Reference," is a detailed reference with many code examples. Combined, these chapters provide thorough coverage of the JUnit framework.

If code has no automated test case written for it to prove that it works, it must be assumed not to work. An API that does not have an automated test case to show how it works must be assumed un-maintainable. Software without automated test cases cannot be economically refactored. Software that that cannot be refactored cannot be extended economically—and believe me, your code will likely be in circulation longer than you think. Your alternative to automated unit-level testing is writing expensive, un-maintainable, rigid, brittle software systems that cannot be easily extended or refactored. Your code base will go the way of the dodo bird or, worse, you will be stuck maintaining it forever—a fitting punishment! When you consider the alternatives, automated unit-level is not optional.

A common argument for not writing automated unit-level test cases is that you just don't have the time. Malarkey. This statement becomes a self-fulfilling prophecy. Productivity is directly related to the stability of your code base. The fewer test cases you write, the less stable your code base becomes. You spend all your time fixing unintended side effects and bugs that are coming out of the woodwork. Soon you have even less time to write tests, not to mention a stomach ulcer. Situation like this can have you running to be another member of the management ranks—and no good developer should want to do that. Get off the hamster wheel and take the time to write test cases.

In Chapter 1, "Introduction to Extreme Programming," we discussed the synergy between refactoring and unit-level testing at length. To sum up those thoughts, without refactoring your system becomes overly complex. Refactoring means keeping your code as simple as possible and yet providing all the features for that iteration of the release. Unit-level testing proves that the code you refactored did not break: The features still work. Testing enables you to have confidence in your ability to refactor and instills courage to refactor often, which keeps your code base solid and maintainable. Working under these conditions is fruitful and rewarding—you can achieve inner peace and contentment with your code.

Where to Get JUnit

JUnit was written by Erich Gamma and Kent Beck. Kent Beck defined the XP methodology and is the author of the first XP book, *Extreme Programming Explained: Embrace Change* as well as subsequent books about XP. JUnit is distributed on SourceForge under the IBM Public License: http://sourceforge.net/projects/junit/

It's hard to measure the progress of your project without testing. In this chapter, when we talk about *testing* we mean automated testing. Testing is not a metric that is typically tracked; however, it can tell you when something begins working or, more importantly, when something that used to work stops working. The next section will show you how to incrementally build a test suite full of test cases that will help you measure the progress of your project and identify unintended side effects of refactoring.

System.out.println Is Not Enough

To prove that their code works, some people watch the code using System.out.println or their IDE's debugger. This approach has three problems: scroll blindness, subjectivity, and lack of automation.

First, it is hard to tell if a complex system is working because so many System.out.println methods are printing so much garbage. Second (and this is very subjective), you must determine if something works by looking at a String

scrolling by on a console. The string of text scrolling by may make sense the day you wrote it, but will it still make sense in three months? Third, when you make changes, things can break in unexpected ways. If you don't have an automated test, you may not test the subsystem that you broke. In fact, it may not be directly related to the subsystem you are working on for quite a while—long enough for the cobwebs of confusion to grow in your mind. Conversely, if you run an automated test several times a day or more, then you will find errors early and often. Simply put, you don't check your code into source control until all the tests run successfully.

Overview of JUnit

JUnit is a framework for writing unit tests. This section helps you focus your development efforts around proving that the code you wrote works and that later, when you refactor to add more features, it still works.

Let's clarify the following concepts: test case, test fixture, and test suite. A *test case* defines a fixture to run a related set of tests. Typically, every class that you write should have a test case. A *test fixture* provides resources: primitive variables and objects that tests need to run. A *test suite* is a collection of related test cases.

For example, if we write a HashMap class, we write a test case for it. The test case has a test fixture object for each test so that we can put objects into the map, pull them out of the map, and perhaps compare them as part of the test. However, if we write a library of collection objects, we write a test suite for it that contains the test case we wrote for the HashMap class—think of a test suite as a collection of test cases.

Let's put these concepts into practice. In order to write a test case, we do the following:

1. Subclass junit.framework.TestCase.
2. If we need fixture objects, override the setUp() method.
3. Define a number of tests that return void and whose method name begins with test, such as testAdd(), testPut(), and testIterator().
4. If we need to release resources that were part of the fixture, override the tearDown() method.
5. If we need to group a related set of test cases, define a suite of tests.

The next section discusses writing your own test case based on java.util. HashMap.

Writing a Test Case

An excellent example of creating a test case is provided in the samples that ship with JUnit. The example is called VectorTest, and it shows how you would go about writing a test case for java.util.Vector. The good thing about this example is that most people are familiar with the Vector class. In the same spirit, we created a simple example based on the java.util.HashMap (Listing 7.1). We will go through this example step by step.

```
/*
 * HashMapTest.java
 *
 * Created on September 16, 2001, 12:27 PM
 */

package xptoolkit.junit.example;

import junit.framework.*;
import java.util.Map;
import java.util.HashMap;
import junit.extensions.*;

/**
 *
 * @author  Rick Hightower
 * @version 1.0
 */
public class HashMapTest extends TestCase {

    private Map testMap;
    private Map testMap2;

    public HashMapTest(String name) {
        super(name);
    }

    public static Test suite() {
          return new TestSuite(HashMapTest.class);
    }

    public static void main (String[] args) {
         junit.textui.TestRunner.run (suite());
    }

    private static final String APPLE_KEY = "AppleCEO";
    private static final String APPLE_VALUE = "AppleCEO";
```

Listing 7.1 HashMapTest test case example. (continues)

```
    protected void setUp() {
        testMap = new HashMap();
        testMap.put(APPLE_KEY, APPLE_VALUE);
        testMap.put("OracleCEO","Larry Ellison");

        testMap2 = new HashMap();
        testMap2.put("1", "1");
        testMap2.put("2", "2");

    }


    public void testPut(){
        String key = "Employee";
        String value = "Rick Hightower";

                //put the value in
        testMap.put(key, value);

                //read the value back out
        String value2 = (String)testMap.get(key);
        assertEquals("The value back from the map ", value, value2);
    }

    public void testSize(){
        assertEquals (2, testMap.size());
    }

    public void testGet(){
        assertEquals(APPLE_VALUE, testMap.get(APPLE_KEY));
        assertNull(testMap.get("JUNK_KEY"));
    }

    public void testPutAll(){
        testMap.putAll(testMap2);
        assertEquals (4, testMap.size());
        assertEquals("1", testMap.get("1"));
        testGet();
    }

    public void testContainsKey(){
          assertTrue("It should contain the apple key",
                       testMap.containsKey(APPLE_KEY));

    }
```

Listing 7.1 HashMapTest test case example. (continues)

```
    public void testContainsValue(){
        assert(testMap.containsKey(APPLE_VALUE));
    }

    public void testRemove(){
        String key = "Employee";
        String value = "Rick Hightower";

                //put the value in
        testMap.put(key, value);

                //remove it
        testMap.remove(key);

                //try to read the value back out
        assertNull(testMap.get(key));

    }


}
```

Listing 7.1 HashMapTest test case example.

Let's break down the example based on the steps we defined in the last section for writing a test case. Step 1 is to define a class that derives junit.framework.TestCase, as follows:

```
import junit.framework.*;
...
public class HashMapTest extends TestCase {
```

Next, if our test case needs a fixture, we override the setUp() method (Step 2), which the HashMapTest does as follows:

```
    protected void setUp() {
        testMap = new HashMap();
        testMap.put(APPLE_KEY, APPLE_VALUE);
        testMap.put("OracleCEO","Larry Ellison");

        testMap2 = new HashMap();
        testMap2.put("1", "1");
        testMap2.put("2", "2");
    }
```

Here we see that the fixture the test case sets up is actually instances of the class under test: the HashMap class. In addition, the test fixture adds some objects (int wrapper) to the HashMap instance. Because the objects that the setUp() method creates will be garbage-collected when we are done with them, we don't have to write a tearDown() method (Step 4). If the setUp() method allocated resources like network connections or database connections, then we would override the tearDown() method to release those resources (Step 4).

Next, the HashMapTest class defines several tests to test the HashMap class, as follows (Step 3):

```
public void testPut(){
    String key = "Employee";
    String value = "Rick Hightower";

            //put the value in
    testMap.put(key, value);

            //read the value back out
    String value2 = (String)testMap.get(key);
    assertEquals("The value back from the map ", value, value2);
}

public void testSize(){
    assertEquals (2, testMap.size());
}

public void testGet(){
    assertEquals(APPLE_VALUE, testMap.get(APPLE_KEY));
    assertNull(testMap.get("JUNK_KEY"));
}

public void testPutAll(){
    testMap.putAll(testMap2);
    assertEquals (4, testMap.size());
    assertEquals("1", testMap.get("1"));
    testGet();
}

public void testContainsKey(){
    assertTrue("It should contain the apple key",
            testMap.containsKey(APPLE_KEY));
}

public void testContainsValue(){
    assertTrue(testMap.containsKey(APPLE_VALUE));
}

public void testRemove(){
    String key = "Employee";
    String value = "Rick Hightower";

            //put the value in
    testMap.put(key, value);
```

```
            //remove it
        testMap.remove(key);

            //try to read the value back out
        assertNull(testMap.get(key));
    }
```

Note that each test method becomes a test. The JUnit framework uses reflection to look for methods whose names begin with *test* and uses them as test cases. It does this when we invoke the TestSuite constructor in the static suite() method, as follows:

```
    public static Test suite() {
         return new TestSuite(HashMapTest.class);
    }
```

A test suite (TestSuite) is a collection of test cases. The test cases themselves can be other test suites. Thus the test suite is a composite of tests using the composite design pattern.

Notice that each test performs an operation on one or both of the HashMaps and then asserts that some condition is true, as follows:

```
    public void testPutAll(){
        testMap.putAll(testMap2);
        assertEquals (4, testMap.size());
        assertEquals("1", testMap.get("1"));
        testGet();
    }
```

The assertTrue() method asserts that a condition is true; if you are an old C/C++ programming dog, this assert works similar to the one in assert.h. If the condition is not true, then the assert method throws an AssertionFailedError, which is an unchecked exception that causes the test to fail. The JUnit API includes various forms of assert methods; for example, we could put a description of the assertion as in the testContainsKey() method, as follows:

```
    public void testContainsKey(){
        assertTrue("It should contain the apple key",
                            testMap.containsKey(APPLE_KEY));
    }
```

Or we can opt to leave it out, as follows:

```
    public void testContainsValue(){
        assertTrue(testMap.containsKey(APPLE_VALUE));
    }
```

Note that the setUp() and tearDown() methods are called before and after every text*X*() method that is run. Because the setUp() method does not allocate any resources that need to be released, the HashMapTest does not need to override the tearDown() method. If it did, the code would look something like this:

```
protected void setUp() {
            //get db connection
      connection = DriverManager.getConnection();
      statement = connection.createStatement();
      results = statement.executeQuery("select count(*) from Pet");

 }
 protected void tearDown() {
          //get db connection
      results.close();
      statement.close();
      connection.close();
 }
```

So far, we've created a test case and fixture objects and tested with assert, but how do we group these test cases into a suite of related test cases? The authors of JUnit have also provided an example of how to do this. They define two tests in the JUnit samples directory: VectorTest and MoneyTest. Then, they define a test suite to run the test cases in the class AllTest, defined in Listing 7.2.

```
package junit.samples;

import junit.framework.*;
import junit.samples.money.MoneyTest;


/**
 * TestSuite that runs all the sample tests
 *
 */
public class AllTests {

      public static void main (String[] args) {
          junit.textui.TestRunner.run (suite());
      }
      public static Test suite ( ) {
         TestSuite suite= new TestSuite("All JUnit Tests");
            suite.addTest(VectorTest.suite());
            suite.addTest (new TestSuite(MoneyTest.class));
            suite.addTest(junit.tests.AllTests.suite());
         return suite;
      }

}
```

Listing 7.2 AllTest test suite setup.

The code in Listing 7.2 compiles several suites of test into one suite. Notice that the main method calls junit.textui.TestRunner.run, passing it the returned value from the static suite() method. The suite() method creates an instance of TestSuite and then adds suites of tests from VectorTest, MoneyTest, and junit.tests.AllTests. Notice that when the AllTest suite() method adds the VectorTest, it calls the VectorTest's suite() method, which is defined as follows:

```
public static Test suite() {
    return new TestSuite(VectorTest.class);
}
```

As you can see, the VectorTest's static suite() method creates a new TestSuite instance by passing itself as a class. TestSuite uses reflection to extract the test methods that make up the suite. The end effect is that you can group related tests into larger and larger test suites. Thus, you could have suites of tests nested in a larger suite. The alternative would be to run every TestCase independently, which would take a long time and would be tedious. Nesting suites of tests enables you to test large portions of code quickly.

We have now covered the basics of JUnit. In the next section, we integrate the test suite in Listing 7.2 with Ant.

Integrating JUnit with Ant

JUnit and Ant go together like a horse and carriage. Ant automates the build-and-deploy process. JUnit automates testing. Put them together, and Ant can automate the build, deploy, and test process. Ant has several tags to support JUnit.

For the integration to work, we need the Extensible Style Language Transformation (XSLT) transform engine JAR file installed; refer to the Ant User Manual documentation or Chapter 12, "Ant Tag Reference" for more information. We also need to put the JAR file for JUnit on the Ant classpath, and we must download the optional.jar file from the Apache site (go to http://jakarta.apache.org/ant/index.html and select the "download" option). The easiest way to put these JAR files on the Ant classpath is to copy them to the lib directory in the ANT_HOME directory (ANT_HOME/lib).

Once we have the required JAR files, we can build and test the last example with the following Ant buildfile, which we put in the ANT_HOME directory:

```
<project name="junitSample" default="test">

        <target name="init">
                <property name="outdir" value="/tmp/junitSample" />
        </target>

        <target name="prepare" depends="init">
                <mkdir dir="${outdir}" />
```

```
        </target>

        <target name="compile" depends="prepare">
                <javac srcdir="." destdir="${outdir}"
                                classpath="junit.jar"/>
        </target>

        <target name="test" depends="compile">

           <junit printsummary="true" >
                   <test name="junit.samples.AllTests" />

                   <classpath>
                           <pathelement location="${outdir}" />
                   </classpath>

           </junit>

        </target>


</project>
```

Let's quickly break down this buildfile. The name of the project is junitSample, and it has the typical targets, as follows: init, prepare, compile, and test. The test target is the default target of the junitSample project's buildfile. The init target creates an "outdir" property that holds the location of the output directory. The prepare tag creates the output directory (outdir). The compile tag builds the Junit sample source code (discussed in the last section) to the output directory (outdir). The interesting target is the test target, as follows:

```
<target name="test" depends="compile">

        <junit printsummary="true" >

                <test name="junit.samples.AllTests" />

                <classpath>
                       <pathelement location="${outdir}" />
                </classpath>

        </junit>
</target>
```

The test target depends on the compile target. The test target uses the junit task defined in the optional.jar file—note that you must have junit.jar on the classpath in order for this task to work. The junit task can run a test created with the junit framework, such as junit.samples.AllTest, described in the last section. The junit task has a sub-element called test. We use the sub-element test to set the classname of the test case we are going to run. In addition, we set up the classpath for JUnit so that it can find the sample classes we compiled in the compile target. Running the code yields these results:

```
C:\tools\junit> ant
Buildfile: build.xml

init:

prepare:

compile:

test:
    [junit] Running junit.samples.AllTests
    [junit] Tests run: 86, Failures: 0, Errors: 1, Time elapsed: 0.911
sec
    [junit] TEST junit.samples.AllTests FAILED

BUILD SUCCESSFUL

Total time: 2 seconds
```

The sample test for our JUnit distribution failed! This event is a nice segue to our next point. As you can see, the summary report for running the test is not very verbose—in fact, it's terse. It is hard to tell which test failed. This result may not be what you want. In fact, we are sure that in the real world, you probably want to know which test failed. All we have to do is add a formatter subelement that directs JUnit to print out a more detailed report. To do so, we add the following to the test target under the junit task (<formatter type="plain" usefile="false"/>):

```
<target name="test" depends="compile">

        <junit printsummary="true" >
                <formatter type="plain" usefile="false"/>

                <test name="junit.samples.AllTests" />

                <classpath>
                        <pathelement location="${outdir}" />
                </classpath>

        </junit>
</target>
```

Now we get much more detailed information, as follows:

```
Buildfile: build.xml

init:
```

```
prepare:

compile:

test:
    [junit] Running junit.samples.AllTests
    [junit] Tests run: 86, Failures: 0, Errors: 1, Time elapsed: 0.941
sec
    [junit] Testsuite: junit.samples.AllTests
    [junit] Tests run: 86, Failures: 0, Errors: 1, Time elapsed: 0.941
sec
    [junit]
    [junit] Testcase: testCapacity took 0 sec
    [junit] Testcase: testClone took 0 sec
    [junit] Testcase: testContains took 0 sec
     . . .
     . . .
    [junit] Testcase: testFailAssertNotNull took 0 sec
    [junit] Testcase: testSucceedAssertNotNull took 0 sec
    [junit] Testcase: testFilter took 0 sec
    [junit]     Caused an ERROR
    [junit] null
    [junit] java.lang.NullPointerException
    . . .
    . . .

    [junit] Testcase: testJarClassLoading took 0.01 sec
    [junit] TEST junit.samples.AllTests FAILED

BUILD SUCCESSFUL
```

We can clearly see that the testFilter failed. What a bummer! But let's not leave this section on a bad note. We'll change the Ant buildfile to build and test the VectorTest described in the previous section so we can show a test that passes. The test target changes as follows:

```
<target name="test" depends="compile">

      <junit printsummary="true" >

           <formatter type="plain" usefile="false"/>

           <test name="junit.samples.VectorTest" />

           <classpath>
                  <pathelement location="${outdir}" />
           </classpath>

      </junit>

</target>
```

Then we run it as follows:

```
Buildfile: build.xml

init:

prepare:

compile:

test:
    [junit] Running junit.samples.VectorTest
    [junit] Tests run: 6, Failures: 0, Errors: 0, Time elapsed: 0.01 sec
    [junit] Testsuite: junit.samples.VectorTest
    [junit] Tests run: 6, Failures: 0, Errors: 0, Time elapsed: 0.01 sec
    [junit]
    [junit] Testcase: testCapacity took 0 sec
    [junit] Testcase: testClone took 0 sec
    [junit] Testcase: testContains took 0 sec
    [junit] Testcase: testElementAt took 0 sec
    [junit] Testcase: testRemoveAll took 0 sec
    [junit] Testcase: testRemoveElement took 0 sec

BUILD SUCCESSFUL

Total time: 1 second
```

Perhaps you were hoping for a little more from your reporting. It would be nice if you could display the results in a Web page. Then you could have an automated build that would run every night, send out a status email, and post the results on your department's intranet Web site. You can do that with the JUnitReport junitreport task.

First we must change the formatter sub-element's "type" attribute to "xml"; it was set to "plain". This setting outputs the test information in XML format. We also need to set the "usefile" attribute to "true"; for the last example, it was "false". The default "usefile" attribute value is "true", so we will remove it altogether. Here is the updated test target:

```
<target name="test" depends="compile">

      <junit printsummary="true" >

           <formatter type="xml" />

           <test name="junit.samples.VectorTest" />
```

```
            <classpath>
                   <pathelement location="${outdir}" />
            </classpath>

        </junit>

    </target>
```

Now, when we run the buildfile, it creates an XML file named TEST-junit.samples.VectorTest.xml. The contents of the XML file are as follows:

```
<?xml version="1.0"?>
<testsuite errors="0" failures="0" name="junit.samples.VectorTest"
tests="6" time="0.201">
  <testcase name="testCapacity" time="0"></testcase>
  <testcase name="testClone" time="0"></testcase>
  <testcase name="testContains" time="0"></testcase>
  <testcase name="testElementAt" time="0"></testcase>
  <testcase name="testRemoveAll" time="0"></testcase>
  <testcase name="testRemoveElement" time="0"></testcase>
</testsuite>
```

Because we now have the output in XML, we can use the junitreport task, which takes the XML and transforms it to HTML using XSLT. You don't have to know XSLT to use the junitreport task. There are two types of reports: those with frames and those without. We add the junitreport task tag after the junit task tag, as follows:

```
        <junitreport todir="./reports">

            <fileset dir=".">

                <include name="TEST-*.xml"/>

            </fileset>

            <report format="frames" todir="./report/html"/>

        </junitreport>
```

When we run this buildfile it generates the report shown in Figure 7.1 in the reports directory.

As you can see from Figure 7.1, the report that is generated allows you to navigate the tests that were run. Therefore, instead of building large suites, you may want to use Ant and the junit task and just specify the tests you want to run as file sets; you will be able to generate really nice reports.

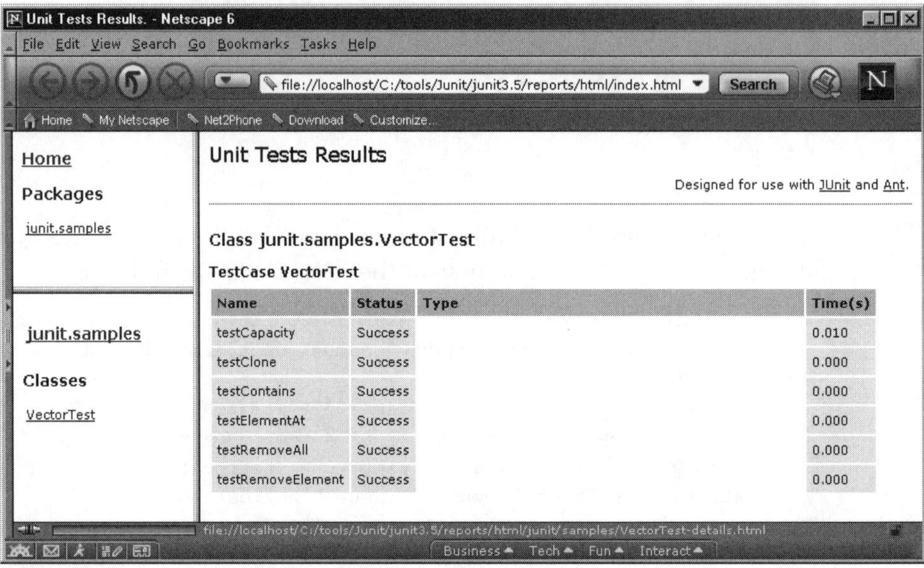

Figure 7.1 Test report.

Case Study: Adding an Entity Bean to the Pet Store

This section explains the test cases for the baseline version of the pet store. We discuss adding an entity bean and Web form to manage product data over the Web (that is, to add, delete, and modify product data). Once we add the entity bean, we add more test cases to test it, and then we integrate those tests into the test buildfile. Thus we will cover building and deploying an entity bean to our EJB server. Before we talk about including EJBs, let's look at what we already have for testing the system. Remember, before you refactor, you should have tests set up so you know that what you refactor does not break.

Overview of Existing JUnit Tests

The test buildfile runs four JUnit tests, as follows:

- CategorySystemTest
- CategoryTest
- SubcategoryTest
- ProductTest

Each test class tests its corresponding counterpart in the model—that is, the public interface to the system. Complete code listings for these tests and their interfaces can be found in Chapter 3, "Example Applications." Because the structure of these four tests are very similar, this section describes only two of them in detail for purposes of illustrating unique elements and techniques. These tests are run by the test project buildfile, demonstrated with this test buildfile snippet (the complete code will be discussed later in Listing 7.5):

```
    <target name="test" depends="compile">
...

            <test  name="test.xptoolkit.model.CategorySystemTest"
                   todir="${reports}" />

            <test  name="test.xptoolkit.model.CategoryTest"
                   todir="${reports}" />

            <test  name="test.xptoolkit.model.SubcategoryTest"
                   todir="${reports}" />

            <test  name="test.xptoolkit.model.ProductTest"
                   todir="${reports}" />
...
```

The tests are designed to test all the functionality of the public interface—everything that could possibly break. The CategorySystemTest (Listing 7.3) tests the CategorySystem.

```
package test.xptoolkit.model;
import xptoolkit.petstore.model.CategorySystem;

import junit.framework.*;

public class CategorySystemTest extends TestCase {
    CategorySystem system;

    public CategorySystemTest(java.lang.String testName) {
        super(testName);
    }

    public static void main(java.lang.String[] args) {
        junit.textui.TestRunner.run(suite());
    }

    public static Test suite() {
        TestSuite suite = new TestSuite(CategorySystemTest.class);

        return suite;
    }
```

Listing 7.3 CategorySystemTest. (continues)

```
protected void setUp()throws Exception {
    system = new CategorySystem();
}


/** Test of getCurrentCategory method, of class
    xptoolkit.petstore.model.CategorySystem. */
        public void testGetCurrentCategory() throws Exception{
            assertNotNull(system.getCurrentCategory());
        }

        /** Test of getSubcategory method, of class
            xptoolkit.petstore.model.CategorySystem. */
        public void testGetSubcategory() throws Exception{
            assertNotNull(system.getSubcategory(111));
        }

        /** Test of getProduct method, of class
            xptoolkit.petstore.model.CategorySystem. */
        public void testGetProduct() throws Exception {
            testGetSubcategory();
            assertNotNull(system.getProduct(1));
        }

            /** Test of getCurrentSubcategory method, of class
                xptoolkit.petstore.model.CategorySystem. */
        public void testGetCurrentSubcategory() throws Exception{
            testGetSubcategory();
            assertNotNull(system.getCurrentSubcategory());
        }

        /** Test of getCurrentProduct method, of class
            xptoolkit.petstore.model.CategorySystem. */
        public void testGetCurrentProduct() throws Exception{
            testGetSubcategory();
            testGetProduct();
            assertNotNull(system.getCurrentProduct());
        }
    }
```

Listing 7.3 CategorySystemTest.

As you may remember from Chapter 3, we populate the database with default values. The JUnit tests use that information to navigate the category hierarchy (for example, Listing 7.4, which shows the CategoryTest).

```
package test.xptoolkit.model;

import java.util.*;
import junit.framework.*;

import xptoolkit.petstore.model.Category;
import xptoolkit.petstore.model.Product;
import xptoolkit.petstore.model.Subcategory;


public class CategoryTest extends TestCase {

    Category category; //object under test

    public CategoryTest(java.lang.String testName) {
        super(testName);
    }

    public static void main(java.lang.String[] args) {
        junit.textui.TestRunner.run(suite());
    }

    public static Test suite() {
        TestSuite suite = new TestSuite(CategoryTest.class);

        return suite;
    }


    public void setUp()throws Exception{
        category = Category.getCategory();
        category.setId(777);
    }

    /** Test of getCategory method, of class
        xptoolkit.petstore.model.Category. */
    public void testGetCategory() throws Exception{
        System.out.println("testGetCategory");
        Category category = Category.getCategory();
        category.setId(777);
        this.assertNotNull("category", category);

    }
```

Listing 7.4 CategoryTest. (continues)

```
    /** Test of getSubcategories method, of class
        xptoolkit.petstore.model.Category. */
    public void testGetSubcategories() throws Exception {
        Subcategory [] categories = category.getSubcategories();
        assertNotNull("categories", categories);
        for (int index=0; index < categories.length; index++){
            assertNotNull("subcategory", categories[index]);
        }
    }

        /** Test of getSubcategory method, of class
            xptoolkit.petstore.model.Category. */
    public void testGetSubcategory() throws Exception {
        Subcategory [] categories = category.getSubcategories();
        assertNotNull("categories", categories);
        for (int index=0; index < categories.length; index++){
            Subcategory subcat=categories[index];
            int id = subcat.getId();
            assertNotNull("subcategory", category.getSubcategory(id));
        }
    }


    public void testGetters() throws Exception {
        assertNotNull("name", category.getName());
        assertNotNull("description", category.getDescription());

    }

}
```

Listing 7.4 CategoryTest.

There are four tests to test the public interface of xptoolkit.petstore.model.Category, as follows:

- testGetCategory
- testGetSubcategories
- testGetSubcategory
- testGetters

The setUp() method creates a category instance and sets it to the main test category.

```
        category = Category.getCategory();
  category.setId(777);
```

Remember, setUp() is called for each test. Thus, each test gets its own copy of category. For example, testGetSubcategories gets its own copy of category, which it uses to test the getSubcategories() method of xptoolkit.petstore. model.Category as follows:

```
    public void testGetSubcategories() throws Exception {
        Subcategory [] categories = category.getSubcategories();
        assertNotNull("categories", categories);
        for (int index=0; index < categories.length; index++){
            assertNotNull("subcategory", categories[index]);
        }
    }
```

Because the test data is known, we could check for specific values of subcategories in specific locations. For example, look at testGetters() from the ProductTest class:

```
/** Test of getters method of class
                        xptoolkit.petstore.model.Product. */
    public void testGetters() {
        this.assertEquals("name", product.getName(), "Poodle");
        this.assertEquals("description", product.getDescription(),
                                                "Poodle description");
        testSetters();
        this.assertEquals("name", product.getName(), "Boo");
        this.assertEquals("description", product.getDescription(),
                                                "Designer");

    }
```

Note that each main model class in the model project has a corresponding test class in the test project (see Figure 7.2).

The test buildfile is responsible for executing the tests in an automated fashion (Listing 7.5). Typically, you write the tests as you develop your classes. Once you are done writing your tests and using them to incrementally test your code as you write it, you put them in your test buildfile so they are included in your automatic build and deploy. Then, not only can you break the build by checking in code that does not compile, you can break the build by writing code that breaks the tests.

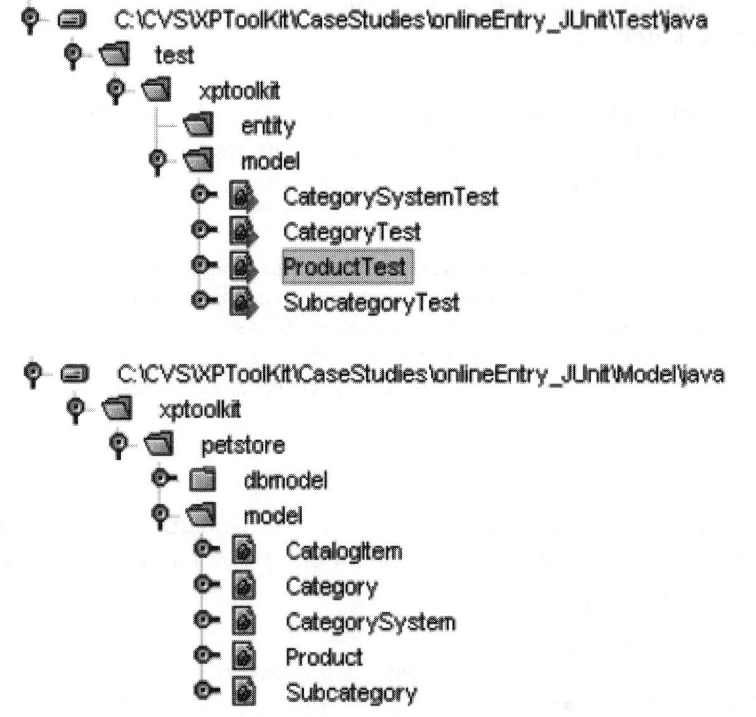

Figure 7.2 Parallel class structure test and model.

```
<project name="test" default="all" >
    <target name="setProps" unless="setProps"
                            description="setup the properties.">
        <property name="outdir" value="/tmp/petstore" />

    </target>


    <target name="init" depends="setProps"
                            description="initialize the properties.">
        <tstamp/>
        <property name="local_outdir" value="${outdir}/pettest" />
        <property name="lib" value="${outdir}/lib" />
        <property name="dist" value="${outdir}/dist" />
        <property name="reports" value="${outdir}/reports" />
        <property name="build" value="${local_outdir}/testclasses" />
        <property name="build_lib" value="./../lib" />
        <property name="test_lib" value="./../testlib" />
        <property name="test_jar" value="${lib}/pettest.jar" />
    </target>
```

Listing 7.5 Test project buildfile. (continues)

```
<target name="clean" depends="init"
                      description="clean up the output directories.">
    <delete dir="${local_outdir}" />
    <delete dir="${reports}" />
</target>


<target name="prepare" depends="init"
                      description="prepare the output directory.">
    <mkdir dir="${build}" />
    <mkdir dir="${dist}" />
    <mkdir dir="${reports}" />
    <mkdir dir="${reports}/html" />
</target>


<target name="compile" depends="prepare"
                      description="compile the Java source.">

    <javac srcdir="./java" destdir="${build}">
        <classpath >
            <fileset dir="${lib}">
                <include name="**/*.jar"/>
            </fileset>

            <fileset dir="${build_lib}">
                <include name="**/*.jar"/>
            </fileset>

            <fileset dir="${test_lib}">
                <include name="**/*.jar"/>
            </fileset>

        </classpath>
    </javac>
</target>

<target name="package" depends="compile">

    <jar jarfile="${test_jar}"
       basedir="${build}" />

</target>

<target name="test" depends="compile">

    <junit printsummary="true" fork="yes">
```

Listing 7.5 Test project buildfile. (continues)

```
        <formatter type="xml" />

        <test  name="test.xptoolkit.model.CategorySystemTest"
               todir="${reports}" />

        <test  name="test.xptoolkit.model.CategoryTest"
               todir="${reports}" />

        <test  name="test.xptoolkit.model.SubcategoryTest"
               todir="${reports}" />

        <test  name="test.xptoolkit.model.ProductTest"
               todir="${reports}" />


        <classpath>
           <fileset dir="${lib}">
               <include name="**/*.jar"/>
           </fileset>

           <fileset dir="${build_lib}">
               <include name="**/*.jar"/>
           </fileset>

           <fileset dir="${test_lib}">
               <include name="**/*.jar"/>
           </fileset>

           <fileset dir="/tools/ant/lib">
               <include name="**/*.jar"/>
           </fileset>

           <fileset dir="${build}" />

        </classpath>

   </junit>

   <junitreport todir="${reports}">

       <fileset dir="${reports}">

           <include name="TEST-*.xml"/>

       </fileset>

       <report format="frames" todir="${reports}/html"/>
```

Listing 7.5 Test project buildfile. (continues)

```
        </junitreport>
    </target>


    <target name="cleanTest" depends="clean,package,test" />

    <target name="all" depends="package,test"
                        description="perform all targets."/>

</project>
```

Listing 7.5 Test project buildfile.

The focal point of the test buildfile is the test target. The test target runs each of the tests that we defined, such as test.xptoolkit.model.CategoryTest. The test target uses the junit and junitreport tasks as follows:

```
<target name="test" depends="compile">

    <junit printsummary="true" fork="yes">

         <formatter type="xml" />

         <test  name="test.xptoolkit.model.CategorySystemTest"
                todir="${reports}" />

. . .
         <classpath>
. . .

            <fileset dir="${test_lib}">
                <include name="**/*.jar"/>
            </fileset>

. . .

         </classpath>

    </junit>

    <junitreport todir="${reports}">

        <fileset dir="${reports}">

            <include name="TEST-*.xml"/>

        </fileset>

        <report format="frames" todir="${reports}/html"/>
```

```
    </junitreport>
</target>
```

Notice that the classpath sub-element of the JUnit class uses the JAR files in ${test_lib}. This is where we store the JAR file (junit.jar) that contains the JUnit framework classes.

The junitreport task specifies the output directory as "${reports}/html" and the input test files that are the XML files generated from the output of the junit task. The junitreport task also specifies the output directory in which to put the report HTML files. (You can see examples of the output HTML displayed in a browser in Chapter 3.) Figure 7.3 shows the output of this test.

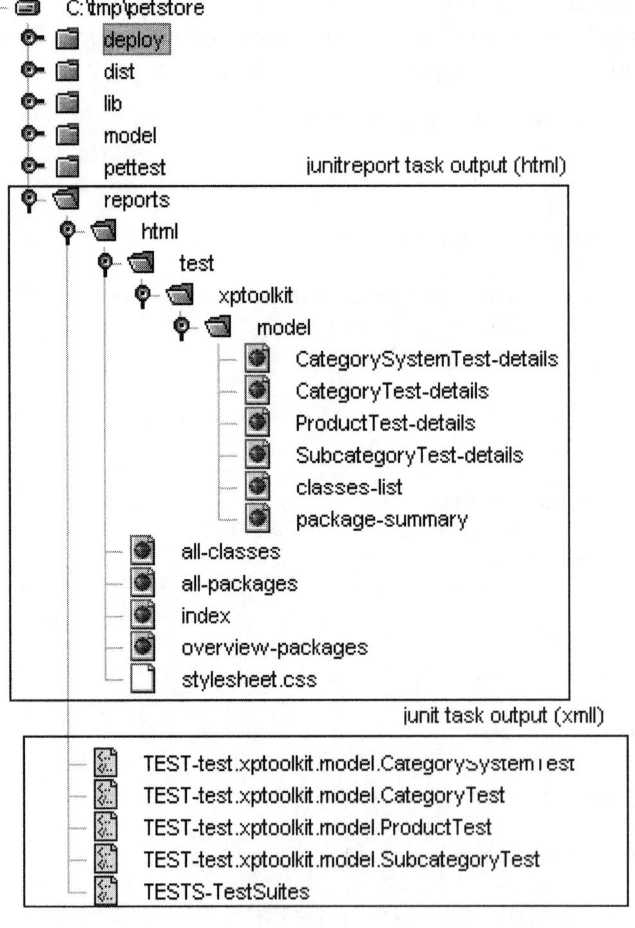

Figure 7.3 Directory structure output of junit and junitreport tasks.

Adding an Enterprise JavaBean to the Pet Store

This section adds a feature to the baseline pet store application: the ability to add, edit, and delete products from the Web. We have decided to use a container-managed entity EJB. Thus, we need to do the following:

1. Create the product entity bean.
2. Add a new subproject buildfile for EJBs.
3. Add a new test case class to test our Product EJB.
4. Update our categorySystem class.
5. Create an HTML form.
6. Add additional JSPs to handle the form submission and the backend navigation.

Figure 7.4 shows a block diagram of how the output will look when we are done.

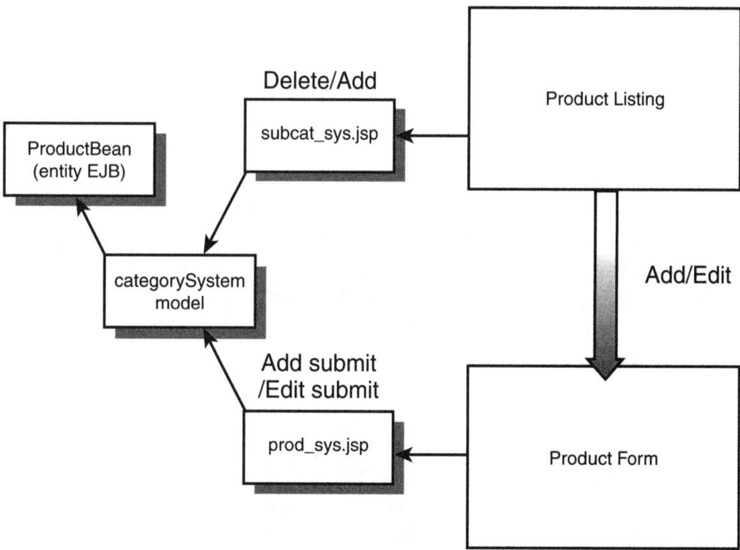

Figure 7.4 Block diagram of product management.

Security and Authentication

In the real world, you should password-protect your product entry management. Servlets 2.3 enables you to do this with a servlet filter. Or, you can do this with Web authentication provided by your application server or Web server. This example does not demonstrate authentication, but you can add it without changing the JSPs introduced with any of the methods we use.

The entity bean is fairly simple, because it is uses container managed persistence (CMP). The container takes care of persisting the bean to the database. See Listings 7.6, 7.7, and 7.8 for the complete product entity bean: its interface, implementation, and home, respectively. With this product entity bean we add, delete, and edit product entries. You can use a number of techniques and design patterns to reduce the number of remote procedure calls; for simplicity, we don't use them here.

```
package xptoolkit.petstore.entity;

import javax.ejb.*;
import java.rmi.RemoteException;

public interface Product extends EJBObject {

    public String getDescription()throws RemoteException;
    public String getName()throws RemoteException;
    public Integer getId()throws RemoteException;
    public int getSubcategoryId()throws RemoteException;
    public int getQty()throws RemoteException;
    public java.math.BigDecimal getPrice()throws RemoteException;


    public void setDescription(String description)throws RemoteException;
    public void setName(String name)throws RemoteException;
    public void setId(Integer ID)throws RemoteException;
    public void setSubcategoryId(int subcat)throws RemoteException;
    public void setQty(int qty)throws RemoteException;
    public void setPrice(java.math.BigDecimal price)throws RemoteException;

}
```

Listing 7.6 Product entity bean interface.

```
package xptoolkit.petstore.entity;

import javax.ejb.*;

public class ProductBean implements EntityBean {

    EntityContext ctx;
    public String description;
    public String name;
    public Integer id;
    public int subcategoryId;
    public int qty;
    public java.math.BigDecimal price;

    public Integer ejbCreate (Integer id, String name, int qty,
                    String description, int subCat,
                    java.math.BigDecimal price){
      this.id = id;
      this.name=name;
      this.description=description;
      this.qty=qty=0;
      subcategoryId=subCat;
      this.price= price;
      return null;
    }

    public void ejbPostCreate(Integer _id, String name, int qty,
                    String description, int subCat,
                    java.math.BigDecimal price){
        id = (Integer)ctx.getPrimaryKey();
        System.out.println("Product ID " + id);
    }

    public String getDescription(){return description;}
    public String getName(){return name;}
    public Integer getId(){return id;}
    public int getSubcategoryId(){return subcategoryId;}
    public int getQty(){return qty;}
    public java.math.BigDecimal getPrice(){return price;}

    public void setDescription(String description)
                                {this.description =description;}
    public void setName(String name){this.name=name;}
    public void setId(Integer id){this.id=id;}
    public void setSubcategoryId(int subcategoryId)
                              {this.subcategoryId=subcategoryId;}
```

Listing 7.7 Product entity bean implementation. (continues)

```
    public void setQty(int qty){this.qty=qty;}
    public void setPrice(java.math.BigDecimal price){this.price=price;}

    public void setEntityContext(EntityContext ctx) { this.ctx = ctx; }
    public void unsetEntityContext() { ctx = null; }
    public void ejbActivate() { }
    public void ejbPassivate() { }
    public void ejbLoad() { }
    public void ejbStore() { }
    public void ejbRemove() { }

}
```

Listing 7.7 Product entity bean implementation.

```
package xptoolkit.petstore.entity;

import javax.ejb.*;
import java.util.*;

import java.rmi.RemoteException;

public interface ProductHome extends EJBHome {


    public Product create(Integer id, String name, int qty,
                          String description, int subCat,
                         java.math.BigDecimal price)
                              throws RemoteException, CreateException;

    Product findByPrimaryKey(Integer key)
                              throws RemoteException, FinderException;

    Collection findAll()throws RemoteException, FinderException;

    Collection findBySubcategoryId()throws RemoteException, FinderException;

}
```

Listing 7.8 Product entity bean home.

```
<ejb-jar>

<description>
This ejb-jar files contains the Enterprise beans for the
Petstore Case Study
</description>
<enterprise-beans>
  <entity>
    <ejb-name>ProductBean</ejb-name>
    <home>xptoolkit.petstore.entity.ProductHome</home>
    <remote>xptoolkit.petstore.entity.Product</remote>
    <ejb-class>xptoolkit.petstore.entity.ProductBean</ejb-class>
    <persistence-type>Container</persistence-type>
    <prim-key-class>java.lang.Integer</prim-key-class>
    <primkey-field>id</primkey-field>
    <reentrant>False</reentrant>
    <cmp-field><field-name>description</field-name></cmp-field>
    <cmp-field><field-name>name</field-name></cmp-field>
    <cmp-field><field-name>id</field-name></cmp-field>
    <cmp-field><field-name>subcategoryId</field-name></cmp-field>
    <cmp-field><field-name>qty</field-name></cmp-field>
    <cmp-field><field-name>price</field-name></cmp-field>
  </entity>

</enterprise-beans>
<assembly-descriptor>
   <container-transaction>
      <method>
        <ejb-name>ProductBean</ejb-name>
        <method-name>*</method-name>
      </method>
      <trans-attribute>Required</trans-attribute>
    </container-transaction>
</assembly-descriptor>
</ejb-jar>
```

Listing 7.9 Product deployment descriptor.

The new ProductTest (test.xptoolkit.petstore.entity.ProductTest) is used to test the entity bean (xptoolkit.petstore.entity.Product). The ProductTest simulates a client; thus, it must import the needed client-side EJB classes. It must import the Java Naming and Directory Interface (JNDI) support and the RMI PortableRemoteObject as follows:

```
import javax.rmi.PortableRemoteObject;
import javax.naming.*;
```

Of course, it must import the bean's home and remote interface, as follows:

```
import xptoolkit.petstore.entity.Product;
import xptoolkit.petstore.entity.ProductHome;
```

Because every test needs to access the home interface to create, find, and delete Products, we locate an instance of the home interface using JNDI in the setUp() method as follows:

```
protected void setUp()throws Exception{

        Object ref;
        InitialContext jndiContext=null;
        jndiContext = new InitialContext(env);
        ref  = jndiContext.lookup("ProductBean");
        home = (ProductHome)
                     PortableRemoteObject.narrow (ref, ProductHome.class);
}
```

This is fairly standard client-side EJB code. The first test uses the home interface to create a product entity with test data.

```
     public void testCreate()throws Exception{
          product = home.create(new Integer(876662), "Rick", 5, "you ",
                               555,
                    new java.math.BigDecimal(1200));
          assertNotNull("product", product);
          assertEquals("name", "Rick", product.getName());

     }
```

As you can see, the first and second tests depend on each other; they are order dependent. The scenario works because the test framework uses reflection, and reflection uses the methods in the order they are declared. This code is brittle and depends on some minutia in the Java reflection API. You can ensure the order of execution by explicitly setting it in the suite() method instead of relying on the generic reflection-based methods. The TestSuite has an addTest() method that lets you add test cases to it.

The second test finds the entity created with the first test and then deletes that entity by calling the product entities' remove() method. Then, to make sure the entity was removed, the test tries to find it again. If the home interface's findByPrimaryKey() method does not find the object, we return; otherwise, we force a fail by calling fail(), as follows:

```
     public void testRemove()throws Exception{
          product = home.findByPrimaryKey(new Integer(876662));
          product.remove();
```

```
        try{
            product = home.findByPrimaryKey(new Integer(876662));
        }
        catch(javax.ejb.ObjectNotFoundException e){
            return;

        }

        fail("Product entity should already be gone and not findable.");
    }
```

The other methods test the setter and getter methods of the product, as follows:

```
    /** Test of setter methods, of class
                            xptoolkit.petstore.model.Product. */
    public void testSetters() throws Exception{
        testCreate();
        product.setName("Boo");
        product.setDescription("Designer");
        product.setQty(5);
        testRemove();
    }

    /** Test of getter methods, of class
                            xptoolkit.petstore.model.Product. */
    public void testGetters() throws Exception{
        testCreate();
        this.assertEquals("name", product.getName(), "Rick");
        this.assertEquals("description", product.getDescription(),
                                                           "you ");

        product.setName("Boo");
        product.setDescription("Designer");
        product.setQty(5);


        this.assertEquals("name", product.getName(), "Boo");
        this.assertEquals("description", product.getDescription(),
                                                "Designer");
        testRemove();

    }
```

The tests in ProductTest are quite simple. They ensure that we have set up and created our entity bean correctly. See Listing 7.10 for the complete ProductTest code.

```
package test.xptoolkit.petstore.entity;
import junit.framework.*;
import java.util.Properties;
import javax.rmi.PortableRemoteObject;
import javax.naming.*;

import xptoolkit.petstore.entity.Product;
import xptoolkit.petstore.entity.ProductHome;


public class ProductTest extends TestCase {

    Product product;
    ProductHome home;

    protected void setUp()throws Exception{

      Object ref;
      InitialContext jndiContext=null;
      jndiContext = new InitialContext(env);
      ref  = jndiContext.lookup("ProductBean");
      home = (ProductHome)
               PortableRemoteObject.narrow (ref, ProductHome.class);
    }


    public ProductTest(java.lang.String testName) {
        super(testName);
    }

    public static void main(java.lang.String[] args) {
        junit.textui.TestRunner.run(suite());
    }

    public static Test suite() {
        TestSuite suite = new TestSuite(ProductTest.class);

        return suite;
    }

    public void testCreate()throws Exception{
        product = home.create(new Integer(876662), "Rick", 5, "you ", 555,
                new java.math.BigDecimal(1200));
        assertNotNull("product", product);
```

Listing 7.10 Product test code. (continues)

```
        assertEquals("name", "Rick", product.getName());

    }

    public void testRemove()throws Exception{
        product = home.findByPrimaryKey(new Integer(876662));
        product.remove();

        try{
            product = home.findByPrimaryKey(new Integer(876662));
        }
        catch(javax.ejb.ObjectNotFoundException e){
            return;

        }

        fail("Product entity should already be gone and not findable.");
    }


    /** Test of getSetter methods, of class
                                xptoolkit.petstore.model.Product. */
    public void testSetters() throws Exception{
        testCreate();
        product.setName("Boo");
        product.setDescription("Designer");
        product.setQty(5);
        testRemove();
    }

    /** Test of getter methods, of class
                                xptoolkit.petstore.model.Product. */
    public void testGetters() throws Exception{
        testCreate();
        this.assertEquals("name", product.getName(), "Rick");
        this.assertEquals("description", product.getDescription(), "you ");

        product.setName("Boo");
        product.setDescription("Designer");
        product.setQty(5);
        this.assertEquals("name", product.getName(), "Boo");
        this.assertEquals("description", product.getDescription(),
                                                        "Designer");
        testRemove();
```

Listing 7.10 Product test code. (continues)

```
    }

    static Properties env = new Properties();
    static {
        env.setProperty("java.naming.factory.initial",
                          "org.jnp.interfaces.NamingContextFactory");
        env.setProperty("java.naming.provider.url",  "localhost:1099");
        env.setProperty("java.naming.factory.url.pkgs",
                                          "org.jboss.naming");
    }
}
```

Listing 7.10 Product test code.

IDEs support JUnit and Ant

Plug-ins are available for Forte, NetBeans, TogetherSoft ControlCenter, JBuilder, VisualAge, and so on for both JUnit and Ant. We create many of our tests by generating the tests' started code in the NetBeans IDE. The ProductTest started code was initially generated with NetBeans support for JUnit. You specify the class, and NetBeans generates the started skeleton to test your class. Cool beans!

It's our considered opinion that no JSP should know whether you are using JDBC, flat files, or entity beans to manage the persistence of the system. Thus, we decided to add support for adding and removing products behind the CategorySystem façade class. In fact, the implementation of the client-side piece of the Product entity is in CategoryDB, and the public interface is defined in the Category abstract class.

Here are the additional methods that we added to the CategorySystem class (xptoolkit.petstore.model. CategorySystem):

```
public void createProduct(Product product) throws Exception{
    currentCategory.createProduct(product);
    if(currentSubcategory!=null)currentSubcategory.invalidate();
}
public void editProduct(Product product) throws Exception{
    currentCategory.editProduct(product);
    if(currentSubcategory!=null)currentSubcategory.invalidate();
}
public void deleteProduct(int id) throws Exception{
    currentCategory.deleteProduct(id);
    if(currentSubcategory!=null)currentSubcategory.invalidate();
}
```

Here are the corresponding methods we added to the Category class:

```
public abstract void createProduct(Product product) throws Exception;
public abstract void editProduct(Product product) throws Exception;
public abstract void deleteProduct(int id) throws Exception;
```

The actual implementation of these methods is in the CategoryDB class, as follows:

```
public void createProduct(Product product) throws Exception{
    getHome().create(new Integer(product.getId()),
                    product.getName(),
                    product.getQty(),
                    product.getDescription(),
                    product.getFkSubcategoryId(),
                    new java.math.BigDecimal(product.getPrice()));
}
public void editProduct(Product product) throws Exception{
    xptoolkit.petstore.entity.Product p
               =getHome().findByPrimaryKey(
               new Integer(product.getId()));
    p.setName(product.getName());
    p.setDescription(product.getDescription());
    p.setPrice(new java.math.BigDecimal(product.getPrice()));
    p.setQty(product.getQty());
}

public void deleteProduct(int id) throws Exception{
      getHome().findByPrimaryKey(new Integer(id)).remove();
}

private ProductHome getHome() throws Exception{
  Object ref;
  InitialContext jndiContext=null;
  jndiContext = new InitialContext(env);
  ref  = jndiContext.lookup("ProductBean");
  return (ProductHome)
          PortableRemoteObject.narrow (ref, ProductHome.class);
}
```

This code should look familiar. It is much like the code in our test, except that now we are using it to implement the public interface to our Web application. You should add tests at the boundary points to every tier in an n-tier architecture. That way, you test the public interface of each tier. This approach becomes particularly useful if things begin to go wrong; when debugging a distributed multitiered application, it's helpful to be able to test access to each tier independently from the rest of the added business logic in the encapsulating tier.

Because the CategorySystem is a very thin wrapper in the case of adding, removing, and editing products, we decided to add the tests in the CategoryTest as follows:

```
public void testCreateDeleteProduct() throws Exception {
   . . .
    Product p = new Product(){};
    p.setId(1119996);
    p.setFkSubcategoryId(111);
    p.setName("Test1");
    p.setDescription("Test1 Description");
    p.setPrice(11);
    p.setPrice(6);
    category.createProduct(p);

    Product p2 = category.getProduct(1119996);
    assertEquals("name after create",p2.getName(), p.getName());

    p.setName("Test2");
    category.editProduct(p);
    Product p3 = category.getProduct(1119996);
    assertEquals("name after edit", p3.getName(), p.getName());


    category.deleteProduct(p.getId());
    Product p4 = category.getProduct(1119996);
    this.assertEquals("product should be gone", -1, p4.getId());
}
```

This code is fairly simple, because the actual product implementation is tested thoroughly in the entity ProductTest. Essentially, the test creates a product, edits it, and deletes it. It makes sure the product data is added, edited, and removed. Here the test creates the product by calling the category createProduct() method:

```
Product p = new Product(){};
p.setId(1119996);
p.setFkSubcategoryId(111);
p.setName("Test1");
p.setDescription("Test1 Description");
p.setPrice(11);
p.setPrice(6);
category.createProduct(p);
```

Next, the test makes sure that the product actually was created by looking it up:

```
Product p2 = category.getProduct(1119996);
assertEquals("name after create",p2.getName(), p.getName());
```

Here the test edits the product by changing the product object and then submitting it. Then, the test makes sure the product was edited:

```
p.setName("Test2");
category.editProduct(p);
```

```
Product p3 = category.getProduct(1119996);
assertEquals("name after edit", p3.getName(), p.getName());
```

Finally, the test removes the product, as follows:

```
category.deleteProduct(p.getId());
Product p4 = category.getProduct(1119996);
this.assertEquals("proudct should be gone", -1, p4.getId());
```

One thing is wrong with this test. It should be further functionally decomposed. For example, let's say the create part fails or the delete part fails. The output of the test will not make clear which functionality was not working. There is a fine line between being over-cautious and sloppy. The more you functionally decompose, the better your reports will be able to point you to the correct failure point.

So, let's decompose the test a little further. We can see that we are doing four things: creating a product, getting a product from the data store, editing a product, and deleting a product from the data store. We begin by moving the test data that the tests will share to the setUp() method, as follows:

```
Product p;

public void setUp()throws Exception{
    . . .
    . . .
    p = new Product(){};
    p.setId(1119996);
    p.setFkSubcategoryId(111);
    p.setName("Test1");
    p.setDescription("Test1 Description");
    p.setPrice(11);
    p.setPrice(6);

}
```

Notice that the test object p is now an instance variable, so it can be used in all four tests. The next step is to break the method testCreateDeleteProduct() into four methods. We add the product from the setUp() method:

```
public void testCreateProduct() throws Exception {
      category.createProduct(p);
}
```

The next test tests the ability to get the product out of the database. Notice that you could combine this get-product test and the previous test, because this one validates the create-product test:

```
public void testGetProduct()throws Exception {
    Product p2 = category.getProduct(1119996);
    assertEquals("name after create",p2.getName(), p.getName());
}
```

The next test tests the ability to edit an existing product:

```
public void testEditProduct() throws Exception {
    p.setName("Test2");
    category.editProduct(p);
    Product p3 = category.getProduct(1119996);
    assertEquals("name after edit", p3.getName(), p.getName());
}
```

Finally, we test the deletion of the product as follows:

```
public void testDeleteProduct()throws Exception {
    category.deleteProduct(p.getId());
    Product p4 = category.getProduct(1119996);
    this.assertEquals("proudct should be gone", -1, p4.getId());
}
```

You really need to endeavor to keep tests small and as atomic in operation as possible. If something breaks in the future, the test will identify exactly what broke. If we had left the test as it was and something broke, it would be hard to tell what broke—not impossible, but difficult. Plus, these methods describe exactly what we are testing.

Creating an Ant Buildfile to Deploy Our Entity Bean

Just like the Hello World example, the EJB source, libraries, and buildfile are self-contained in their own directory structure (see Figure 7.5).

The src directory holds the source files. The jboss-clientlib directory holds the library files needed by JBoss (the EJB server). The META-DATA directory holds the deployment descriptor and the entity property to SQL table field mapping file. The buildfile project name is enterprise_beans; refer to Listing 7.11.

```
<project name="enterprise_beans" default="all" >


    <target name="setProps" unless="setProps"
                          description="setup the properties.">
        <property name="outdir" value="/tmp/petstore" />
        <property name="jboss" value="/tools/jboss/jboss/deploy" />
    </target>

    <target name="init" depends="setProps"
                          description="initialize the properties.">
```

Listing 7.11 enterprise_beans project buildfile. (continues)

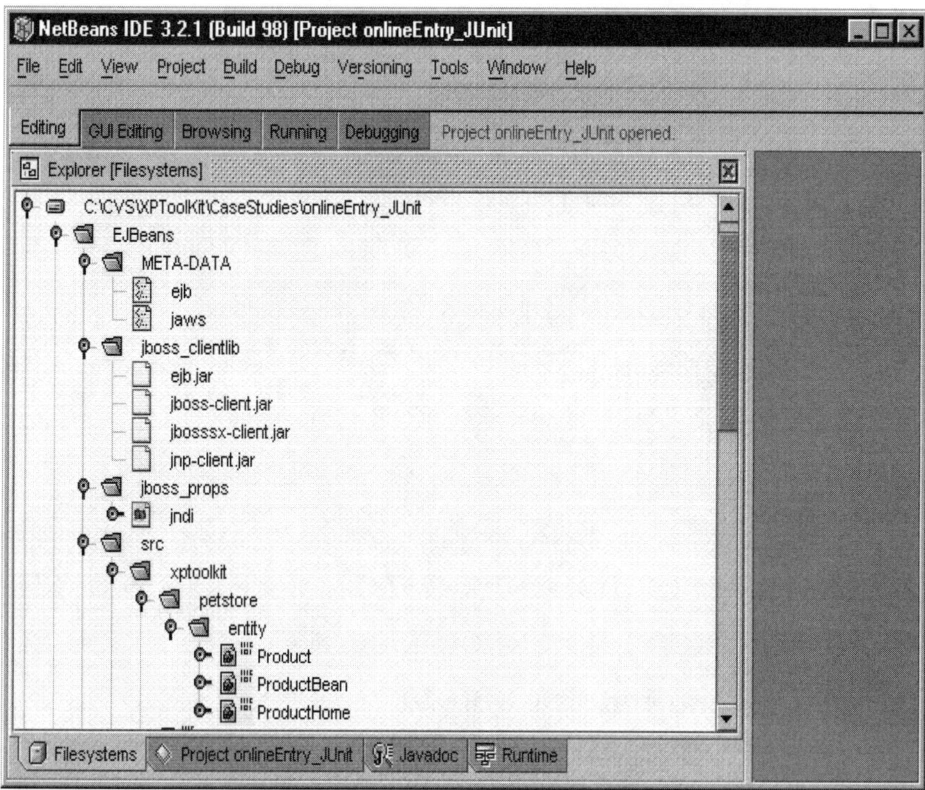

Figure 7.5 EJBeans subproject.

```
        <tstamp/>
        <property name="ejbout" value="${outdir}/ejbs" />
        <property name="build" value="${ejbout}/ejb-jar" />
        <property name="client" value="${ejbout}/ejb-jar-client" />
        <property name="dist" value="${outdir}/dist" />
        <property name="lib" value="${outdir}/lib" />
        <property name="meta-data" value="${build}/META-INF" />
        <property name="build_lib" value="./../lib" />
        <property name="jar_name" value="petbeans.jar" />
    </target>

    <target name="clean_jboss" if="jboss">
        <delete file="${jboss}/${jar_name}" />
    </target>
```

Listing 7.11 enterprise_beans project buildfile. (continues)

```
<target name="clean" depends="init,clean_jboss"
                     description="clean up the output directories.">
    <delete dir="${build}" />
    <delete dir="${meta-data}" />
    <delete dir="${client}" />
    <delete dir="${dist}/${jar_name}" />
</target>


<target name="prepare" depends="init"
                     description="prepare the output directory.">
    <mkdir dir="${build}" />
    <mkdir dir="${lib}" />
    <mkdir dir="${meta-data}" />
    <mkdir dir="${client}" />
    <mkdir dir="${dist}" />
</target>

<target name="compile" depends="prepare"
                     description="compile the Java source.">
    <javac srcdir="./src" destdir="${build}" >
        <classpath >
            <pathelement location="." />

            <fileset dir="${build_lib}">
                <include name="**/*.jar"/>
            </fileset>

            <fileset dir="${lib}">
                <include name="**/*.jar"/>
            </fileset>

        </classpath>
    </javac>
</target>

<target name="config_jboss_jndi" if="jboss">
    <copy todir="${client}" >
         <fileset dir="./jboss_props" />
    </copy>

</target>

<target name="config_jndi" depends="config_jboss_jndi" />
```

Listing 7.11 enterprise_beans project buildfile. (continues)

```
    <target name="package" depends="compile,config_jndi"
                      description="package the Java classes into a jar.">
        <copy todir="${client}" >
             <fileset dir="${build}" excludes="**/*Bean*"
                                      includes="**/*.class*" />
        </copy>

        <jar jarfile="${lib}/client-${jar_name}"
          basedir="${client}" />


          <copy file="./META-DATA/ejb.xml"
                            tofile="${meta-data}/ejb-jar.xml"/>
          <copy file="./META-DATA/jaws.xml"
                            tofile="${meta-data}/jaws.xml" />

         <jar jarfile="${dist}/${jar_name}"
           basedir="${build}" />


    </target>

    <target name="deploy_jboss" depends="package" if="jboss">
        <copy file="${dist}/${jar_name}" todir="${jboss}" />
        <copy todir="${lib}"  >
            <fileset dir="./jboss_clientlib" />
        </copy>
    </target>

    <target name="deploy" depends="package,deploy_jboss"
                  description="deploys the jar file to the ejb server.">
    </target>


    <target name="all" depends="clean,deploy"
                         description="perform all targets."/>

</project>
```

Listing 7.11 enterprise_beans project buildfile.

Let's break down the buildfile and explain the important parts step by step. The setProps task defines a property called "jboss", which it sets to the deploy directory of JBoss:

```
<target name="setProps" unless="setProps"
                        description="setup the properties.">
    <property name="outdir" value="/tmp/petstore" />
    <property name="jboss" value="/tools/jboss/jboss/deploy" />
</target>
```

JBoss has a deploy directory; any Enterprise JavaBean copied to the deploy directory will be automatically read and deployed by the JBoss server. The buildfile uses this property to conditionally delete the EJB JAR file during a clean, to copy the JNDI properties needed for JBoss during a package, and to copy the EJB JAR file to the JBoss deploy directory during a deploy:

```
<target name="clean_jboss" if="jboss">
    <delete file="${jboss}/${jar_name}" />
</target>

. . .

<target name="config_jboss_jndi" if="jboss">
    <copy todir="${client}" >
         <fileset dir="./jboss_props" />
    </copy>

</target>

. . .

<target name="deploy_jboss" depends="package" if="jboss">
    <copy file="${dist}/${jar_name}" todir="${jboss}" />
    <copy todir="${lib}"  >
        <fileset dir="./jboss_clientlib" />
    </copy>
</target>
```

Obviously, your application server may need extra tasks executed. If you have several application servers to deploy to, you can use this technique to create tasks that are executed conditionally.

The compile target of this application is fairly vanilla—that is, it is a lot like the other subprojects. However, the package is interesting because we have to create two JAR files: one for clients and one for the EJB server:

```
<target name="package" depends="compile,config_jndi"
                description="package the Java classes into a jar.">
    <copy todir="${client}" >
         <fileset dir="${build}" excludes="**/*Bean*"
                                 includes="**/*.class*" />
```

```
        </copy>

        <jar jarfile="${lib}/client-${jar_name}"
           basedir="${client}" />


          <copy file="./META-DATA/ejb.xml"
                              tofile="${meta-data}/ejb-jar.xml"/>
          <copy file="./META-DATA/jaws.xml"
                              tofile="${meta-data}/jaws.xml" />

        <jar jarfile="${dist}/${jar_name}"
           basedir="${build}" />


    </target>
```

The package task first creates a client-side JAR file by copying the needed files to a staging area and then jarring them. The first step to create a client-side JAR is to use the copy task to copy all the class files except the implementation to a temporary staging directory, as follows:

```
<copy todir="${client}" >
     <fileset dir="${build}" excludes="**/*Bean*"
                             includes="**/*.class*" />
</copy>
```

Notice how this copy task uses the excludes pattern **/*Bean* to exclude any class file containing the substring *Bean*. This step effectively excludes the product implementation class (ProductBean), which is not needed for the client-side JAR. Now that all the needed client-side files are in the ${client} directory, the buildfile can jar the client-side files, as follows:

```
<jar jarfile="${lib}/client-${jar_name}"
  basedir="${client}" />
```

The client JAR file is put in the output directory lib where the Web application buildfile can get it and put it in the WAR file.

The JAR file for the EJB server must contain not only the implementation class but also the deployment descriptor and the CMP mappings file. (Note that we copy in a mapping file specific to JBoss. In a real buildfile, you may want to do this in a target that is executed only if the "jboss" property is set.) Here are the tasks to build the server EJB JAR file:

```
      <copy file="./META-DATA/ejb.xml" tofile="${meta-data}/ejb-
jar.xml"/>
      <copy file="./META-DATA/jaws.xml" tofile="${meta-data}/jaws.xml"
/>

      <jar jarfile="${dist}/${jar_name}"  basedir="${build}" />
```

When this buildfile executes, we get a JAR file in lib (client-petbeans.jar) and a JAR file in the distribution directory (petbeans.jar); see Figure 7.6.

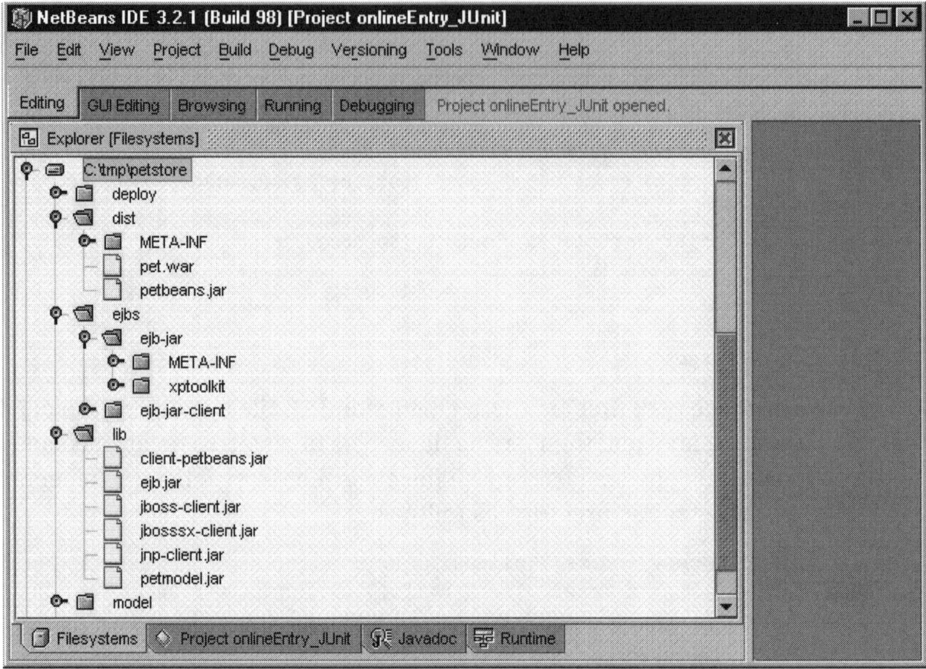

Figure 7.6 Output of the enterprise_beans buildfile.

In addition to the client-side JAR file, in the case of JBoss the Web application needs the following: naming, RMI, and EJB support libraries (the JAR files ejb.jar, jboss-client.jar, and jbosssx.jar, shown in Figure 7.7). Thus the deploy target depends on the jboss_deploy target, which copies the files to the lib directory where they can be picked up by the Web application buildfile and packaged in the WAR file, as follows:

```
    <target name="deploy_jboss" depends="package" if="jboss">
        <copy file="${dist}/${jar_name}" todir="${jboss}" />
        <copy todir="${lib}"  >
            <fileset dir="./jboss_clientlib" />
        </copy>
    </target>


    <target name="deploy" depends="package,deploy_jboss"
                   description="deploys the jar file to the ejb
server.">
    </target>
```

When the WAR file is deployed, the needed libraries are in the WEB-INF/lib directory where they can be used by the Web applications class loader (see Figure 7.7).

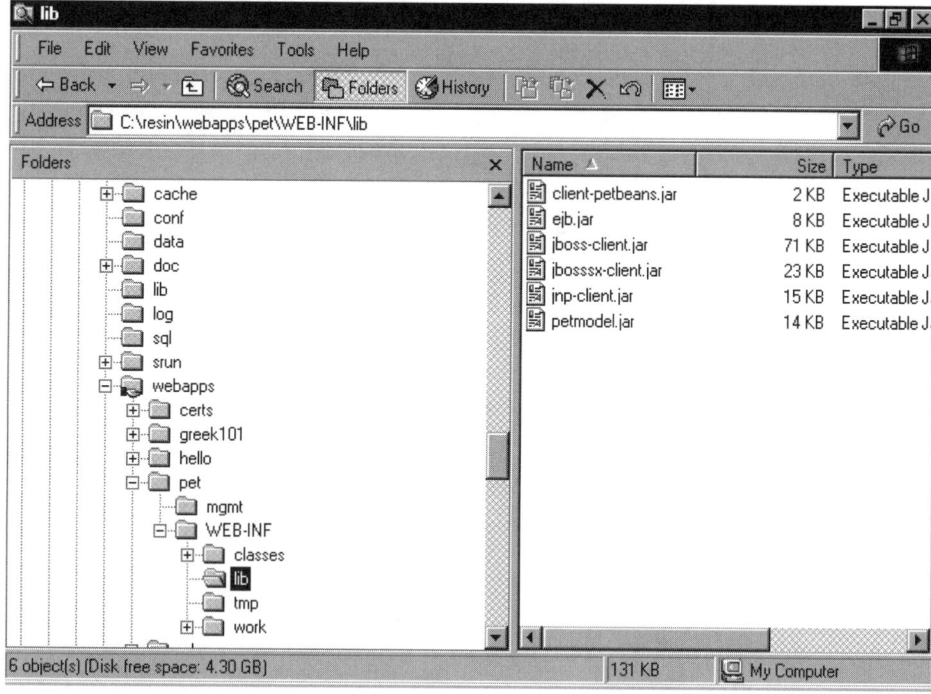

Figure 7.7 The Web application has the needed JAR files.

Now that we have created the classes, tests, and buildfiles to build and deploy the features to add, edit, and delete products, let's update the test buildfile so that it can automatically test the files.

Modifying the Test Buildfile to Test Our Entity Bean

In Listing 7.12, we added the lines in bold to the test target of the test buildfile:

```
<target name="test" depends="compile">

    <junit printsummary="true" fork="yes">

        <formatter type="xml" />

        <test  name="test.xptoolkit.model.CategorySystemTest"
               todir="${reports}" />

        <test  name="test.xptoolkit.model.CategoryTest"
               todir="${reports}" />
```

Listing 7.12 Adding the entity ProductTest to our test buildfile. (continues)

```
        <test  name="test.xptoolkit.model.SubcategoryTest"
               todir="${reports}" />

        <test  name="test.xptoolkit.model.ProductTest"
               todir="${reports}" />

        <test  name="test.xptoolkit.petstore.entity.ProductTest"
               todir="${reports}" />


        <classpath>
           <fileset dir="${lib}">
               <include name="**/*.jar"/>
           </fileset>

           <fileset dir="${build_lib}">
               <include name="**/*.jar"/>
           </fileset>

           <fileset dir="../EJBeans/jboss_clientlib">
               <include name="**/*.jar"/>
           </fileset>


           <fileset dir="${test_lib}">
               <include name="**/*.jar"/>
           </fileset>

           <fileset dir="/tools/ant/lib">
               <include name="**/*.jar"/>
           </fileset>


           <fileset dir="${build}" />

        </classpath>

    </junit>

    <junitreport todir="${reports}">

        <fileset dir="${reports}">

            <include name="TEST-*.xml"/>

        </fileset>
```

Listing 7.12 Adding the entity ProductTest to our test buildfile. (continues)

```
        <report format="frames" todir="${reports}/html"/>

    </junitreport>
</target>
```

Listing 7.12 Adding the entity ProductTest to our test buildfile.

Note that we didn't add much, because the additional test methods were added to CategoryTest and CategorySytemTest. The only test we have to add is the entity ProductTest, as follows:

```
<test  name="test.xptoolkit.petstore.entity.ProductTest"
             todir="${reports}" />
```

Because the junitreport task uses a file set, the output from the entity ProductTest is automatically included with the rest. The important point here is that once the testing buildfile is set up, adding new tests and reports is easy. Please look at the output for the entity ProductTest in Figure 7.8.

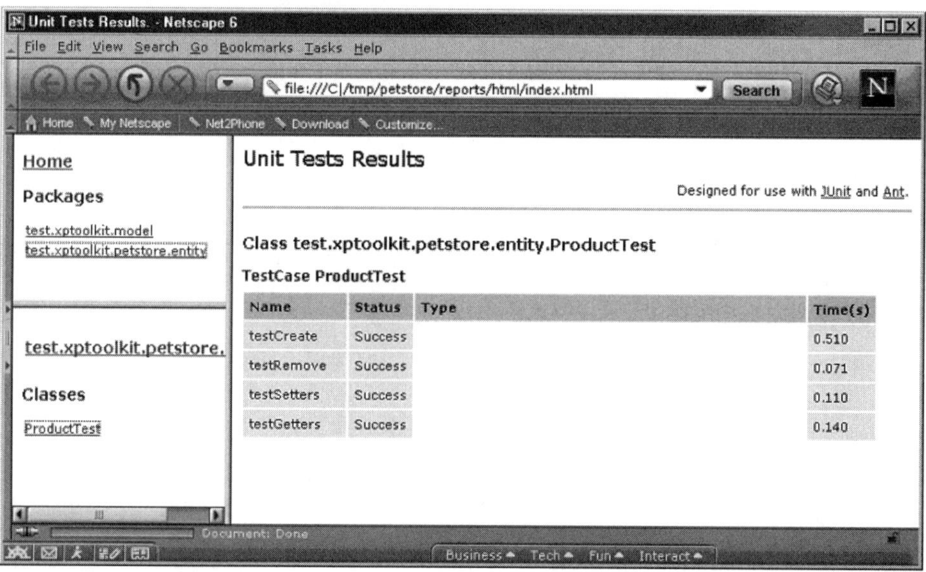

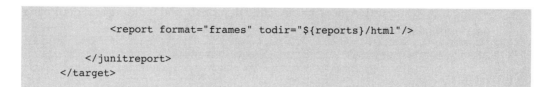

Figure 7.8 Entity ProductTest.

Case Study Conclusion

This case study included test cases used for the baseline version of the pet store. We added an entity bean and Web form to manage product data over the Web (add, delete, and modify product data). Once we added the entity bean, we added test cases to test it, and then we integrated them into the test buildfile.

Using this example, we more realistically demonstrated building and deploying an entity bean to our EJB server.

Summary

This chapter covered the basics of using JUnit (a framework for writing automated unit tests) to create automated testing for your project. We discussed some of the reasons why you would want to use automated testing. Unit-level testing shows that the code you just refactored did not break. Automated testing gives you confidence in your ability to refactor. Ant and JUnit together can automate the build, deploy, and test process, which is essential for continuous integration and refactoring. In addition, Ant allows you to create snazzy HTML reports on your project using the junit and junitreport tasks. This reports allows you to see the state of your project at a glance.

CHAPTER 8

Testing Container Services with Cactus

This chapter shows how to use Cactus for in-container testing, a vital concern of any XP/J2EE developer. To phrase it another way, this chapter attempts to answer the question, "How do I do unit tests on servlets and other J2EE components?" This chapter assumes familiarity with JUnit and J2EE components—especially servlets and JSPs.

Where to Get Cactus

Originally, Cactus was called J2EEUnit, a name that captured the intent of the framework nicely. However, Sun owns the J2EE trademark, so The Apache Software Foundation changed the framework's name to Cactus. Cactus was recently accepted as a top-level project under Jakarta, putting it on par with Ant, Tomcat, and Struts. Simultaneously with this move, the package names for Cactus were changed from org.apache.commons.cactus to org.apache.cactus. Be sure to check the Cactus site for further developments.

Cactus is distributed under The Apache Software License, Version 1.1 and can be downloaded at:

http://jakarta.apache.org/

Why In-Container Testing?

You need a framework like Cactus to test J2EE code. Why? Because of the special relationship that J2EE code—servlets, JSPs, EJBs, and so on—holds with its *container*. Naturally, unit testing focuses on *units* of program code. However, no code exists in a vacuum. Even the simplest program is dependent upon other units of code (any Java program, for instance, is dependent upon the JVM). One of the biggest challenges of unit testing is how to tease the unit apart from its context so that its behavior can be asserted independently.

Testing in Isolation: Mock Objects

A new unit testing technique termed Mock Objects or Endo-Testing was just beginning to make an appearance as we were writing this book. The idea behind Mock Object testing is to define "mock objects" that test cases can pass to the code being exercised. These mock objects take the place of domain objects and have dummy behavior that test cases can configure at runtime. A typical mock object interaction might go something like:

```
public void testFilter() {
  mockFilter.setExpectedFilterCalls(1);
  filterableObject.apply(mockFilter);
  mockFilter.verify();
}
```

The verify() function would ensure that the expected calls to the filter's filter() function occurred.

Endo-testing solves the problem of code in context by providing an ultra-lightweight emulation of that context on a per-test basis. The Mock Object passed to code under test should encompass all of the state that the code needs to operate correctly.

Advantages to Mock Objects

Using Mock Objects refines the practice of unit testing by ensuring almost totally independent operation of the code under test. This provides a variety of advantages. Certain application states may be impossible, difficult, or time-consuming to reproduce. Mock Objects avoid this problem by keeping all of the "state" setUp in the Mock Object. Mock Objects also improve code design according to the authors of *Endo-Testing: Unit Testing with Mock Objects* (a paper presented by Tim Mackinnon, Steve Freeman, and Philip Craig at "eXtreme Programming and Flexible Processes in Software Engineering - XP2000"). An isolating unit test, "improves domain code by preserving encapsulation, reducing global dependencies, and clarifying the interactions between classes."

Disdvantages to Mock Objects

Mock Objects require some effort to design and implement. Mackinnon, et. al. point to this difficulty: "In some cases it can be hard to create Mock Objects to represent types in a complex external library. The most difficult aspect is usually the discovery of values and structures for parameters that are passed into the domain code." In the case of J2EE container services, the complexity and scope of the libraries can be very high. With time, as the Java community develops reusable mock libraries and perfects code generation tools for Mock Objects this disadvantage will lessen. Several projects dedicated to theses goals already exist, however, at the time of this writing, most were in their early stages. One promising candidate is the Mock Objects project (http://www.mockobjects.com) an open source project hosted on SourceForge with contributors from the Cactus team.

Testing in Context: Integration Testing

Integration or in-container J2EE testing eliminates the problem of isolating tests by embracing it. Integration tests attempt to test the domain code (as far as is possible) from within the context provided by the container. For instance, an in-container test for a servlet would exercise its doGet() method by passing it actual or thinly wrapped versions of real ServletRequest and ServletResponse objects.

Advantages to Integration Testing

The chief advantage to in-container testing is verification of the interaction between domain code and container services. J2EE containers grow in complexity and scope every year, providing such diverse services as object lifecycle maintenance, security, transactions, object persistence, and so on. Containers rely on declarative deployment descriptors to specify and configure many of these services. Although many J2EE services are governed by the specifications released through the Java Community Process, the specifications leave many implementation details to container providers. Furthermore, there are no guarantees that a given container will be bug-free or that it will implement the specification exactly.

A Real-World Example

I worked on a project recently where we wanted to take advantage of some of the new features of the EJB 2.0 specification. We were working with a small application server (Resin) that had recently implemented the parts of the specification (specifically Container Managed Persistence) that we were interested in. Using integration tests helped us refine our understanding of the domain because we had to precisely specify our expectations about the container and helped us uncover some pitfalls early. We were getting an intermittent error that showed up in about one out of three test runs. It turned out that the service we were requesting needed to be isolated in a transaction to avoid modification to underlying database tables while the service was running. Integration tests helped us focus our attention on the specific container service that we were calling—without the surrounding context of an application to distract us.

Integration testing allows developers to verify all the aspects of testing that elude verification in the domain code. Proper in-container tests can validate assumptions about the way the application is configured (is such-and-such a servlet mapped correctly?), whether services perform as expected, and help track down bugs that result from component interaction.

Disadvantages to Integration Testing

By its nature, integration testing is less "unit" than Mock Object testing. While it helps verify interaction with the container, it does not provide especially good verification of domain code. Integration testing generates less pressure to refine the underlying design, since integration tests work perfectly well with systems of interdependent components. On the flip side, the context that in-container tests provide cannot be exactly identical to the code's production context. Integration testing is white-box testing—it gets inside the container to test pieces of logic. The intrusion of test code into the container must necessarily alter the surrounding context. As an example, Cactus provides wrappers for several container objects. Although the extra behavior added by these wrappers should not affect testing adversely, it could cause results that would not occur in a normal context. Black-box testing (with a framework such as HttpUnit) that calls an application externally can replicate a production environment more closely.

A Blend of Approaches

Ideally a full test suite would include verification of the domain logic with Mock Objects, integration testing with Cactus, and functional tests with a framework such as HttpUnit. However, integration testing is a critical part of this picture. J2EE applications rely can on container services so heavily that not having at least a "smoke test" of interaction with the deployment container amounts to a significant project risk.

Why Cactus?

Cactus is an open source framework that provides in container testing services for Servlets, JSP custom tags, and Servlet Filters. Other container components such as connection pools, EJBs, and JSPs can be easily tested through Cactus, although as of version 1.2, the framework does not include any services *specifically* designed to facilitate their testing. EJB testing services do loom on the horizon.

Cactus works by providing objects called "redirectors," which serve as points of entry to the container. These redirectors execute test cases written for Cactus in the container and provide access to container objects such as HttpServletRequest, PageContext, and FilterChain. There is one proxy per directly supported API: one for servlets, one for filters, and one for custom tags. More are planned for the future. Developers who wish to work with components that are indirectly supported can choose any the most appropriate redirector (usually ServletRedirector) to gain access to the container.

In addition to providing an entry into the container and access to the implicit objects, Cactus integrates with the JUnit framework and makes the business of talking to the redirector transparent to the user (well, almost transparent). Writing Cactus test cases can be as easy as extending a Cactus base class and using the objects that Cactus provides.

Cactus vs. HttpUnit

Cactus and HttpUnit both test Web application components, so questions naturally arise about their relationship and respective domains. Although there is some overlap, the basic difference is that Cactus is the more unit-oriented of the two. Cactus tests are designed to exercise the behaviors of specific classes and methods, whereas HttpUnit is designed to exercise requests to specific resources on a server.

A Cactus test might target the behavior of HelloWorldServlet, whereas an HttpUnit test might target http://myserver.com/hello/HelloWorldServlet. Depending on the server configuration, this path could invoke several filters and/or kick the user out to a login page before allowing access to HelloWorldServlet. Cactus tests *pieces* of the chain of objects that generates a response, and HttpUnit tests the *whole* chain. Although each tool has its separate place (Cactus for unit testing and HttpUnit for functional testing), the line sometimes blurs. For instance, a simple servlet might be in charge solely of writing some data to the response. In this case, inspection of the servlet response is all the testing the servlet needs. HttpUnit, Cactus, or a combination of the two would serve.

HttpUnit ships with an interesting companion API called ServletUnit. This framework essentially provides a stub container for Servlets to reside in and allows these servlets to be accessed as if they were running in a remote Web server. Although ServletUnit could be useful, it still leans towards the functional end of testing—its domain does not overlap that of Cactus.

Installing Cactus

We have avoided giving installation instructions in this book because we have no desire to duplicate the documentation. However, we made an exception for Cactus because the process is not simple. Installation involves the coordination of the two halves of the Cactus equation: the client side, where requests are composed and sent to the Web container, and the server side, where the tests are actually executed. (This is a simplified explanation. The exact relationship between the server and client sides of Cactus is explored in the next section, "Cactus Architecture.") The prerequisites for a Cactus installation are trivial (for anyone intending to write code that Cactus would test): a JVM capable of running JDK 1.2 and a servlet engine compliant with the Servlet 2.2 (or better) specification.

Open source development moves fast, and the Cactus user community constantly suggests improvements to the installation process. Furthermore, the Cactus Web site provides several Ant buildfiles that simplify the building and test-deployment process. Be sure to check the Web site for the most up-to-date information: http://jakarta.apache.org/commons/cactus/index.html.

Server-Side Installation

Installing Cactus components on the server involves the following steps:

1. Put the Cactus libraries on the server's classpath. commons-cactus.jar and junit.jar must both be on the server's classpath. In most cases, this means you must put these JAR files into the WEB-INF/lib folder of the Web application that will contain your Cactus tests.
2. Put the test classes on the server's classpath. This step is necessary because Cactus executes any given test case both on the server and on the client. Omitting this step will cause a ClassNotFoundException when the redirector servlet attempts to load a test case that is not on the server. It is important not only to put tests on the server initially, but to keep them up to date. If a test is changed and the server is not updated with a new copy of the test, it will continue to use the old one—causing unexpected results. For this reason, an automated build and deployment tool such as Ant is a practical necessity for development with Cactus.
3. Put the classes under test on the server's classpath. Naturally, the latest copy of all the code that the tests depend upon also needs to reside on the server for the tests to run.
4. Map URLs to the various Cactus redirectors. Ordinarily, doing so will involve adding mappings to the web.xml file of the Web application that contains the Cactus tests. Cactus operates by calling these redirectors with HTTP requests from the client; they must have URL mappings so they can be called externally. Listing 8.1 shows the web.xml file that we will be using for the first example (assuming the Web application is named cactus-tests); its general form should be familiar to anyone who has worked with servlets before. This example includes mappings for the servlet, JSP custom tag, and filter redirectors.

```
<?xml version="1.0" encoding="ISO-8859-1"?>

<!DOCTYPE web-app
    PUBLIC "-//Sun Microsystems, Inc.//DTD Web Application 2.2//EN"
    "http://java.sun.com/j2ee/dtds/web-app_2.2.dtd">

<web-app>

    <!-- Mappings for the Servlet Redirector -->
    <servlet>
```

Listing 8.1 Sample deployment descriptor demonstrating Cactus mappings. (continues)

```
        <servlet-name>ServletRedirector</servlet-name>
        <servlet-class>
            org.apache.cactus.server.ServletTestRedirector
        </servlet-class>
    </servlet>

   <servlet-mapping>
        <servlet-name>ServletRedirector</servlet-name>
        <url-pattern>/ServletRedirector/</url-pattern>
    </servlet-mapping>

    <!-- Mappings for the FilterRedirector -->
    <filter>
        <filter-name>FilterRedirector</filter-name>
        <filter-class>
            org.apache.cactus.server.FilterTestRedirector
        </filter-class>
    </filter>

    <filter-mapping>
        <filter-name>FilterRedirector</filter-name>
        <url-pattern>/FilterRedirector/</url-pattern>
    </filter-mapping>

    <!-- Mappings for the JspRedirector -->
    <servlet>
        <servlet-name>JspRedirector</servlet-name>
        <jsp-file>/redirector.jsp/</jsp-file>
    </servlet>

    <servlet-mapping>
        <servlet-name>JspRedirector</servlet-name>
        <url-pattern>/JspRedirector/</url-pattern>
    </servlet-mapping>
</web-app>
```

Listing 8.1 Sample deployment descriptor demonstrating Cactus mappings.

5. If custom tag tests are on the horizon, add redirector.jsp (the JSP redirector) to your Web application in the location specified in the previous step. (In the example, this will be the root of the Web application.) This step is necessary because the commons-cactus jar that contains the classes for the other redirectors cannot contain JSPs.

Client-Side Installation

Client side setup involves less work. First, make sure that junit.jar and commons-cactus.jar are on the client's classpath (along with your Cactus test cases, of course). Second, create a properties file called cactus.properties and put it on your classpath. cactus.properties will contain entries that correspond to the URLs of the redirectors that were mapped during the server-side installation. Cactus needs these properties set so that it can direct requests to the server-side test runners from within the client test runners.

Here are the contents of the cactus.properties file we will use to develop our first example:

```
cactus.servletRedirectorURL=
                    http://localhost:8080/cactus-tests/ServletRedirector/

cactus.jspRedirectorURL=
                    http://localhost:8080/cactus-tests/JspRedirector/

cactus.filterRedirectorURL=
                    http://localhost:8080/cactus-tests/FilterRedirector/
```

Each entry is a URL. “cactus-tests” is simply the name of the example Web application. (The example lists the host as localhost:8080 on the assumption that the tests will be run on a local Web server—be sure to specify the actual name and port of the machine on which you want your tests to run.)

NOTE:

With some help from Ant, the cactus.properties file can be generated just before test suite execution. Generating the file allows for on-the-fly customization of the redirector URLs to account for differences between local and integration servers.

A Simple Example

Now that Cactus is installed in a Web application called cactus-tests on our Web server, let’s try to run a test to prove that it works. The class we want to test is simple: It maps all the request parameter into session attributes (and returns a java.util.Map of the parameters and values). It has a single static method:

```
public static Map mapRequestToSession(HttpServletRequest request){
  HttpSession session = request.getSession();
  Map paramsMap = new HashMap();
  for(Enumeration e = request.getParameterNames(); e.hasMoreElements();){
    String paramName = (String)e.nextElement();
    String paramValue = request.getParameter(paramName);
    session.setAttribute(paramName, paramValue);
    paramsMap.put(paramName, paramValue);
  }
  return paramsMap;
}
```

Our Cactus test for the SessionMapper class follows the standard JUnit test case template. It has a couple of differences: The class descends from org.apache.cactus.ServletTestCase, and there is another method in addition to the testSessionMapper()—beginSessionMapper(WebRequest request). Here is the code for the test case:

```
package xptoolkit.cactus;
import org.apache.cactus.*;
import junit.framework.*;

public class MapperTest extends ServletTestCase{
  /*standard constructor omitted */

  public void beginSessionMapper(WebRequest clientSideRequest){
    clientSideRequest.addParameter("xp", "rules!");
  }

  public void testSessionMapper(){
    Map map = SessionMapper.mapRequestToSession(request);
    String val = (String)session.getAttribute("xp");
    assertEquals("rules!", val);
    val = (String)map.get("xp");
    assertEquals("rules!", val);
  }

  /*standard main and suite methods omitted */
}
```

The beginSessionMapper() method is executed on the client, and it sets up the request that will eventually arrive at the redirector servlet and thereby at the SessionMapper class. We'll cover this type of method in more detail in the section "Writing Cactus Tests."

The testSessionMapper() method passes the request instance variable inherited from ServletTestCase into mapRequestToSession(HttpServletRequest request). The request variable implements the HttpServletRequest interface because it wraps an instance of the request generated by the Web server. Once mapRequestToSession() has completed its work, we expect to find a session attribute mapped under the key XP. ServletTestCase also provides an instance variable session (type HttpSession). We pull our value from this variable, assert that it is equal to the String we expect, and voilà! Our test is complete.

To execute the test, first we make sure that the server has the latest version of both SessionMapper and MapperTest. Once the server has been made aware of the new classes, we use one of the usual JUnit test runners to execute the test normally on the client side. When the test executes, Cactus automatically sends an HTTP request to the servlet redirector specifying that MapperTest should be instantiated and that its testMapRequestToSession() method should be invoked. The server runs the test and returns the results to the client for Cactus to interpret. Barring any setup issues, the test should run. As pair-programming partners, we give each other a high-five and begin integrating our test and code into the system.

Cactus Architecture

In order to generate the implicit objects available in a Web server, Cactus needs to replicate the request-response cycle of HTTP communication. To do this (and also to allow verification of the response returned by the Web server) Cactus test cases are fully executed in two instances that pretend to run as one—the first on the client side and the second on the server side. The framework authors made this decision to simplify the creation of test cases: the alternative would be to have one class for the server and one for the client. This process operates so smoothly that it often appears that Cactus test cases are standard JUnit test cases. Occasionally, test execution can produce unexpected behavior because, although the two objects operate as one, they do not actually share a common state. However, with caution and a solid understanding of the Cactus architecture, writing test cases that execute in the container is a snap.

In this section, we'll give you an in-depth look at how Cactus goes about executing a test case (including which steps happen where) by examining the life cycle of a subclass of ServletTestCase. We chose ServletTestCase because it's slightly simpler than the other two redirector test cases. However the steps outlined in the following sections could apply equally to any of Cactus' TestCases. It's probably a good idea to read this section and the next section, "Writing Cactus Tests," together, because the material is difficult to separate.

Beginning Execution

A Cactus test is started from a usual JUnit test runner (see Figure 8.1). If you are not familiar with JUnit's way of executing test cases, it's probably a good idea to review Chapter 7, "Unit Testing with JUnit," and skim Chapter 14, "JUnit API Reference."

An instance of the test case is instantiated, and its test method is selected by the name passed into the constructor.

Client Side
FooTest instance
(testDoSomething selected)

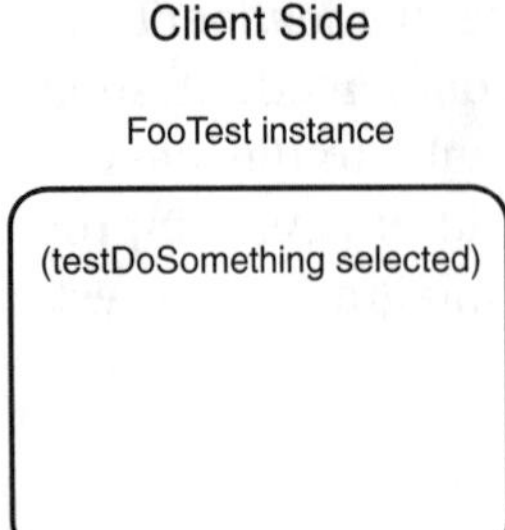

Figure 8.1 A diagram of the first stage of Cactus test case execution.

The begin*XXX*() Method

Based on the name of the test method (a method named test*XXX*()), ServletTestCase will look for and execute a method in the TestCase named begin*XXX*() (see Figure 8.2). For example, if Cactus were executing the testFoo() method of your test case, it would execute your beginFoo() method during this step. The begin*XXX*() method is used to set up any request parameters required by the test.

Calling the Redirector Servlet

After begin*XXX*() completes, ServletTestCase opens an HTTP connection to the redirector servlet (see Figure 8.3). In addition to sending any request parameters added in begin*XXX*, Cactus sends some internal parameters that specify which test (and which test method) to execute on the server.

Server-Side Setup

When the redirector servlet receives the request, it inspects the internal parameters and instantiates a new copy of the correct test case on the server (see

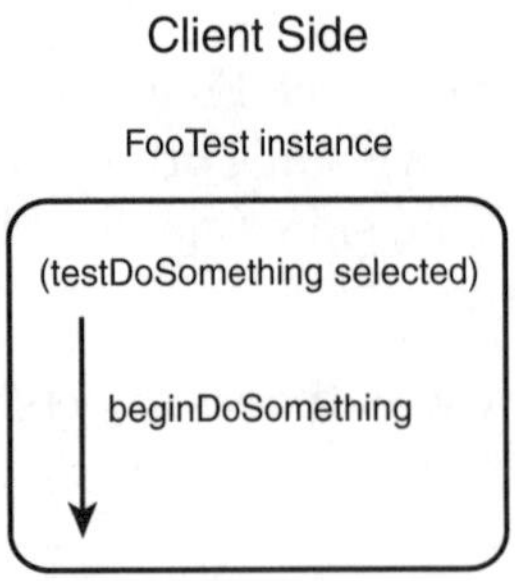

Client Side
FooTest instance
(testDoSomething selected)
beginDoSomething

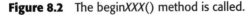

Figure 8.2 The begin*XXX*() method is called.

Figure 8.4). Once the class is instantiated, the redirector servlet uses reflection to copy the standard servlet variables (request, response, and so on) into the new test case instance. These variables are wrapped versions of the variables available to the redirector servlet.

Server-Side Execution

Once the server-side test case has been fully initialized, server-side execution begins (see Figure 8.5). The setUp(), test*XXX*(), and tearDown() methods are executed at this point. (Note that these are executed only in the copy of the test case that runs on the server.) The results of the test (including errors or failure, if any) are captured and stored in an application scope variable.

Results Collection and Post-Processing

Once the test has finished executing, the copy of the test on the client makes another request to the redirector servlet asking for the results (see Figure 8.6). The redirector servlet pulls the results from the application scope variable where they were stored and sends them to the client. If any exceptions or failures were stored in the results, they are rethrown so the JUnit test runner will log them normally. If the result was successful, a final end*XXX*() method is executed on the client.

The end*XXX*() takes a WebResponse parameter. The WebResponse object contains response data written to the client, if any. The end*XXX*() method can perform assertions against contents of the response using the methods of the WebResponse object. Test execution is complete after end*XXX*() returns. Please note that there are actually two types of WebResponse objects—we will cover these in the next section.

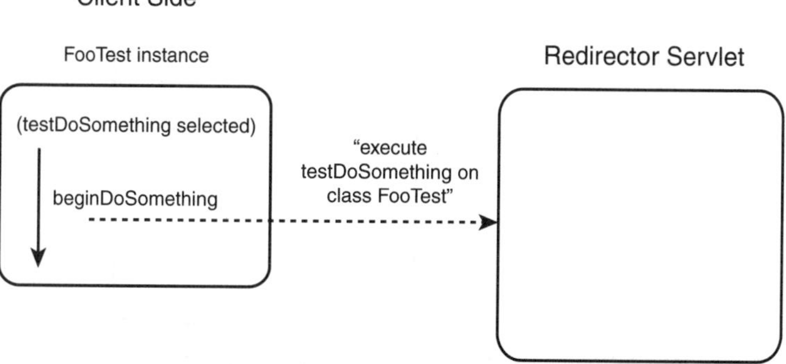

Figure 8.3 The client-side test case sends a request to the redirector servlet.

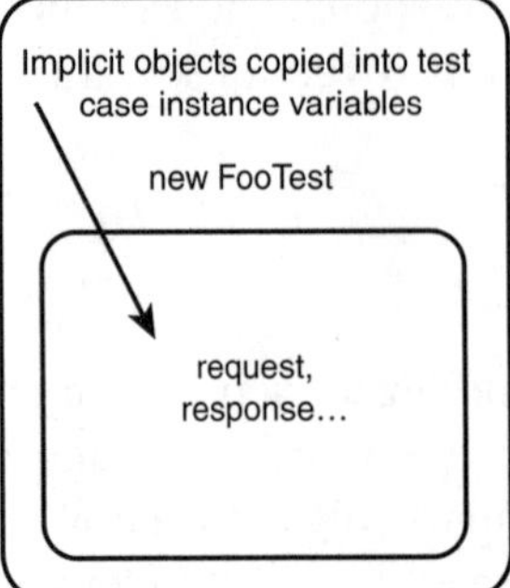

Figure 8.4 The redirector initializes the server-side test case.

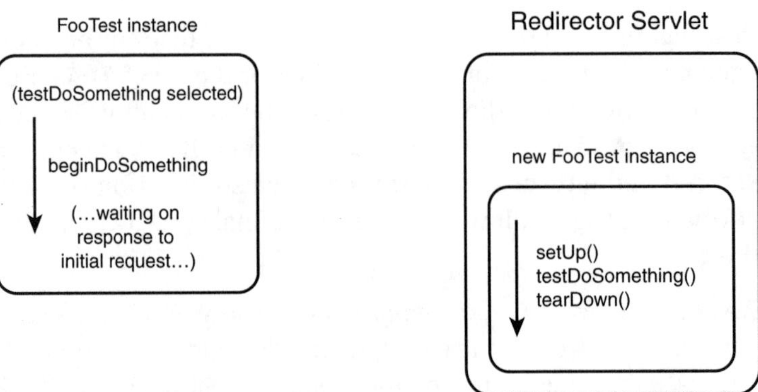

Figure 8.5 The test case runs on the server.

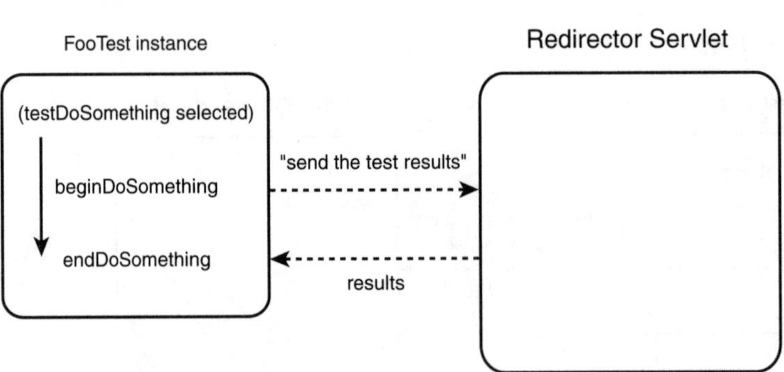

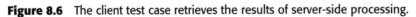

Figure 8.6 The client test case retrieves the results of server-side processing.

Writing Cactus Tests

At this point in the chapter, you probably have a pretty good idea of what writing a Cactus test case will be like. This section will attempt to fill in the gaps in your knowledge with an in-depth look at the various pieces of a Cactus test case. We will examine at a ServletTestCase. Again, most of the principles that apply to writing a ServletTestCAse apply to the other types of Cactus TestCase. However, JspTestCase is covered in "JspTestCases and Custom Tags," and FilterTestCase is covered in "Testing Filters."

The Code Under Test

The code under test is a servlet that wraps the behavior of the SessionMapper class as seen in the "Installing Cactus" section. Listing 8.2 gives the code for the MapperServlet. In addition to mapping the results of the request into the session, this servlet prints all the request parameters to the response in the format "key=value". Although we could use HttpUnit to check on the response, we need Cactus to ensure that the the request parameters are appropriately mapped into the session. In addition, the MapperServlet responds to initialization parameters (specifically, it varies the capitalization of its output if the "ALL_CAPS" parameter is set to "true"). With Cactus, we can set different initialization parameters without having to modify the deployment descriptor for the Web application.

```
package xptoolkit.cactus;
import javax.servlet.http.HttpServlet;
import javax.servlet.http.HttpServletRequest;
import javax.servlet.http.HttpServletResponse;
import java.util.*;
import java.io.PrintWriter;
import java.io.IOException;

public class MapperServlet extends HttpServlet{

  public void doGet(HttpServletRequest request,
                    HttpServletResponse response)throws IOException{

    Map paramMap =  SessionMapper.mapRequestToSession(request);
    PrintWriter writer = response.getWriter();
```

Listing 8.2 The MapperServlet to be tested. (continues)

```
        Set mapEntries = paramMap.entrySet();
        Map.Entry e = null;
        for(Iterator iter = mapEntries.iterator(); iter.hasNext();){
          Map.Entry entry = (Map.Entry)iter.next();
          String entryStr = entry.getKey() + "=" + entry.getValue();
          if(useAllCaps()){
            entryStr = entryStr.toUpperCase();
          }
          writer.println(entryStr);
        }
      }

      public boolean useAllCaps(){
        String useAllCapsStr =getServletConfig().getInitParameter("ALL_CAPS");
        return useAllCapsStr.equalsIgnoreCase("true");
      }
    }
```

Listing 8.2 The MapperServlet to be tested.

Listing 8.3 contains the complete code for MapperServletTest, a subclass of Cactus's ServletTestCase. Don't worry if you don't fully understand it; the following sections will explore each part in detail.

```
package xptoolkit.cactus;
import org.apache.cactus.*;

import junit.framework.*;

public class MapperServletTest extends ServletTestCase{

    private MapperServlet servlet;

    public MapperServletTest(String name) {
        super(name);
    }

    public void beginDoGet(ServletTestRequest request){
        request.addParameter("foo","manchu");
    }

    public void setUp()throws Exception{
        this.config.setInitParameter("ALL_CAPS","true");
        servlet = new MapperServlet();
```

Listing 8.3 The test case for the MapperServlet. (continues)

```
        servlet.init(config);
    }

    public void testDoGet() throws Exception{
        servlet.doGet(request, response);
        /*maps the parameters into the session as a side effect*/
        String value = (String)session.getAttribute("foo");
        assertEquals("request param not mapped into session",
                    "manchu", value);
    }

    public void tearDown(){
        /*no significant server-side resources to release*/
    }

    public void testUseAllCaps(){
        assertTrue("servlet set to use all caps",servlet.useAllCaps());
    }

    public void endDoGet(WebResponse respons) throws Exception{
        String responseString = response.getText();
        System.out.println(responseString);
        boolean paramInResponse =
                responseString.indexOf("FOO=MANCHU") > -1;
        assertTrue("param not found in response", paramInResponse);
    }


    public static TestSuite suite(){
        TestSuite suite = new TestSuite(MapperServletTest.class);
        return suite;
    }

    public static void main(String[] args){
        junit.textui.TestRunner.run(suite());
    }
}
```

Listing 8.3 The test case for the MapperServlet.

Extending the Appropriate Class

Cactus tests are JUnit tests. Their execution is started using JUnit's TestRunners outside the container, and in format they follow the basic JUnit test case. There are a couple of key differences, however. The most obvious is that Cactus test cases extend one of Cactus' TestCases (such as ServletTestCase or

JspTestCase). These base classes provide hooks into the Cactus framework for remote execution and specify several instance variables (such as request and response) that correspond to objects that are readily available to the redirector during execution. The presence of these objects allows you to test methods that depend on these portions of the API in question.

The begin*XXX*() Method

If your test method name will eventually be testRiotHandler, then you may choose to write an additional public method called beginRiotHandler(). This method is referred to generally as the begin*XXX*() method and is run on the client before execution of the test proper. The begin*XXX*() method must accept one argument—an org.apache.cactus.WebRequest. The WebRequest represents a client-side request that the ServletTestCase will send to the redirector servlet, and that will eventually (in a modified form) be copied into the test case's request instance variable. The begin*XXX*() method serves primarily to add parameters and other information to this request object. Because begin*XXX*() is executed in a different copy of the test case from the one that runs on the server, its only method of communicating with the server-side test execution code is through the WebRequest.

Adding Information to the Request

The WebRequest defines several methods that set up the state of the request. Chapter 15, "Cactus API Reference," contains more detailed descriptions of these methods; however, they are worth outlining here. addCookie(), addHeader(), and addParameter() add request cookies, headers, and parameters, respectively. These can be retrieved from the request variable during server-side execution with the methods defined in the HttpServletRequest interface. setMethod() sets the HTTP method (GET or POST) that the request will use. setAutomaticSession() determines whether a session will automatically be created for this request; the default value is true. If begin*XXX*() calls setAutomaticSession(false), the session instance variable in the ServletTestCase will not be instantiated by the redirector (and calls to request.getSession(false) will return null.).

The setURL() method of ServletTestRequest is provided because the actual URL of the request sent to the server will be the URL of the redirector servlet. If the code under test does URL processing setURL() allows for a mock URL. See the ServletURL class description in Chapter 15 for more details. The beginDoGet() method in our MapperServletTest uses addParameter() to add a single parameter "foo" with the value "manchu" to the request:

```
public void beginDoGet(ServletTestRequest request){
  request.addParameter("foo","manchu");
}
```

A Possible Trap

The begin*XXX*() method seems like an ideal place to do method-specific setup above and beyond request parameters. However, the following begin*XXX*() method will not work:

```
public void beginCyborgAttack{
  someImportantInstanceVariable = someSpecificSetupMethod();
}
```

If someImportantInstanceVariable is referenced in testCyborgAttack, a NullPointerException will result because beginCyborgAttack() executes in a different copy of the test case. If a test method requires specific setup, you should use the following code instead:

```
public void testCyborgAttack{
  someImportantInstanceVariable = someSpecificSetupMethod();
  //..rest of testMethod
}
```

The Implicit Objects

A major feature of Cactus is the presence of implicit objects as public member variables of ServletTestCase. Server-side methods can pass these variables as parameters to tested methods that require them. ServletTestCase defines four implicit objects: request, response, session, and config. These variables are initialized just prior to the calling of setUp() and are available only in the copy of the test case that runs on the server. (They contain null on the client.) Each implicit object is either the exact version or a thinly wrapped version of the same object available to the redirector servlet. The reasons for the wrapping are explored under the individual section.

request

The request variable implements HttpServletRequest. Its actual class is org.apache.cactus.server.HttpServletRequestWrapper, which delegates almost all its calls to the original HttpServletRequest. This means that the wrapper contains all of the request parameters that were specified in the begin*XXX*(). The only exceptions are the methods that return information about the URL. These methods return the simulated URL specified with ServletTestRequest.setURL in begin*XXX*(). The request variable also returns a Cactus-wrapped version of a

RequestDispatcher from getRequestDispatcher() to avoid problems resulting from the mocked URL.

response

This variable is set to the actual response object passed into the redirector servlet's doGet()/doPost() method.

session

Unless setAutomaticSession(false) was called in begin*XXX*(), this variable contains the result of HttpServletRequest.getSession(true). Otherwise, it contains null.

config

This variable contains a wrapped version of the ServletConfig object returned by a call to getServletConfig() in the redirector. The wrapper delegates almost all its methods; the key difference is its handling of initialization parameters. In addition to being able to return init parameters of the redirector servlet (as mapped in the deployment descriptor), you can set further init parameters with setInitParameter(). The values set with this method take precedence over the values of the redirector servlet.

The config object also returns a wrapped ServletContext from getServletContext(). The ServletContext wrapper handles forwards and includes correctly (additional logic is needed to cope with the simulated URL of the HttpServletRequestWrapper); it also saves all calls to its logging methods so that they can be easily retrieved and inspected by test code.

In the Example

In the setUp() method, we use the config object to initialize the MapperServlet. First the "ALL_CAPS" init parameter is set to "true" so the test can evaluate the servlet's capitalization handling. Take a look at the following section on setUp() and tearDown() to see the actual code.

setUp() and tearDown()

The setUp() and tearDown() methods mark the beginning and end of server-side execution, respectively. The use of these methods is analogous to their use in regular JUnit. They are not specific to any test method and are the ideal place to construct a test fixture. All the implicit objects are available in setUp() and tearDown().

In the Example

MapperServletTest.setUp() demonstrates proper use. An init parameter is set on the config object to simulate the expected initialization parameters for the MapperServlet. Then setUp() creates an instance of MapperServlet, and it is initialized with the modified config object. Notice that this is done manually by the setUp() method; ordinarily, the servlet engine would handle this housekeeping chore. Here, the "unit" nature of Cactus becomes more apparent. The framework does not invoke servlets; it merely provides access to the container:

```
public void setUp()throws Exception{
  this.config.setInitParameter("ALL_CAPS","true");
  servlet = new MapperServlet();
  servlet.init(config);
}
```

test*XXX*()

The test method, as in JUnit, defines the meat of the testing logic. In the example, it consists of passing two of the implicit objects to the servlet under test and then running assertions against other implicit objects to verify that they were modified correctly:

```
public void testDoGet() throws Exception{
  servlet.doGet(request, response);
  /*maps the parameters into the session as a side effect*/
  String value = (String)session.getAttribute("foo");
  assertEquals("request param not mapped into session", "manchu",
value);
}
```

However, the implicit objects do not need to be used. The test method can verify any code that relies on container services. Imagine the following static method, which performs a JNDI lookup:

```
public static XAConnection connectionLookup() throws Exception {
  InitialContext ctx = new InitialContext();
  XADataSource src =
      (XADataSource)ctx.lookup("java/comp/env/webDatabase");
  return src.getXAConnection();
}
```

This method could be tested in a Cactus test case as follows:

```
public void testJNDILookup()throws Exception{
  javax.sql.XAConnection conn = JNDILookup.connectionLookup();
```

```
    assertNotNull(conn);
  }
```

end*XXX*()

The final (optional) method that ServletTestCase expects subclasses to define is end*XXX*(). This method is called only after the results of the server-side execution have been retrieved from the server. If the results do not contain any failures or errors, end*XXX*() is called. This method is used to verify the final output sent by the server. This can be useful for cases where the code you are testing generates a full HTML response, as well as cases (such as custom tags) where only a small amount of data is written to the client. Needless to say, the servlet implicit objects are not available in end*XXX*(); nor are any variables that were set during server-side execution.

You can define end*XXX*() with one of two signatures, which differ based on the type of the single parameter they accept. The two possible parameter types are org.apache.cactus.WebResponse and com.meterware.httpunit.WebResponse. Each one provides different assertion capabilities, detailed in the subsections below:

Basic Assertions: Cactus' WebResponse

The Cactus version of the WebResponse supports simple assertions. It allows the transformation of the server's response into a searchable String with getText() or into an array of Strings with getTextAsArray(). It also provides facilities to retrieve and perform assertions on cookies returned with the response by the server; this can be done by using getCookies() and getCookie(String). Chapter 15, "Cactus API Reference" contains an example of how to work with client-side cookies in Cactus.)

In the Example

In the example, the getText() method of the WebResponse returns the a String. Then, the String is searched for the occurrence of the capitalized request parameters:

```
public void endDoGet(WebResponse response) throws Exception{
  String responseString = response.getText(conn);
  boolean paramInResponse = responseString.indexOf("FOO=MANCHU") > -1;
  assertTrue("param not found in response", paramInResponse);
}
```

Complex Assertions: HttpUnit's WebResponse

The alternate signature for end*XXX* is end*XXX*(com.meterware.httpunit. WebResponse). HttpUnit's WebResponse class supports significantly more sophisticated assertions, but operates primarily on HTML documents. For plain text or XML responses, for example, you are probably better off with Cactus' WebResponse. Using the two frameworks together allows easy access to these powerful assertion facilities without tying test development to the black-box model of HttpUnit.

Using the HttpUnit WebResponse class is a piece of cake. The HttpUnit API reference details the available methods, but a few examples here will illustrate their general capabilities. getLinks() returns an array of WebLink objects, which provide accessors for their target URLs. getDOM() returns the org.w3c.dom.Node corresponding to the underlying HTML document, and getText() returns a String containing the raw HTML. In order to access these features, the content type of the response must be set to "text-html"; however, a suggestion has been submitted to the HttpUnit team to allow this to be assumed if necessary (although the response will still have to contain HTML).

For more information on the WebResponse class, check out Chapter 9, "Functional Testing with HttpUnit," as well as Chapter 16, "HttpUnit API Reference." If you are only interested in Cactus integration, after reading these pages go straight to the section on the WebResponse class in Chapter 16.

An Example of end*XXX*() using HttpUnit

Listing 8.4 contains the source of a simple servlet that prints a link into the response object. Listing 8.5 contains the relevant methods of a Cactus test that verifies the output using HttpUnit.

```
public class HappyServlet extends javax.servlet.http.HttpServlet {

  public void doGet(HttpServletRequest request,
                    HttpServletResponse response)throws IOException{
    response.setContentType("text/html");
    PrintWriter writer = response.getWriter();
    writer.println("<a href='http://www.dextrose.com/pika.html'>");
    writer.println("I'm so happy!</a>");
  }
}
```

Listing 8.4 A simple servlet that outputs HTML.

```
private HappyServlet servlet;

public void setUp()throws Exception{
  servlet = new HappyServlet();
  servlet.init(config);
}

/** Test of doGet method, of class xptoolkit.cactus.HappyServlet. */
public void testDoGet()throws Exception{
  System.out.println("testDoGet");
  servlet.doGet(request, response);
}

public void endDoGet(com.meterware.httpunit.WebResponse response)
                                               throws Exception{
  WebLink link = response.getLinkWith("I'm so happy!");
  assertNotNull(link);
  System.out.println(resp.getText());
  org.w3c.dom.Node = resp.getDOM();
}
```

Listing 8.5 The key methods of the Cactus/HttpUnit test for HappyServlet.

Cactus with Ant

As you saw in Chapter 2, "J2EE Deployment Concepts," deploying J2EE applications is no picnic. If you've already read the sections on Ant and J2EE application assembly, then you probably have an idea of how you might use Ant to get test code onto the server for execution. Deploying test cases with Ant requires no new technical knowledge, but rather some strategic knowledge and some organization. The Cactus Web site (http://jakarta.apache.org/commons/cactus/index.html) provides an in-depth tutorial on Ant integration and supplies custom tasks suited for Ant deployment (such as starting the server if it isn't already running). It's worth checking out these tutorials (or re-reading Chapters 4, 5, and 6 on Ant), because this section will give you an overview of strategy rather than specific instructions.

The Strategy

In order to run Cactus tests, you must have several pieces in place. Namely:

- The code under test must be deployed in the container.

- The test cases themselves (including the Cactus and JUnit JARs) must also be deployed on the server.
- If the server does not support hot deployment, the server must be restarted after a deployment.
- Before test execution, the server must be running.
- A test runner must call the Cactus test cases on the client side (thereby activating the server-side test code).

Ant is a natural choice to automate these tasks. In fact, if you accomplish all these steps, and the test suite exercises all the code, then you are practically in the presence of continuous integration! Of course, although the strategy appears simple, the execution is slightly more complex. In particular, the deployment of test code raises the question of how to deploy it in relation to the tested code.

A Web Application Just for Testing

The Ant integration tutorial on the Cactus Web site suggests creating a separate WAR file used only for testing purposes. The advantage to this approach is that it is self-contained. The testing WAR can be deployed easily alongside a production Web application, and builds and execution of test code will have their own space to run in. JARs used only by test cases (the Cactus and JUnit JARs spring to mind) don't pollute the classpath of the working application. The chief drawback is having to pull all the code under test into the testing application.

Testing as Part of the Production Application

An alternate strategy is to build the testing into the application that it tests. This avoids duplication of code in two different WAR files. Also, test cases may be harder to separate from their code than to keep together. However, the production Web application will be laden with unexecuted test code. Of course, you could modify the Ant script so that a release build excluded the test code, but at the cost of added build script complexity.

The best solution is probably to experiment with different organization patterns and see which ones work and which don't. Unlike bare JUnit tests, Cactus tests demand at least deployment automation, and at that point it's worth going the extra mile to achieve continuous integration.

Testing Filters

NOTE

This section covers a material in a pre-release version of Cactus 1.2. As such, there may be some changes between what we describe and the actual behavior of Cactus 1.2. Check our Web site for errata.

The Servlet 2.3 specification introduced the concept of Filters, reusable components that would execute before and/or after a given resource. Cactus 1.2 includes a redirector and TestCase to facilitate the testing of Filters and other components that depend on the implicit objects available in a Filter.

Before any filter tests can begin, the FilterRedirector must be mapped into the web.xml file (Listing 8.1 contains a web.xml with an entry for the FilterRedirector) and the entry for cactus.filterRedirectorURL in cactus.properties must be correctly pointed at the redirector:

```
cactus.filterRedirectorURL=
       http://localhost:8080/cactus-tests/FilterRedirector/
```

Writing a Filter test case is, for the most part, straightforward. Complications arise from the fact that Filters are meant to be executed in a chain. Each Filter has the option of continuing the chain of execution by calling doFilter() on the FilterChain object that the container passes to it. Continuing (or discontinuing) the chain is an important part of Filter behavior—good unit tests should verify that the chain of filters is handled correctly. At the time of this writing, the preferred method of verifying the chain behavior of the Filter is to pass it a Mock FilterChain and assert that the Mock did or did not receive a call to its doFilter() method. The following example illustrates how to create and work with a Mock FilterChain.

An Example

The code under test is a simple Filter that verifies that a user is logged onto the server (checks for a "User" object exists in the session). If the user record exists in the session, the filter continues the chain. If not, the Filter breaks the chain and forwards to a login page specified in an initialization parameter.

```
public class AuthFilter implements Filter {
  private FilterConfig config;

  public void init(FilterConfig config) throws ServletException{
    this.config = config;
  }
```

```
  public void doFilter(ServletRequest request,
  ServletResponse response, FilterChain chain)
  throws IOException, ServletException {
    String loginPage = config.getInitParameter("LOGIN_PAGE");
    HttpSession session = ((HttpServletRequest)request).getSession();
    Object user = session.getAttribute("USER");
    if(user != null){
      chain.doFilter(request, response);
    }
    else{
      RequestDispatcher d = request.getRequestDispatcher(loginPage);
      d.forward(request, response);
    }
  }

  public void destroy() {}

}
```

The basics of writing a FilterTestCase are almost the same as those for writing a ServletTestCase. As with Servlets, the Filter in question must be created and initialized manually (usually in the setUp() method):

```
public void setUp()throws Exception {
  filter = new AuthFilter();
  filter.init(config);
  config.setInitParameter("LOGIN_PAGE", "/login_test.html");
  recordingChain = new RecordingChain();
}
```

The config variable of FilterTestCase stores the Filter redirector's FilterConfig object (in wrapped form). The wrapper allows us to specify the initialization parameter "LOGIN PAGE" without having to add it to the web.xml entry for the FilterRedirector.

In the case of AuthFilter, we need to verify the Filter's behavior in two states: user logged in and user not logged in. Here are the two test methods:

```
public void testDoFilter() throws Exception{
  RecordingChain recordingChain = new RecordingChain();
  /*put "user" in session*/
  request.getSession().setAttribute("USER", "not a real user");
  filter.doFilter(request, response, recordingChain);
  assertTrue(recordingChain.verify());
}


public void testNoUser() throws Exception{
  RecordingChain recordingChain = new RecordingChain();
  /*no user in session*/
  filter.doFilter(request, response, recordingChain);
```

```
    assertTrue(!recordingChain.verify());
  }
```

In both cases, we create an instance of a RecordingChain, which is a Mock-type object invented for this Test. FilterChain is easy to mock up because the interface contains only one method: doFilter(). RecordingChain implements FilterChain and adds a verify() method that returns true or false depending on whether doFilter() was called on the chain. Both test methods call verify() to discover whether the chain was continued. Here is the source code:

```
class RecordingChain implements FilterChain{
  boolean doFilterInvoked = false;
  public void doFilter(ServletRequest servletRequest,
                       ServletResponse servletResponse) {
    doFilterInvoked = true;
  }

  public boolean verify(){
    return doFilterInvoked;
  }
}
```

One final method asserts that the forward to the login page actually occurred. This is done by running assertions in end*XXX* on the response returned from the testNoUser method:

```
public void endNoUser(WebResponse response){
  String text = response.getText();
  assertEquals("test login page contents", text);
}
```

If you need to test more complex behavior, you are free to implement filterChain in such a way that it emulates more complex behavior (perhaps it writes some data to the response).

That's about all there is to basic Filter testing. Additional testing techniques are being perfected to allow testing of more complex filter chains based on more complicated entries in the deployment descriptor, however, at press time none of these were ready for release.

JSPTestCases and Custom Tags

JspTestCase was designed to exercise code that depends on the JSP API, specifically that require the pageContext and out objects availiable in every JSP. This section covers testing of JSP custom tags, the main type of J2EE component that uses these objects.

Then How Can I Test My JSPs?

Cactus can be used to test actual JSPs as well as JSP components. However, the technique was still being perfected by the Cactus team as we went to press. Essentially, you can have JspTestCase map Mock versions of objects that the JSP depends on into the appropriate scopes and then forwards control to the tested JSP. The output of the JSP can then be verified in end*XXX*().

In any case, you should be working to minimize the need for JSP testing. JSPs should be contain very little logic, so that you can concentrate on testing the classes the JSPs depend on and still ensure good coverage. The output of a JSP should not vary *radically* depending on its context—at least not unless the radical variation is encapsulated in a bean or a custom tag. If it the output *does* vary, maybe the page needs some refactoring.

Custom tags are both powerful and complicated. A custom tag consists of a *tag handler* class combined with entries in a deployment descriptor file (and possibly a TagExtraInfo class that specifies additional features of the tag). Like a servlet or an applet, tags have a specific lifecycle that is maintained by the container. In the case of custom tags, the tag handler class is deeply intertwined with the container code. Because of this complexity, test developers can struggle with creating proper unit tests—after all, how do you unit test a deployment descriptor? However, in a complicated situation, unit testing increases in importance. You can ferret out subtle container-interaction bugs with ease if you are confident that your code behaves as expected.

Spending the time to understand how a custom tag works, so that this behavior can be replicated in isolation (in other words, in a test), pays off. This section illustrates how to use the context provided by JspTestCase to exercise different types of custom tags, but it is beyond the scope of this book to examine the nuances of, say, the custom tag lifecycle in detail. One of the easiest and most practical ways of deciphering custom tag behavior is to examine the generated servlet for a JSP that uses custom tags. Many IDEs (in particular, the Open Source NetBeans) offer JSP translation and compilation, along with the ability to view the translated servlet. Also, most servlet containers keep a copy of the JSP servlets somewhere close to the original (usually in some sort of working directory). If your IDE won't translate your JSPs, look for these files. Once you have the translated servlets, spend some time putting in custom tags, recompiling, and examining the generated code. Although the generated code is implementation specific, there are only so many ways to conform to the JSP specification. Examine the output from a couple different servlet engines and cross reference your findings with the J2EE tutorial, a reference work, and/or the JSP specification.

Testing Simple Tags

You can quickly put together a unit test for a simple tag. Let's start with the equivalent of "hello world," a custom tag that prints one line of output to the page's JspWriter and ignores any body. The tag handler class appears in Listing 8.6.

```
public class ExampleTag extends BodyTagSupport {

  public int doStartTag() {
    try {
      JspWriter out = pageContext.getOut();
      out.print("simple tag");
    } catch(IOException ioe) {
      throw new RuntimeException(ioe.toString());
    }
    return(SKIP_BODY);
  }
}
```

Listing 8.6 A simple tag handler class.

This tag submits to Cactus testing without a whimper. Because the tag handler implements only one method, all we have to do is initialize the custom tag, call its one method (doStartTag ()), and inspect the results.

We begin creating the test case by extending JspTestCase. JspTestCase operates like ServletTestCase (which we explored earlier in this chapter), except that it uses a JSP to execute the test methods and provides two additional implicit variables available in JSPS: pageContext and out. These variables are simply set to the variables of the same name in redirector.jsp. To test our tag, we initialize it in the setUp() method. The initialization consists of two steps: instantiating the tag and setting the pageContext:

```
public void setUp(){
  tag = new ExampleTag();
  /*pageContext set with the JspTestCase instance variable*/
  tag.setPageContext(this.pageContext);
}
```

The pageContext object grants the tag access to all the servlet implicit objects, as well as the output writer from the page.

Once the test case has initialized the tag, we exercise its behavior in our test method. In this case, we call doStartTag() and verify that it returns the SKIP_BODY constant from the javax.servlet.jsp.tagext.Tag interface:

```
public void testDoStartTag() {
  System.out.println("testDoStartTag");
  int result = tag.doStartTag();
  assertEquals(tag.SKIP_BODY, result);
}
```

But wait! How do we verify that the String "simple tag" was written to the output? Easy enough: We simply use the end*XXX*() method and inspect the response. Because doStartTag() is the only candidate for writing to the output, it must be responsible for anything that shows up in the response. Here is the endDoStartTag() method:

```
public void endDoStartTag(WebResponse resp) throws Exception{
  String response = resp.getText();
  boolean containsText = response.indexOf("simple tag") > -1;
  assert(containsText);
}
```

These are the basic steps in any tag test: Set up the tag according to the specification, call the tag handler's lifecycle method in isolation, and inspect the response if necessary. Of course, a test like this will not verify the whole tag because it does not interact with the tag deployment descriptor and/or TagExtraInfo class. See the "Testing Auxiliary Tag Components" section for strategies related to these extra elements of a custom tag.

Testing Tag Attributes and Page Interaction

Attributes of a custom tag are implemented as setter methods on the tag handler class, to be called before the tag's processing methods begin. The mapping of tag attributes to methods is specified in the tag library descriptor file, which includes an "attribute" element for each tag attribute, with sub-elements specifying the name, whether the attribute is required, and whether its value can be specified as a runtime expression. To examine how to test a tag that uses attributes, we'll look at a simple tag from the popular Struts framework. The ifParameterEquals tag checks the request for a named parameter and evaluates the tag body if the parameter is equal to a specified value. In the following snippet, ifParameterEquals prints "Consuelo Jones" to the page writer if the "iWantConsuelo" request parameter is set to "true":

```
<struts:ifParameterEquals name="iWantConsuelo" value="true">
    Consuelo Jones
</struts:ifParameterEquals>
```

Listing 8.7 contains the tag handler class for ifParameterEquals.

```
public class IfParameterEqualsTag extends TagSupport {

    /**
     * The name of the parameter being compared.
     */
    protected String name = null;


    /**
     * The value to compare this parameter to.
     */
    protected String value = null;


    /**
     * Return the parameter name.
     */
    public String getName() {
      return (this.name);

    }


    /**
     * Set the parameter name.
     *
     * @param name The new parameter name
     */
    public void setName(String name) {
      this.name = name;
    }


    /**
     * Return the comparison value.
     */
    public String getValue() {
      return (this.value);
    }


    /**
     * Set the comparison value.
     *
     * @param value The new comparison value
     */
```

Listing 8.7 The Struts ifParameterEquals tag handler. (continues)

```
    public void setValue(String value) {
      this.value = value;
    }


    /**
     * Compare the specified parameter to the specified value, and decide
     * whether or not to include the body content.
     *
     * @exception JspException if a JSP exception has occurred
     */
    public int doStartTag() throws JspException {

      // Retrieve the value of the specified parameter
      HttpServletRequest request =
        (HttpServletRequest) pageContext.getRequest();
      String compare = request.getParameter(name);
      if (compare == null)
        compare = "";

      // Conditionally evaluate the body of our tag
      if (compare.equals(value))
          return (EVAL_BODY_INCLUDE);
      else
          return (SKIP_BODY);

    }


    public void release() {
      super.release();
      name = null;
      value = null;
    }

}
```

Listing 8.7 The Struts ifParameterEquals tag handler.

A quick examination of the generated servlet shows us how Tomcat would set up the tag:

```
org.apache.struts.taglib.IfParameterEqualsTag
_jspx_th_struts_ifParameterEquals_0 =
                    new org.apache.struts.taglib.IfParameterEqualsTag();
_jspx_th_struts_ifParameterEquals_0.setPageContext(pageContext);
_jspx_th_struts_ifParameterEquals_0.setParent(null);
_jspx_th_struts_ifParameterEquals_0.setName("iWantConsuelo");
_jspx_th_struts_ifParameterEquals_0.setValue("true");
```

Our test case will attempt to replicate this. First we add the required parameter to the request:

```
public void beginPresent(ServletTestRequest request){
  request.addParameter("iWantConsuelo", "true");
}
```

Then, we initialize the tag's attributes in setUp(). Notice that we do not have to write special steps to allow the tag access to the request; the pageContext variable takes care of that for us:

```
public void setUp(){
  tag = new IfParameterEqualsTag();
  tag.setPageContext(this.pageContext);
  tag.setName("iWantConsuelo");
  tag.setValue("true");
}
```

We write the test method to call doStartTag() and check that it returns EVAL_BODY_INCLUDE:

```
public void testPresent() throws Exception{
  assertEquals(tag.EVAL_BODY_INCLUDE, tag.doStartTag());
}
```

This verifies that the tag will include the body—we don't need to add body content and check that it shows up in the response. In order to check that the tag works when the request does not contain the expected parameter, we write another test method:

```
public void testNotPresent()throws Exception{
  assertEquals(tag.SKIP_BODY, tag.doStartTag());
}
```

Because we have not specified a beginNotPresent() method, no parameters will be added to the request.

Managing Information in Scopes

Tag handler classes have access to information in four possible scopes: page, request, session, and application. As we saw in the previous example, the pageContext object manages access to these scopes. The pageContext view of the scopes is *live*, so that anything set in, say, the request object immediately becomes available through a call to pageContext.getAttribute("name", PageContext.REQUEST_SCOPE). This relationship works in reverse as well, so you can use it to verify that your tags are properly modifying the various implicit objects. For instance, to check that a tag has mapped a String into the session under the key "hotProductChoice," you could use:

```
tag.doStartTag()//or the appropriate tag lifecycle method
assertNotNull(session.getAttribute("hotProductChoice"));
```

See " Testing Auxiliary Tag Components" for a more involved example.

Testing Body Tags

Tags that perform processing on their body use a BodyContent object to access their page content. BodyContent extends JspWriter and nests within another JspWriter, possibly another BodyContent object. You should keep these facts in mind; they indicate that the BodyContent object contains the *result* of the evaluation of the body, not the unaltered content of the body as it appears on the JSP page. Imagine that one tag nests within another like this:

```
<parent>
  <child/>
</parent>
```

In this situation, *child* is evaluated first and simply writes its output (if any) into the BodyContent object of parent. When *parent* begins execution, its BodyContent object only contains the String results of *child*'s processing. Although the concept may elude immediate understanding, it simplifies the testing of BodyTags. To test a tag that processes its body, simply write some test data into a BodyContent object and pass it to the tag in question. See the section "Working with Nested Tags" for further information.

To obtain a suitable BodyContent, use pageContext.pushBody(). This method returns a new BodyContent object nested within the previous JspWriter. This operation also updates the value of the JspWriter contained in the page scope (available with pageContext.getOut()) to the new BodyContent. Most translated servlets perform the operation like this:

```
out = pageContext.pushBody();
tag.setBodyContent((BodyContent) out);
```

(out is the standard JSP implicit variable.) Let's look at an example.

productLink Tag Example

The productLink tag turns its contents into a hyperlink that points to the product page on the current Web site. The product page requires an id in the request, so the productLink tag accepts an "id" attribute. JSP designers use productLink tags like this:

```
<example:productLink productId="3">
    Check out the Bastion of Fun (TM)
</example:productLink>
```

The tag handler class is simple. It writes out the opening <a> tag, then the content of the tag, and finally the closing </a>. Listing 8.8 displays the code.

```
public class ProductLinkTag extends BodyTagSupport{

  private String productId;

  public void setProductId(String id) {
    this.productId = id;
  }

  public int doAfterBody()throws JspTagException{
    try{
      JspWriter writer = bodyContent.getEnclosingWriter();
      writer.print("<a href='product.jsp?id="+productId+"'>");
      bodyContent.writeOut(writer);
      writer.println("</a>");
    }
    catch(java.io.IOException e){
      throw new JspTagException(e.toString());
    }
    return BodyTag.EVAL_PAGE;
  }
}
```

Listing 8.8 The handler class for the productLink tag.

The test case builds upon the other test cases designed so far. A couple of extra steps are included to deal with the BodyContent object. Here is the setUp() method:

```
public void setUp() throws Exception{
  tag = new ProductLinkTag();
  tag.setPageContext(this.pageContext);
  out = pageContext.pushBody();
  tag.setBodyContent((BodyContent)out);
  /*not necessary since product link tag does not implement it,
    but this is where it would go in the standard lifecycle*/
  tag.doInitBody();
}
```

Once the out variable is converted to an instance of BodyContent and registered with the tag, the test method can write sample content to it to be processed by the tag. In testDoAfterBody(), we print a manifest constant (for easy assertions later) as the body of the tag. Then we call doAfterBody() (which handles the body processing) and verify that it returns SKIP_BODY:

```
public void testDoAfterBody() throws Exception{
  /*violates strict life cycle order...but that should not have any
    effect on this tag, and results in better separation between setUp
and
    test method*/
  tag.setProductId(TEST_PRODUCT_ID);

  out.println(TEST_LINK_TEXT);
  int afterBodyResult = tag.doAfterBody();
  assertEquals(tag.SKIP_BODY, afterBodyResult);
}
```

endDoAfterBody() does most of the assertion work for us. First define the signature that uses HttpUnit's WebResponse, and then we use the convenience method getLinkWith(String) on WebResponse to search for the link with the text we specified earlier. If the search succeeds, we verify that the "href" attribute of the link indeed points to the product page:

```
/*using HttpUnit's WebResponse*/
public void endDoAfterBody(WebResponse resp)throws Exception{
 WebLink link = resp.getLinkWith(TEST_LINK_TEXT);
  assertNotNull(link);
  String pointsTo = link.getURLString();
  assertEquals(TEST_LINK_TARGET, pointsTo);
}
```

Testing Iteration Tags

The iteration tag lifecycle specified by JSP 1.2 can be roughly represented with the following boilerplate code (ignoring extra stages that might occur because the tag might also be a BodyTag):

```
if(tag.doStartTag() != SKIP_BODY){
  do{
    /*body processing*/
  }while(tag.doAfterBody() == EVAL_BODY_AGAIN);
}
/*evaluate doEndTag*/
```

To test an iteration tag, all we have to do is replicate this type of loop in a test method. If possible, we should also attempt to verify each lifecycle method in isolation. For instance, if the tag stops iterating after a certain variable in the page scope reaches a certain value, we could design a test method to verify that this was the case:

```
public void testAfterBodyConditions(){
  pageContext.setAttribute("shouldStop", new Boolean(true));
  assertEquals(tag.SKIP_BODY, tag.doAfterBody());
}
```

However, the boundary conditions of the loop may depend on an unexposed internal state. Although the tag under test can be modified to expose state, doing so may violate encapsulation. In these cases, the best option is to re-create the entire loop and verify that the tag body was processed the expected number of times.

Repeat Tag Example

We use this method to verify the behavior of a simple repeat tag. The tag takes a single attribute, "repetitions", which governs the number of times the tag body repeats without modification. This is how the repeat tag might appear in a JSP:

```
<%int count = 0;%>
<example:repeat repetitions="3">
    <%count++;%>
    Some content: <%=count%>
</example:repeat>
```

Listing 8.9 shows the code for the handler class.

```
public class RepeatTag extends javax.servlet.jsp.tagext.BodyTagSupport{

  private int repetitions;
  private int count;

  public void setRepetitions(String repetitions) {
    this.repetitions = Integer.parseInt(repetitions);
  }

  public void doInitBody(){
    /*doStartTag dicatates that the tag body will always be processed at
     *least once.
     */
    count = 1;
  }

  public int doStartTag(){
    if(repetitions > 0){
      return EVAL_BODY_INCLUDE;
    }
```

Listing 8.9 The handler class for the repeat tag. (continues)

```
    return SKIP_BODY;
  }

  public int doAfterBody(){
    if(++count < repetitions){
      return EVAL_BODY_AGAIN;
    }
    return SKIP_BODY;
  }
}
```

Listing 8.9 The handler class for the repeat tag.

Testing an iteration tag requires no special setup (beyond that required for any custom tag). First we verify that doStartTag() will go forward only if the number of repetitions has been set to a number greater than zero:

```
public void testDoStartTag() {
  tag.setRepetitions("0");
  int result = tag.doStartTag();
  assertEquals(tag.SKIP_BODY, result);
  tag.setRepetitions("2");
  result = tag.doStartTag();
  assertEquals(tag.EVAL_BODY_INCLUDE, result);
}
```

The second test method will validate the tag's behavior in the standard iteration loop:

```
public void testDoAfterBody() throws Exception {
  tag.setRepetitions("3");
  int count = 0;
  do{
    count++;
    out.print("Some content: " + count);
  }while(tag.doAfterBody() == tag.EVAL_BODY_AGAIN);
  assertEquals(3, count);
}
```

Before anything else, testDoAfterBody() sets the tag's repetitions attribute to a reasonable value. Then the method declares a local count variable to keep track of the number of loop executions. After running the do-while loop (terminated by the return value of doAfterBody()), the method verifies that the loop body has executed the expected number of times. The out.print(...) statement was inserted for illustration; because the tag includes the body without performing any tag-specific processing, it does not matter what goes on within the loop—only that it exists.

Server-side Assertion Facilities

As of Cactus 1.1, (Cactus 1.2 is still pre-release at the time of wrting, and this area has not been finalized), the inspection of the response sent to the client was the best facility available for inspecting the output of custom tags. After some experience with the classes surrounding custom tags, we can see that there may be another way.

Another Use for BodyContent

JspTestCase provides an instance variable out that corresponds to the JSP implicit variable of the same name. out is an instance of JspWriter, which declares no methods that allow the inspection of the underlying buffer. However, the BodyContent class (which extends JspWriter) explicitly allows the inspection of it contents. Because of its subclass relationship to JspWriter, the contents of out in JspTestCase could be replaced with a BodyContent object without necessitating changes in usage. Doing so would allow us to inspect the response without waiting to return the output to the client. For example, the out object could be examined and cleared after each call to a doAfterBody() method, thereby making the test method more isolated.

We can obtain a BodyContent object through a call to pageContext.pushBody(). As we saw in the "Testing Body Tags" section, this method call also updates the out object stored in the pageContext object. Therefore, any custom tags that, for instance, call pageContext.getOut() will automatically be using the new BodyContent object instead of the standard JspWriter. Further calls to pushBody() will function transparently. The only problem so far relates to the buffered nature of the BodyContent object. Because BodyContent was intended for use with tags that might never want to write the contents to the client, using pushBody() to replace the out instance variable in JspTestCase prevents any data written to out from reaching the response unless special steps are taken.

To write the data to the underlying servlet response, we use BodyContent.writeOut(Writer) to copy the buffer of the BodyContent object into the specified writer. We can combine this with BodyContent's getEnclosingWriter() method to print the BodyContent's data back into the original JspWriter object. A typical usage pattern might go something like this:

```
private BodyContent tempOut;

public void setUp(){
  tag = new TestedTag();
  tag.setPageContext(pageContext);
  tag.setSomeAttribute("testValue");
```

```
    tempOut = pageContext.pushBody();
  }

  public void testDoStartTag()throws Exception {
    /*produces some output based on attribute set above*/
    tag.doStartTag();
    String result = tempOut.getString();
    assertTrue(result.indexOf("testValue ") > -1);
  }

  public void tearDown()throws Exception{
    tempOut.writeOut(tempOut.getEnclosingWriter());
  }
```

If you are testing nested tags, you need to watch out for the creation of new BodyContent objects with subsequent calls to PageContext.pushBody(). In the examples thus far, we have omitted calls to PageContext.popBody() because after the test method finishes executing, no code remains to make use of the writers. However, if you adopt this trick to simplify your assertions, you will have to be sure that each *further* pushBody() call is balanced by a popBody() after the test finishes using the BodyContent object.

Working with Nested Tags

The JSP specification allows tags to be nested within other tags. Most of the time, nested tags operate independently. However, tag designers can build child tags that interact with their enclosing parent tags. (The relationship does not work the other way; enclosing tags cannot act on their children unless they communicate through shared page data.) To adequately test this complex situation, we need two sets of tests. First, simulate the effects of the child on the parent and verify that the parent behaves as expected. Second, test the child tag to be sure that the parent tag provides access to the correct services or data. This section will walk through both sets of tests.

Two tags form the basis for our example: parent and child. The parent element (taking a single attribute, "name") simply prints out a message stating its name and whether it contains children. The child elements each obtain the name of their parent and print a message declaring who they belong to. The tag might be used like this:

```
<example:parent name="Papa Smurf">
    <example:child/>
    <example:child/>
</example:parent>
```

The generated output would be:

```
Child tag nested within parent named 'Papa Smurf'. Child tag nested
within parent named 'Papa Smurf'. Parent tag named 'Papa Smurf' does
contain children.
```

The tag handler classes (minus class imports) in shown in Listing 8.10.

```
public class ParentTag extends TagSupport{

  private boolean containsChildren;
  private String name;

  public boolean getContainsChildren() {
    return containsChildren;
  }

  public void setContainsChildren(boolean containsChildren) {
    this.containsChildren = containsChildren;
  }

  public String getName() {
    return name;
  }

  public void setName(String name) {
    this.name = name;
  }

  public int doAfterBody() throws JspTagException{
    JspWriter out = pageContext.getOut();
    try{
      out.print("Parent tag named '" + name + "' does ");
      if(!containsChildren){
        out.print("not ");
      }
      out.print("contain children.");
    }
    catch(java.io.IOException e){
      throw new JspTagException(e.toString());
    }
    return this.SKIP_BODY;
  }

}
```

Listing 8.10 Tag handler classes for a pair of nested tags. (continues)

```
public class ChildTag extends TagSupport{
  public int doStartTag() throws JspTagException{
    JspWriter out = pageContext.getOut();
    ParentTag parent =
      (ParentTag)TagSupport.findAncestorWithClass(this, ParentTag.class);

    parent.setContainsChildren(true);
    String parentName= parent.getName();
    try{
      out.print("Child tag nested within parent named '" +
                parentName+"'.");
    }
    catch(java.io.IOException e){
      throw new JspTagException(e.toString());
    }
    return this.EVAL_BODY_INCLUDE;
  }
}
```

Listing 8.10 Tag handler classes for a pair of nested tags.

The child tag interacts with the parent by setting a property in the parent tag (containsChildren). Depending on the value of containsChildren, the message printed from ParentTag's doAfterBody() method will differ. Instead of attempting to test a full nested interaction right off the bat, we begin by testing this interaction. Listing 8.11 shows the setUp() method (the test uses the BodyContent trick discussed in the section "Server-side Assertion Facilities") and two test methods (each exercising a different state of the ParentTag class).

```
public void setUp(){
  tag = new ParentTag();
  tag.setPageContext(pageContext);
  tag.setName("testName");
  tempOut = pageContext.pushBody();
}

public void testNoKids()throws Exception {
  tag.setContainsChildren(false);
  tag.doAfterBody();
  String result = tempOut.getString();
  /*should print "does not contain children"*/
  assertTrue(result.indexOf("not") > -1);
}
```

Listing 8.11 setUp() and two test methods for the ParentTag class. (continues)

```
public void testKids()throws Exception{
  tag.setContainsChildren(true);
  tag.doAfterBody();
  String result = tempOut.getString();
  /*should print "does contain children"*/
  assertTrue(result.indexOf("not") == -1);
}
```

Listing 8.11 setUp() and two test methods for the ParentTag class.

Once we verify the basic mechanism of interaction, we can move on to the ChildTag class. The setUp() method performs some extra steps:

```
private ChildTag tag;
private ParentTag p;
private BodyContent tempOut;

public void setUp()throws Exception{
  startParentTag();
  tag = new ChildTag();
  tag.setPageContext(this.pageContext);
  tag.setParent(p);

  /*the BodyContent trick*/
  tempOut = pageContext.pushBody();
}

public void startParentTag() throws Exception{
  p = new ParentTag();
  p.setPageContext(this.pageContext);
  p.setName("test parent name");
  p.doStartTag();
}
```

As you can see, setUp() creates both a ParentTag and a ChildTag class. setUp() instantiates and initializes ParentTag first, including a call to doStartTag() (which remains the default implementation in this case). Once setUp() has reached the point in parent tag's lifecycle where its body would be processed, it creates the child tag and sets p (the instantiated ParentTag object) as the child tag's parent. ChildTag now awaits testing.

The test method calls doStartTag() (the only implemented lifecycle method) on the child and then checks the containsChildren property of the parent tag—tag.doStartTag() should have changed the property to "true":

```
public void testDoStartTag() throws Exception{
  tag.doStartTag();
  /*child's doStartTag method should have modified the parent's
    containsChildren property.
```

```
        */
       assertTrue(p.getContainsChildren());
       String outputOfDoStartTag = tempOut.getString();
       assertEquals("Child tag nested within parent named '"+ p.getName()+"'.",
                    outputOfDoStartTag);
    }
```

Assuming that this first assertion passes, testDoStartTag() uses the BodyContent trick (see the section "Server-side Assertion Facilities") to obtain the output from the child tag. The test method uses a call to assertEquals() to verify that the output contains the name of the parent tag and is formatted correctly.

Having simulated the effects of the child tag upon the parent and also verified that the child tag was finding and using the parent tag correctly, our test cases cover most of the territory available to them. However, nested tag interactions can get very complex. Creating several actual-use examples in a real JSP and then examining the translated servlet yields valuable insight into how to model tag interactions in a test context.

Testing Auxiliary Tag Components

The definition of a custom tag extends beyond the behavior of the tag handler class. In order to test a custom tag thoroughly, we need test cases to verify that the tag library descriptor entry and/or the TagExtraInfo class perform as expected.

TagExtraInfo Classes

The tag element in the tag library descriptor file contains an optional <tei-class> sub-element. The tei-class element contains the fully qualified name of a subclass of javax.servlet.jsp.tagext.TagExtraInfo. The TagExtraInfo class for a given tag provides two possible services: specifying scripting variables to be defined as part of the tag's execution (with getVariableInfo()) and providing translation-time validation of a tag's attributes (with isValid()). Both methods surrender to testing without complaint; in fact, TagExtraInfo tests do not need to be run in the container. Both methods depend on a single TagData object, which you can construct manually from a Hashtable or Object[][] (the TagData object represents name-value pairs for all of the attributes used in a given tag at translation time). Simply construct a TagData object and pass it to the method, then assert that the result is as expected.

Tag Library Descriptor Testing

Because deployment descriptors are declarative specifications of container behavior rather than executable program code, they evade most Java-based unit testing techniques. However, creating a simple JSP that uses a tag in its intended manner provides a common-sense check that no major errors have crept in. Making this sanity-check JSP part of a unit testing suite takes a small amount of effort and provides important test coverage. If you need to change the deployment descriptor to support a new feature, these JSP-based tests allow rapid discovery of any incompatibilities. Let's examine JSP-based descriptor tests by applying them to a common problem in tag testing: verifying the creation of a scripting variable.

Scripting variables can be defined by a tag either in its TagExtraInfo class or in the tag's <variable> sub-elements in the tag library descriptor (in JSP 1.2). Both methods of defining a scripting variable rely on the container to generate the necessary servlet code. For example, the custom tag var specifies VarTei as its TagExtraInfo class in the deployment descriptor. According to the JUnit test, VarTei behaves correctly: specifying a single scripting variable var, to be newly created and available from the beginning of the tag onwards. To test the container-generation process, we give the container a JSP that depends upon the presence of var. Here is what such a page might look like:

```
<%@page import="junit.framework.Assert"%>
<%@taglib uri="WEB-INF/example.tld" prefix="example"%>
<example:var/>
<%
  Assert.assertNotNull(var);
  Assert.assertEquals("foo", var);
%>
```

If the container does not create var correctly, the attempt to access it in the scriptlet will cause a compilation error. So, this JSP constitutes a test. The value of the scripting variable (set in the VarTag handler class with pageContext.-setAttribute("var", "foo")) is verified with assertions called directly from junit.framework.Assert. These assertions round out this sanity test, but we sense it's a bad idea to put *too* many assertions in the JSP-based test—it's probably better to use actual test cases because of the greater control they afford.

To provide error logging and to make these hybrid tests part of the regular suite, we call the test JSPs from within ordinary Cactus tests. We begin by extending JspTestCase to provide access to the pageContext implicit object. Then, we implement a test method that calls pageContext.include() with an argument specifying the JSP test we wish to run:

```
public void testVarCreate() throws Exception{
  pageContext.include("/var_create.jsp");
}
```

Any uncaught exceptions (including compilation exceptions!) are propagated up the stack to the test method where they are trapped and logged by the Cactus error handler.

NOTE

This method of verifying the tag library descriptor may be useful, but it may also possess some problems. We don't guarantee perfect results, and you may need to pursue a variety of strategies to ensure that the container does not use older JSP translations. (For instance, occasionally you need restart some versions of Resin to ensure that it will retranslate JSPs.) That being said, we feel more comfortable with a unit test verifying that our code works as intended—and creating a sample JSP that illustrates possible tag configurations fulfills one of the most important functions of automated tests: serving as executable documentation.

Case Study: The Pet Store with Custom Tags

So far, we have explored the access Cactus provides to the servlet container and the ways in which Cactus test cases can be leveraged to unit- or integration-test various J2EE components. Now it's time to put the rubber to the road and see how Cactus-based unit tests can verify our code and speed the refactoring process on our sample application. We will use Cactus to test a custom tag we develop to simplify the JSPs used in the front end of the AAA Pets online store.

The Business Need

Let's suppose that the developers who designed the JSPs for the front end of the AAA pet store were more concerned with getting a site up and running than with design. Now, several months after the initial launch, the AAA marketing director has authorized a redesign. Furthermore, in the time since development began, our shop has adopted Extreme Programming. As a result, our XP coach reminds us constantly of the value of adding unit tests to the existing code. The original JSPs contain a lot of logic, and a few near-disasters have reminded us of the fragility of untested code. This week, we are scheduled to refactor the JSPs to use custom tags, separating some of the logic so that we can test it.

Finding a Starting Point

We begin looking over the JSPs. The J2EE blueprints available on Sun's Web site suggest that, "JSP pages should contain no code written in the Java programming language (that is, no expressions or scriptlets). Anything a JSP page needs to do with Java code can be done from a custom tag" (http://java.sun.com/j2ee/blueprints/web_tier/qanda/index.html). We ponder that for a while and begin to boggle at the enormity of our task. We decide to keep the blueprint's suggestion as our eventual goal and tackle a small chunk at first. After an examination of the main navigation pages, we find a for loop whose basic structure appears on two separate pages. The loop iterates through all the subcategories available in the current category and prints out a link to each one. Listing 8.12 displays the code fragment from header.jsp.

```
<%
  Category category = categorySystem.getCurrentCategory();
  Subcategory [] subcategories = category.getSubcategories();
  for (int index=0; index < subcategories.length; index++){
    Subcategory subcategory = subcategories[index];
 %>
  <td width="20%" align="center">
    <a href="subcategory.jsp?id=<%=subcategory.getId()%>">
      <%=subcategory.getName()%>
    </a>
    <br />
  </td>
<%}%>
```

Listing 8.12 A for loop using scriptlets in the old header.jsp.

subcategory.jsp creates a similar loop (the contents do not include table cells) that displays the subcategories in the sidebar. The IterationTag interface provides easy hooks into just this sort of functionality. This seems a likely place to begin our refactoring, and we sit down to work.

The TestCase

We begin by writing the test first, a practice recommended by XP that helps us think through the problem domain before attempting to solve it. "What will our custom tag have to accomplish?" we ask ourselves. We decide that the custom tag should assume responsibility for obtaining a valid list of subcategories. Then, the tag should step through the subcategories and print the body of the tag once for each member of the array. However, we need to vary some elements of the body on each pass. The old solution does this by making method calls in scriptlets:

```
<%=subcategory.getName()%>
```

We decide to move this Java code into the custom tag and create a couple of temporary variables that exist strictly within the body of the tag and change their values with each body iteration.

The setUp() Method

To test custom tags, we extend JspTestCase. Then, we proceed with the setup code that is common to almost all custom tags: creating the tag, setting its page context, and calling doStartTag(): (We don't know that we'll need doStartTag for sure, but doStartTag oftern serves to initialize the "first pass" of the tag—we guess we'll need it in a minute.)

```
private SubcategoryListTag tag;
private CategorySystem categorySystem;

public void setUp()throws Exception{
  categorySystem = new CategorySystem();
  session.setAttribute("categorySystem", categorySystem);
  tag = new SubcategoryListTag();
  tag.setPageContext(this.pageContext);
  tag.doStartTag();
}
```

In addition to the tag set up we map an instance of the CategorySystem model object into the session. We allow this dependency because most of the existing pages do this already using a <jsp:useBean> tag.

The Tag Loop

Now that our tag is ready to run, we need to write code that verifies its entire lifecycle. Because we know it will iterate, we type in the standard tag do-while loop used by most servlet containers:

```
do{

}while(tag.doAfterBody() == tag.EVAL_BODY_AGAIN);
```

Now we ask, "What do we need to test?" We must check if we have created our scripting variables, and according to the JSP specification, these variables are made available to the container by nesting them in one of the accessible scopes (usually the PAGE scope). This approach seems promising, so we code to pull the variables from where they should have been placed by the tag:

```
do{
  pageContext.getAttribute("subCatId");
  pageContext.getAttribute("subCatName");
}while(tag.doAfterBody() == tag.EVAL_BODY_AGAIN);
```

"But how," we wonder, "will we verify that these objects are correct?" We could set up an array that parallels the one used by the loop, and we could even get the data the same way. This seems like a good verification, so we implement this logic and add a final check to verify that the tag iterates once per element in the array (lest the test terminate prematurely). Now that we've completed the test, it's time to write the actual code. Listing 8.13 contains the final version of the test method.

```
public void testList() throws Exception{
  Category category = categorySystem.getCurrentCategory();
  Subcategory [] subcategories = category.getSubcategories();
  int count = 0;
  do{
    Subcategory subCat = subcategories[count++];

    int id = subCat.getId();
    assertEquals(""+id, pageContext.getAttribute("subCatId"));

    String name = subCat.getName();
    assertEquals(name, pageContext.getAttribute("subCatName"));
  }
  while (tag.doAfterBody() == tag.EVAL_BODY_AGAIN);

  /*tag has repeated as many times as there are array members*/
  assertEquals(count,subcategories.length);
}
```

Listing 8.13 A test method that exercises a full run of our proposed tag.

Writing the Tag

Writing the test simplifies writing the code. We have the following facts clearly in mind:

- We must set up the initial tag state in doStartTag(), including retrieval of the data and preparation for the first evaluation.
- The container calls doAfterBody() once after each body evaluation to determine whether to continue processing.

We begin to brainstorm about code that fulfills these criteria. An iterator would keep track of our position, and it has a handy hasNext() method that we can use to determine the return value for doAfterBody(). Using this utility class prevents us from having to maintain an internal count and do numeric comparisons.

My first impulse had been to use the array without the Iterator, since that's what the original JSP did. Because we have a test to validate the class, we don't feel so bound to the previous implementation. Already the tests have helped. We set to work.

We write a private helper method to initialize our iterator (stored in an instance member variable). Aside from some exception checking, the method is straightforward: First we pull a CategorySystem object from the session scope using pageContext. Then, we retrieve an array of Subcategories to iterate over. Finally, we use the static method asList() from java.util.Arrays to turn the array into a java.util.List, and from there we get its iterator. The code for the helper method is shown in Listing 8.14.

```
private Iterator iter;

public int doStartTag() throws JspTagException{
  initializeIterator();
  if(!iter.hasNext()){
    return SKIP_BODY;
  }

  updatePageVariables();
  return EVAL_BODY_INCLUDE;
}

private void initializeIterator() throws JspTagException{
  CategorySystem categorySystem =
    (CategorySystem) pageContext.getAttribute("categorySystem",
                                              pageContext.SESSION_SCOPE);
  if(categorySystem == null){
    throw new JspTagException("categorySystem not found in session");
  }

  Category category = categorySystem.getCurrentCategory();
  Subcategory [] subcategories = null;
  try{
    subcategories = category.getSubcategories();
  }
  catch(Exception e){
    throw new JspTagException("subcategories cannot be retrieved: " + e);
  }
```

Listing 8.14 A helper method retrieves an iterator view of Subcategories. (continues)

```
    //iter is an instance variable.
    iter = Arrays.asList(subcategories).iterator();
}
```

Listing 8.14 A helper method retrieves an iterator view of Subcategories.

We use another private helper method to update the scripting variables in the pageContext, and we use Iterator.hasNext() to determine the return value of doAfterBody() (see Listing 8.15).

```
public int doAfterBody(){
  if(iter.hasNext()){
    updatePageVariables();
    return EVAL_BODY_AGAIN;
  }
  return SKIP_BODY;
}

private void updatePageVariables(){
  Subcategory subCat = (Subcategory)iter.next();
  /*new values repalce previous ones, if any*/
  pageContext.setAttribute("subCatId", String.valueOf(subCat.getId()));
  pageContext.setAttribute("subCatName", subCat.getName());
}
```

Listing 8.15 doAfterBody() and updatePageVariables() complete the tag.

Now all we have to do is build and run the tests. We discover that they all pass! Next, we ask ourselves, "Have we tested everything that could possibly break?" We haven't put the tag into its native JSP context yet, and until we do we can't be sure of it. We whip up a one-tag JSP to demonstrate use and verify that our tag library descriptor also works. We use the method outlined in section "Tag Library Descriptor Testing" earlier in this chapter—using pageContext.include() to load and process the JSP. Listing 8.16 gives the test method from the JspTest-Case as well as the test JSP itself.

```
/*test method from Catus test case*/
public void testListWithJsp() throws Exception{
  pageContext.include("subcategory_list_test.jsp");
}

/**** subcategory_list_test.jsp ****/
```

Listing 8.16 A simple JSP validates that all the pieces fit together. (continues)

```
<%@taglib uri="WEB-INF/petstore-taglib.tld" prefix="petstore"%>

<petstore:subcategoryList>
  Name = <%= subCatName%>.<br>
  ID = <%= subCatId %>
</petstore:subcategoryList>
```

Listing 8.16 A simple JSP validates that all the pieces fit together.

The error message Cactus dumps when we run the improved test reveals that we never wrote the tag library descriptor entry! (Unit tests are great for catching coarse errors as well as subtle ones.) We quickly write the deployment descriptor entry. See Listing 8.17 for the code.

```
<tag>
  <name>subcategoryList</name>
  <tagclass>xptoolkit.petstore.tag.SubcategoryListTag</tagclass>
  <info>
    Iterates over all of the available subcategories. Provides two
    nested variables, "subCatName" and "subCatId" corresponding to
   same attributes of current subcategory.
  </info>
  <bodycontent>JSP</bodycontent>
  <variable>
    <name-given>subCatId</name-given>
    <declare>true</declare>
    <!-- default is nested -->
  </variable>
  <variable>
    <name-given>subCatName</name-given>
    <declare>true</declare>
    <!-- default is nested -->
  </variable>
</tag>
```

Listing 8.17 The tag library descriptor entry for our new tag.

Once we verify that our code passes all our automated tests, we begin adding the tag to our JSPs. Here is the end result of one such replacement:

```
<petstore:subcategoryList>
        <a href="subcategory.jsp?id=<%= subCatId%>"><%= subCatName %></a>
        <br>
</petstore:subcategoryList>
```

One minor issue crops up while we are manually verifying that the pages do indeed still work (in a way, we are testing our tests). The variable names we have defined inside the subcategoryList tag conflict with other variables in the JSPs. We make the change (a very minor one), run our tests, and redeploy. Now all the modified pages (along with our tag code) have become production candidates. Because our tests let an error through, however, we are not content. We decide to add the link-checking spider (developed in the Chapter 9, "Functional Testing with HttpUnit") to the suite of tests that are run with each build. I concur, and we add functional testing to our list of tasks.

Review of the Case Study

During this refactoring episode, we pulled code out of JSPs (the view in an MVC architecture) and encapsulated it in JSP custom tags. In the process, we made portions of the site's logic amenable to testing. This result represents a victory. Every piece of code that is paired with a unit test is a safe piece of code—one that you're not afraid to touch and redesign. Would we have written these tests without Cactus? Maybe not. Faced with mocking up portions of the servlet specification (and JSP, and custom tag specifications to boot!), even the most dedicated programming pair might have released their inner pig and relied upon total visual inspection. Not only do we have better code for the future, but the test helped us write our tag today. Because we were forced to think through what defined a successful tag execution, we were able to meet that definition all the more rapidly.

Summary

This chapter examined the importance of in-container integration testing and the role the Cactus framework plays in implementing it. Cactus enables Extreme Programming on the J2EE platform by providing tests access to the inner workings of a J2EE container. By doing so, Cactus allows and encourages scores of unit tests that might not otherwise have been writtenThe test cases it enables are often those that most need to be run—tests of code that intertwines with container services. Also, because it allows access to the real thing rather than Mock Objects or stub framework, you can gain valuable insight into your container as well as into your application. With Cactus, when you feel tempted to grouse about the application server, you can write a quick test case to prove yourself wrong (or right!). Personally, we couldn't live without Cactus—unit tests of server-side code should be easy to write, and Cactus makes that a reality.

CHAPTER 9

Functional Testing with HttpUnit

This chapter explains the techniques for performing functional testing of Web applications with the HttpUnit framework. The chapter opens with a consideration of the role of functional testing in XP; it then explains how to use the HttpUnit tool. The chapter concludes with a case study covering the development of a link-checking spider using HttpUnit.

Why Functional Testing?

HttpUnit is not unit testing at all. HttpUnit more closely approximates functional testing, or black-box testing. Web application tests written using HttpUnit do not test *pieces* of the application code but rather query the Web server externally and examine the responses received. Extreme Programming does not usually focus on this sort of testing because of its inherent complexities. Testing an entire Web application can be a daunting task; many different combinations of user behavior exist, and attempting to replicate them all seems difficult. Faced with the challenge of writing code that verifies each possible permutation of "The system could not process your request because…," programmers will hide out in the nearest dark room and attempt to port Linux to the Sega Dreamcast instead. So XP focuses on unit testing—testing small, manageable pieces of code so that each building block of the system is verified as being good.

However, functional testing holds an important place in Extreme Programming. XP stresses that functional tests are written for (and largely *by*) the customer so that they receive high-level feedback about the state of the system. Because functional tests verify the whole system, they can catch subtle bugs that emerge only in a close-to-production environment (server configuration issues, subsystem-interaction bugs, user-experience issues, and so on). As a system matures (and XP says that the natural state of a project is in deployment), it becomes more possible (and necessary) to devote time to ensuring that the system performs as expected. Automated functional tests relieve someone (even, gasp!, a developer) of the grim duty of manually inspecting unchanged areas of the site before a new build is released to production.

Furthermore, in a Web environment, the line between unit and functional testing blurs. Because each request-response cycle is somewhat atomic, a page view can be treated as a "unit" of code. Testing that sales_report.jsp returns a view of sales reports is a legitimate verification of a component. Also, when using technologies such as JSP, testing the raw HTML output may be the only useful way to determine whether a component has behaved as expected.

Where to Get HttpUnit

HttpUnit is an open source, automated Web site testing tool created by Russell Gold. HttpUnit is written in Java and is distributed for free on SourceForge at: http://sourceforge.net/projects/httpunit/

Why HttpUnit?

Plenty of functional testing products for Web applications clutter the market. Most of them are aimed at Quality Assurance engineers looking for graphical automation tools. Given that HttpUnit is competing in the same space as all these fine beasts, why should an XP developer turn to HttpUnit?

One obvious answer is price. HttpUnit is an open source API that can be put into place without licensing fees or concerns about software piracy. Another advantage is HttpUnit's simplicity. The HttpUnit classes encapsulate in Java the basic mechanisms of maintaining client state, sending requests, retrieving responses, and following links. In addition, they provide handy shortcut methods to extract meaningful elements from an HTTP response (headers, tables, and so on). That's about all. HTTPUnit offers no proprietary GUI, automated test scheduling, graphical reports, or similar features.

Although these might seem like arguments against the software, they also mean that developers are free to provide their own customized solutions for these areas. For instance, HttpUnit tests could be combined with JUnitPerf's test decorators to provide a quick load-test. In addition, because HttpUnit tests are written in Java, they can be structured in almost any imaginable way. With other testing tools, test choices are limited to those anticipated by the team who wrote the tool. Finally, HttpUnit does not directly extend JUnit—meaning that it can be put to use outside of a testing context (perhaps posting HTTP requests to a remote server from within a Java application).

HttpUnit provides fertile ground on which to build complex test suites; however, this flexibility comes at a price. A typical test case for a Web page that contained a form might be to fill out the form in several wrong ways, verifying that validation worked in each case, and then to fill it out correctly, checking that the appropriate subsequent page was displayed. Writing the Java code to perform this test could become cumbersome, because much of it would be repeated with minor changes (which form fields to fill out, which failure message was returned, and so on). Ideally, testing applications would be developed on top of HttpUnit to address some of these issues. One interesting technique (still in its early stages) is to create XML "scripts" for HttpUnit tests. The script defines which pages were consulted in what order and which assertions were performed on the results. New scripts could be written as new functionality arose, and the test suite would execute one test for each script. One such system has already been developed, based on JXUnit (http://jxunit.sourceforge.net/).

Because much of the value of functional testing comes in its thoroughness and scope (testing every user-visible feature of the whole application), and because the tests cannot be incrementally developed with the same ease as unit tests (many smaller components must be assembled before the test can be written), HttpUnit tests are not as lightweight or critical to XP as other types of tests. However, they can be deployed somewhat incrementally, and the features that HttpUnit provides to aid assertion writing (the ability to easily find hyperlinks in a response, for example) are unparalleled. It's worth considering HttpUnit as a developer if you have to write any assertions against a returned HTML page for any reason or if you need automated functional tests for your Web site and wish to leverage the flexibility of a framework instead of a tool.

HttpUnit vs. Cactus

HttpUnit and Cactus overlap each other's functionality. However, the basic difference is clear: HttpUnit performs functional tests, whereas Cactus performs unit/integration tests. See Chapter 8, "Testing Container Services with Cactus," for a clearer delineation of the frameworks' respective roles, as well as for instructions on how use them together.

HttpUnit Basics

HttpUnit can be thought of as two clusters of functionality:

- A Web client that maintains state and provides the facility to send requests and retrieve responses
- A variety of methods that simplify the verification of response content

The first cluster of functionality allows for the basics of talking to a Web server and is easily explained. The second cluster allows for the unit testing of individual pages. Used together, the clusters can verify complex behavior such as page flow. The rest of this section will explain how to employ the basics of HttpUnit.

WebClient Functionality

HttpUnit's WebClient class, appropriately enough, models a Web client. (Actually, WebClient is an abstract class; WebConversation provides the implementation that test developers will use.) WebClient/WebConversation acts basically like a standard Web browser: It maintains client state—including persistent response headers such as cookies, relative URLs, and frame sets—and allows a user to send requests for specific resources and retrieve the responses.

Natural collaborators with WebConversation are WebRequest and WebResponse. WebRequest (naturally) represents a request to a remote server, and WebResponse encapsulates the reply. Using these classes is simple:

```
WebConversation conversation = new WebConversation();
WebRequest simpleRequest =
    new GetMethodWebRequest("http://httpunit.sourceforge.net/");
WebResponse response = conversation.getResponse(simpleRequest);
```

Note that GetMethodWebRequest is a subclass of the abstract class WebRequest (specifically one that uses HTTP GET). The last two lines occur so often that WebConversation implements a convenience method to shorten them into one line:

```
WebResponse response =
    conversation.getResponse("http://httpunit.sourceforge.net/");
```

Building on these core classes, HttpUnit provides the facility to follow links contained in WebResponses:

```
WebLink link = response.getLinkWith("automated web site testing");
WebRequest request = link.getRequest();
response = conversation.getResponse(request);
```

Note that the text searched for in getLinkWith is the clickable text, not the value of the "href" attribute. Also, getLinkWith will return the first link that contains the matching text. HttpUnit provides other methods for link searching; see Chapter 16, "HttpUnit API Reference," for details.

Response Inspection and Multiple Pages

Requesting and retrieving pages is great—but how do you use HttpUnit to verify that the responses are in order? Several methods on the WebResponse object are designed to allow easy inspection of the response. These run the gamut from the quick and dirty (return the response as text with response.getText()) to the specific (find a table with response.getTableWithSummary()) to the ultra-powerful (get the XML DOM for the HTML page with response.getDOM()). The results of these methods can be used in combination with JUnit assertions to check that the requested pages are as expected.

The following example introduces a fully working functional Web test. You can download the JSPs and HTML files that serve as the application under test, as well as the test itself, from the book's Web site at www.RickHightower.com/JavaXP. The folder on this chapter contains a short read-me file describing how to download and set up the example code. The component under test is the annual sales report page (presumably generated dynamically from the database). Because sales reports are naturally sensitive matters, a login page protects the page. To test this component, the test developer might decide that the following facts should be verified:

Login

- The sales report page will redirect to the login page if the user is not logged in.
- The login page will redirect to the private page if filled out correctly.
- The login page will display a message if the username and/or password are entered incorrectly.

Sales Report Page

- The sales report page will contain two tables: projected and current sales.
- Each table will contain dollar amounts representing the sales for a given year.
- The sales report page will contain a list of the board of directors.

Feedback

- The feedback form on the bottom of each page is structured correctly.
- The feedback form submits correctly.

It's easy to see how many different testable facts can be contained in a relatively simple set of user actions. This is only natural, and it makes thorough functional testing somewhat daunting. Still, the task of functional testing with HttpUnit can be made easier with good design. The first step is to try to break down the testable facts into small groups that can be unit tested.

For this example, the entire test will be contained inside a JUnit TestCase (see Chapter 7, "Unit Testing with JUnit," if you are unfamiliar with its functionality). Each of the groups of facts will be verified with its own test method—for example, testLogin(). The setUp() method will initialize the instance variable conversation with a new WebConversation to avoid having to create one in each test method.

Login Testing

The test method for the login page will verify the testable fact summarized under "Login" in the previous section. The test simulates the following page flow: A user attempts to access a private page. She is redirected to the login page and fills it out incorrectly. Her login is processed, and the application takes her back to the login page, displaying an error message. Finally she logs in correctly and arrives at the private page. Listing 9.1 contains the code for login testing.

```
public void setUp(){
  conversation = new WebConversation();
}

private WebResponse goToPrivatePage() throws Exception{
  /*try to get to a protected page*/
  return conversation.getResponse(
      "http://localhost:8080/examples/private.jsp");
}

public void testLogin() throws Exception{
  WebResponse response = this.goToPrivatePage();
  /*verify that we are at the login page*/
  assertLoginPage(response);
```

Listing 9.1 Login test code (part of a larger TestCase). (continues)

```
    /*try to login with a bad username and password*/
    response = login(response, "xxx", "notAPassword");
    assertLoginPage(response);

    /*check that an error message has been displayed*/
    String pageStr = response.getText();
    assertTrue(pageStr.indexOf("Password or User name not correct.")>-1);

    /*login correctly*/
    response = login(response, "user", "muffinWaste77");
    assertTrue(!response.getTitle().equals("Login"));
  }

  public void assertLoginPage(WebResponse response)throws Exception{
    /*
    page title is often a quick verification that the correct page is
    being examined.
    */
    assertEquals("redirected successfully to login",
                 "Login", response.getTitle());
  }

  public WebResponse login(WebResponse loginPage, String userName,
                           String pass) throws Exception{
    /* since the forms are not named, get the first form on the page */
   WebForm form = loginPage.getForms()[0];

    /*Get the request from the form*/
    WebRequest loginRequest = form.getRequest();

    /*set the user name and password*/
    loginRequest.setParameter("userName", userName);
    loginRequest.setParameter("password", pass);

    /*return the response for the login*/
    return conversation.getResponse(loginRequest);
  }
```

Listing 9.1 Login test code (part of a larger TestCase).

Notice that Listing 9.1 breaks the code into four separate methods (in addition to setUp). login() and goToPrivatePage() were originally inlined. After we began work on the other two tests (which needed similar tasks performed), we devised separate methods to avoid code duplication (one of the cardinal rules of code design in XP). Eventually, as the testing application grew, methods such as these would probably find a home in a separate utility class. Another note on design: Almost all the methods in this TestCase declare Exception in the throws clause. HttpUnit classes declare some exceptions that are somewhat difficult to deal with (SAXException, IOException, and MalformedURLException). In most cases there is nothing that a test can do about the underlying cause, aside from bringing it to a developer's attention. Therefore, it makes sense to allow the JUnit framework to handle and log the errors as test failures once they bubble up past the TestCase. Later on, if one of the exceptions becomes meaningful, this behavior can be changed; but for now it makes sense to throw most exceptions through our TestCase.

The first method, goToPrivatePage(), uses HttpUnit functionality covered earlier in the chapter and serves mostly to save some typing. assertLoginPage() simply asserts that the page title retrieved with reponse.getTitle() is equal to "Login". These utility methods (along with login()) support testLogin(), which simulates requesting a protected page, logging in incorrectly, and then logging in correctly and being directed to the originally requested resource.

The login() method submits a login request and introduces form handling in HttpUnit. The first step is to obtain a WebForm from the WebResponse that simulates the login page. This is taken care of with:

```
WebForm form = loginPage.getForms()[0];
```

getForms() returns an array, and we select its first member, corresponding to the first form on the page. WebForm supports the verification of its contents (which we will cover later in this example), but in order to submit it, we first have to get a request that corresponds to a submission of this form:

```
WebRequest loginRequest = form.getRequest();
```

Now, form parameters for the username and password are set in the request:

```
loginRequest.setParameter("userName", userName);
```

Finally, the request is submitted to the server with conversation.getResponse(request).

The testLogin() method contains barely any new HttpUnit code. It uses the utility methods to simulate page flow, and uses JUnit asserts to verify that the results are correct. The only new feature employed is response.getText(), which returns a String equivalent to what View Source would return for the same page in a Web browser. A quick way to check for simple HTML output is to use String.indexOf() to search the returned text for the specified content:

```
String pageStr = response.getText();
assertTrue(pageStr.indexOf("Password or User name not correct.")>-1);
```

Testing the Sales Report Page

Now that the login feature has been tested, we will dive into table manipulation with HttpUnit. The sales report page is laid out (minus the feedback form at the bottom) in one top-level table with two rows (Figure 9.1). The first row contains two other tables, each contained in a cell, that display the report information. We also know that the sales report page has a complex table layout based on figures retrieved from the company database. This means that we cannot assert the specific textual contents of the page, only its general form. We begin by examining the output of the sales report page contained in Listing 9.2.

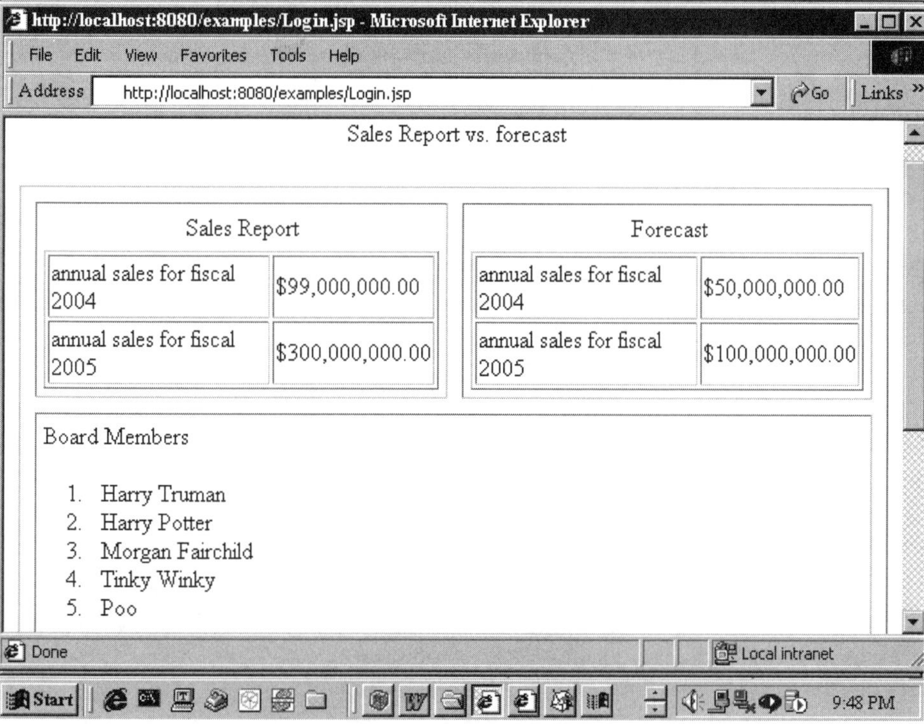

Figure 9.1 The sales report page we are attempting to verify.

```
<!-- head and body tags skipped -->
<table border='true' cellspacing='10' cellpadding='5'>
<caption>
Sales Report vs. forecast
</caption>
<tr>
 <td width="50%">
    <table border='true' title='Sales Report'>
```

Listing 9.2 HTML generated by the sales report page. (continues)

```
        <caption>
            Sales Report
        </caption>
        <tr>
            <td width='40%'>
                annual sales for fiscal 2004
            </td>
            <td width="20%">
                $99,000,000.00
            </td>
        </tr>

        <tr>
            <td width='40%'>
                annual sales for fiscal 2005
            </td>
            <td width='20%'>
                $300,000,000.00
            </td>
        </tr>
    </table>
</td>

<td width="50%">
    <table title='forecast' border="true">
        <caption>
            forecast
        </caption>
        <tr>
            <td width='40%'>
                annual sales for fiscal 2004
            </td>
            <td width='20%'>
                $50,000,000.00
            </td>
        </tr>

        <tr>
            <td width='40%'>
                annual sales for fiscal 2005
            </td>
            <td width='20%'>
                $100,000,000.00
            </td>
        </tr>
    </table>
 </td>
```

Listing 9.2 HTML generated by the sales report page. (continues)

```
</tr>
<tr>
  <td colspan='2'>
    Board Members <br />
    <ol title='Board Members'>
        <li>Harry Truman</li>
        <li>Harry Potter</li>
        <li>Morgan Fairchild</li>
        <li>Tinky Winky</li>
        <li>Poo</li>
    </ol>
    <br/>
    Note that the actual sales are a lot higher than the projected sales.
  </td>
</tr>
</table>
<!--Feedback form follows-->
```

Listing 9.2 HTML generated by the sales report page.

HttpUnit recognizes the importance of tables as a page-structuring tool and gives you several handy tools for interacting with them. This example verifies three facts:

- There will be current and forecast sales report tables.
- Each table will contain sales data for a number of years.
- A list of the Board of Directors will appear on the page.

In order to test the first of these, we need to access each table individually. The WebResponse class has several methods for retrieving tables:

```
public WebTable[] getTables()
public WebTable getTableStartingWith(String text)
public WebTable getTableStartingWithPrefix(String text)
public WebTable getTableWithID(String text)
public WebTable getTableWithSummary(String text)
```

Of these, only getTables() will return an array of the top-level tables on this page. This seems like a good way to narrow the results. However, the getTableWith*XXX*() methods will recurse into tables in search of a match. It would be nice to use one of those methods. The getTableStartingWith*XXX*() methods return tables based on the text of their first (non-empty) cell. These methods do not suit our needs because the two tables begin identically ("Sales report," and "forecast" are contained in the <caption> tag). The other two methods will search for a table based on the "id" and "summary" attributes of the table. However, upon examination of the HTML output, the page designers have included neither attribute in their tables. According to XP's principle of common code ownership, we should change the class that generates this page. If the tables are summarized or given IDs, they are easier to test. In the real world, we would consider this refactoring. For the purposes of our example, we will leave the page design alone in order to explore more of HttpUnit's functionality.

Because the page includes only one top-level table, we go ahead and get it:

```
WebTable topLevelTable = response.getTables()[0];
```

WebTable represents an HTML table and has a method that returns a specific cell: getTableCell(int row, int column). We use this to get the first cell of the first row (which contains the sales report table):

```
TableCell reportCell = topLevelTable.getTableCell(0,0);
```

TableCell is in turn an object representation of an HTML table cell. It shares many of the methods of WebResponse (in fact, they share an interface, HTMLSegment), including the ability to retrieve contained tables. At this point we want to verify that we have two distinct tables, the report and the forecast. Examining the HMTL, we see that the tables are identified only by their captions. Again, if we had summaries or IDs, we could make short work of this problem. However, none exist, and we have no quick way to determine a specific subtag (we could access the HTML DOM, but let's leave that for later in the chapter). So, we decide again to use a quick substring search that verifies the caption exists in the cell at all:

```
String cellStr = cell.asText();
assertTrue(cellStr+ "contained " +caption,cellStr.indexOf(caption)>-1);
```

Now that we have checked to be sure we are seeing the cell containing the correct table, we can get the actual cell and verify its structure:

```
WebTable table = cell.getTables()[0];
this.assertGenericSalesTable(table);//a custom method
```

The assertGenericSalesTable() method uses a for loop to iterate over the contents of one of the sales tables. It also uses WebTable.asText(), which returns the table as a two-dimensional String array. (This is only a convenience, because the same result can be obtained with TableCell.asText()—in fact, WebTable uses TableCell.asText() internally.) Each row in the table is checked—the first cell must start with "annual sales for fiscal," and the second cell must begin with a dollar sign.

Listing 9.3 contains the full code for this portion of the test.

```
/*
  Sets up the sales report page to be checked by
  assertSalesReportPage(WebResponse response)
 */
public void testReportsPage() throws Exception{

  WebResponse response = this.goToPrivatePage();

  /*redirected automatically to login page, so attempt to log in*/
  response = login(response, "user", "muffinWaste77");

  /*now we should be on the sales report page*/
  assertSalesReportPage(response);
}

public void assertSalesReportPage(WebResponse response) throws Exception{
  /*will return null—designers have unhelpfully forgotten to specify
    'summary' attribute!
  */
  //response.getTableWithSummary("Sales Report");

  /*
    Also unusable—both the "Forecast" and "Sales Report" tables
    start with the same cell!
  */
  //response.getTableStartingWith("Annual sales for fiscal 2004");

  WebTable topLevelTable = response.getTables()[0];
  TableCell reportCell = topLevelTable.getTableCell(0,0);
  assertSalesCell("Sales Report", reportCell);
  //WebTable reportTable = reportCell.getTables()[0];
  TableCell forecastCell = topLevelTable.getTableCell(0,1);
  assertSalesCell("Forecast", forecastCell);

  TableCell boardCell = topLevelTable.getTableCell(1,1);
  assertBoardCell(boardCell);
}

public void assertSalesCell(String caption, TableCell cell)throws Exception{
  /*verify the cell contains the caption*/
  String cellStr = cell.asText();
  assertTrue(cellStr+ "contained " +caption,cellStr.indexOf(caption)>-1);
```

Listing 9.3 Sales report test code (part of a larger TestCase). (continues)

```
    /*get the table and verify its structure*/
    WebTable table = cell.getTables()[0];
    this.assertGenericSalesTable(table);
  }

  public void assertGenericSalesTable(WebTable table) throws Exception{
    String[][] tableArray = table.asText();
    for(int i =0; i< tableArray.length; i++){
      assertTrue("row correctly captioned",
              tableArray[i][0].startsWith("annual sales for fiscal "));
      assertTrue("row contains dollar figure",
              tableArray[i][1].startsWith("$"));
    }
  }

  public void assertBoardCell(TableCell cell) throws Exception{
    /*should span 2 columns*/
    assertEquals(2, cell.getColSpan());

    /*
      Turn the cell into text and verify that it contains "Board Members"
    */
    String cellStr = cell.asText();
    assertTrue(cellStr.indexOf("Board Members ") > -1);
  }
```

Listing 9.3 Sales report test code (part of a larger TestCase).

The Feedback Form

At this point, the sales report page is all but verified. Verifying that the board member list exists involves only another substring search through a text rendering of a cell. All that remains in this TestCase is to check on the feedback form at the bottom of the page (Figure 9.2).

To complete our functional test of this component of the Web application, we have to check that the form at the bottom of the page is structured correctly and that it will accept average user input. The page designers have named this form so that it can be retrieved with this simple code:

```
WebForm feedbackForm = response.getFormWithName("feedback");
```

WebForm (naturally) represents an HTML form. If we examine the page's HTML, we can see that this form is laid out internally using a table—this layout should not affect anything we are doing, because WebForm models the form itself, not the exact HTML on which it is based. The first check we can run is

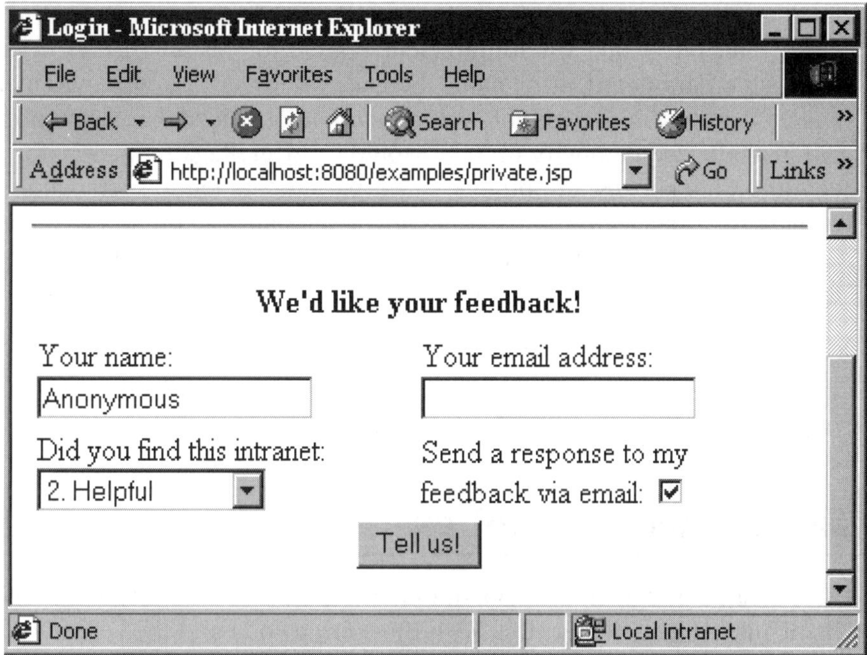

Figure 9.2 The feedback form that appears below every page.

that the form contains all of the possible parameters we expect. First we retrieve the possible parameters with:

```
String[] parameters = feedbackForm.getParameterNames();
```

Then we can check these versus our expectations with a custom assert function:

```
String[] expected = {"name", "email", "reply", "usefulness"};
assertArraysEqual(expected, parameters);
```

Now we can verify that the “usefulness” drop-down box contains the correct parameters using a similar technique:

```
String[] usefulnessValues  = feedbackForm.getOptionValues("usefulness");
String[] expectedValues  = {"1","2","3"};
assertArraysEqual(expectedValues, usefulnessValues);
```

We can also assert that a given parameter has a default value:

```
assertEquals("2", feedbackForm.getParameterValue("usefulness"));
```

Once we have checked on the state of the form in the received page, we can fill it out and submit it. We have already covered the basics of form submission with the login page; only a couple of wrinkles remain undiscussed. First, all form parameters are set with request.setParameter(). Parameters that accept more than one value (multiple select boxes, for instance) can be set with request.setParameter(String name, String[] values). By default, parameters are checked against the acceptable values in the underlying form. Attempting to set the "usefulness" parameter to "600" would yield an IllegalRequestParameterException. Checkboxes and other request parameters can be removed from the request with request.removeParameter(String name). Note that HttpUnit does *not* check whether you are removing a parameter that could not be removed from the browser. The statement

```
feedbackRequest.removeParameter("usefulness");
```

would be just fine by HttpUnit. Once all the request parameters are set, the request can be submitted in the usual manner.

Advanced Topics in HttpUnit

If you have gotten this far in the chapter, you already know enough about HttpUnit to begin developing. With the source code and the reference chapter at your side, you should be able to write some mean Web testing code. The rest of this chapter will be devoted to giving an overview of the remaining issues in the HttpUnit framework and developing a more sophisticated testing program that leverages the power of HttpUnit's Java base. This section covers topics in HttpUnit such as DOM inspection, headers and validation, and HttpUnit's configurable options.

DOM Inspection

HttpUnit provides the ability to inspect an HTML document or part of an HTML document as a DOM. The Document Object Model (DOM) is a standard developed by the World Wide Web Consortium (www.w3.org/DOM/) that treats documents as objects that can be manipulated. DOM was developed to allow programmatic access to data in languages such as XML and HTML. A full discussion of DOM lies outside the scope of this book; if you need a primer, every-Java journal with online archives is sure to have several articles on XML and its two common program interfaces, DOM and SAX (Simple API for XML). What you need to know about DOM and HttpUnit is that HttpUnit uses JTidy—an HTML parser—to turn a server response into an in-memory DOM whose contents can be accessed at random. Almost all of HttpUnit's powerful assertion capabilities (WebResponse.getTables(), for instance) rely on DOM manipulation under the hood. For instance, WebResponse.getLinks() uses

```
NodeList nl = NodeUtils.getElementsByTagName( _rootNode, "a" );
Vector list = new Vector();
for (int i = 0; i < nl.getLength(); i++) {
  Node child = nl.item(i);
  if (isLinkAnchor( child )) {
    list.addElement( new WebLink( _baseURL, _baseTarget, child ) );
  }
}
```

to find all the Nodes (roughly corresponding to tags, in this case) with the name "a" (as in <a href="blah">) in the underlying HTML.

Using the DOMs provided by HttpUnit can be somewhat difficult, simply because DOM programming can be difficult. The DOM API (the Javadocs can be found at www.w3.org/DOM/2000/12/dom2-javadoc/index.html) was designed to be language independent and thus doesn't jibe with Java as well as it might.

JDOM

JDOM, a lightweight API for XML interaction, is available under an Apache-style open source license from www.jdom.org. Its API is significantly more intuitive and Java-like than DOM, and in a book covering top-quality open source tools, it seemed worth mentioning.

Manipulating the HTML DOM can yield information that would otherwise be unavailable for assertion. As an example, let's return to our earlier test of the sales report page. The sales report tables were labeled with captions, an element not specifically searched for or returned by HttpUnit. Let's say that it becomes essential to validate these captions. The following DOM code could find the value of the <caption> element for inspection:

```
/**
 * @param cell A table cell containing a single nested table.
 */
private String findCaption(TableCell cell) throws Exception{
  Node node = cell.getDOM();
  Element elem = (Element)node;
  NodeList listOfCaptions = elem.getElementsByTagName("caption");

  /*presume only 1*/
  Node firstCaption = listOfCaptions.item(0);

  /*contents are actually contained in a child node of the caption
  Node*/
  Node contents = firstCaption.getFirstChild();
  return contents.getNodeValue();
}
```

As you can see, DOM code can get a bit involved. But, on the bright side, our sales report test is now more accurate!

Headers and Cookies

HttpUnit's WebConversation class internally stores all the headers that will be sent to the Web server with each request. Naturally, this storage covers cookies, authentication headers, and various other request headers. In order to set a header for transmission to the server with all future requests, use WebConversations's setHeaderField(String fieldName, String fieldValue) method. Shortcut methods exist for commonly used headers, such as authorization headers: setAuthorization(String userName, String password). Setting a header field to null will remove the header from all subsequent requests.

Cookies are handled slightly differently. WebConversation has methods (getCookieNames() and getCookieValue()) that return all of the cookie's names to be sent as well as an individual cookie's value. addCookie(String name, String value) adds a cookie to the list of cookies to send. Unlike with header fields, there is no way to remove an individual cookie from the list.

As for server-defined cookies, the WebResponse class allows inspection of new cookies through two methods: getNewCookieNames() and getNewCookieValue(). For example, the following code would print all the new cookies set in a Web server response:

```
for(int i =0; i < names.length; i++){
  System.out.print(names[i] + " – ");
  System.out.println(response.getNewCookieValue(names[i]));
}
```

This facility allows verification that the server has tried to set a specific cookie in the response.

Frames

HttpUnit handles frames in a straightforward manner. We give an extensive example on working with frames in the description of the WebClient class in Chapter 16, "HttpUnit API Reference," which won't be reproduced here; however, the brief explanation is that the WebClient stores a Hashtable of frames internally. The contents of a given frame can be accessed by name with

```
WebResponse response = WebClient.getFrameContents("someFrameName")
```

If a test follows a link from within one frame that updates another frame, the response from the WebConversation will be the contents of the target frame (which will also be accessible through getFrameContents).

SSL

HttpUnit can test sites that use Secure Sockets Layer (SSL), but doing so is somewhat involved. The process requires two basic steps: The server must have an SSL certificate installed, and the JVM used by HttpUnit must trust the installed certificate. (Certificates from Verisign or Thawte are automatically trusted.) A number of technical details surround SSL support in Java/HttpUnit, most of which are covered in the SSL FAQ hosted on HttpUnit's SourceForge site (http://httpunit.sourceforge.net/doc/sslfaq.html).

HttpUnitOptions

The HttpUnitOptions class provides a series of static properties that configure the behavior of HttpUnit. HttpUnitOptions provides options that determine whether link searches are case-sensitive, whether to follow page refresh requests automatically, and whether to print headers to the System.out stream as they are sent and received. Chapter 16, "HttpUnit API Reference," contains more detailed information on each of these options. It is worth noting that because these properties are merely static variables, you need to exercise some care in using them in a multithreaded testing environment (such as running JUnitPerf with HttpUnit) if the options are set to conflicting values in different tests.

Technical Limitations

HttpUnit provides much of the functionality of a Web browser from within a Java application. However, a number of things remain outside its purview. JavaScript is an obvious example. There is no way to verify that a JavaScript function will be called upon form submission, that a rollover will happen, and so on. No add-on to HttpUnit is planned to address this issue, although Russel Gold (the framework's primary author) says in the project FAQ, "If you feel ambitious enough to add JavaScript support yourself, I would be happy to accept submissions" (http://httpunit.sourceforge.net/doc/faq.html#javascript).

HttpUnit does not forgive bad HTML. This feature can cause problems when you test pages that display correctly in major browsers but do not strictly adhere to the HTML specification. Frequently, the problem has to do with <form> tags, which must be nested correctly within tables. Unfortunately, the HTML must be corrected to fix this problem, although calling HttpUnitOptions.setParserWarningsEnabled(true) will at least indicate HTML problems encountered during parsing. See the WebForm class documentation in Chapter 16, "HttpUnit API Reference," for details on this problem.

Spider Example

HttpUnit's Java foundations mean that it's possible to devise all sorts of interesting testing applications. The API merely offers objects for test developers to employ at their convenience. In fact, verifying page output from individual requests (as we did with the sales report page in our previous examples) is perhaps the lowest-order use of the framework. The code for verifying three simple pages was over 100 lines long. Writing a test like that could take several hours, especially as you slowly tweak it to account for wrinkles in the underlying site. To quote one developer I worked with, "You could check the output manually in three seconds." Clearly, writing code like that is not the best option. Instead, test developers should seek ways to automatically verify portions of Web applications without manually asserting every single page. The spider example illustrates this approach by attempting to solve a common problem: how to quickly verify that a new site deployment has no major errors.

Spider Development: First Iteration

Our criteria for basic verification of a deployment is that each user-accessible link will display a page without an exception (HTTP code 500 Internal Server Error). HttpUnit helpfully turns these exceptions into HttpInternalErrorExceptions, which will fail tests for us. So, we have a starting point. If we can retrieve a response for every link on the site without an exception, the site must at least be up and running.

Is This a Valid Test?

Checking all the internal links is not a thorough test for most sites because it omits things like user-interaction, customization, correct page sequence (private.jsp should redirect to the login page), and so on. However, imagine a dynamically generated catalog site. The online catalog contains more than 10,000 products. A link-checking spider could automatically verify that all the product pages are at least displaying—something that even the most dedicated tester would be loath to do. Some added logic to verify the general structure of a product display page could provide testing coverage for more than 90 percent of the accessible pages on such a site.

Using HttpUnit's classes, coding such a spider becomes easy. All we need to do is start at the front page and try to go to every internal link on it. If we encounter a link we have checked before, we ignore it. For each page we successfully retrieve, we check all the links on it, and so on. Eventually, every link will have been checked and the program will terminate. If any page fails to display, HttpUnit will throw an exception and stop the test.

We begin by initializing a WebConversation to handle all the requests and a java.util.HashSet to keep track of which links we have followed so far. Then we write a test method that gets the response for a site's homepage and checks all the links on it:

```
private WebConversation conversation;
private Set checkedLinks;
private String host = "www.sitetotest.com";

public void setUp(){
        conversation = new WebConversation();
        checkedLinks = new HashSet();
}

public void testEntireSite() throws Exception{
  WebResponse response = conversation.getResponse("http://"+host);
  checkAllLinks(response);
  System.out.println("Site check finished. Link's checked: " +
         checkedLinks.size() + " : " + checkedLinks);
}
```

The checkAllLinks() method is also simple:

```
private void checkAllLinks(WebResponse response) throws Exception{
  if(!isHtml(response)){
    return;
  }
  WebLink[] links = response.getLinks();
  System.out.println(response.getTitle() + " -- links found = " +
        links.length);
  for(int i =0; i < links.length; i++){

    boolean newLink = checkedLinks.add(links[i].getURLString());
    if(newLink){
      System.out.println("Total links checked so far: " +
                          checkedLinks.size());
      checkLink(links[i]);
    }
  }
}

private boolean isHtml(WebResponse response){
  return response.getContentType().equals("text/html");
}
```

The isHtml() method checks to be sure that the response in which we are checking the links is in fact HTML (HttpUnit doesn't parse Flash content, for instance). After the available links in the response have been retrieved, checkAllLinks() iterates over the link array and attempts to put the text of each link into the checkedLinks set. If it is successful (indicating a new link), then checkAllLinks() attempts to verify the link with checkLink():

```
private void checkLink(WebLink link) throws Exception{
  WebRequest request = link.getRequest();
  java.net.URL url = request.getURL();
  System.out.println("checking link: " + url);
  String linkHost = url.getHost();
  if(linkHost.equals(this.host)){
    WebResponse response = conversation.getResponse(request);
    this.checkAllLinks(response);
  }
}
```

The java.net.URL is retrieved from the link through getRequest().getURL() (shown in expanded form). If the host part of the URL matches the host under test, then checkLink() retrieves the response (here is where an exception would be thrown) and then attempts checkAllLinks() in it. Finally, all of the links will be checked and the test will terminate.

At this point, the spider is perfectly usable. However, it has one major flaw: All the testing is carried out in one test method. That means that if one link fails, the entire test fails. This approach does not granularize the test output—if .1 percent of product pages (10 of 10,000) in a hypothetical catalog test suffer from a rare bug because of bad data in the database, we don't want the whole test to fail. We want to record the error, but have the test results reflect that 99.9 percent of the site is working.

Spider Development: Second Iteration

Because the spider is a testing class, our benchmark for the newly added functionality is that given the same input as our first iteration, it should yield the same results. With that quick and dirty test in mind, we begin integrating the HttpUnit spider into JUnit's framework. The integration shouldn't affect the core logic of the spider; it will still use a Set to keep track of already spidered links, ignore links outside a specified host, and so on. However, the test we ran as a method will be refactored into a separate object. The setup for the test (which we ran in testEntireSite) now exists in a separate class:

```
public class SpiderSiteTest {

public static Test suite(){
    String host = "www.eblox.com";
    TestSuite suite = new TestSuite();
    WebRequest homePage = new GetMethodWebRequest("http://" + host);
    SpiderPageTest test =
          new SpiderPageTest(homePage, new HashSet(), host);
    suite.addTest(test);
    return suite;
  }

  public static void main(String[] args){
    /*
      junit.swingui.TestRunner.main(
          new String[]{"xptoolkit.httpUnitSpiderSiteTest"}
    );
    */
    junit.textui.TestRunner.run(suite());
  }
}
```

The class declares a static suite method, which allows it to be accessed by JUnit's test runners as demonstrated in the main() method. The suite consists of a single instance of SpiderPageTest—the object that performs all the logic of spidering pages, checking results, and so on. SpiderSiteTest merely serves as a convenient test launcher. It could be replaced with a more sophisticated launcher class that, say, read in the host initial page from a properties file or some such.

The SpiderPageTest object is the critical piece of the testing application. Its public interface consists of two constructors that parameterize the behavior of the test as well as the methods specified in junit.framework.Test (see Chapter 14, "JUnit API Reference," for details). The constructors specify the WebRequest (or, for convenience, the WebLink from which the request is derived), a java.util.Set of links that have already been tested, and the host of the site to test (offsite links are ignored).

The Test interface specifies two methods: run(junit.framework.TestResult result) and countTestCases(). run() is supposed to execute the Test and report the outcome to the TestResult. We will cover this method in a moment. countTestCases() returns the total number of TestCases run by this Test. In this case, we have to cheat and return 1, because we have no way of knowing in advance how many pages will be tested and, hence, how many tests will run. This clues us in to imperfect integration with JUnit. JUnit's designers expected TestCases to be the objects that actually execute a test (as opposed to aggregate or modify tests). Perhaps SpiderPageTest should be a TestCase. We write this down on our task list as something to investigate after our SpiderSiteTest runs. Once we have all the logic, we may be able to see how to reshape SpiderPageTest for better integration. See Listing 9.4 for the constructors and class initialization.

```
private WebConversation conversation = new WebConversation();
private WebRequest request;
private WebLink link;
private Set alreadyChecked;
private String host;

public SpiderPageTest(WebRequest request, Set alreadyChecked, String host) {
  this.request = request;
  this.alreadyChecked = alreadyChecked;
  this.host = host;
}

public SpiderPageTest(WebLink link, Set alreadyChecked, String host) {
  request = link.getRequest();
  this.alreadyChecked = alreadyChecked;
  this.host = host;
}
```

Listing 9.4 Constructors and initialization for SpiderPageTest.

JUnit's TestRunners (and, later on, the class itself) will call the run() method of SpiderPageTest to execute the object's testable behavior, so it makes sense to examine this method first:

```
public void run(TestResult result) {
  if(notSameHost()){
    System.out.println(this + " not run because host for test (" +
                       host + ") does not match URL being tested.");
    return;
  }

  WebResponse response = runTest(result);

  if(response != null){
    try{
      spiderPage(response, result);
    }
    catch(SAXException e){
      result.addError(this, e);
    }
  }
}
```

Its first step is to verify that the host of the request matches the host under test. If it does not, the method returns; external links are neither failures nor successes—they are simply ignored. Then, the runTest() method checks the page and reports the outcome to the test result. If this step is successful, the response from that page is sent to spiderPage(), which acts almost exactly like checkAllLinks() in the first iteration of the spider (we will cover this method in detail in a moment).

The runTest() method takes care of accessing the page and logging exceptions (read test failures) that occur in the process:

```
private WebResponse runTest(TestResult result){
  WebResponse response = null;

  result.startTest(this);
  try{
    response = this.accessPage();
  }
  catch (ThreadDeath e) { throw e; }
  catch (AssertionFailedError e) {
    result.addFailure(this, e);
  }
  catch (Throwable t) {
    result.addError(this, t);
  }
  /*furture requests are wrapped in their own test,
    so this test ends here*/
  result.endTest(this);

  return response;
}

private WebResponse accessPage() throws Exception{
  return conversation.getResponse(request);
}
```

First, the start of the test is registered with the result using result.startTest(this). Then the test() method is run and the errors (if any) are registered with the result using the result.addError() and result.addFailure() methods. Finally, result.endTest(this) is called to signal test completion to the result.

Errors or Failures?

Should we log HttpUnitExceptions (that is, page failures, commonly 404 or 500 status responses) as errors (unanticipated) or failures (anticipated)? There are reasons for either approach. Logging them as failures seems proper because the test is meant to check for exactly this type of exception. Logging them as errors is easier, and we did not specifically raise an AssertionFailedError with an assertion, so the exception could be regarded as unexpected.

The run() method calls spiderPage()if there are no failures in runTest(). The only difference between spiderPage() and its earlier incarnation (checkAllLinks()) is that instead of executing a method on each link it finds, it instantiates a new SpiderPageTest and calls run() on it:

```
SpiderPageTest linkTest =
        new SpiderPageTest(links[i], alreadyChecked, host);
linkTest.run(result);
```

Thus, a call to the run() method of a SpiderPageTest will probably execute calls to the run() methods of several SpiderPageTests. For this reason, SpiderPageTest is more like a combination of a test runner and a test than a pure test. The full code for spiderPage() appears in Listing 9.5.

```
private void spiderPage(WebResponse response, TestResult result)
                        throws SAXException{

  if(!isHtml(response)){
    return;
  }
  WebLink[] links = response.getLinks();

  for(int i =0; i < links.length; i++){

    boolean newLink = alreadyChecked.add(links[i].getURLString());

    if(newLink){
      System.out.println("Total links checked so far: "
                         + alreadyChecked.size());

      SpiderPageTest linkTest =
          new SpiderPageTest(links[i], alreadyChecked, host);
      linkTest.run(result);
    }
  }
}

private boolean isHtml(WebResponse response){
      return response.getContentType().equals("text/html");
}
```

Listing 9.5 The spiderPage() method of SpiderPageTest.

Future Work on the Spider

As we discovered in implementing countTestCases with a "cheat" return value, this example still has wrinkles to be ironed out. Tighter integration with JUnit would probably be beneficial. Also, we could extend the spider with new launchers. For example, imagine a site where a logged-in user is able to access more or different areas than a non-authenticated user. With a few lines of HttpUnit code, we might write a launcher that spidered the site, logged in, and then spidered the site again.

Summary

HttpUnit provides a flexible Java API for interacting with Web servers while maintaining client state and a powerful set of utilities that make writing assertions against HTTP responses easy. This chapter has covered the mechanics of writing basic HttpUnit code; explored the specifics of interacting with forms, tables, and cookies; and opened the door to sophisticated automated testing with the development of a link-checking spider.

Functional testing with HttpUnit is more complex than unit testing with JUnit. Web site tests must be carefully structured, and you must strike a constant balance between thoroughness and time spent in test development. Writing a generic test framework like the link checker in this chapter can increase coverage without increasing time spent. The best argument in favor of the framework is that HttpUnit's flexibility lends itself to this type of development.

CHAPTER 10

Measuring Application Performance with JMeter

Ideally, during the design phase of a project, you will receive important performance criteria such as the target number of simultaneous users the system should support and the hardware the system will run on. Of course, we don't always live in an ideal world, but you will still be responsible for delivering an application that meets all performance criteria. Don't wait until the end of the project to begin measuring performance.

You should build tracer bullets for the system incrementally—single slices of business value that utilize major pieces of your expected final architecture—and then measure performance of those tracer bullets. If you don't, expect to work some late hours and weekends the first few weeks after product launch. The faster you can identify potential bottlenecks, the quicker you can re-architect and avoid them.

Where To Get JMeter

JMeter is distributed by The Apache Software Foundation, under The Apache Software License, Version 1.1, at:

http://jakarta.apache.org/builds/jakarta-jmeter/release/

Being a Hero Is No fun

One company hired me three days before launch. I spent the first three days untangling a connection-pooling problem. The product (an e-commerce Web site) launched the same day the customer company was showing the Web site at a convention. You could say the Web site was the star of the show. Expectations grew.

Unfortunately, the Web site did not scale. I spent the month working 100-hour weeks in an effort to re-architect a site that was in production, making many patch releases. We made steady improvements, and before the end of the month the site was performing very well. Then, without warning, the customer company did a major marketing blitz and the site got twice as many hits as before in a matter of days. At this point, I began sleeping at work because I was there so much.

It took another month of 100-hour+ work-weeks to get the site up to speed again. The moral of the story is that a little planning and performance monitoring up front can save you a lot of heartache and late nights, and you may avoid angering your customer and burning out your employees.

Overview of JMeter

JMeter, from The Apache Software Foundation, is a 100% pure Java desktop application created to load-test and measure system performance. It originally focused on Web applications but was made extensible and extended. Thus, JMeter can load and performance-test HTTP, FTP, and RDBMS with its support for Java Database Connectivity (JDBC). And, you can write pluggable samplers that perform tests, pluggable timers, and data analysis and visualization plugins. For example, you could write a plugin that allows you test Enterprise JavaBeans (EJBs), Simple Object Access Protocol (SOAP), or Common Object Request Broker Architecture (CORBA) by writing your own custom sampler.

Typically, you use JMeter to measure your system performance. At first it may seem that JMeter overlaps with JUnitPerf or HttpUnit. Rather, it complements these tools: You can use JMeter to simulate load while you use JUnitPerf in conjunction with HttpUnit to ensure that your Web application still responds in a timely manner.

You can use JMeter to simulate a heavy load on your system, server, and network. JMeter has a full multithreading framework that allows concurrent sampling by many threads and simultaneous sampling of different functions by separate ThreadGroups. Thus, you can also use JMeter to test system performance under different load types, such as heavy updates, heavy browsing, heavy transactions, or under different combination of load profiles simultaneously. An advantage of using JMeter is that you get instant visual feedback of system performance with its graphs and splines.

Because JMeter can load test a site using HTTP, it can be used to test performance of both static and dynamic resources: files, Java servlets, Perl CGI, Python CGI, PHP, JavaServer Pages (JSP), Cold Fusion, Active Server Pages, and more.

JMeter Concepts

To use JMeter, you must construct and then run a TestPlan. A *TestPlan* consists of one to many ThreadGroups. You can think of a thread as a simulated user, and a ThreadGroup as a list of simulated users. The general rule is that the more threads you add, the harder your system resources will get hit.

Once you create all the elements in the TestPlan, you begin your test. JMeter then compiles your test elements and creates a single TestPlan object. From the TestPlan, a JMeterEngine is formed. The JMeterEngine creates threads, and each thread iterates through the test cases.

When you start JMeter, you see two top-level nodes in its tree: the TestPlan node and the WorkBench node. The TestPlan node holds the active TestPlan you are ready to run. In the WorkBench area, you can construct and configure tests. You must move the test elements and configuration to the TestPlan node before you actually run it. Figure 10.1 shows an active test loaded in the TestPlan node and a test under construction in the WorkBench node.

A *timer* is a simple element that is added to a ThreadGroup. Remember, we said that a thread is like a simulated user; without a timer, that thread becomes a hyper user. If you do not add a timer, the simulated user will keep hitting the site with no delay; however fun this scenario might be, it rarely simulates a real-world user. Thus you add timers to slow down the simulated users (threads) so they behave like real-world users. JMeter has three types of timers: constant timer, Gaussian random timer, and uniform random timer. We typically use the constant timer to create a repeatable test, and we use a Gaussian random timer to simulate real-world user activity.

Another element you'll typically add to a ThreadGroup is a *controller*. JMeter uses two types of controllers: testing and logic. You use a testing controller to test your system with various protocols (JDBC, HTTP, FTP, and so on). The testing controller does the sampling, but it does not record the results—for that, you need to add something else.A logical controller controls the flow. It controls the iterative behavior of sub-controllers.

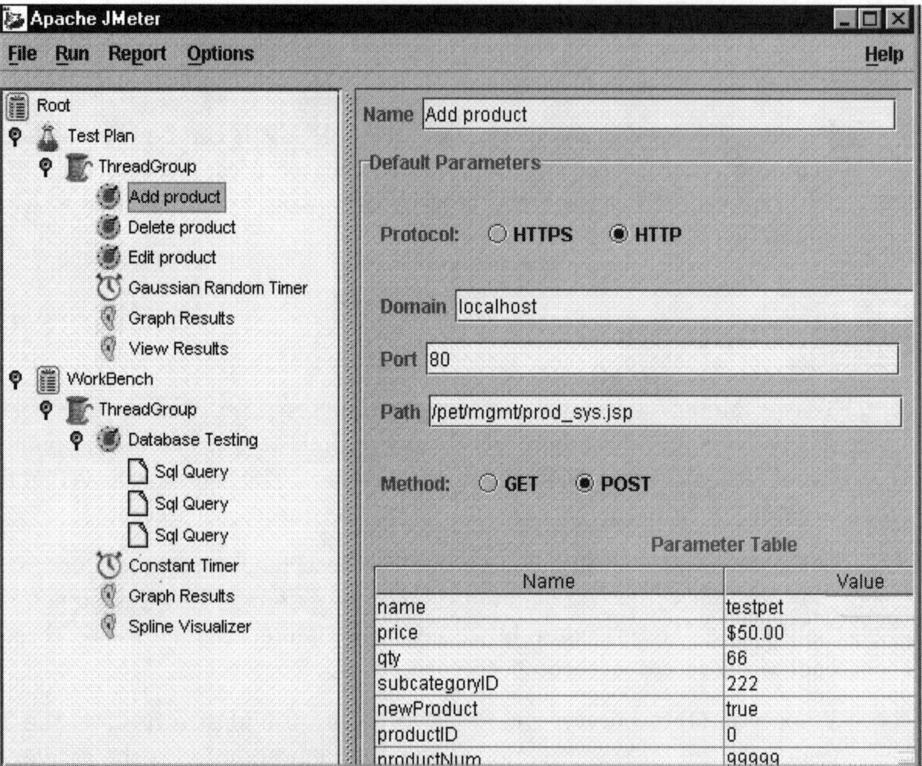

Figure 10.1 JMeter WorkBench and TestPlan nodes.

A controller may contain many config elements that help you configure the controller. When you run a test, every element in the TestPlan receives every config element that is above it. For example, a timer inserted into the TestPlan at the highest level applies to all testing controllers.

You'll also typically add a listener to a ThreadGroup. A *listener* receives sampling data and either graphs it or stores it. Thus JMeter uses two types of listeners: visualizers and reporters. A testing controller collects sampling data and publishes it to one or more listeners, which may store the data in a file or display it in a graph. The View Results listener shows the text returned from a Web site. We use it to make sure the Web application is returning real HTML and not an error page.

Enough theory, concepts, and overview: Let's dive in and use JMeter to test a Web application; then, later in this chapter, we'll test some JDBC queries. The following sections walk step by step through building a TestPlan that first tests navigating through our pet store example and then tests filling out forms on the backend management piece created in the JUnit chapter.

Using JMeter to Test a Web Application Navigation

In this example, we'll set up a ThreadGroup, add Web-test controllers to the ThreadGroup, set up a timer, and set up a graph listener. We follow these steps:

1. Start JMeter. After installing JMeter, you will see a directory called bin in the JMeter home directory. Go to bin and type "jmeter"; this script will work under Unix and Windows because the makers of JMeter created both types of start-up scripts.
2. We'll add a ThreadGroup to the TestPlan. Right-click on the TestPlan node, select Add, and select ThreadGroup from the pop-up menu (see Figure 10.2).
3. Expand the TestPlan node and select the ThreadGroup node. Note that the number of threads is set to 1. Although one thread is not a realistic load test, it's great when we are developing a test. We don't want to launch 100 simulated users (threads) when we don't know if our TestPlan works.

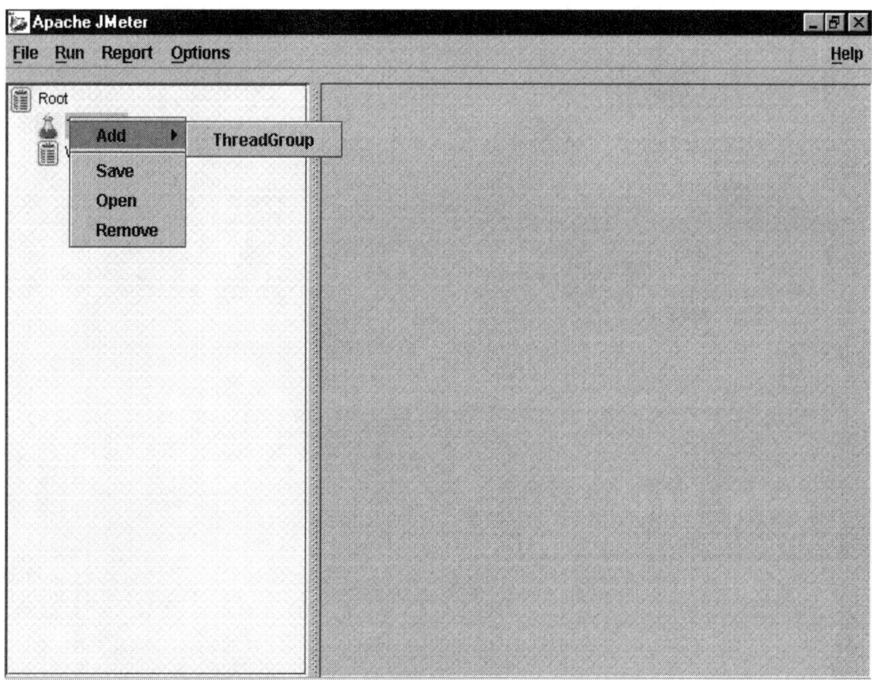

Figure 10.2 Adding a ThreadGroup to the JMeter TestPlan.

4. Change the name of the ThreadGroup to Navigation, because we're going to set up this type of test.
5. In order for the test to do something, we need to add a controller. Right-click the ThreadGroup node and add a WebTesting Controller, as shown in Figure 10.3.
6. We need to configure the Web-testing controller. We will set up several Web-testing controllers to simulate navigating down the Web application from the home page to the product page of the pet store sample application. Set up the first controller as follows:
   - Set the name to HomeWebTest.
   - Set the domain to localhost (or wherever petstore is running).
   - Set the port to 80, which is the default (or whatever port the Web application server is set to run on).
   - Set the path to pet (as in http://localhost/pet).

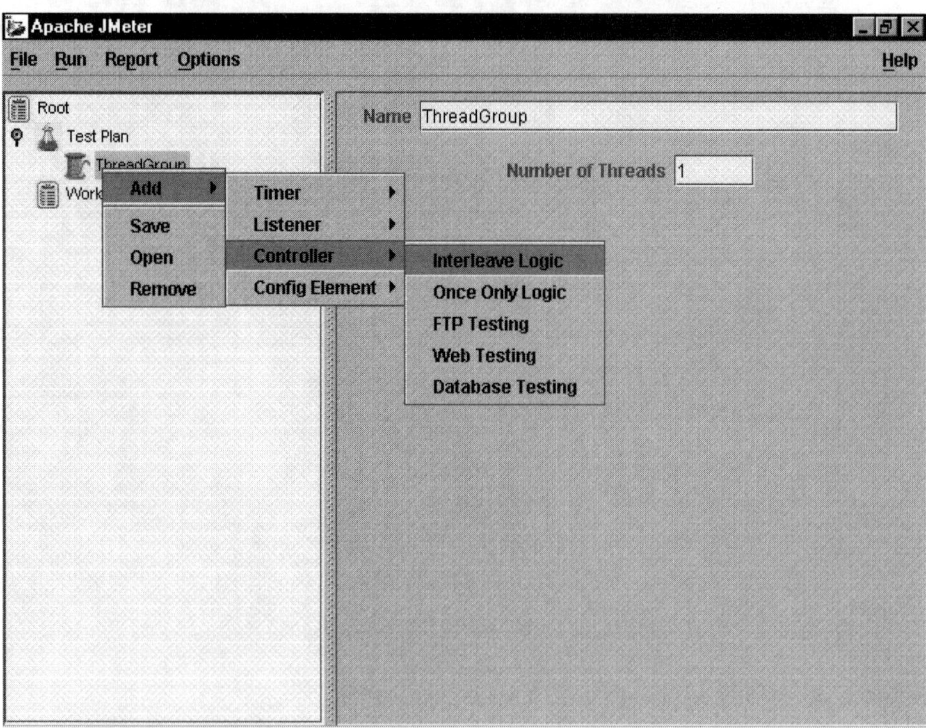

Figure 10.3 Adding a WebTesting Controller.

7. Set up the ability to access the subcategory, as in http://localhost/pet/subcategory.jsp?id=222. Add another Web-testing controller as follows:
   - Set the name to SubcategoryWebTest.
   - Set the domain to localhost.
   - Leave the port at 80.
   - Set the path to pet/subcategory.jsp (as in http://localhost/pet/subcategory.jsp?id=222).
8. Add the "id" parameter and set it to a valid subcategory id. Note that 222 should be a valid subcategory identifier, but we need to check the DB just in case we deleted it. To add an "id" parameter, click on Add in the Web-controller configuration pane. Type "id" for the name and "222" for the value. The pane should look like Figure 10.4. Figure 10.5 shows the corresponding browser view of the same URL defined in Figure 10.4.

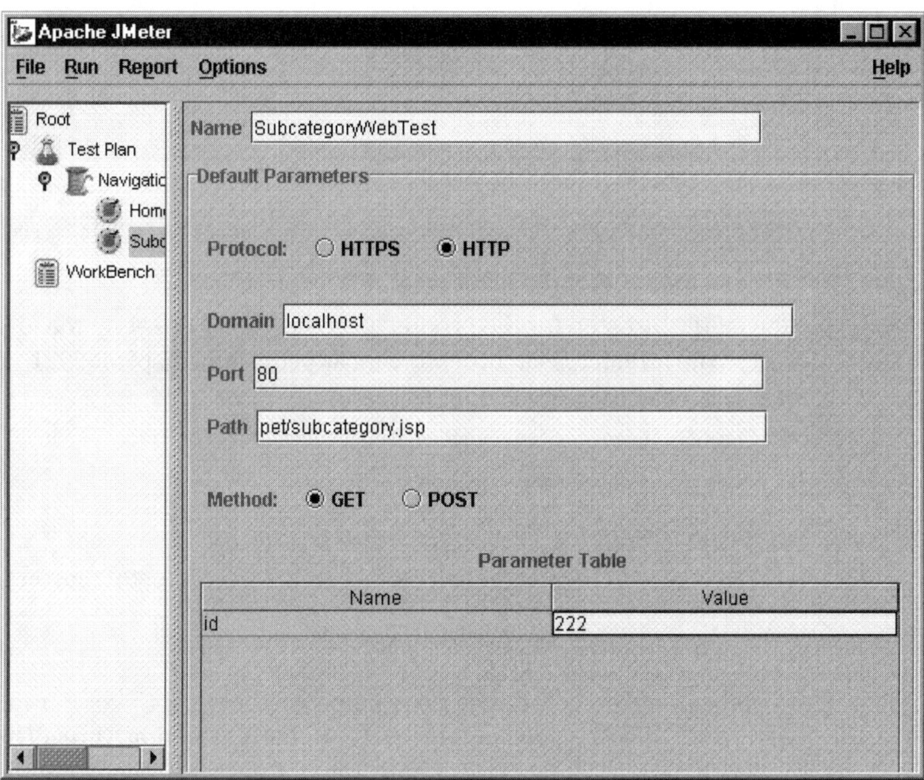

Figure 10.4 SubcategoryWebTest configuration pane.

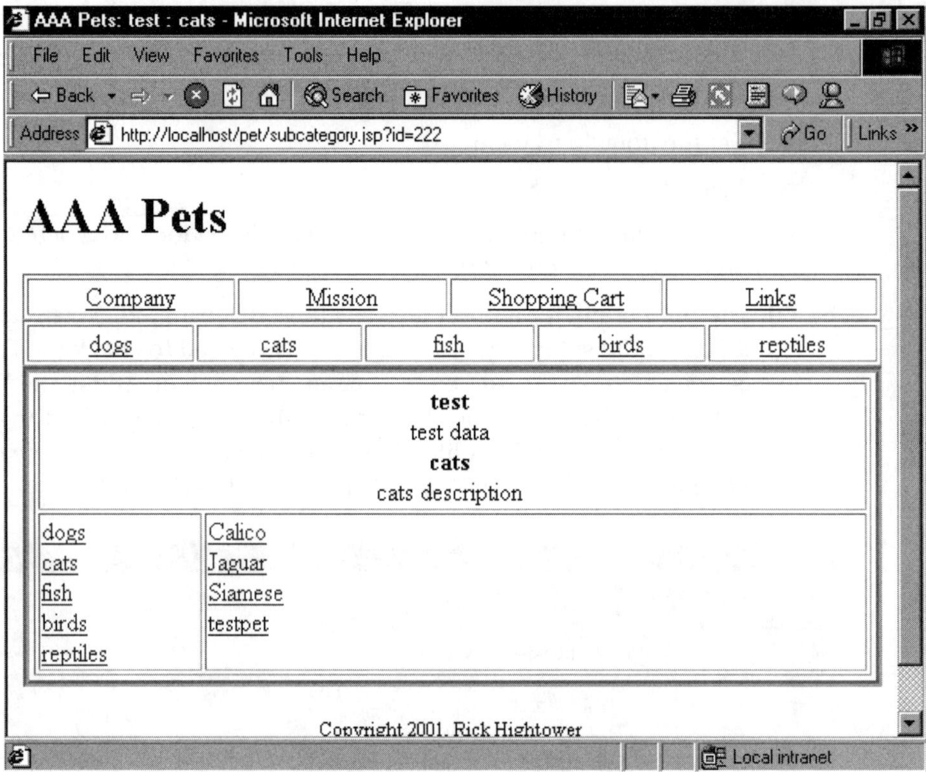

Figure 10.5 Browser equivalent to the subcategory Web test in Figure 10.4.

9. Repeat the last step for the product page test. That is, set up the ability to access the product, as in http://localhost/pet/product.jsp?id=2221. Add another Web-testing controller as follows:
   - Set the name to ProductWebTest.
   - Set the domain to localhost.
   - Leave the port at 80.
   - Set the path to pet/product.jsp (as in http://localhost/pet/product.jsp?id=2221).
   - Add an "id" parameter set to "2221".
10. Now that the Web controllers are set up, we'll set up a timer. For this example, we will use a constant timer. Go to the Navigation ThreadGroup node, right-click it, and choose Add, Timer, Constant Timer from the pop-up menu. When we are setting up a test, we like to slow down the timer so we can see if the test is really doing what we expect it to. To set the timer interval to 3 seconds, use a value of 3000 (the timer works with milliseconds).

11. We need a way to view our results. Right-click the Navigation Thread-Group, and choose Add, Listener, Graph Results from the pop-up menu. As we stated earlier, the first time a test runs, it is good to see the real HTML flying by; so, add a View Results listener, as well (select Add, Listener, View Results from the pop-up menu).

Now that we can see the results, let's run the test. Select the Navigation Thread-Group and then select Run, Start from the main menu bar.

There are two ways to know the test is working: We can look at the View Results listener and see the pages of HTML, or we can look at the data being spit out to the console by JMeter, as follows:

```
Sampling url: http://localhost:80/pet
Original location=http://localhost/pet/
Modified location=http://localhost/pet/
Sampling url: http://localhost:80/pet/
Sampling url: http://localhost:80/pet/subcategory.jsp?id=222
```

The console indicates test errors on the product.jsp because the current subcategory is in the Web application session information. We have not set up JMeter to track session information. The error when trying to load product.jsp is as follows:

```
Sampling url: http://localhost:80/pet/product.jsp?id=2221
java.io.FileNotFoundException:
http://localhost:80/pet/product.jsp?id=2221
        at sun.net.www.protocol.http.HttpURLConnection.getInputStream
  (Unknown Source)
        at java.net.HttpURLConnection.getResponseCode
(Unknown Source)
        at org.apache.jmeter.protocol.http.sampler.HTTPSampler.getError-
Level
(HTTPSampler.java:191)
        at
org.apache.jmeter.protocol.http.sampler.HTTPSampler.sample(HTTPSample
```

This happened quite by mistake. Remember, we said the pet store Web application was not robust. Well, we did not lie; as it happens, the pet store Web application needs session data to traverse to the products correctly. You don't want this feature in a real Web application, but this Web application is non-robust by design.

However, a real Web application may hold important session information like user id, preferences, affiliations, and so on. This information may provide a customized view or provide some filtering on a per-user/per-session basis. Therefore, this snafu lends an excellent opportunity to show you how JMeter can track session information.

The default behavior of many JSP and Servlet engines is to send a special cookie to the client to track session information. A cookie is a name/value pair that is stored on the client's machine. The cookie is associated with a particular URL, and it's sent when you access pages under that URL. Thus, we must set up JMeter to receive and transmit the cookie back to the Web application server. Fortunately, this is easy to do with JMeter: All we have to do is add a cookie manager to the thread navigation ThreadGroup (Add, Config Element, Cookie Manager), and JMeter does the rest. When we rerun the test, it will work this time.

So far we've been lobbing softballs at our Web application. Now that we know it runs, it's time to play hard ball. Set the thread count to 100 on the Navigation ThreadGroup, and reduce the time to 300 milliseconds on the timer. Save any work in open programs before starting this test. Run the test—let 'er rip! (See Figure 10.6.)

We find the graph useful, but we also like to dump the data out to a file and read it in with a spreadsheet application (Excel) and some Python stats package we

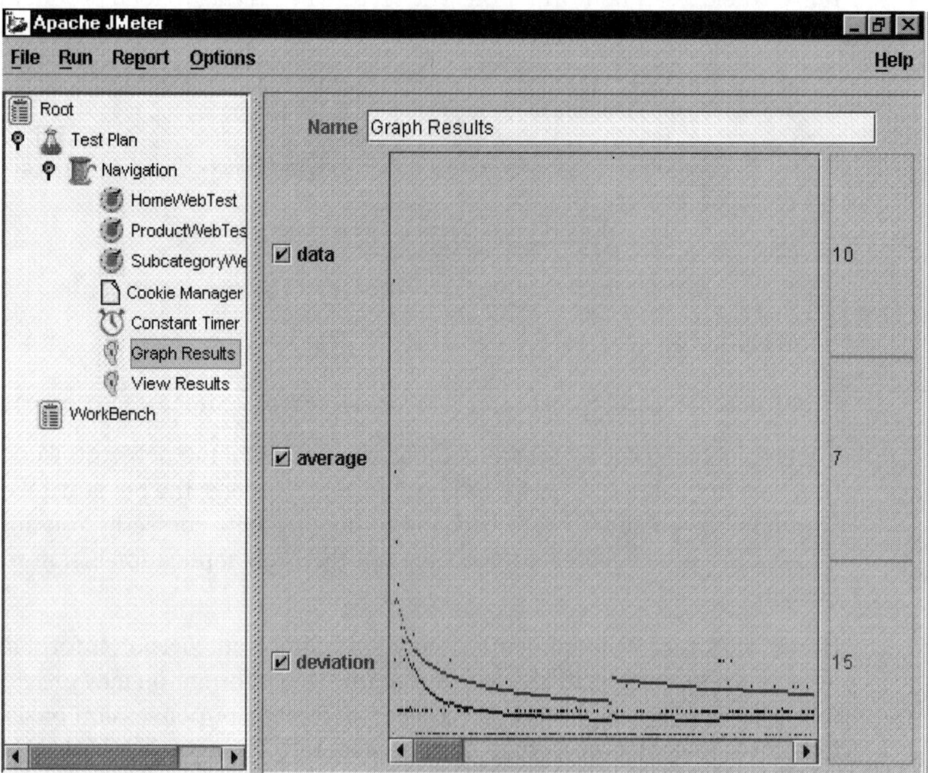

Figure 10.6 Graph of the test case running against the Web application.

wrote. In addition, we find the spline visualizer useful in seeing the runtime performance of the system. Add the spline visualizer to the Navigation ThreadGroup by right-clicking and choosing Add, Listener, Spline Visualizer from the pop-up menu. Now, add the file reporter to the Navigation ThreadGroup (select Add, Listener, File Reporter). Click on the File Reporter element and set the output file location (for example, /tmp/output.log). Now, let's run it again.

After running the spline visualizer, we can see that the average access time is around 444 milliseconds, and we get a very interesting view of the runtime data (see Figure 10.7).

In addition to the data in Figure 10.7 and the graph from the first run, we can import the output data recorded by the File Reporter into our favorite spreadsheet or other analysis software and create a custom report. Here is a sample file listing of the date in verbose mode:

```
http://localhost:80/pet/product.jsp?id=2221  200
http://localhost:80/pet/subcategory.jsp?id=222  220
http://localhost:80/pet/subcategory.jsp?id=222  230
http://localhost:80/pet/  220
```

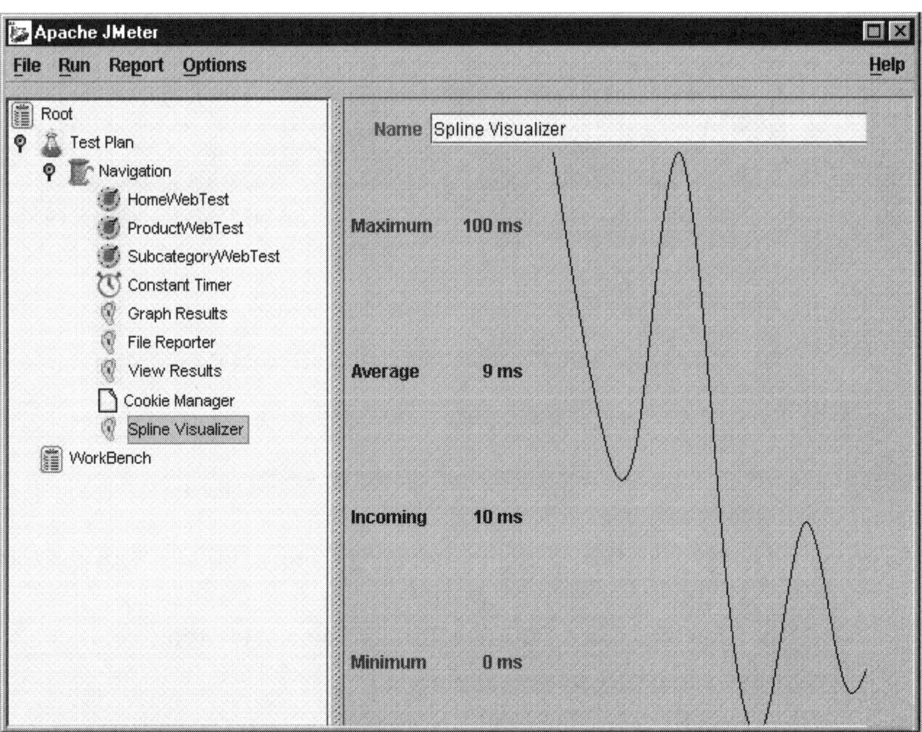

Figure 10.7 Spline visualizer running the navigation test.

In this example, we set up a ThreadGroup; added Web-test controllers to the ThreadGroup; set up a timer; added a cookie manager; and set up a graph, file reporter, and spline visualizer listener. In the next section, we'll create a script that can simulate form entry.

Using JMeter to Test the Web Application's Form Entry

In this example, we will test the back-end product form entry. In Chapter 7, "Unit Testing with JUnit," we created a case study that added to the pet store example the functionality to add, delete, and edit products. In this section, we will write code that tests this feature. Then, we will combine this test with the last test so we can simulate customers browsing the Web site at the same time we simulate the pet store clerk adding new pets, to see what happens to performance.

First we will add a Web-application test that tests adding products. If we open the backend product page (http://localhost/pet/mgmt/product.jsp?id=2221) in a browser and view the source, the form looks like this:

```
<form method="POST" action="prod_sys.jsp">
  <p>Name: <input type="text" name="name" value="" size="20"></p>
  <p>Price: <input type="text" name="price" value="$0.00" size="20"></p>
  <p>Qty: <input type="text" name="qty" value="0" size="20"></p>
  <input type="hidden" name="subcategoryID" value="222" size="20">
  <input type="hidden" name="productNum" value="4" size="20">
  <input type="hidden" name="newProduct" value="true" size="20">
  <input type="hidden" name="productID" value="0" size="20">


  <p>Description:</p>
  <p><textarea rows="8" name="description" cols="84" ></textarea></p>
  <p> </p>
  <p><input type="submit" value="Submit" name="submit"><input
type="reset"
                  value="Reset" name="reset"></p>
</form>
```

All we have to do with JMeter is simulate adding a product with this form. Thus we need to fill in the form parameters:

- "name" is the name of the new product we are creating.
- "price" can be set to any valid price.
- "qty" can be set to any valid quantity.

- "subcategoryID" must be set to a valid subcategory id. Consult the ID field of the subcategory table to see a valid id. If the test data hasn't changed, "222" is the subcategory id for Cats.
- "productNum" is the number of products in the current subcategory. We don't have to know how many products are in the subcategory; instead, we just make productNum really large—in this case, "99999".
- "newProduct" should be set to "true", which just means that we are adding a new product rather than editing an existing product.
- "productID" can be set to "0" because this value simulates adding a new product. (This parameter really is not used.)
- "description" can be any value.

We add all these parameters to the Web-application controller we added, and then change the method from GET to POST to match the HTML form. We set everything else just as we did in the earlier example, and we set the path to pet/mgmt/prod_sys.jsp to match the "action" attribute in the HTML form. Our Web controller configuration panel looks like the one in Figure 10.8.

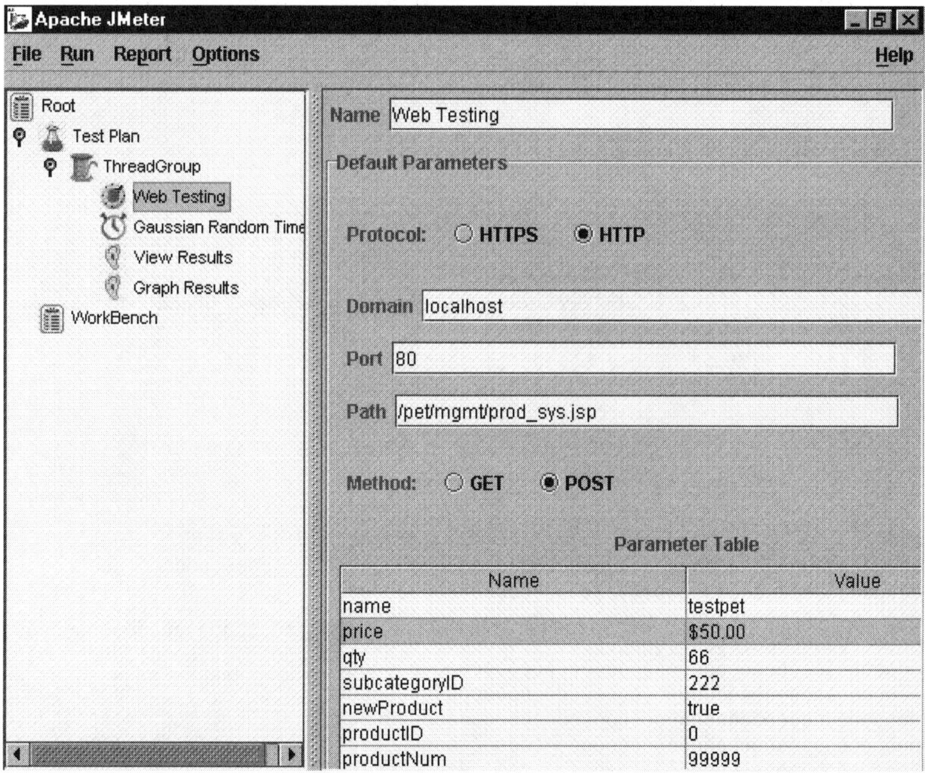

Figure 10.8 Adding a product using JMeter.

We can run this test now, but we will only be able to run it once—the test is essentially hard-coding the primary key of the product, which must be unique. To run the test many times, we need to create another test to delete the product we set up in this test. So, we add another Web-testing controller to delete the one we just added.

The form we are trying to simulate is the backend subcategory form (http://localhost/pet/mgmt/subcategory.jsp?id=222), shown in Figure 10.9. The HTML for the form we are tying to simulate is as follows:

```
<form method="POST" action="subcat_sys.jsp">
  <table border="1" width="100%">




    <tr>
      <td width="9%">
         <input type="checkbox" name="delete_2221"
value="OFF">delete</td>
      <td width="86%">
        <a href="product.jsp?id=2221" target="_blank">Calico</a>
       <br>
    </td>
    </tr>


    <tr>
      <td width="9%">
         <input type="checkbox" name="delete_2222"
value="OFF">delete</td>
      <td width="86%">
         <a href="product.jsp?id=2222" target="_blank">Jaguar</a>
       <br>
    </td>
    </tr>


    <tr>
      <td width="9%">
          <input type="checkbox" name="delete_2223"
              value="OFF">delete</td>
      <td width="86%">
        <a href="product.jsp?id=2223" target="_blank">Siamese</a>
       <br>
    </td>
    </tr>


    <tr>
      <td width="9%">
```

```
        <input type="checkbox" name="delete_22299999"
               value="OFF">delete</td>
      <td width="86%">
        <a href="product.jsp?id=22299999" target="_blank">testpet</a>
        <br>
    </td>
    </tr>

  </table>
  <p>
        <input type="submit" value="Submit" name="submit">
        <input type="reset" value="Reset" name="Reset">
        <input type="submit" value="Add" name="add"></p>
</form>
```

If we examine the JSP code to which we need to submit this form, we see that the id is embedded in the name of the check box in bold, as follows:

```
        <input type="checkbox" name="delete_22299999"
                 value="OFF">delete</td>
```

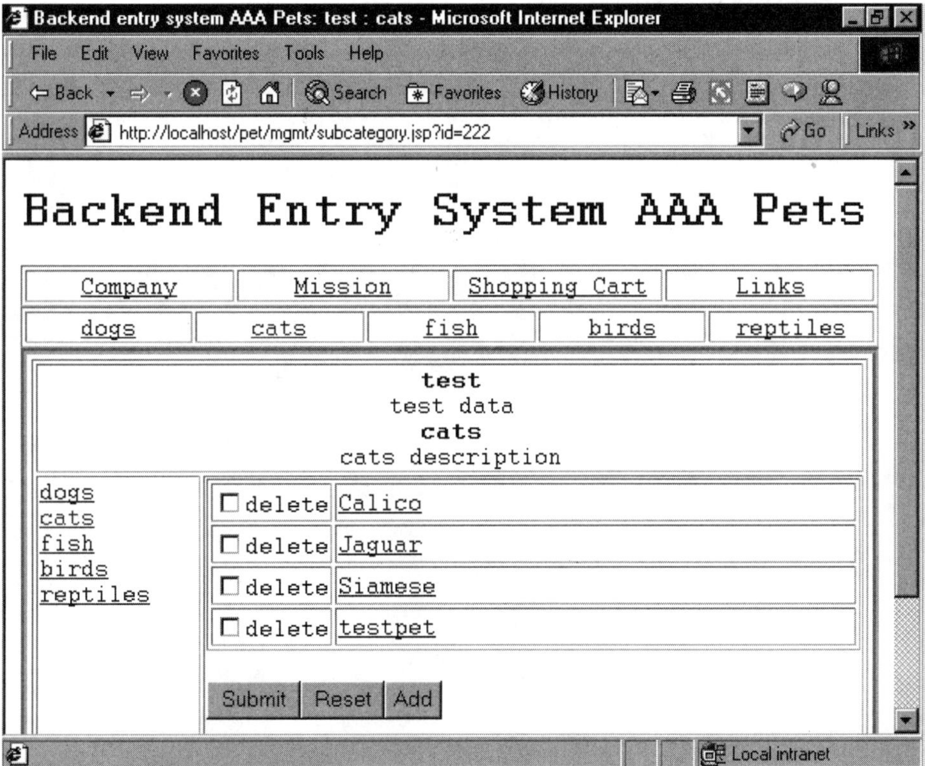

Figure 10.9 Backend subcategory form.

We need to add a parameter to our Web testing controller, as follows:

- Set the name to "Delete product".
- Set the domain to localhost.
- Leave the port at 80.
- Set the path to pet/mgmt/subcat_sys.jsp.
- Change the method to POST (default is GET).
- Add a parameter to delete_22299999 and set the value to "ON".

When we are done, the configuration panel looks like Figure 10.10.

Finally, for completeness, let's add the ability to test editing a product. We'll set up two of these tests: one to edit a product and one to change it back. To set up the editing test, we add a new Web-controller tester and configure it as follows:

- Set the name to "Edit product".
- Set the domain to localhost.
- Leave the port at 80.

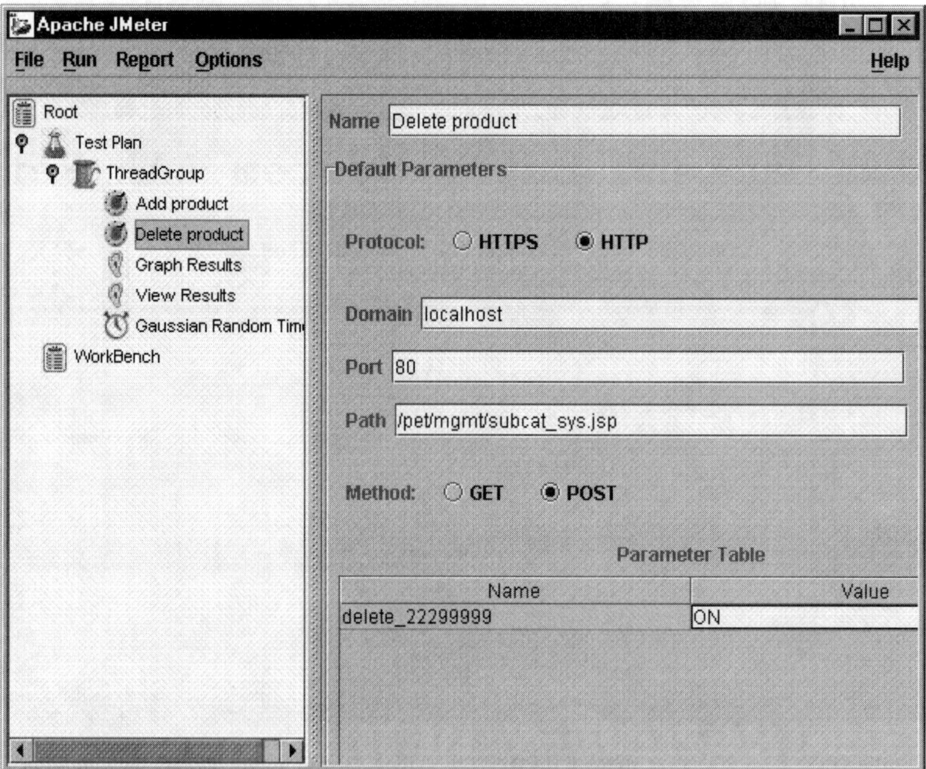

Figure 10.10 Using JMeter to delete a product in the pet store application.

- Set the path to pet/mgmt/prod_sys.jsp.
- Change the method to post (default is get).
- Add the following name/value pairs to the parameter list:
    - "name"="Calico"
    - "price"="$500"
    - "qty"="5"
    - "subcategoryID"="222"
    - "newProduct"="false"
    - "productNum"="0"
    - "description"="Calico data has been edited!"

When we are done, the configuration panel looks like the one in Figure 10.11.

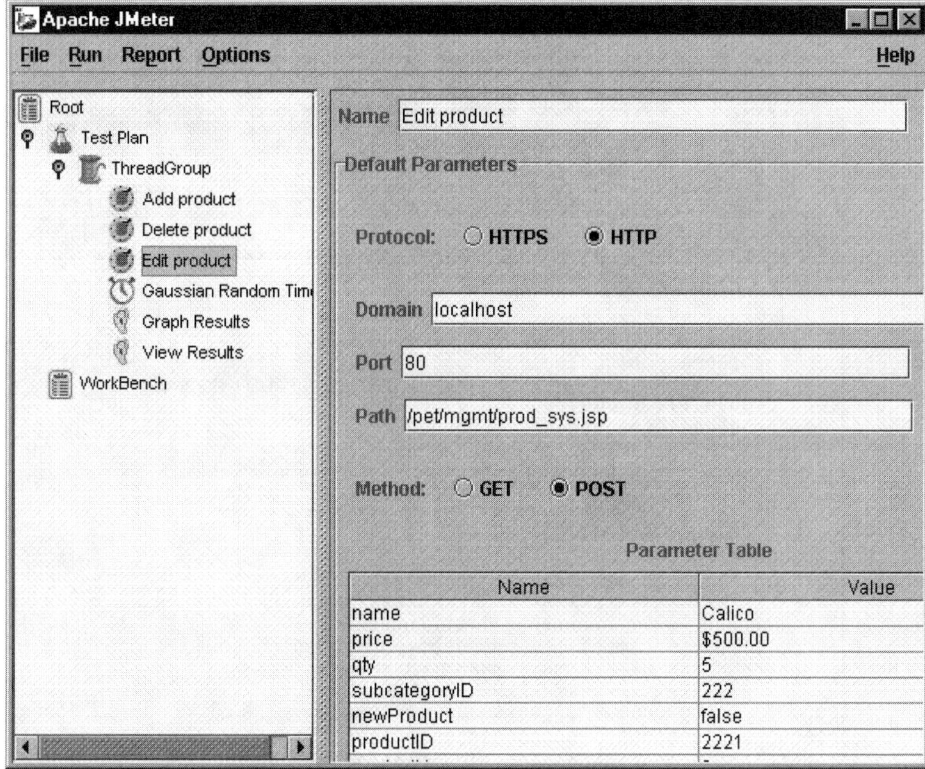

Figure 10.11 Using JMeter to edit a product.

We recommend setting the thread count to 1 and then using the timer to adjust the frequency of edits, because these tests should execute in order. Before running the test, add some listeners and a timer as in the last example. Go ahead and run the test and examine the results.

Notice that we can save any node. Let's save this test and create or reload the last test, and then save it at the ThreadGroup node. Then we can load both the front-end browsing and the backend product management into the test case by selecting Open from the popup-menu, and they will run at the same time.

Because the nodes are saved as XML, we could write a program that reads the test data or that generates it quite easily. Figure 10.12 shows the XML text for the test we just created as displayed in Internet Explorer.

JMeter has other ways of creating the setup XML for tests. We can set up a proxy server that listens to requests and records them in an XML text that we can use for test cases. Refer to the user guide under Recording Browser Activity to learn how to do this. This technique can shave off some of the time it takes to create tests. In the next section, we will create a JDBC test.

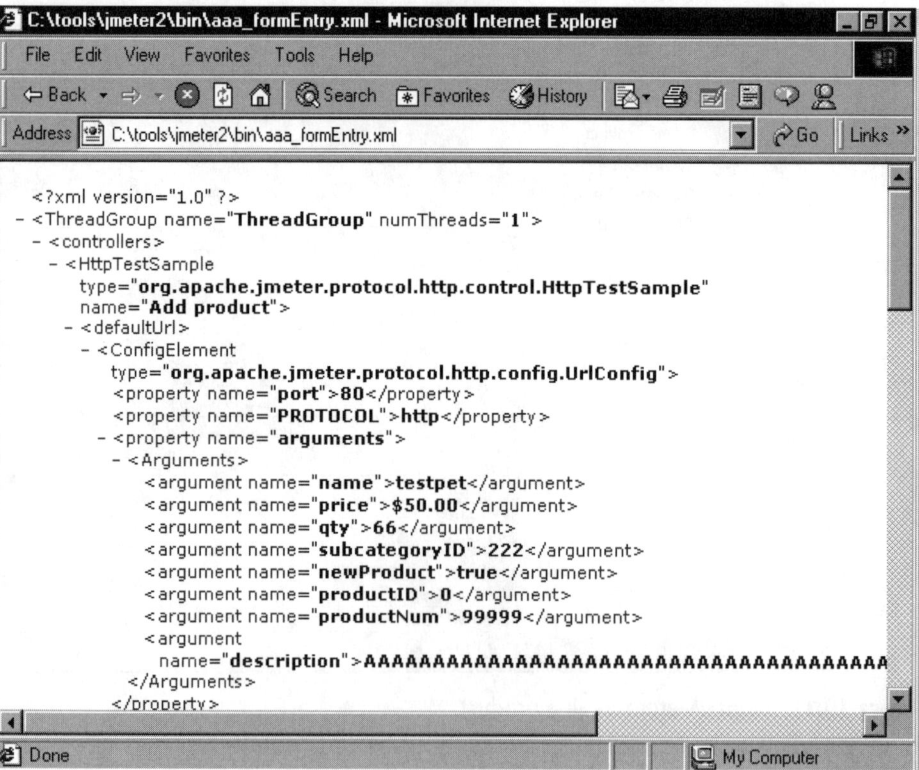
C:\tools\jmeter2\bin\aaa_formEntry.xml - Microsoft Internet Explorer
File Edit View Favorites Tools Help
Back Search Favorites History
Address C:\tools\jmeter2\bin\aaa_formEntry.xml Go Links
<?xml version="1.0" ?>
- <ThreadGroup name="ThreadGroup" numThreads="1">
- <controllers>
- <HttpTestSample type="org.apache.jmeter.protocol.http.control.HttpTestSample" name="Add product">
- <defaultUrl>
- <ConfigElement type="org.apache.jmeter.protocol.http.config.UrlConfig">
<property name="port">80</property>
<property name="PROTOCOL">http</property>
- <property name="arguments">
- <Arguments>
<argument name="name">testpet</argument>
<argument name="price">$50.00</argument>
<argument name="qty">66</argument>
<argument name="subcategoryID">222</argument>
<argument name="newProduct">true</argument>
<argument name="productID">0</argument>
<argument name="productNum">99999</argument>
<argument name="description">AAAAAAAAAAAAAAAAAAAAAAAAAAAAAAAAAAAAA
</Arguments>
</property>
Done
My Computer

Figure 10.12 XML text for testing forms in IE.

Using JMeter to Test Performance of Our RDBMS

For completeness, we want to add a test to test the RDBMS server for our pet store application. If your system was experiencing some lag, you could rule out the RDBMS system by load testing. Perhaps you need to adjust some indexes or add a vertical or horizontal split to reduce lock contention and deadlocks. After you do this, you want to be sure your throughput is what you expect—that you got the improvements you were hoping for.

Start JMeter as before and add a new ThreadGroup. Then, add a database testing controller to the ThreadGroup (right-click the ThreadGroup and select Add, Controller, Database Testing). Now, configure the controller as shown in Figure 10.13.

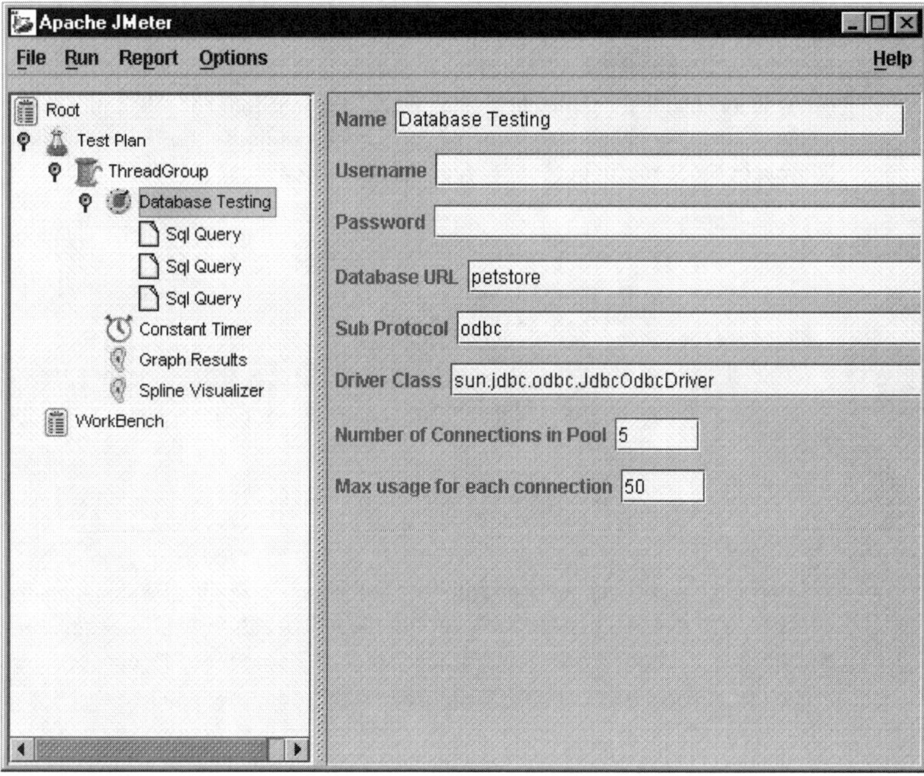

Figure 10.13 Database configuration.

Right-click the Database Testing controller and add three SQL queries to it with the following SQL query statements:

```
select name, description, id from category where ID = 777
select name, description, id, fk_category_id from subcategory
where ID = 111
select name, description, price, id, fk_subcategory_id from product
where id = 1
```

These queries essentially test navigation of the front-end pet store. To complete the test, we need to add a timer and a listener. When we are done we can run the test, and the JMeter instance will look like the one in Figure 10.13.

Advantage of Open Source

We tried using the JDBC-ODBC bridge driver and it did not work with JMeter (sun.jdbc.odbc.JdbcOdbcDriver). The JDBC-ODBC bridge expects a URL in the form jdbc:odbc:petstore, where petstore is the Open DataBase Connectivity (ODBC) DSN. No matter what we did, JMeter passed a URL that caused an ODBC error. In order to get the JDBC-ODBC bridge to work, we modified the DBConfig class in package org.apache.jmeter.protocol.jdbc.config. We made the following change (shown in bold) to the getConnectionString method:

```
        public String getConnectionString()
        {
            if (getSubProtocol() == null ||
getSubProtocol().length()==0){
                return getUrl();
            }
            else if (getSubProtocol().equals("odbc")){
                return "jdbc:odbc:" + getUrl();
            }
            else {
                return "jdbc:"+getSubProtocol()+"://"+getUrl();
            }
        }
```

JMeter ships with an Ant buildfile and the source code for JMeter. So, after we made the change, we just had to run "ant clean" and then "ant" at the command prompt. We submitted this patch; if it is not in the version of JMeter you are using and you are using the JDBC-ODBC bridge, you know what to do.

Case Study: The Pet Store

We will use JMeter to gather performance metrics on a new prototype of the AAA Pet Store and compare the performance of a new technology (XML/XSLT) to the existing technology (straight JSP). These numbers will help us decide whether to make the switch in the near future.

Business Need

XML and Extensible Style Language Transformation (XSLT) have garnered a lot of media attention recently. Therefore, let's imagine that our chief technology strategist has suggested that the design team look into porting the AAA Pet Store's presentation logic to this new technology. Always cautious, the engineering team decided that before they could create any estimates related to XML use, we had to know more.

So, we went ahead and built a prototype of the pet store that converts model data into XML using an open-source API called JDom. One of our enterprising design team members learned XSL and wrote style sheets to turn the XML into HTML. Then, we used Apache's Xalan engine to perform the transformation. Voilà! We had a working prototype. Management was ready to move again, but a couple of programmers had doubts. Something bothered us about the prototype—it seemed as though we were just adding the XML/XSLT on top of our existing code. After all, we still had JSPs pushing out HTML; they were just going through some extra steps. XP says, "Listen to your gut."

Before management commits us to a new schedule involving XML, we decide to do some quick performance analysis to see what kind of price we are paying for these extra steps. It may be that the prototype, while functional, doesn't represent a design that will work under load.

Prototype Architecture

Let's take a look at the prototype's structure so we can get a better sense of what we are about to test. The new interface reuses the application's model code, so there's nothing new there. The changes begin to happen at the JSP level. Instead of spitting out HTML, the JSPs generate XML elements using JDOM (www.jdom.org). The XML generation looks like this (from productlist.jsp):

```
Element eProduct = new Element("CURRENT_PRODUCT");
  Element id = new Element("ID");
    id.addContent(String.valueOf(product.getId()));
  eProduct.addContent(id);

  Element name = new Element("NAME");
    name.addContent(product.getName());
  eProduct.addContent(name);

  Element description = new Element("DESCRIPTION");
    description.addContent(product.getDescription());
  eProduct.addContent(description);

  Element ePrice = new Element("PRICE");
    ePrice.addContent(price);
```

```
    eProduct.addContent(ePrice);

  root.addChild(eProduct);
```

This page looks like a good candidate for refactoring. Perhaps if we pursue this architecture, we can write use some object-to-XML mapping tools. Also, this code probably should execute in a separate class so that we can test it more easily. We take down these ideas as notes for later. The XML that this page produces looks something like the following:

```
<CURRENT_PRODUCT>
  <ID>1</ID>
  <NAME>Poodle</NAME>
  <DESCRIPTION>Poodle description</DESCRIPTION>
  <PRICE>$1.00</PRICE>
</CURRENT_PRODUCT>
```

After all, the XML has been modeled in JDOM objects; the JSP writes the XML out to a String and then pass it to Xalan's XSLT processing engine. We note this operation as a potential performance bottleneck. JDOM may already represent its object in a form that an XSLT engine can read—reading from and writing to Strings could be unnecessary. The XSLT engine uses a style sheet specified by the JSP to transform XML output of the page into HTML. Here is the XSL for the product element:

```
<xsl:if test="CURRENT_PRODUCT">
  <table width="100%" cellpadding="0" cellspacing="0" border="0">
    <tr>
      <td align="center">
        <b>
          <xsl:value-of select="CURRENT_PRODUCT/NAME" />
        </b>
        <br />
        <xsl:value-of select="CURRENT_PRODUCT/DESCRIPTION" />
        <br />
        <b>
          <xsl:value-of select="CURRENT_PRODUCT/PRICE" />
        </b>
      </td>
    </tr>
  </table>
</xsl:if>
```

The end result is a page that mimics the page created by the regular pet store application (we could even use HttpUnit to verify that they are structurally identical). However, with some refactoring, XML data generated by the page could be transformed in a number of different ways, or even sent to partners without transformation. If those are pressing business needs, maybe this will be a viable architecture. We have to weigh these potential advantages (and XP says we should treat *potential* advantages with suspicion) against the results of our JMeter testing in order to give management good feedback about the decisions they make.

Creating the Test

We decided to compare the XSL prototype's performance against that of the existing system. By taking this as our goal, we simplify our task. Real-world performance conditions can be hard to replicate, making absolute performance difficult to measure. By testing two alternatives side by side, we develop an idea of their *relative* worth. When deciding between the two options, that's all the data we need.

The Test Plan

We decide to subject both Web applications to the same series of tests. Several simulated users will access a series of pages over and over again. While the system is under this load, we will gather its performance metrics. We will test each application four times: with 10, 30, 100, and 500 users. We know that the AAA Pet Store gets an average of 10 to 30 concurrent users during the day, but the customer worries about the potential increase in use connected to their upcoming promotional campaign.

We model the test case after typical user behavior: We enter at the index page, go to a pet category, and then view a couple of animals within the category. This test exercises every major page in the prototype—another excellent feature. We note a couple of complicating factors: The Web server, the database, and the testing application (JMeter) are collocated. This fact eliminates one type of test noise (data transfer over an open network) but generates another: If the load becomes too high, the three applications might begin to compete with one another for scarce resources, increasing test times artificially. We decide to accept this risk, especially in light of the fact that Distributed JMeter (http://jakarta.apache.org/jmeter/user_manual/rmi.html) was developed precisely to eliminate uncertain network bottlenecks. Also, we are testing two applications side by side, and any box issues should affect both equally. Still, we minimize our risk by reducing the number of extraneous processes running on the test box.

The simulated users will hit an average of one page per second, with a variation of one second (users might request another page immediately, or could wait two seconds before doing so). Real users are probably more variable, but we choose to ignore that fact for this test. Without research, have no idea what a real use pattern would look like, and (again) the side-by-side test minimizes risk.

Creating the Test in JMeter

We create a ThreadGroup in JMeter's test tree area and set the initial number of threads to 10. We will go back and manually edit this value before each test run. Then, we add a Web Testing controller to the ThreadGroup. (By the way, you can see the final test configuration in the sidebar of any of the screenshots in this section.) To the Web Testing controller, we add URL samples for each page we want a test user to visit (index, product, and so on). A Cookie Manager element takes care of maintaining client state for the entire test (important for the pet store's navigation system). Right before the listeners, we add a Gaussian random timer. We set the values as decided earlier.

The Listeners

We add several listeners to the test, each with a different purpose. The View Results listener allows us to verify that all the pages are coming through OK. After we are sure the test works, we remove this listener because it clutters the interface and adds a slight performance drag to the test. The three main visualizers we employ are the graph, the spline visualizer, and the file reporter. The graph is our best friend: It provides a quick visual analysis while also providing a running average and deviation count along its side. It also automatically scales its view of the data to keep the data in eyesight. This works for a quick check, but it prevents good visual comparisons between systems under different loads (a heavily loaded system might appear to have better response times because its response times vary so widely—to keep the data in view, JMeter shrinks the Y axis of the graph). The spline visualizer tracks minimum and maximum response times for us, and also provides a picture of the performance relative to time. This is handy, but because response times can vary so widely (under heavy load, both applications have occasional sharp spikes), the spline visualizer's averaging behavior can create a strange picture of the data. We keep it in this test only for its quick statistics.

The file reporter is probably our biggest asset in the long term. We use it to store all the response times from each test. Then, we can run a more detailed analysis if the data warrants (if both systems perform identically, we can probably skip this step). We manually change the output file for each test run to keep the data for different loads and applications separate (we use names like XSLT_100.txt).

Execution

Executing the tests is as simple as clicking on Start and then clicking on Stop after enough data has been gathered. We do not enforce any particular policy on the length of test runs—average behavior interests us more, and without a few hours for each test run, a real-world test length cannot be simulated. To switch test applications, we remove the Web testing controller from the TestPlan and replace it with a new one. This leaves the listeners, timer, and cookie manager properly configured.

Results

Even under the lightest load, the XSLT prototype takes longer to respond. As the user load increases, the XSLT times increase more rapidly than do those of the plain-JSP application. We punch the numbers we gathered (by simply writing down JMeter's analyses) into a table, shown in Table 10.1.

As you can gather from the statistics, the JSP version of the site with 100 users performs much like the XSLT version with 10.

Figures 10.14 and 10.15 show two of the test graphs. We discard most of the graphs generated by JMeter during the test because they are so difficult to compare visually. If we need valid graphs later, we will generate them from the report files.

Both graphs reveal a strong tendency to have occasional response times much higher than the average response time (the light gray line). Figure 10.16 shows how response times degrade as users are added to the load (this naturally happens as JMeter starts more threads.)

Analysis

Obviously, the XSLT prototype does not scale as well as the plain JSP solution. However, this is just the first step of a comprehensive evaluation. We begin by determining the actual performance needs of the client. Yes, the JSP version outperforms the XSLT version, but the difference between the two implementations barely registers to the end user under light load. A careful analysis of the pet store's current usage (and/or future projections) could define how *much* worse XSLT must perform to be ruled out. We also know that the tests do not accurately model user behavior—more time could be spent on that issue. Also, what other performance issues might affect the end user's experience? If the time to retrieve data from a production database (as opposed to a collocated one) adds a reliable one second to every response, the page-view time could

Table 10.1 Summary of test results (all times are in milliseconds).

	10 USERS		30 USERS		100 USERS		500 USERS	
	PLAIN JSP	XSLT	PLAIN JSP	XSLT	PLAIN JSP	XSLT	PLAIN JSP	XSLT
Maximum	20	891	51	851	991	6019	39000	33408
Average	0	58	2	195	66	3324	584	8233
Deviation	3	151	7	151	82	1260	784	11000

Note: The minimum time was usually for the first request, before the system became loaded, and so was always near 0.

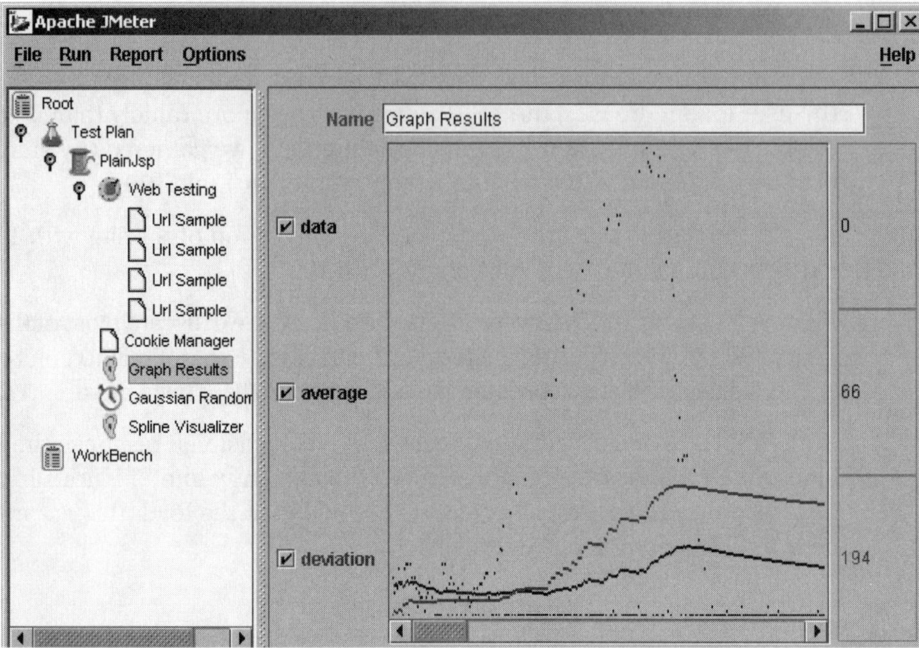

Figure 10.14 The XSLT prototype with 30 users.

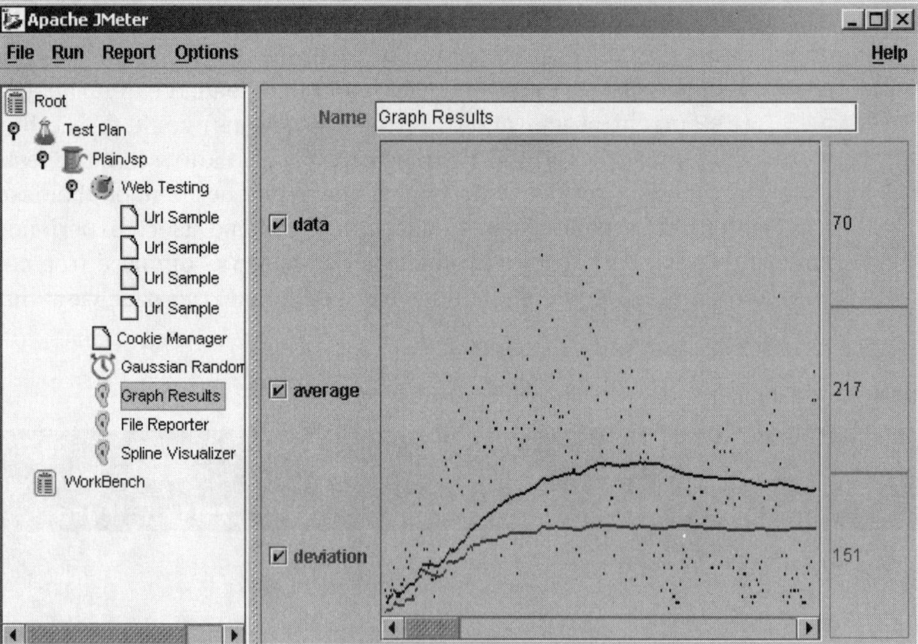

Figure 10.15 The JSP application with 100 users.

change from acceptable to unacceptable. Finally, what is acceptable or unacceptable to a user? How many seconds or milliseconds occupy the space between "zippy" and "I'll take my business elsewhere"? Any or all of these questions could yield avenues for further research.

What Do We Do?

If all the questions have been resolved and the client decides that AAA Pet Store must go forward with XSLT, and that it must handle 100 concurrent users at one second per page or less, then we need to examine what can be done to speed things up. The JMeter tests we ran could be rewritten in HttpUnit and turned into functional tests for the customer—then they would know when we had achieved their performance goals. After that, we could use profiling tools to expose bottlenecks in the system. With the bottlenecks in sight, we could refactor components, testing our performance expectations with JUnitPerf. Our prototype isn't necessarily fatally flawed—some caching and refactoring might bring it well within the functional test's "pass" range.

One thing is certain: A sensible team would not build new functionality around the unaltered prototype without at least devoting some resources to the task of improving performance. Even in that situation, the client would have to hear that there was significant risk in going forward without more exploratory development.

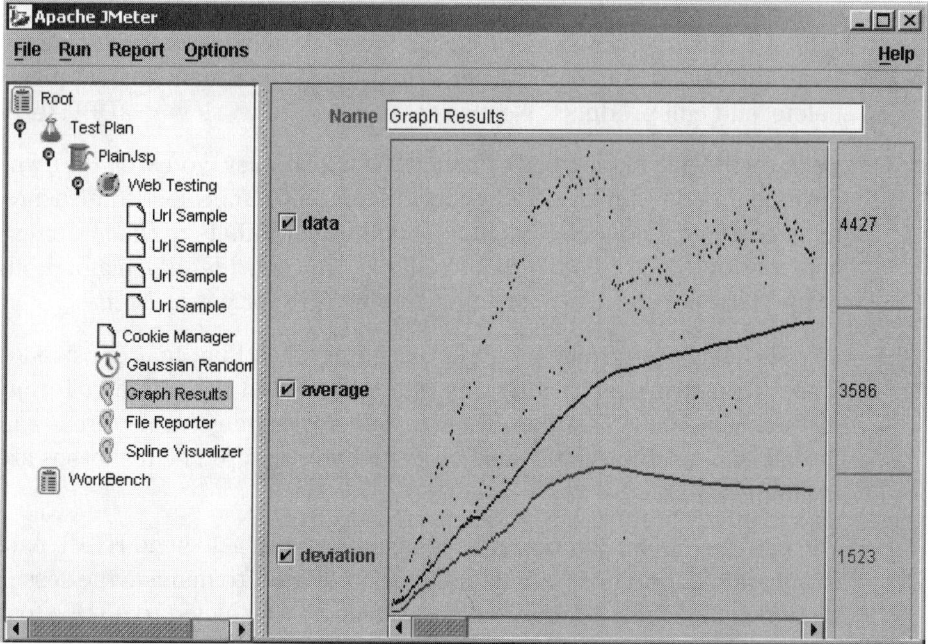

Figure 10.16 The XSLT prototype with 100 users.

Conclusion

We developed a "rubber to the road" prototype of a proposed redesign of AAA Pet Store using XSLT. Along the way, we (re)learned the value of XP's *rapid feedback* principle. A half-day's worth of testing with JMeter was enough to give the team some solid data about the relative performance characteristics of the two frameworks. Real numbers (even if gathered quickly) are worth a thousand conversations like this:

> **XSL Enthusiast:** "XML-based technology performs just fine! You just have to make sure you're using the right Fozzenbanger."
>
> **XSL Naysayer:** "XSLT will never be fast enough for a high-performance site because of the inherent performance penalties associated with glarzing the wondabanger."

Imagine that the XSLT prototype was constructed to model the future architecture of a multimillion-dollar Web site. Using JMeter to gather feedback about its potential performance could save someone a costly mistake. An XP team always looks for hidden difficulties and lurking problems so they can be avoided. JMeter is a good flashlight to shine into the dark crannies of performance.

Summary

In this chapter, we discussed testing our Web application with JMeter. We used JMeter to test the front end of the pet store: the navigation. And, we used JMeter to test the back end of the pet store: the product management piece to add, delete, and edit products. We also set up a test to work with JDBC testing.

Because JMeter makes performance testing so easy, you won't do what some developers do—you won't wait until the end of the project to measure performance. You can now incrementally build tracer bullets of the system and measure performance of the tracer bullets. You can identify major bottlenecks before they become the overriding architecture for your system.

To use JMeter, you must construct and run a TestPlan that consists of one to many ThreadGroups. A thread is like a simulated user. JMeter forms a JMeterEngine from the TestPlan. Then, the JMeterEngine creates threads, and each thread iterates through the test cases that you set up. The test cases are stored in simple XML.

You can use JMeter to post and get pages. You can also send HTML parameters to simulate a form post. Sometimes you may want to manage the session information cookie with a JMeter cookie manager. We needed to do this to navigate to the Product page of the pet store, because the current subcategory was stored in the session information.

CHAPTER 11

Load Testing with JUnitPerf

As part of the planning phase of any project, you should be given performance criteria for the completed system. By using JUnitPerf to decorate your existing JUnit test cases, you can ensure that your system meets its performance criteria. For example, you can test each Web page to ensure that it loads in 10 seconds or less and that the average load time is less than 5 seconds while the site is handling 1,000 concurrent users.

JUnitPerf 1.4 requires the use of JUnit 3.2 or higher. JUnitPerf consists of a small set of test decorators and related classes that extend the JUnit API; thus JUnitPerf tests extend a JUnit test by using the decorator pattern. You must have pre-existing JUnit tests to use JUnitPerf. JUnitPerf allows you to easily load tests and have tests fail if they do not respond in a certain time. You should be judicious in deciding when to use JUnitPerf. Using JUnitPerf to test every line of code is usually time-consuming and unnecessary. JUnitPerf is most effective in situations where you have specific performance criteria to meet. It is often a good idea to first use a performance-profiling tool, such as JProbe, to identify areas of code that have the highest potential for scalability and performance issues. Then you can focus your JUnitPerf tests on those relatively few bottleneck class methods.

You can use JUnitPerf in conjunction with HttpUnit and JMeter to test performance of a Web site under load. For example, write a set JUnit test that uses HttpUnit tests that simulate a user navigating to a product in a Web catalog. Use JMeter to flood the site with requests, while you run a navigation test under a JUnitPerf timed test and set the test to fail if it does not navigate the site to the product page in 15 seconds.

Where To Get JUnitPerf

JUnitPerf was developed by Mike Clark from Clarkware Consulting, Inc. and is distributed under the BSD license. You can download JUnitPerf at www.clarkware.com/software/JUnitPerf.html.

JUnitPerf Concepts

There are two major types of tests for JUnitPerf: the timed test and the load test, defined by the TimedTest class and LoadTest class, respectively.

When you create a TimedTest test decorator, you pass it an existing JUnit test and a maximum elapsed time in milliseconds. A TimedTest is a JUnit TestDecorator, which fails the decorated test after a specified time. You can use the TimedTest in two ways: Wait until the test completes and check the elapsed time, or fail immediately if the elapsed time exceeds the maximum.

A LoadTest is also a test decorator that runs a test with a number of simulated users for a certain amount of iterations. You can slowly ramp the load or turn it on all at once.

TimedTest Example

To show the concepts of the TimedTest put into practice, we'll create a simple JUnit test case and then decorate it with a TimedTest (see Listing 11.1 for the complete code listing). We will step through this test in the remainder of this section.

```
package xptoolkit.junitperf;
import junit.framework.TestCase;
import junit.framework.Test;
import junit.framework.TestSuite;
import junit.textui.TestRunner;


import java.util.Random;
import java.util.Vector;
import java.util.Iterator;
import com.clarkware.junitperf.TimedTest;
```

Listing 11.1 Loop test case. (continues)

```
public class SimpleTest extends TestCase{
    public SimpleTest(String testName){
        super(testName);
    }

    private final static int MAX_STRINGS = 55555;
    private final static String hiddenString = "Hi Mom";
    private final static int LENGTH = hiddenString.length();
    private static String [] strings = new String[MAX_STRINGS];
    private static Vector vector = new Vector();
    private static int hiddenLocation;

    static {
        Random random = new Random();
        for (int index=0; index < MAX_STRINGS; index++){
            strings[index]=random.nextLong() + " Not Mom";
            vector.add(strings[index]);
        }
        hiddenLocation= MAX_STRINGS-1;
        strings[hiddenLocation]=hiddenString;
        vector.setElementAt(hiddenString,hiddenLocation);

    }

    public final void testForLoop(){
        boolean found = false;
        char [] chars = null;
        int index;
        for (index=0; index < strings.length; index++){
            chars = strings[index].toCharArray();
            if (chars.length != LENGTH) return;
            if(chars[0]!='H') continue;
            if(chars[1]!='i') continue;
            if(chars[2]!=' ') continue;
            if(chars[3]!='M') continue;
            if(chars[4]!='o') continue;
            if(chars[5]!='m') continue;
            found =  true;
            break;
        }
        assertEquals("Index", hiddenLocation, index);
        assertEquals("Found", true, found);
    }

    public final void testIteration(){
        boolean found=false;
```

Listing 11.1 Loop test case. (continues)

```
        Iterator iterator = vector.iterator();
        int index=0;

        while(iterator.hasNext()){
            String string = (String) iterator.next();
            if (string.equals(hiddenString)){
                found = true;
                break;
            }
            index++;
        }
        assertEquals("Index", hiddenLocation, index);
        assertEquals("Found", true, found);
    }

    public final void testVector(){
        boolean found=false;
        Object [] items = vector.toArray();

        int index;
        String string;

        for (index=0; index < items.length; index++){
            string = (String)items[index];
            if (string.length() != LENGTH) return;
            if (string.equals(hiddenString)){
                found = true;
                break;
            }
            index++;
        }
        assertEquals("Index", hiddenLocation, index);
        assertEquals("Found", true, found);
    }


    static final int TIMES = 2000;

    public void testForLoopAlot(){
        for(int index=0; index < TIMES; index++){
            testForLoop();
        }
    }

    public void testVectorAlot(){
        for(int index=0; index < TIMES; index++){
```

Listing 11.1 Loop test case. (continues)

```
            testVector();
        }
    }


    public void testIterationAlot(){
        for(int index=0; index < TIMES; index++){
            testIteration();
        }

    }

    public static Test suite2() {
        TestSuite suite= new TestSuite();
        suite.addTest(new SimpleTest("testIterationAlot"));
        return suite;
    }

    public static Test suite1() {
        TestSuite suite= new TestSuite();
        suite.addTest(new SimpleTest("testForLoopAlot"));
        return suite;
    }

    public static void main(String [] args){
        TestRunner.run(suite1());
        TestRunner.run(suite2());
        TestRunner.run(new SimpleTest("testVectorAlot"));

        long maxElapsedTime = 5000;
        Test testCase = suite1();
        Test timedTest = new TimedTest(testCase, maxElapsedTime);
        TestRunner.run(timedTest);

        testCase = suite2();
        timedTest = new TimedTest(testCase, maxElapsedTime);
        TestRunner.run(timedTest);

        timedTest = new TimedTest(new SimpleTest("testVectorAlot"),
                                  maxElapsedTime);
        TestRunner.run(timedTest);


    }
}
```

Listing 11.1 Loop test case.

The JUnit test case has two tests that iterate through a list of strings in two different ways searching for a target string. For this scenario, we decided that a vector should be passed around; after some performance analysis, we decided that the test of the code must execute in five seconds or less so that the code will not be a bottleneck in the system's performance. The first test gets an Iterator object from a vector collection, casts each element to a string, and then checks to see if the string is equal to the hidden string as follows:

```
public void testIteration(){
    boolean found=false;
    Iterator iterator = vector.iterator();
    int index=0;

    while(iterator.hasNext()){
        String string = (String) iterator.next();
        if (string.equals(hiddenString)){
            found = true;
            break;
        }
        index++;
    }
    assertEquals("Index", hiddenLocation, index);
    assertEquals("Found", true, found);
}
```

Notice that the test asserts that the index is the same as the hiddenLocation, and that it asserts that the string was found.

The second test has the same functionality as the first, but it tries to reduce the number of method calls, casts, and lines of executed code, as follows:

```
public void testForLoop(){
    boolean found = false;
    char [] chars = null;
    int index;
    for (index=0; index < strings.length; index++){
        chars = strings[index].toCharArray();
        if (chars.length != LENGTH) return;
        if(chars[0]!='H') continue;
        if(chars[1]!='i') continue;
        if(chars[2]!=' ') continue;
        if(chars[3]!='M') continue;
        if(chars[4]!='o') continue;
        if(chars[5]!='m') continue;
        found =  true;
        break;
    }
    assertEquals("Index", hiddenLocation, index);
    assertEquals("Found", true, found);
}
```

Because the testForLoop() method runs extremely fast, we put the tests in another loop that executes 2,000 times, as follows:

```
static final int TIMES = 2000;

public void testForLoopAlot(){
    for(int index=0; index < TIMES; index++){
        testForLoop();
    }
}

public void testIterationAlot(){
    for(int index=0; index < TIMES; index++){
        testIteration();
    }

}
```

Now that we have created the tests, we need to give the tests enough data so that they will register a measurable time (this was not an issue when we all had 8080 PCs).

The code to set up the test data is not in the setUp() method as you might expect, because code in the setUp() and tearDown() methods is counted by the TimedTest decorator class. So, when we decorate this JUnit test with a JUnit-Perf TimedTest, the setup code will not be counted in the test, which makes the test of our code more accurate. The code to set up the test data is therefore all initialized in a static initializer block, as follows:

```
private final static int MAX_STRINGS = 55555;
private final static String hiddenString = "Hi Mom";
private final static int LENGTH = hiddenString.length();
private static String [] strings = new String[MAX_STRINGS];
private static Vector vector = new Vector();
private static int hiddenLocation;

static {
    Random random = new Random();
    for (int index=0; index < MAX_STRINGS; index++){
        strings[index]=random.nextLong() + " Not Mom";
        vector.add(strings[index]);
    }
    hiddenLocation= MAX_STRINGS-1;
    strings[hiddenLocation]=hiddenString;
    vector.setElementAt(hiddenString,hiddenLocation);

}
```

To run the above previous test, Iwe use JUnit TestRunner., IWe added the following code to use the TestRunner (you may recall that the TestRunner's run()

method runs a suite of tests and reports status via stdio). Notice that the main method calls junit.textui.TestRunner.run, passing it the returned value from the static suite() method:

```
public static Test suite2() {
    TestSuite suite= new TestSuite();
    suite.addTest(new SimpleTest("testIterationAlot"));
    return suite;
}

public static Test suite1() {
    TestSuite suite= new TestSuite();
    suite.addTest(new SimpleTest("testForLoopAlot"));
    return suite;
}

public static void main(String [] args){
    TestRunner.run(suite1());
    TestRunner.run(suite2());
}
```

The default behavior of the test runner prints out the time it takes to run the test. The results from running this test are as follows:

```
Time: 0.01

OK (1 tests)

.
Time: 26.071

OK (1 tests)
```

As you can see, the testForLoop executes a lot faster than the testIteration. Now that we have two working JUnit tests, let's decorate them with a JUnitPerf TimedTest. As you have likely realized by now, these two JUnits tests are supercilious. However, let's pretend for the sake of learning that it is not, and that we want to get the execution time so that the test always runs in less than five seconds. To do this, we create a JUnitPerf TimedTest. First we import the TimedTest class:

```
import com.clarkware.junitperf.TimedTest;
```

Then we run the forLoopTest through the TimedTest decorator:

```
long maxElapsedTime = 5000
Test testCase = suite1();
Test timedTest = new TimedTest(testCase, maxElapsedTime);
TestRunner.run(timedTest);
```

Notice that we pass the timedTest the TestSuite that has the testForLoop in it, and we tell it to fail if the operation takes longer than five seconds. Next we run the test for the testIteration:

```
testCase = suite2();
timedTest = new TimedTest(testCase, maxElapsedTime);
TestRunner.run(timedTest);
```

Because we know that suite2(), the testForIteration test, takes about 28 seconds, we know that it will fail. Here is the output from this test:

```
. . .
.TimedTest (WAITING): junit.framework.TestSuite@5debc3: 0 ms
. . .

.TimedTest (WAITING): junit.framework.TestSuite@218aa2: 26187 ms
1) junit.framework.TestSuite@218aa2 "Maximum elapsed time exceeded!
Expected 5000ms, but was 26187ms."

FAILURES!!!
Tests run: 1,  Failures: 1,  Errors: 0
```

We can see that the test failed. Just for kicks, let's try to optimize the test to pass. Suppose it would make the code much simpler if we were able to use a vector. However, instead of grabbing the iterator, we decide to see how much faster would it be if we get the array from the vector. Here is the code we add to try this new search function:

```
    public final void testVector(){
        boolean found=false;
        Object [] items = vector.toArray();

        int index;
        String string;

        for (index=0; index < items.length; index++){
            string = (String)items[index];
            if (string.length() != LENGTH) return;
            if (string.equals(hiddenString)){
                found = true;
                break;
            }
            index++;
        }
        assertEquals("Index", hiddenLocation, index);
        assertEquals("Found", true, found);
    }

. . .
```

```
        public void testVectorAlot(){
            for(int index=0; index < TIMES; index++){
                testVector();
            }
        }
    . . .
            TestRunner.run(new SimpleTest("testVectorAlot"));
    . . .
            timedTest = new TimedTest(new SimpleTest("testVectorAlot"),
                 maxElapsedTime);
            TestRunner.run(timedTest);
```

We set up JUnitPerf as before, but notice when we run this test it now passes, and we are still using a vector. Here is the output from this code:

```
.
Time: 4.617


.
TimedTest (WAITING): testVectorAlot(xptoolkit.junitperf.SimpleTest):
4606 ms

Time: 4.606

OK (1 tests)
```

Just to cap off what we have done, we created a simple JUnit test that showed different ways to loop through a list of string searching for a string. We set up a JUnitPerf test for each test to see if each test could finish the test in under five seconds. We had two extreme version of the search. One version used a String array and a for loop, and it was really fast. The other version used the iterator utility to iterate through the strings in a vector and search for the string. In our contrived example, we decided that we had to use a vector, so we wrote another loop that met the criteria (and was a lot more readable than the really fast version), and then we used JUnitPerf TimedTest to prove that the new loop met the criteria.

LoadTest Example

Like the TimedTest, a LoadTest is a test decorator. The LoadTest runs a test with a number of simulated concurrent users and iterations. When you create a LoadTest class instance, you pass it a number of concurrent users. Each user runs the test once, unless you set the iteration higher when you construct a LoadTest.

First, to see a simple usage of the LoadTest, let's take our testVectorAlot (Listing 11.1) and this time load-test with five threads. Because we are running this test on a machine with one processor, we expect the time to go up by a factor of five or so. Here is the code to run the LoadTest:

```
int users = 5;
Test loadTest = new LoadTest(
                new SimpleTest("testVectorAlot"), users);
TestRunner.run(loadTest);
```

Notice that the LoadTest constructor is a lot like the TimeTest constructor in the last section when we wrapped the SimpleTest in the TimedTest. Now, instead of using the TimedTest and passing the max time out, we are using the LoadTest class and passing the number of user threads to simulate.

Here is the output from this test:

```
.....
Time: 27.75

OK (5 tests)
```

The JUnit framework uses the decorator design pattern to add additional functionality to tests dynamically. Thus, you can nest a test inside a decorator test that adds additional functionality but still has the same public interface as the nested test. You can nest the test to decorate the nested test. If we wanted a test where each user ran 5 tests, the test had to complete in 150 seconds, and the test failed as soon as 150 seconds passed, we could create it as follows.

We first import the RepeatedTest from JUnit (we could have used this approach instead of the forXXXAlot tests earlier):

```
import junit.extensions.RepeatedTest;
```

Next, we create the simpleTest to run the testVector as follows:

```
Test simpleTest = new SimpleTest("testVector");
```

We create the repeated test to execute 2,000 iterations:

```
int iterations = 2000;
Test repeatedTest = new RepeatedTest(simpleTest, iterations);
```

Notice that the simpleTest is passed to the repeated test constructor, along with the number of iterations that we want the test run. We decorated the simple test with a repeated test.

Next, we decorate the repeated test with a load test:

```
int users = 5;
Test loadTest = new LoadTest(repeatedTest, users);
```

Finally, we decorate the loadTest with the timedTest and run the timedTest as follows:

```
long maxElapsedTime = 150 * 1000;
Test timedTest = new TimedTest(loadTest, maxElapsedTime);
TestRunner.run(timedTest);
```

In this section, we covered how to decorate test with different tests. As we can see, you can nest these tests pretty deep.

Case Study

In this case study, we incorporate JUnitPerf, HttpUnit, and JMeter. Basically, we pound on the site with JMeter at the same time we run an HttpUnit test decorated with a JUnitPerf timed test. We essentially scale up the user until we no longer meet the timed requirement.

HTTPUnit Test

JUnitPerf needs a host JUnit test to work. Thus, the first part of this case study is writing an HttpUnit test that will test the site. For this case study, I we took the code for the pet store HttpUnit case study at the end of Chapter 7, "Unit Testing with JUnit." We won't cover the code in detail, again here, but briefly, the test code performs navigation and form entry. Here is a concise overview of the code to test the site.

First, we import the needed HttpUnit and support classes as follows:

```
import com.meterware.httpunit.*;
import java.io.IOException;
import java.net.MalformedURLException;
import org.xml.sax.*;
import org.w3c.dom.*;
import junit.framework.*;
```

Next, we define some constants that point to our site.

```
    protected static String HOST = "http://localhost/pet/";
    protected static String MGMT = "mgmt/";
    protected static String INDEX_PAGE = "index.jsp";
    protected static String SUBCATEGORY_PAGE = "subcategory.jsp?id=222";
```

In the real world, you may make the host a command- line argument. For this example, we just hard-coded it. First let's cover look at the navigation tests.

Here is the code to test the main page.

```
    public void testIndex() throws Exception {
        WebConversation wc = new WebConversation();
        WebResponse resp = wc.getResponse(HOST+INDEX_PAGE);
```

```
        WebTable table = resp.getTables()[2];

        assertEquals("# of tables", 3, resp.getTables().length);
        assertEquals("message in third table",
                     "Welcome to AAA Pets",
                     table.getCellAsText(0,0));
    }
```

This code verifies that the index page has exactly three HTML tables and displays the message "Welcome to AAA Pets" in the body of the third table.

Here is the code to test the subcategory page. This test verifies that there are three links corresponding to the products (breeds) associated with the subcategory "cats":

```
    public void testSubCategory() throws Exception {
        WebConversation wc = new WebConversation();
        WebResponse resp = wc.getResponse(HOST + SUBCATEGORY_PAGE);

        assertNotNull("Cat Breed #1", resp.getLinkWith("Calico"));
        assertNotNull("Cat Breed #2", resp.getLinkWith("Jaguar"));
        assertNotNull("Cat Breed #3", resp.getLinkWith("Siamese"));
    }
```

Notice that the test is checking for the data that was populated with the sample data from the buildDB.xml ant buildfile discussed in the last case study on JUnit. There is also a test on Product (testProduct) that we haven't listed here because we covered it in the HttpUnit case study.

In addtion to these navigation tests, three tests examine the form entry on the product management price (testCreate, testDelete, and testEdit). For example, here is the code to test creating a product.

```
   /**
     * Verifies that it can create a new product.
     */
    public void testCreate() throws Exception {

        WebConversation wc = new WebConversation();
        WebResponse   resp = wc.getResponse(
                              HOST + MGMT + SUBCATEGORY_PAGE);

        WebForm form = resp.getForms()[0];
```

```
        WebRequest req = form.getRequest("add");
        resp = wc.getResponse(req);

        form = resp.getForms()[0];
        req = form.getRequest();
        req.setParameter("name", "Persian");
        req.setParameter("price", "$10.00");
        req.setParameter("qty", "2");

        resp = wc.getResponse(req);
        resp = wc.getResponse(HOST + MGMT + SUBCATEGORY_PAGE);

        assertNotNull("link for 'Persian'", resp.getLinkWith("Persian"));
    }
```

Now that you get the gist of the HttpUnit test for the Web navigation and product management, let's look at the JMeter test.

JMeter Configuration

For the JMeter configuration, like HttpUnit, we will navigate the site and manage products (add, delete, edit) on the backend. For this test, we will set up the back end with one simulated users that edits a site randomly distributed every 30 seconds with a standard deviation of 5 seconds using the Gaussian random timer. A front-end user will hit the site every three seconds with a standard deviation of five seconds using the Gaussian random timer.

Chapter 10, "Measuring Application Performance with JMeter," explained in depth how to set up JMeter to do perform this magic. For completeness, Figure 11.1 shows the configuration panel for adding a test product to the Web site using JMeter.

Figure 11.1 also shows that we have two thread groups, one to perform product management and one to handle front-end navigation of the site similar to testProduct, testIndex, and testSubcategory in the earlier HttpUnit test. Notice that even though Figure 11.1 shows the Product Management thread group and the Navigation thread group in the same JMeter instance, we run them in two different instances because JMeter sums the times; we want the simulated users that are navigating to be faster than the simulated users that are performing product management.

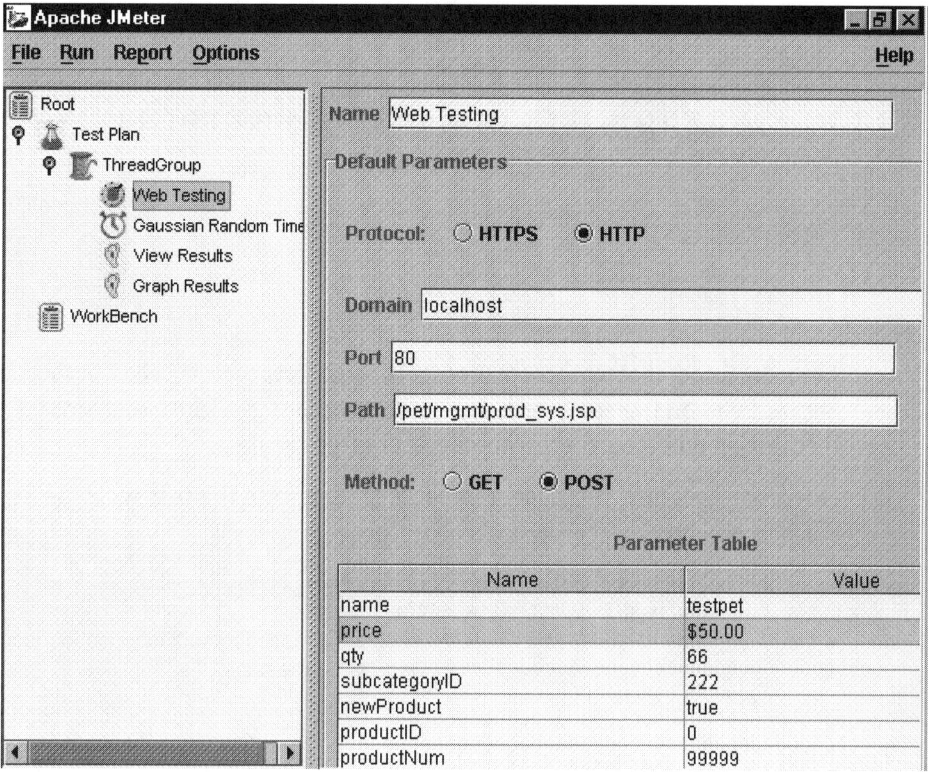

Figure 11.1 Adding a product with JMeter.

Putting It All Together

Now that we have the JMeter test and the HttpUnit test, let's require the test that navigates and edits a product to complete in less that five seconds., In addition, we want to determine how many simultaneous users we can have and still meet this threshold. After viewing the Web logs of an existing site, we model the behavior of the existing site and created a JMeter test from the previous section).

We want to will decorate the HttpUnit test with a JUnitPerf timed test. The existing HttpUnit test starts its test as follows:

```
public static void main(String args[]) {
    junit.textui.TestRunner.run(suite());
}
```

```
    public static Test suite() {
        return new TestSuite(HttpUnitTest.class);
    }
```

When we run this test a few times to make sure that Resin (the servlet engine) compiles the JSPs, we get the following output:

```
......
Time: 1.202

OK (6 tests)
```

Keep in mind that we are running Resin, JBoss (the EJB server), and SQL Server 2000 on the same box. If you are running in a more distributed environment or on a beefier box, you may get better results.

Now that we know the baseline test, let's decorate the test with the TimedTest class to execute in five seconds as follows:

```
    public static void main(String args[]) {
         int maxElapsedTime = 5000;
         Test timedTest = new TimedTest(suite(), maxElapsedTime);
         junit.textui.TestRunner.run(timedTest);
    }
```

Just for a baseline, we run both thread groups for a while with one thread each and get the following results:

```
......TimedTest (WAITING):
test.xptoolkit.petstore.httpunit.HttpUnitTest: 1292 ms

Time: 1.302

OK (6 tests)
```

Now, increase the number of front-end simulated users in JMeter to five users. We stop and start the Navigation thread group and rerun the JUnitPerf-decorated HttpUnit test. We get the following results:

```
......TimedTest (WAITING):
test.xptoolkit.petstore.httpunit.HttpUnitTest: 1232 ms

Time: 1.232

OK (6 tests)
```

We run this test a few times to make sure we get the same results. Now, we crank up the number of users to 50, because we want to see some action. We also notice that we're running the TimedTest several times, so we decide to decorate it with a RepeatedTest as follows:

```
public static void main(String args[]) {
     //junit.textui.TestRunner.run(suite());
     int maxElapsedTime = 5000;
     Test timedTest = new TimedTest(suite(), maxElapsedTime);
     Test repeatTest = new RepeatedTest(timedTest,5);
     junit.textui.TestRunner.run(repeatTest);
 }
```

The results with 50 users are as follows:

```
......TimedTest (WAITING):
test.xptoolkit.petstore.httpunit.HttpUnitTest:
 1382 ms
......TimedTest (WAITING):
test.xptoolkit.petstore.httpunit.HttpUnitTest:
 501 ms
......TimedTest (WAITING):
test.xptoolkit.petstore.httpunit.HttpUnitTest:
 591 ms
......TimedTest (WAITING):
test.xptoolkit.petstore.httpunit.HttpUnitTest:
 500 ms
......TimedTest (WAITING):
test.xptoolkit.petstore.httpunit.HttpUnitTest:
 461 ms

Time: 3.435

OK (30 tests)
```

As you can see, the overall performance has improved after the first iteration because the test class was created already.

Now it's time to get nasty. We increase the JMeter test to run 5,000 simulated users with the Navigation Thread group. We get the following results:

```
......TimedTest (WAITING):
test.xptoolkit.petstore.httpunit.HttpUnitTest:
 3305 ms
```

```
......TimedTest (WAITING):
test.xptoolkit.petstore.httpunit.HttpUnitTest:
 6670 ms
F......TimedTest (WAITING):
test.xptoolkit.petstore.httpunit.HttpUnitTest:
 420 ms
......TimedTest (WAITING):
test.xptoolkit.petstore.httpunit.HttpUnitTest:
 301 ms
......TimedTest (WAITING):
test.xptoolkit.petstore.httpunit.HttpUnitTest:
 330 ms

Time: 11.026
There was 1 failure:
1) test.xptoolkit.petstore.httpunit.HttpUnitTest "Maximum elapsed time
 exceeded! Expected 5000ms, but was 6670ms."

FAILURES!!!
Tests run: 30,  Failures: 1,  Errors: 0
```

As we can see, on my current machine we can handle around 5,000 users attacking the site before we start to fail the test and go over five seconds (we are still under five seconds on average). The same techniques could be used on a real Web application with real requirements to help you determine what hardware you need, how to partition your Web application, and so on.

Real Test

For a real test, you should increase the number of users at a slower pace, and have the JUnitPerf test repeat 30 times. If any of the 30 times failed, then the test would fail. This way, passing the test passing would not be a fluke fluctuation of system performance, but a realistic result.

Conclusion

We incorporated JUnitPerf, HttpUnit, and JMeter in this case study to pound on the site with JMeter and measure performance of the site under load; JUnitPerf wrapped a test done in HttpUnit that navigated the site and edited the back end. We essentially scaled the simulated navigation users until we no longer meet the timed requirement.

Summary

This chapter demonstrated the extensibility of the JUnit framework by showing several test decorators from JUnitPerf and the JUnit extensions. We also gave a real-world example of how to create TimedTest for code we that is about to be optimized or code that has a strict requirement to be optimized.

JUnitPerf works with existing JUnit tests. If you have performance criteria for a certain piece of code, then create a JUnitPerf test to show your code meets the criteria and continues to meet the criteria after you refactor the code.a

CHAPTER 12

Ant Tag Reference

Another Neat Tool (Ant), despite its modest name, is a powerful platform-independent build tool. By creating XML files to develop build tasks, you can extend Ant to solve a host of problems, taking it far beyond simple code compilation. Ant's focus on code completion and application building is its strength and weakness. Ant does solve some problems programmatically. However, it is not intended to be a programming language. This reference covers most of Ant's built-in tasks and a few optional tasks that relate to the content of this book. The task descriptions are concise and organized into logical groupings for easier reference.

Ant Command Line Options

After following Ant's installation instructions, you can execute build.xml files by simply typing "ant" at the command prompt. If you're using someone else's buildfile, you should investigate its purpose and functionality before running it. If the creator of the buildfile has described its main tasks, that extended help/usage will be available using the projecthelp switch.

NOTE

Throughout this chapter, an asterisk (*) after a parameter name indicates that this is a required parameter in the task's simplest form.

The general syntax for the ant command line is as follows:

```
ant [options] [target [target2 [target3] ...]]
```

Simple buildfiles won't require most of these switches. However, if your buildfile is not named build.xml, you will need to specify the buildfile's name by using the -buildfile option; to execute a target other than the default, use the following:

```
ant -buildfile [ANT file] [target]
```

Command line options displayed from Ant's help option are as follows:

```
-help                    print this message
-projecthelp             print project help information
-version                 print the version information and exit
-quiet                   be extra quiet
-verbose                 be extra verbose
-debug                   print debugging information
-emacs                   produce logging information without adornments
-logfile [file]          use given file for log output
-logger [classname]      the class that is to perform logging
-listener [classname]    add an instance of class as a project listener
-buildfile [file]        use specified buildfile
-find [file]             search for buildfile towards the root of the
                         filesystem and use the first one found
-Dproperty=[value]       set property to value
```

XML Tag

Ant uses XML files to execute. The default name of Ant's XML file is build.xml. If an Ant user types "ant" with no other commands, Ant will attempt to open build.xml. Ant's build.xml file must contain the XML version and encoding:

```
<?xml version="1.0" encoding="UTF-8"?>
```

If you are not familiar with XML encoding, be aware that comments are written as follows:

```
<!-- comment goes here -->
```

Ant Parent Elements

There are many parent tags in Ant, which are described in this section.

Project Tag

All targets are nested within a parent tag that defines the Ant project:

```
<project basedir="[working directory]" default="[default task]"
name="[project name]">
```

```
        <!--All tasks will be nested within targets here-->

</project>
```

Parameters

name Name of the project

default* The target to use when one is not specified in the Ant command line execution

basedir The working directory for the project or root path for the project; defaults to the parent directory of the build file

Target Tag

All of Ant's tasks fit into a parent target element:

```
<target name="[target name]"/>
```

All tasks reside within target tags. The parent target tag defines the order of execution by declaring dependences. All dependent tasks will then execute before the task that defined it. This relationship is the primary way to define execution order within Ant files. Alternatively, the antcall and ant tasks can be used to execute tasks by target name. For more information, refer to these tasks under the section "Ant's Key Tasks" later in this chapter for more detail.

Parameters

name* Name of the target.

depends A comma-separated list of tasks that must execute all of their task's dependences, listed in their task parameter, before the task will execute:

```
<target name="[target name]" depends="[dependent target name]"/>
```

When the target is called, the dependent target will execute will execute first. For example, consider the following usage:

```
<target name="A"/>
<target name="B" depends="A"/>
<target name="C" depends="B"/>
<target name="D" depends="C,E"/>
<target name="E" depends="C,B,A"/>
```

If we execute the following command, the order of execution will be A, B, C, E, and then D:

```
ant d
```

If we execute the following command, the order of execution will be A, B, C, and then E. No dependency is defined for D, so target D will not execute:

```
ant e
```

if Name of a property that must exist in order for the task to run. It does not evaluate against the value of a property, it only checks to see if the property exists:

```
<target name="[target name]" if="[property name]"/>
```

When the target executes, it looks to see if a property with that name exists. If it does, the task will execute.

unless Name of a property that must not be set in order for the task to execute. The "unless" parameter does not depend on the "if" parameter. It only evaluates that a property does not exist; it does not evaluate against the value of a property:

```
<target name="[target name]" unless="[property name]"/>
```

When the target executes, it will look to see if a property with that name exists. If it does, the task will not execute.

description A short description of the task.. These descriptions do not print to the screen:

```
<target name="[target name]" description="[task description]"/>
```

When you use Ant's command line option –projecthelp, all the tasks and their descriptions will be printed to the screen.

Path Tag

The path element allows for paths to be used by many tasks:

```
<path id=[property] path="[path]"/>
```

Parameter

id* Property to represent many path and class path references. The property is referred to as a *reference id*. Many tasks allow the use of a path task via the reference id.

Nested Parameters

pathelement A class used to specify both paths and class paths. It is often used as a child of a project to create a set of reusable paths and class paths:

```
<path>
    <pathelement path="[path]"/>
</path>
```

path A comma-separated list of paths:

```
<path>
    <pathelement path="[path]"/>
</path>
```

location A comma-separated list of paths relative to the base directory of the project:

```
<path>
    <pathelement location="classes"/>
</path>
```

fileset groups a set of files and directories. The following buildfile snippets groups all jar files in the /cvs/jars directory as follows:

```
<path>
    <fileset dir="/cvs/jars" >
        <include name="**/*.jar"/>
    </fileset>
</path>
```

Filter Tag

Filters can be used for file-copying tasks. All instances of a specified token can be replaced with a specified value.

A *token* is a value that can be automatically expanded in a set of text files when they are copied. Tokens are encased in the @ character as in @filename@. If a token exists in a file but no token is defined in the buildfile then no action will be taken, i.e., the token defined in the file will not be changed.

You define a token using the filter tag as follows:

```
<filter token="filename" value="autoexec.bat"/>
```

Later if you copied a text file with that contained the text "@filename@" and filtering is on, the text "@filename@" is replaced with "autoexec.bat". Demonstrated as follows:

```
<copy todir="/tmp" filtering="true">
  <fileset dir="/src/config"/>
</copy>
```

Parameters

token* Value of the string of text to be replaced in the file. An at sign (@) will be placed around this value automatically.

value* Replacement value to be applied to the token in the file.

filtersfile File containing one name/value pair per line. This file creates filters for every entry in the properties file.

filtersfile* A properties file from which to read the filters.

Tstamp Tag

The tstamp task sets several properties to the current date and time. From the system time:

DSTAMP The date formatted as “yyyymmdd”

TSTAMP The time formatted as “hhmm”

TODAY The current date formatted as “month day year”

The tag is as follows:

```
<tstamp/>
```

Nested Parameters

property A property to set to a particular time/date format

pattern Time/date pattern to use:

```
<tstamp>
    <format property="TODAY_UK" pattern="d MMMM yyyy">
</tstamp>
```

Ant Key Tasks

A key task is something that must be done for Ant. In contrast, most other tasks have more to do with accomplishing things for the application we are building.

Ant Task

The ant task executes an Ant buildfile from the currently executing Ant script:

```
<ANT antfile="[ant file name]"/>
```

It will execute the project’s default target.

Parameters

antfile* The name of the Ant file to execute; defaults to build.xml

dir The directory where the Ant file is located The root path of this file is specified in the project tag’s basedir parameter, at the beginning of the Ant file.

```
<ANT antfile="[ant file] dir="[location of ant file]"/>
```

target A specific target to be run, located in the Ant file:

```
<ANT antfile="[ant file] target="[target]"/>
```

output A file to hold the output of the Ant script:

```
<ANT antfile="[ant file] output="[log file]"/>
```

Antcall Task

The antcall task executes an Ant target:

```
<antcall target="[target]"/>
```

All of the dependent Ant targets will execute, followed by the specific target specified.

Parameters

target* The target name that antcall will execute.

Nested Parameters

param A property to be set before running the tasks in the target.

name Name of a property to be assigned a value.

value Value to assign to the property.

This example will set a property to a value when the antcall task is executed:

```
<antcall target="[target name]">
        <param name="[property]" value="[property value]"/>
</antcall>
```

Available Task

You can use the available task to determine if a file, class, or Java Virtual Machine (JVM) system property is available. If it is not present, the task sets the value of a given property to "false" (the value defaults to "true").

In the following example, if the file is not available, the property will be set to "false":

```
<available file="[resource]" property="[property]"/>
```

Parameters

property* Name of the property to set, as defined by the property task.

value The text that will be assigned to the property if the resource is available. The default value is "true":

```
<available file="[file name]" property="[property]" value="[property
    value]"/>
```

classname Name of a class file; used to determine if the class file is available:

```
<available classname="[class file]" property="[property]"/>
```

resource Name of a JVM resource; used to determine if the resource is available:

```
<available resource ="[JVM Resource]" property="[property]"/>
```

file* Name of a file; used to determine if the file is available.

classpath A class path to use when looking up class files with the classname attribute:

```
<available classpath="[class path]" classname="[class file]"/>
```

classpathref A classpathref is used to look into a classpath that has already been defined with a path element demonstrated in the buildfile snippet below.

The following example will determine if a class file within a given path exists, by using the property that references a path:

```
<project…
     <path id="[property]">
          <pathelement path="[path]/"/>
     </path>

     <task…
          <available classname="[class file]" classpathref="[property
               of path]"/>
     </task>
```

Nested Parameter

classpath Allows tasks to use paths and class paths efficiently (see section "Frequently Used Nested Parameters and Elements" at the end of this chapter).

Echo Task

The echo task sends message to Ant's system output or to a specified file:

```
<echo message="Hello world"/>

<echo>
This is a longer message stretching over
two lines.
</echo>
```

Parameters

message* Text of the message to display.

file Name of a file to direct output to.

append Boolean value of "true" or "false". When set to "true", output will be appended to a file specified by the file element. Defaults to "false".

Fail Task

The fail task stops execution of the current build:

```
<fail/>
```

Parameter

message Text of a message to be displayed when the fail task is executed

Property Task

The property task creates properties by assigning values to names. Properties set outside the current Ant project cannot be reassigned in the current Ant project:

```
<property name="[property]" value="[property value]"/>
```

Parameters

name* A name to be assigned to a name/value pair

value* A value to be assigned to a name/value pair

refid A name used in referring to an attribute specified by the "id" parameter of a path structure (see the path element in the section "Ant Parent Elements"):

```
<property refid="[property]"/>
```

file A reference to an external properties file in which each line specifies a new key value pair:

```
<property file="[file name]"/>
```

location A reference to an external properties file with an absolute path, in which each line specifies a new key value pair in the file:

```
<property location="[absolute path]"/>
```

environment A prefix to be assigned to the property used to get the current systems properties:

```
<property environment="[property]"/>
```

The following line will return the value of the system property:

```
<echo message="[environment property].[system property]"
```

classpath The class path used to determine the properties file for the java.util.Properties class in Sun's JDK

classpathref The class path defined in Ant's path element that is used to determine the properties file for the java.util.Properties class in Sun's JDK

Nested Parameter

classpath Allows tasks to use paths and class paths efficiently (see section "Frequently Used Nested Parameters and Elements" at the end of this chapter).

Taskdef Task

The taskdef task creates a custom task by executing Java classes:

```
<taskdef name="[task]" classname="[java class]"/>
```

Parameters

name* The name of the task

classname* The full class name

classpath The class path used when looking up the class name:

```
<taskdef name="[task]" classname="[java class]" classpath"[classpath]"/>
```

Directory and File System Tasks

These are tasks focusing on file-based issues.

Chmod Task

The chmod task changes file permissions on Unix systems:

```
<chmod file="[file]" perm="[permissions]"/>
```

Parameters

file* File or directory on which to alter permissions.

dir Directory whose files and directories are targeted to have their permissions changed:

```
<chmod dir="[path]" perm="[permissions]"/>
```

perm* Value to which the targeted files' or directories' permissions will be set. On Unix systems, there are typically three groups: User, Group, and Other. The three values used most often to set these values are Read, Write, and Execute.

defaultexcludes A value of "yes" or "no". Indicates whether default excludes are used.

includes A comma-separated list of patterns to include in the file set. All other files are excluded.

includesfile A file source of patterns to include in the file set. All other files will be excluded.

excludes A comma-separated list of patterns to exclude in the file set. All other files are included.

excludesfile A file source of patterns to exclude in the file set. All other files will be included.

parallel If "false", more then one chmod command can be used. Defaults to "true".

type A value of "file", "dir", or "both"; defaults to "file". The file command sends only file names as system commands. The dir command sends the directory name to be used to determine what files to execute. The both command uses the file names and directory names.

Nested Parameters

fileset Specifies a collections of files (see section "Frequently Used Nested Parameters and Elements" at the end of this chapter for more information).

Copy Task

The copy task attempts to create a copy of a file/directory structure and place it in a specified directory:

```
<copy file="[file name]" todir="[directory]"/>
```

Source files that are older then the destination files are not copied unless otherwise specified with the "overwrite" parameter. You can also use this command to copy a source file to a destination of a different name.

Parameters

***file** File name of the source target file. When you're using a nested file set, the "todir" or "tofile" parameter is required, instead.

preservelastmodified Boolean value of “yes” or “no”. It gives the destination files the same creation dates as the source files.

tofile Name of the destination file name target:

```
<copy file="[file name]" tofile="[file name]"/>
```

***todir** Name of the destination directory target.

overwrite When set to “yes”, older source files will overwrite newer files in the destination. Defaults to “no”.

filtering When set to “yes”, turns on token filtering (for more information, see the section “Ant Parent Elements” earlier in this chapter.) Defaults to “no”.

flatten When set to “yes”, the target is identical to the source name and the directory structure is stripped off, effectively making the branch of the directory tree flat. Defaults to “no”.

includeEmptyDirs When set to “no”, the empty directories in a file set are not created in the destination target. Defaults to “yes”.

Nested Parameters

fileset Specifies a collections of files (see section “Frequently Used Nested Parameters and Elements” at the end of this chapter for more information).

mapper A definition can be found under the “Frequently Used Nested Parameters” section at the end of this chapter.

Delete Task

The delete task removes a file or a file structure from a directory structure:

```
<delete file="/lib/foo.jar"/>
```

If the file or directory does not exist, execution is halted, unless the “quiet” parameter is set to “true”.

Parameters

file* File name of the target to be removed.

dir Directory name of the target to be removed:

```
<delete dir="../foo"/>
```

verbose When set to “false”, deleted files will not be written out during execution. Defaults to “true”.

quiet When set to “true”, the build won’t fail if the item does not exist when delete is called. Error messages pertaining to files or directories that don’t exist will also be suppressed. Defaults to “false”.

includeEmptyDirs When set to "true" while using a fileset, empty directories will be deleted. Defaults to "false".

Nested Parameters

fileset Specifies a collections of files (see section "Frequently Used Nested Parameters and Elements" at the end of this chapter for more information).

mapper A definition can be found under the "Frequently Used Nested Parameters" section at the end of this chapter.

Mkdir Task

The mkdir task creates a directory structure, adding directories when needed:

```
<mkdir dir="[directory]>
```

Parameter

***dir** The directory structure to create.

Move Task

The move task attempts to delete the source file or single directory while creating a copy of that file or directory in a new location:

```
<move file="[file]" todir="[directory]"/>
```

Using move in conjunction with a "fileset" parameter enables you to move groups of files and directory structures. This command can also be used to move a source file to a destination with a different name.

Parameters

***file** The file name of the source target file to be removed.

tofile The name that the file will have when written:

```
<move file="[file]" tofile="[file]"/>
```

todir* The name of the destination directory.

overwrite When set to "yes", older source files will overwrite newer files in the destination. Defaults to "no".

filtering When set to "on", token filtering is used. Defaults to "off".

flatten When set to "yes", the target is identical to the source name and the directory structure is stripped off, effectively making the branch of the directory tree flat. Defaults to "no".

includeEmptyDirs When set to "no", the empty directories in a file set will not be created in the destination target. Defaults to "yes".

Nested Parameters

fileset Specifies a collections of files (see section "Frequently Used Nested Parameters and Elements" at the end of this chapter for more information).

mapper A definition can be found under the "Frequently Used Nested Parameters" section at the end of this chapter.

Touch Task

The touch task changes the modification time of existing files to the current time, unless a time is specifically stated. If the file does not exist, it is created:

```
<touch file="[file]"/>
```

Parameters

***file** Name of the file to manipulate or create

millis The modification time in seconds since Jan 1 1970

datetime The modification time in the format "MM/DD/YYYY HH:MM AM":

```
<touch file="[file]" datetime="01/01/2000 12:00 am"/>
```

External Execution Tasks

External execution tasks enable you to invoke other programs and shell scripts.

Apply Task

The apply, exec, and execon tasks all have similar functions, but it is useful to review their capabilities before you decide which one to use. Apply is the most complex of the three. It executes the specified program using both file sets and mappers. The file sets define a group of files that will be applied to the executable. The mapper allows for time and date checking to compare the source files times against the destination files, avoiding unnecessary execution of unwanted sources. The apply task is as follows:

```
<apply executable="[command]" dest="[path]"/>
```

Parameters

***executable** File name of the executable.

***dest** Directory that holds the target files.

dir The working directory of the system command.

os List of operating systems on which the command will run.

output A file to store the output of the command.

timeout Amount of time after which execution will be halted, specified in milliseconds.

failonerror If the program returns a code other then 0, the build will fail.

parallel When set to "true", files are appended as arguments rather than being executed individually. Defaults to "false".

type Value of "file", "dir", or "both". The "file" command sends only file names as system commands. The "dir" command sends the directory name to be used to determine what files to execute. The "both" command uses file names and directory names. Defaults to "file".

Nested Parameters

fileset Specifies a collections of files (see section "Frequently Used Nested Parameters and Elements" at the end of this chapter for more information).

arg Comand line arguments for the command.

srcfile In cases where some arguments come befor and some are after the name of the soure files name, it's relative poison can be marked with the srcfile tag.

```
<apply executable=[file name]>
  <arg value=[argument]/>
  <srfile/>
  <arg value=[argument]/>
  <fileset dir=[path]/>
</apply>
```

targetfile Uses the dest parameter of the apply task to find files to be used as targets. Like the srcfile nested task is marks the location of the targeted files within command line arguments.

env Specifies values available at run time.

- **key** Name of the environmental variable.
- **value** Value of the environmental variable.
- **path** A path value to use with a key.
- **file** A file to use with a given command.
- **mapper** A definition can be found under the "Frequently Used Nested Parameters" section at the end of this chapter.

Exec Task

As we mentioned earlier, the apply, exec, and execon tasks have similar functions. Exec is the simplest of the three—it simply executes the specified program:

```
<exec executable="[commad and switches]"/>
```

Parameters

***command** The whole command line as it would be executed, with all its parameters, on the system.

executable File name of the executable.

dir Working directory of the system command.

os List of operating systems on which the command will run.

output File to store the output of the command.

timeout Amount of time after which execution will be halted, specified in milliseconds.

failonerror If the program returns a code other then 0, the build will fail.

newenvironment When new environment variables are specified, does not propagate the old environment. Defaults to "false".

Nested Parameters

arg Comand line arguments for the command.

env Specifies values available at run time.

- **key** Name of the environmental variable.
- **value** Value of the environmental variable.
- **path** A path value to use with a key.
- **file** A file to use with a given command.
- **mapper** A definition can be found under the Frequently Used Nested Parameters section.

Execon Task

As we've mentioned, the apply, exec, and execon tasks have similar functions. Execon's complexity falls between the other two. It executes the specified program and allows for filesets to be used. The filesets define a group of files that can be applied to the executable:

```
<execon executable="[command]">
  <fileset dir="[directory]" includes="[pateren set]"/>
</apply>
```

Parameters

***executable** File name of the executable.

dir The working directory of the system command.

os List of operating systems on which the command will run.

output File to store the output of the command.

timeout Amount of time after which execution will be halted, specified in milliseconds.

failonerror If the program returns a code other then 0, the build will fail.

newenvironment When new environment variables are specified, does not propagate the old environment. Defaults to "false".

parallel When set to "true", files are appended as arguments rather than being executed individually. Defaults to "false".

type Value of "file", "dir", or "both". The "file: command sends only file names as system commands. The "dir" command sends the directory name to be used to determine what files to execute. The "both" command uses file names and directory names. Defaults to "file".

Nested Parameters

fileset Specifies a collections of files (see section "Frequently Used Nested Parameters and Elements" at the end of this chapter for more information).

arg Comand line arguments for the command.**srcfile** In cases where some arguments come befor and some are after the name of the soure files name, it's relative poison can be marked with the srcfile tag.

```
<apply executable=[file name]>
  <arg value=[argument]/>
  <srfile/>
  <arg value=[argument]/>
  <fileset dir=[path]/>
</apply>
```

targetfile Uses the dest parameter of the apply task to find files to be used as targets. Like the srcfile nested task is marks the location of the targeted files within command line arguments.

env Specifies values available at run time.

- **key** Name of the environmental variable.
- **value** Value of the environmental variable.
- **path** A path value to use with a key.
- **file** A file to use with a given command.

- **mapper** A definition can be found under the Frequently Used Nested Parameters section.

Java Task

The java task executes a Java class:

```
<java classname="java class" />
```

This method of invoking the compiler has many useful options you can use to invoke a new JVM for the Java application to run in. In most cases, it is more robust to invoke a new JVM.

Parameters

***classname** The Java class to execute.

classpath The class path for the Java program execution.

classpathref A reference id to a class path for the Java program execution.

fork Boolean value of "yes" and "no". When set to "yes", a new JVM will be instantiated. Defaults to "no".

jvm Used with the "fork" parameter. Invokes the Java compiler. Defaults to "java".

jvmargs Used with the "fork" parameter. Specifies parameters to pass when invoking the JVM.

maxmemory Used with the "fork" parameter. The maximum amount of memory allocated to theJVM.

failonerror Available only if "fork" is "yes" (true). Stops the build process if the command exits with a returncode other than 0.

dir Used with the "fork" parameter. The working directory for the JVM.

output A file to which to write the output of the JVM.

Nested Parameters

arg Comand line arguments for the java application.

jvmarg Comand line arguments for the JVM.

sysproperty Specifies values available at run time.

- **key** Name of the environmental variable.
- **value** Value of the environmental variable.
- **path** A path value to use with a key.
- **file** A file to use with a given command.

- **mapper** A definition can be found under the Frequently Used Nested Parameters section.

classpath Allows tasks to use paths and class paths efficiently (see section "Frequently Used Nested Parameters and Elements" at the end of this chapter).

Javac Task

This command is used to compile Java source code using the JVM in which Ant is running:

```
<javac srcdir="[directory]"/>
```

Parameters

src* The directory where the Java packages to be compiled are located.

dirdestdir The location where the class files will be placed after they are successfully compiled.

includes Comma-separated list of patterns to use with the src parameter.

includesfile File in which each new line lists patterns to use with the src parameter.

excludes Comma-separated list of patterns not to use with the src parameter.

excludesfile File in which each new line lists patterns not to use with the src parameter.

defaultexcludes A value of "yes" or "no". "Yes" sets the default excludes to be used. Defaults to "no".

classpath Class path to be used by the compiler.

bootclasspath Location of the bootstrap class files

classpathref Class path to be used by the compiler, specified as a reference ID.

bootclasspathref Location of the bootstrap class files, specified as a reference ID.

extdirs Location of installed extensions.

encoding Encoding of source files.

debug When set to "no", debug information from the compiler will be shown as output. Defaults to "off".

optimize When set to "on", the compiler is set to optimize its execution. Defaults to "off".

deprecation When set to “on”, deprecation information from the compiler will be shown as output. Defaults to “off”.

target Tells the compiler to generate class files for a JVM version.

verbose Tells the compiler to use verbose output.

depend Tells the compiler to use dependency tracking, if it supports it.

includeANTRuntime When set to “no”, the lib directory in the ANT_HOME directory will not be used as part of the class path. Defaults to “yes”.

includeJavaRuntime When set to “yes”, the lib directory in the JAVA_HOME directory will be used as part of the class path. Defaults to “no”.

failonerror When set to “false”, the compiler will continue even when it fails to compile a class. Defaults to “true”.

Nested Parameters

fileset Specifies a collections of files (see section “Frequently Used Nested Parameters and Elements” at the end of this chapter for more information).

src Same as srcdir in the javc task.

classpath Same as classpath in the javac task.

bootclasspath Same as bootclasspath in the javac task.

extdirs Same as extdirs in the javac task.

Sql Task

The sql task executes SQL statements using a JBDC source:

```
<sql
    driver="[java class]"
    url="[database url]"
    userid="[user]"
    password="[password]"
    src="[file]"
/>
```

Commands can be executed without an src parameter file, as follows:

```
<sql
    driver=[java class]
    url="[database url]"
    userid="[user]"
    password="[password]"
    >
select *
from tablefoo
```

```
insert into table foo values (1,2,3)
</sql>
```

Parameters

driver Java class name of the Java Database Connectivity (JDBC) driver.

url Database connection URL.

userid Database user name.

password Database password.

src File containing SQL statements separated by semicolons and commented with double slashes (//) or double dashes (—).

autocommit When set to "true", the transactions are committed after execution. Defaults to "false".

print When set to "true", the output returned from the execution of the SQL statement is displayed. Defaults to "false".

showheaders When set to "false", the headers will not be displayed out. Defaults to "true".

output File to write system out information to. Defaults to System.out.

classpath Class path used to load the driver.

onerror Value of "continue", "stop", or "abort". Tells Ant how to handle errors. "Continue" shows the error, and execution is not interrupted. "Stop" halts execution of Ant, and transactions are committed. "Abort" stops execution of Ant, and transactions are not committed.

rdbms Executes commands only if the JBDC driver returns that the RDBMS (Remote Database Message System) is equal to a given value.

version Executes commands only if the JBDC driver returns that the RDBMS (Remote Database Message System) version is equal to a given value.

Nested Parameters

transaction Executes several commands using the same connection.

src File containing SQL statements separated by semicolons and commented with double slashes (//) or double dashes (—).

classpath Allows tasks to use paths and class paths efficiently (see section "Frequently Used Nested Parameters and Elements" at the end of this chapter).

File Library Tasks

Ant's file library tasks enable you to bundles classes and other files into library files such as JARs and WARs.

Jar Task

The jar task creates a Java type Java Application Resource (JAR) file:

```
<jar jarfile="[jar]" basedir="[directory]"/>
```

Parameters

jarfile* Name of the JAR file to create.

basedir The directory from which to recursively make the JAR.

compress Boolean value of "true" or "false". When set to "false", compression won't be used. Defaults to "true".

includes Comma-separated list of patterns to use with a basedir parameter.

includesfile File in which each new line lists patterns to use with a basedir parameter.

excludes Comma-separated list of patterns not to use with a basedir parameter.

excludesfile File in which each new line lists patterns not to use with a basedir parameter.

defaultexcludes A value of "yes" or "no". "Yes" sets the default excludes to be used. Defaults to "no".

manifest The name of the manifest file to use.

whenempty If set to "skip", the JAR file is not made if no files match the pattern. Defaults not to skip.

Nested Parameters

fileset Specifies a collections of files (see section "Frequently Used Nested Parameters and Elements" at the end of this chapter for more information).

War Task

The war task creates a Java type Web Application Resource (WAR) file.

```
<war warfile="[file name]" webxml="[file name]">
  <fileset dir="[path]"/>
    <lib dir="[path]">
```

```
    </lib>
  <classes dir="[path]"/>
</war>
```

Parameters

warfile The name of the WAR (Web Application Resource) file the task will create.

webxml The web.xml file to be used as a deployment descriptor for the WAR file.

basedir The directory that contains the files to put into the Zip. Defaults to the base directory defined in the project.

compress Boolean value of "true" or "false". When set to "false", the files will not be compressed in the Zip. Defaults to "true".

includes Comma-separated list of patterns to use with a directory parameter.

includesfile File in which each new line lists patterns to use with a directory parameter.

excludes Comma-separated list of patterns not to use with a directory parameter.

excludesfile File in which each new line lists patterns not to use with a directory parameter.

defaultexcludes When set to "yes", default excludes are to be used. Defaults to "no".

manifest A manifest to use in the WAR file.

whenempty If set to "skip", the Zip is not made when no files match the pattern. Defaults to not skip.

Nested Parameters

lib Specifies files to go in the WEB-INF/LIB directory of the WAR. All files in the LIB directory will be available when the Web application runs.

- **fileset** Specifies a collections of files (see section "Frequently Used Nested Parameters and Elements" at the end of this chapter for more information).

classes Specifies files to go in the WEB-INF/CLASES directory of the WAR. All files in the CLASSES directory are the compiled source of the Web application.

- **fileset** Specifies a collections of files (see section "Frequently Used Nested Parameters and Elements" at the end of this chapter for more information).

webinf Specifies files to go in the WEB-INF directory of the WAR.

- **fileset** Specifies a collections of files (see section "Frequently Used Nested Parameters and Elements" at the end of this chapter for more information).

zipfileset See section "Frequently Used Nested Parameters and Elements" at the end of this chapter for a definition.

Zip Task

The zip task creates a compressed file library of the Zip type.

```
<zip zipfile="[file]"
     basedir="[path]"
/>
```

Parameters

zipfile* The name of the Zip file the task will create.

basedir The directory that contains the files to put into the Zip. Defaults to the base directory defined in the project.

compress When set to "false", the files will not be compressed in the Zip. Defaults to "true".

includes Comma-separated list of patterns to use with a directory parameter.

includesfile File in which each new line lists patterns to use with a directory parameter.

excludes Comma-separated list of patterns not to use with a directory parameter.

excludesfile File in which each new line lists patterns not to use with a directory parameter.

defaultexcludes When set to "yes", default excludes are to be used. Defaults to "no".

whenempty If set to "skip", the Zip file is not made if no files match the pattern. Defaults not to skip.

Nested Parameters

fileset Specifies a collections of files (see section "Frequently Used Nested Parameters and Elements" at the end of this chapter for more information).

zipfileset See section "Frequently Used Nested Parameters and Elements" at the end of this chapter for definition.

Unjar, Unzip, and Unwar Tasks

The unzip task expands file libraries of the Zip type, including WARs and JARs:

```
<unzip src="[file]" dest="[directory]"/>
```

Parameters

src The file library to expand.

dest The directory in which to expand the files.

File Readers Writers and Tokenizers

This section covers tasks that manipulate the content of text files.

Replace Task

The replace task finds and replaces a string or strings of text within a text file:

```
<replace file="[file]" token="[replacement value]"/>
```

Parameters

file* Specific file in which to replace the tokens.

dir Directory in which to find the files whose tokens will be replaced.

token Value of the string of text to act as an indicator for replacement.

value Text with which to replace the token. Defaults to an empty string.

propertyFile A file containing one name/value pair per line. This file is used by the "replacefilter" nested parameter tag to replace multiple strings at one time with values that can be different.

includes Comma-separated list of patterns to use with a directory parameter.

includesfile File in which each new line lists patterns to use with a directory parameter.

excludes Comma-separated list of patterns not to use with a directory parameter.

excludesfile File in which each new line lists patterns not to use with a directory parameter.

defaultexcludes When set to "yes", default excludes are to be used. Defaults to "no".

token* The value of the string of text to be replaced in the file.

value Replacement value to be applied to the token in the file.

property Replacement value as a property for the token to be replaced in the file:

```
<replace dir="${../mailTemplates}" value="foo@bla.org"
includes="**/*.template" token="&mailAddress&"/>
```

or

```
<replace
    file="mailTemplate.txt"
    value="foo"
    propertyFile="../mailTemplates/mail.properties" >
  <replacefilter
    token="$project.name$" />
  <replacefilter
    token="$email.link$"
    value="http://www.fooBuildStatus.com"/>
  <replacefilter
    token="$build.time$"
    property="build.time"/>
</replace>
```

Nested Parameters

fileset Specifies a collections of files (see section “Frequently Used Nested Parameters and Elements” at the end of this chapter for more information).

replacefilter Defines tokens and replacement values.

- **token** Value of the string of text to act as an indicator for replacement.
- **value** Text with which to replace the token. Defaults to an empty string.
- **property** Property that defines text with which to replace the token.

Mail Task

The mail task sends Simple Mail Transfer Protocol (SMTP) email:

```
<mail from="foo" tolist="bla" subject="Your code doesn't compile bla"
        files="error.log"/>
```

Parameters

from Email address of sender

tolist List of recipients separated by commas

message Text for the body of the email

files List of files to use that contain the text for the body of the email

mailhost Host name of the mail server

subject Text for the subject of the email

Source Control Tasks

Ant's source control tasks enable you to manage Java source and related development files using systems like CVS.

Cvs Task

The cvs task name is based on the acronym for Concurent Versioning System. (CVS is a source control system; you can learn more about it at www.cvshome.org.) This task allows for the handling of CVS modules that contain source files.

Parameters

command CVS command to be executed, and parameters provided with that command.

cvsRoot Root directory of the remote CVS server.

dest Directory other than the project's root directory, where files are checked out locally.

package CVS module to check out.

tag Tag of the CVS module to check out.

date Date which the most recent version of the CVS module to be checked out must be equal to or earlier than.

quiet Boolean value of "true" or "false". When set to "true", prevents CVS information from printing out on the terminal. Defaults to "false".

noexec Boolean value of "true" or "false". When set to "true", only reports will be generated—no files will be modified. Defaults to "false".

output File to which the command's standard output should be output. Defaults to Ant's log MSG_INFO.

error File to which the command's standard error should be output. Defaults to Ant's log MSG_WARN.

Get Task

The get task downloads a file from a URL.

Parameters

src* URL from which to download a file.

dest* File name and location to write the file to.

verbose Boolean value of "on" or "off". When set to "on", messages will be suppressed. Defaults to "off".

ignoreerrors Boolean value of "true" or "false". When set to "true", the build will not fail when errors occur. Defaults to "false".

usetimestamp Boolean value of "true" or "false". When set to "true", the file time and date are compared. If the file is newer than a file specified in the dest parameter, it will be downloaded.

Some Key Optional Tasks

Junit Task

The junit task runs unit-level tests developed in Junit's testing framework.

Parameters

printsummary When set to "on", prints one line of statistics for each test case.

fork When set to "on", runs the test in a JVM separate from the one in which Ant is running.

haltonerror When set to "on", fails the build if an error occurs during the testing.

haltonfailure When set to "on", fails the build if a test fails.

timeout Skips a test if it doesn't finish in a given amount of time. Specified in milliseconds.

maxmemory Maximum amount of memory for the new JVM.

jvm Command used to invoke a new JVM. Default value is "Java".

dir The directory to invoke a new JVM.

Nested Parameters

classpath Allows tasks to use paths and class paths efficiently (see section "Frequently Used Nested Parameters and Elements" at the end of this chapter).

jvmarg Allows properties to be passed to the new JVM:

```
<jvmarg value="-Dfoo=baz"/>
```

- **value** The property key and value specified for the new JVM's use:

```
-D<key>=<value>
```

sysproperty Allows properties to be used by the test classes as they run:

```
<sysproperty key="foo" value="bla"/>
```

- **key** Name of the property
- **value** Text associated with the key

formatter Prints test results with a specified format

- **type*** Either "xml" or "plain"; "plain" outputs a text file, and "xml" outputs XML
- **classname** Name of a custom formatter class
- **extension** Extension on the file name for use with the custom class
- **usefile** When set to "false", the output won't go to a file

test Runs a single Junit test

- **name*** Name of the test class to run
- **fork** When set to "yes", a new JVM will be used
- **fork** When set to "on", runs the test in a separate JVM from the one in which Ant is running
- **haltonerror** When set to "on", fails the build if an error occurs during the testing
- **haltonfailure** When set to "on", fails the build if a test fails
- **todir** Directory the reports will write to
- **outfile** Base name of the report file
- **if** Evaluates whether a property exists before running a test
- **unless** Evaluates whether a property does not exists before running a test

batchtest Runs many Junit test with a nested file set

- **fork** When set to "on", runs the test in a JVM separate from the one in which Ant is running
- **haltonerror** When set to "on", fails the build if an error occurs during the testing
- **todir** Directory the reports will write to
- **if** Evaluates whether a property exists before running a test
- **unless** Evaluates whether a property does not exist before running a test

JunitReport Task

The junitreport task transforms the XML output from a Junit task's tests into an HTML-based report:

```
<junitreport todir="./foo">
  <fileset dir="./bla">
    <include name="TEST-*.xml"/>
  </fileset>
  <report format="frames" todir="./reports"/>
</junitreport>
```

Parameters

tofile File name to hold a list of all the files generated by the Junit task; defaults to TESTS-TestSuites.xml

todir Directory to which to write the file specified in the tofile parameter

Nested Parameters

fileset Specifies a collections of files (see section "Frequently Used Nested Parameters and Elements" at the end of this chapter for more information).

report Generates reports for the Junit tests

- **format** Set to "frames" or "no frames"; defaults to "frames"
- **styledir** Directory where style sheets are defined; defaults to embedded style sheets
- **todir** Directory where the final HTML files are written
- **extension** Extension for the final reports; defaults to HTML

Frequently Used Nested Parameters and Elements

Nested parameters can be used within certain tasks tags, as children. Some of the most frequent ones are listed below in order to shorten the definition a tasks, by avoiding repetition.

Classpath Element

The classpath task allows tasks to use paths and class paths efficiently:

```
<classpath path="[path]"/>
```

Nested Parameters

pathelement Class used to specify both paths and class paths. Pathelement is used as a nested element for many other tasks:

```
<classpath>
       <pathelement path="[path]"/>
</classpath>
```

- **path** A comma-separated list of paths:

  ```
  <classpath>
         <pathelement path="[path]"/>
  </classpath>
  ```

- **location** a comma-separated list of paths, relative to the base directory of the project:

  ```
  <classpath>
         <pathelement location="classes"/>
  </classpath>
  ```

fileset Specifies a collections of files (see section "Frequently Used Nested Parameters and Elements" at the end of this chapter for more information).

```
<fileset dir="/src/java" >
    <include name="**/*.java"/>
    <exclude name="**/*Test*"/>
</fileset>
```

The above example includes all Java source except those with the substring "Test" in their filename.

Mapper Element

The mapper task simply maps a file to a target. Keep in mind that this task is used in conjunction with other tasks.

```
<mapper type="identity"/>
```

In the above the to and from are ignored and the files are copied into a parallel subdirectory hierarchy as the source to the destination (e.g., c:\src\xptool \Hello.java copied to d:\backup\src\xptool\Hello.java).

```
<mapper type="flatten"/>
```

Unlike the first example, copy all the files from the source to the destination, but all in the source directory with no subdirectory hierarchy (e.g., c:\src\xptool\Hello.java copied to d:\backup\Hello.java).

```
<mapper type="glob" from="*.java" to="*.java.bak"/>
```

Copy *.java files to *.java.bak files (e.g., c:\src\xptool\Hello.java copied to d:\backup\src\xptool\Hello.java.bak).

Parameters

type Several types have been defined internally to this class:

- **identity** The target is identical to the source name.
- **flatten** The target is identical to the source name and is stripped of any directory structure, effectively making the branch flat.
- **merge** The type will map all entries to the same target using the mapper's "to" parameter.
- **glob** Patterns will be matched using the mapper's "to" and "from" parameters. The "to" parameter will be used to specify the pattern-matching names. The "from" parameter will be used to specify the target pattern.
- **regexp** Patterns will be evaluated against a regular expression using the mapper's "to" and "from" parameters. The "to" parameter will be used to specify the regular expression to match names. The "from" parameter will be used to specify the regular expression for the target pattern.

classname Specifies the implementation by class name.

classpath The class path to use when looking up the class name.

classpathref A class path used in looking up a class specified by the reference id of one of the build files elements:

```
<project ... >
  <path id="project.class.path">
    <pathelement location="lib/"/>
    <pathelement path="${java.class.path}/"/>
  </path>

<available classname="Foo" classpathref="project.class.path"/>
```

from Refer to the earlier implementations of the "type" parameter of the mapper task to see how and when "from" is used.

to Refer to the earlier implementations of the "type" parameter of the mapper task to see how and when "to" is used.

Nested Parameters

classpath A definition was listed above.

Fileset Element

The fileset task defines groups of files in a branch of a directory structure:

```
<fileset dir="src/" >
```

Parameters

***dir** Base of the branch in the directory structure from which the fileset will be built.

defaultexcludes Value of "yes" or "no"; specifies whether default excludes are used.

includes Comma-separated list of patterns to include in the file set. All other files are excluded.

includesfile File source of patterns to include in the file set. All other files will be excluded.

excludes Comma-separated list of patterns to exclude in the file set. All other files are included.

excludesfile File source of patterns to exclude in the file set. All other files will be included.

Nested Parameters

patternset A definition can be found defined above at the start of thie section "Frequently Used Nested Parameters".

Patternset Element

The patternset task provides a way to group patterns for later use. It is commonly used nested in a fileset task:

```
<patternset id="junit.test.sources" >
<include name="**/*Test*.java" />
     <exclude name="**/AllTests.java" />
</patternset>
```

Parameters

includes Comma-separated list of patterns to include in the file set. All other files are excluded.

includesfile File source of patterns to include in the file set. All other files will be excluded.

excludes Comma-separated list of patterns to exclude in the file set. All other files are included.

excludesfile File source of patterns to exclude in the file set. All other files will be included.

Zipfileset Element

The zipfileset task defines groups of files in a branch of a directory structure:

```
<zipfileset dir="src/" >
```

Parameters

prefix File that specifies the path of a Zip archive where files will be added

fullpath Directory in which a single file is added to an archive

src Zip file whose extracted contents should be included in the archive

dir* Base of the branch in the directory structure from which the file set will be built

defaultexcludes Value of "yes" or "no"; specifies whether default excludes are used

includes Comma-separated list of patterns to include in the file set. All other files are excluded.

includesfile File source of patterns to include in the file set. All other files will be excluded.

excludes Comma-separated list of patterns to exclude in the file set. All other files are included.

excludesfile File source of patterns to exclude in the file set. All other files will be included.

CHAPTER 13

Ant API Reference

The purpose of this chapter is to summarize the part of the Ant API that developers can use to customize an individual build process. The Ant classes documented in this chapter are as follows:

- AntClassLoader
- BuildEvent
- BuildException
- BuildListener
- BuildLogger
- DefaultLogger
- DesirableFilter
- DirectoryScanner
- FileScanner
- IntrospectionHelper
- Location
- Main
- PathTokenizer
- Project
- ProjectHelper
- RuntimeConfigurable

- Target
- Task
- TaskAdapter
- UnknownElement
- XmlLogger

Package org.apache.tools.ant

Class AntClassLoader

```
public class AntClassLoader
```

Inheritance Information

Extends: `java.lang.ClassLoader`

Description

This class is used to load a class in Ant if that class exists within a classpath different from the one used to start Ant. A helper method (forceLoadClass) allows classes to be loaded from the system classpath of the machine running Ant.

Constructors

```
public AntClassLoader(Project project, Path classpath)
```

When constructing a new classloader, you must specify both the Ant project it should be associated with and the classpath from which it will load classes.

```
public AntClassLoader(Project project, Path classpath,
                      boolean systemFirst)
```

This alternate constructor for an AntClassLoader takes a true or false flag indicating whether the system classpath should also be used. This information is helpful if the classloader needs to access classes (or dependencies to classes) loaded in your system path (for example, JUnit).

Methods

```
public void setIsolated(boolean isolated)
```

This method forces Ant to look only in this classloader's classpath (as opposed to also including the base classloader or other loaded classloaders). If isolated mode is turned on, then any classes referenced and not found in this classloader will throw a java.lang.classNotFoundException.

```
public void addSystemPackageRoot(java.lang.String packageRoot)
```

This method adds a new directory (or Java package) to the default path for the system path classloader. Any subdirectories will also be included.

```
public void addLoaderPackageRoot(java.lang.String packageRoot)
```

This method adds a new directory (or Java package) to the default path for this classloader. Any subdirectories will also be included.

```
public java.lang.Class forceLoadClass(java.lang.String classname)
```

This method loads this classloader even if that class is available on the system classpath. Any future class loaded by this object will be loaded using this classloader. If those classes are not available in its classpath, the class loader will throw a java.lang.ClassNotFoundException.

```
public java.lang.Class forceLoadSystemClass(java.lang.String classname)
```

This method loads a class but defers to the system classloader. You use this method to ensure that any objects created by the class will be compatible with the system loader.

```
public java.io.InputStream getResourceAsStream(java.lang.String name)
```

You use this class to get an InputStream to a named resource.

```
protected java.lang.Class loadClass(java.lang.String classname,
                                    boolean resolve()
```

This method loads a given class using this classloader. If the requested class does not exist on the system classpath or this loader's classpath, the method will throw a java.lang.ClassNotFoundException.

```
public java.lang.Class findClass(java.lang.String name)
```

This method finds and loads a given class using this classloader. If the requested class does not exist on the system classpath or this loader's classpath, the method will throw a java.lang.ClassNotFoundException.

Class BuildEvent

```
public class BuildEvent
```

Inheritance Information

Extends: `java.util.EventObject`

Constructors

```
public BuildEvent(Project project)
public BuildEvent(Target target)
public BuildEvent(Task task)
```

Methods

```
public void setMessage(java.lang.String message, int priority)
```

This method sets the default logging message for this event

```
public void setException(java.lang.Throwable exception)
```

This method specifies a custom exception you want this event to throw.

```
public Project getProject()
```

This method returns the Project that fired this event.

```
public Target getTarget()
```

This method returns the Target that fired this event.

```
public Task getTask()
```

This method returns the Task that fired this event.

```
public java.lang.String getMessage()
```

This method returns the logging message.

```
public int getPriority()
```

This method returns the priority value associated with the logging message.

```
public java.lang.Throwable getException()
```

This method returns the exception that was thrown, as a Throwable. This field will be set only for taskFinished, targetFinished, and buildFinished events.

Class BuildException

```
public class BuildException
```

Inheritance Information

Extends: `java.lang.RuntimeException`

DescriptionBuildException signals an error condition during a build.

Constructors

```
public BuildException()
```

This constructor initializes an undescribed build exception.

```
public BuildException(java.lang.String msg)
```

This constructor initializes a build exception with the given descriptive message.

```
public BuildException(java.lang.String msg,
                      java.lang.Throwable cause)
```

This constructor initializes a build exception with the given message and nested exception.

```
public BuildException(String msg, Throwable cause,
                    Location location)
```

This constructor initializes a build exception with the given message and nested exception and a location in a file.

```
public BuildException(java.lang.Throwable cause)
```

This constructor initializes a build exception with a nested exception.

```
public BuildException(java.lang.String msg, Location location)
```

This constructor initializes a build exception with the given message and a location in a file.

```
public BuildException(java.lang.Throwable cause,
                    Location location)
```

This constructor initializes a build exception with a nested exception and a location in a file.

Methods

```
public java.lang.Throwable getException()
```

This is the getter method for the nested exception.

```
public java.lang.String toString()
```

This method overrides toString in String.

```
public void setLocation(Location location)
```

This is the setter method for the file location where the error occurred.

```
public Location getLocation()
```

This is the getter method for the file location where the error occurred.

```
public void printStackTrace()
```

This method overrides Exception.

```
public void printStackTrace(java.io.PrintStream ps)
```

This method overrides Exception.

```
public void printStackTrace(java.io.PrintWriter pw)
```

This method overrides Exception.

Interface BuildListener

```
public Interface BuildListener
```

Inheritance Information

Extends: `java.util.EventListener`

Description

Classes that implement this interface will be notified of events happening in a build.

Methods

```
public void buildStarted(BuildEvent event)
```

This method is called before any events are started.

```
public void buildFinished(BuildEvent event)
```

This method is called after the last target has finished. It will still be called if an error occurs during the build.

```
public void targetStarted(BuildEvent event)
```

This method is called before the target's execution is started.

```
public void targetFinished(BuildEvent event)
```

This method is called after the target has finished. It will still be called if an error occurs during the execution of the target.

```
public void taskStarted(BuildEvent event)
```

This method is called before the task's execution is started.

```
public void taskFinished(BuildEvent event)
```

This method is called after the task has finished. It will still be called if an error occurs during the execution of the task.

```
public void messageLogged(BuildEvent event)
```

This method is executed whenever a message is logged.

Interface BuildLogger

```
public Interface BuildLogger
```

Inheritance Information

Extends: `BuildListener`

Description

Ant uses this interface to log the output from the build. A build logger is very much like a build listener with permission to write to the Ant log, which is usually System.out (unless redirected by the -logfile option).

Methods

```
public void setMessageOutputLevel(int level)
```

This method sets the msgOutputLevel for this logger. Any messages with a level less than or equal to the given level will be logged. The constants for the message levels are in Project.java. The order of the levels, from least verbose to most verbose, is MSG_ERR, MSG_WARN, MSG_INFO, MSG_VERBOSE, MSG_DEBUG.

```
public void setOutputPrintStream(PrintStream output)
```

This method sets the output stream this logger will use.

```
public void setEmacsMode(boolean emacsMode)
```

This method sets this logger to produce emacs-compatible output.

```
public void setErrorPrintStream(java.io.PrintStream err)
```

This method sets the output stream this logger will use for errors.

Class DefaultLogger

```
public class DefaultLogger
```

Inheritance Information

Extends: `java.lang.Object`

Implements: `BuildLogger`

Description

This class writes a build event to a PrintStream. Note that DefaultLogger only writes which targets are being executed and any messages that are logged.

Fields

```
protected java.io.PrintStream out
```

```
protected java.io.PrintStream err
```

```
protected int msgOutputLevel
```

```
protected static java.lang.String lSep
```

```
protected boolean emacsMode
```

Methods

```
public void setMessageOutputLevel(int level)
```

This method sets the msgOutputLevel for this logger. Any messages with a level less than or equal to the given level will be logged. The constants for the message levels are in Project.java. The order of the levels, from least verbose to most verbose, is MSG_ERR, MSG_WARN, MSG_INFO, MSG_VERBOSE, MSG_DEBUG.

```
public void setOutputPrintStream(java.io.PrintStream output)
```

This method sets the output stream this logger will use. It is specified by `setOutputPrintStream` in interface `BuildLogger`.

```
public void setErrorPrintStream(java.io.PrintStream err)
```

This method sets the output stream this logger will use for errors. It is specified by `setErrorPrintStream` in interface `BuildLogger`.

```
public void setEmacsMode(boolean emacsMode)
```

This method sets this logger to produce emacs-compatible output. It is specified by `setEmacsMode` in interface `BuildLogger`.

```
public void buildStarted(BuildEvent event)
```

This method executes before any targets are started. It is specified by `buildStarted` in interface `BuildListener`.

```
public void buildFinished(BuildEvent event)
```

This method executes after all other activity in the build and prints the build's success status and any errors. It is specified by `buildFinished` in interface `BuildListener`.

```
public void targetStarted(BuildEvent event)
```

This method executes when a target is started. It is specified by `targetStarted` in interface `BuildListener`.

```
public void targetFinished(BuildEvent event)
```

This method executes when a target is complete, whether errors occurred or not.

```
public void taskStarted(BuildEvent event)
```

This method executes when a task is started.

```
public void taskFinished(BuildEvent event)
```

This method executes when a task has finished, whether errors occurred or not.

```
public void messageLogged(BuildEvent event)
```

This method executes when a message is logged.

Class DesirableFilter

```
public class DesireableFilter
```

Inheritance Information

Extends: `java.lang.Object`

Implements: `java.io.FilenameFilter`

Description

This class is designed to filter filenames to determine their desirability.

Methods

```
public boolean accept(java.io.File dir, java.lang.String name)
```

This method tests the given filename to determine whether it's desirable. It helps tasks filter temporary files and files used by Concurrent Versioning System (CVS). It is specified by accept in interface java.io.FilenameFilter.

Class DirectoryScanner

```
public class DirectoryScanner
```

Inheritance Information

Implements: `FileScanner`

Description

This class is designed to scan a directory for specific files and subdirectories.

Fields

```
protected static final java.lang.String[] DEFAULTEXCLUDES
```

This field is a string array to hold patterns that should be excluded by default.

```
protected java.io.File basedir
```

This field is the base directory from which to scan.

```
protected java.lang.String[] includes
```

This field is a string array to hold patterns that should be included by default.

```
protected java.lang.String[] excludes
```

This field is a string array to hold patterns that will be excluded.

```
protected java.util.Vector filesIncluded
```

This field specifies all files that were found and matched one or more includes, and matched no excludes.

```
protected java.util.Vector filesNotIncluded
```

This field specifies the files that were found and matched zero includes.

```
protected java.util.Vector filesExcluded
```

This field specifies the files that were found and matched one or more includes, and also matched at least one exclude.

```
protected java.util.Vector dirsIncluded
```

This field specifies the directories that were found and matched one or more includes, and matched zero excludes.

```
protected java.util.Vector dirsNotIncluded
```

This field specifies the directories that were found and matched zero includes.

```
protected java.util.Vector dirsExcluded
```

This field specifies the files that were found and matched one or more includes, and also matched one or more excludes.

```
protected boolean haveSlowResults
```

This field is a true or false value indicating whether the vectors holding results were built by a slow scan.

Methods

```
protected static boolean
matchPath(java.lang.String pattern,java.lang.String str)
```

This method matches a path(str) against a pattern.

```
protected static boolean match(java.lang.String pattern,
                               java.lang.String str)
```

This method matches a path(str) against a pattern.

```
public void setBasedir(java.lang.String basedir)
```

This method sets the basedir from which to scan.

```
public void setBasedir(java.io.File basedir)
```

This method sets the basedir from which to scan.

```
public java.io.File getBasedir()
```

This method returns the basedir from which to scan.

```
public void setIncludes(java.lang.String[] includes)
```

This is the setter method for the includes array.

```
public void setExcludes(java.lang.String[] excludes)
```

This is the setter method for the excludes array.

```
public void scan()
```

This method scans the basedir for files that match one or more include patterns and zero exclude patterns.

```
protected void slowScan()
```

This method invokes a scan.

```
protected void scandir(java.io.File dir,java.lang.String vpath,
                       boolean fast)
```

This method scans the passed dir for files and directories. Found files and directories are placed in the respective collections, based on the matching of includes and excludes. When a directory is found, it is scanned recursively.

```
protected boolean isIncluded(java.lang.String name)
```

This method returns true or false if a name matches at least one include pattern.

```
protected boolean couldHoldIncluded(java.lang.String name)
```

This method returns true or false if a name matches the start of at least one include pattern.

```
protected boolean isExcluded(java.lang.String name)
```

This method returns true or false if a name matches at least one exclude pattern.

```
public java.lang.String[] getIncludedFiles()
```

This is the getter method for the included-files array.

```
public java.lang.String[] getNotIncludedFiles()
```

This is the getter method for the not-included-files array.

```
public java.lang.String[] getExcludedFiles()
```

This is the getter method for the excluded-files array.

```
public java.lang.String[] getIncludedDirectories()
```

This is the getter method for the included-directories array.

```
public java.lang.String[] getNotIncludedDirectories()
```

This is the getter method for the not-included-directories array.

```
public java.lang.String[] getExcludedDirectories()
```

This is the getter method for the excluded-directories array.

```
public void addDefaultExcludes()
```

This method adds the array with default exclusions to the current exclusions set.

Interface FileScanner

```
public Interface FileScanner
```

Description

This is an interface that describes the actions required by any type of directory scanner.

Methods

```
public void addDefaultExcludes()
```

This method adds an array with default exclusions to the current exclusions set.

```
public java.io.File getBasedir()
```

This method gets the basedir to use for scanning.

```
public java.lang.String[] getExcludedDirectories()
```

This method gets the names of the directories that matched one or more of the include patterns and also matched one or more of the exclude patterns.

```
public java.lang.String[] getExcludedFiles()
```

This method gets the names of the files that matched one or more of the include patterns and matched also one or more of the exclude patterns.

```
public java.lang.String[] getIncludedDirectories()
```

This method gets the names of the directories that matched one or more of the include patterns and matched none of the exclude patterns.

```
public java.lang.String[] getIncludedFiles()
```

This method gets the names of the files that matched one or more of the include patterns and matched zero of the exclude patterns.

```
public java.lang.String[] getNotIncludedDirectories()
```

This method gets the names of the directories that matched zero of the include patterns.

```
public java.lang.String[] getNotIncludedFiles()
```

This method gets the names of the files that matched zero of the include patterns.

```
public void scan()
```

This method scans the basedir for files that match one or more include patterns and zero exclude patterns.

```
public void setBasedir(java.lang.String basedir)
```

This method sets the basedir from which to scan, given a String.

```
public void setBasedir(java.io.File basedir)
```

This method sets the basedir from which to scan, given a file.

```
public void setExcludes(java.lang.String[] excludes)
```

This method sets the array of exclude patterns.

```
public void setIncludes(java.lang.String[] includes)
```

This method sets the array of include patterns.

Class IntrospectionHelper

```
public class IntrospectionHelper
```

Description

IntrospectionHelper collects the methods a task or nested element holds to set or create attributes or elements.

Methods

```
public static IntrospectionHelper getHelper(java.lang.Class c)
```

This method implemente the FactoryMethod design pattern for helper objects.

```
public void setAttribute(Project p,  java.lang.Object element,
                         java.lang.String attributeName,
                         java.lang.String value)
```

This method sets the named attribute to the given value.

```
public void addText(java.lang.Object element,
                    java.lang.String text)
```

This method adds PCDATA areas.

```
public java.lang.Object createElement(java.lang.Object element,
                                      java.lang.String elementName)
```

This method creates a nested element with the given name.

```
public java.lang.Class getElementType String elementName)
```

This method returns the type of the nested element with the given name.

```
public Class getAttributeType(String attributeName)
```

This method returns the type of an attribute with the given name.

```
public boolean supportsCharacters()
```

This method returns a true or false value indicating whether the introspected class supports PCDATA.

```
public java.util.Enumeration getAttributes()
```

This is the getter method for an Enumeration of all attributes supported by the introspected class.

```
public java.util.Enumeration getNestedElements()
```

This is the getter method for an Enumeration of all nested elements supported by the introspected class.

Class Location

```
public class Location
```

Inheritance Information

Extends: `java.lang.Object`

Description

Location represents a file location. Although it is not used in an example in this chapter, it is quite useful in file-manipulation actions.

Constructors

```
Location(java.lang.String fileName)
```

This constructor initializes a location with a file name but no line number.

```
Location(java.lang.String fileName, int lineNumber,
        int columnNumber)
```

This constructor initializes a location with a file name and line number.

Field

```
public static final Location UNKNOWN_LOCATION
```

Method

```
public java.lang.String toString()
```

This method overrides toString in class java.lang.Object.

Class Main

```
public class main
```

Description

This class acts as the command-line entry point into Ant and assembles and executes an Ant project.

Field

```
public static final java.lang.String DEFAULT_BUILD_FILENAME
```

This field is the default name of the buildfile.

Methods

```
protected Main(jatva.lang.String[] args)
public static void main(java.lang.String[] args)
```

This method executes a build using either a given target or the default target.

Class PathTokenizer

```
public class PathTokenizer
```

Description

A PathTokenizer returns the components that make up a path. The path can use either colons (:) or semicolons (;) as path separators and slashes (/) or backslashes (\) as file separators.

Constructor

```
public PathTokenizer(java.lang.String path)
```

Methods

```
public boolean hasMoreTokens()
```

This method returns true or false indicating whether the string has more tokens.

```
public java.lang.String nextToken()
```

This method returns the next token.

Class Project

```
public class Project
```

Inheritance Information

Extends: `java.lang.Object`

Description

The Project class is the main focus of an Ant project and represents the build XML file. This class defines a Ant project with all of its targets and tasks. It also has the ability to execute a build given a specific target name.

Project has a single parameterless constructor, so it can be instantiated with the following syntax:

```
Project proj = new Project();
```

Programmatically, the Project class can be used to create an object that will automatically run a set of Ant tasks.

Methods

```
public void init()
```

This method initializes the project. This process involves setting the default task definitions and loading the system properties.

```
public void log(java.lang.String msg)
```

This method writes the given message to the log.

```
public void log(java.lang.String msg,int msgLevel)
```

This method writes the given message to the log at the given message level.

```
public void log(Task task, java.lang.String msg, int msgLevel)
```

This method writes the given message to the log for the given task at the given message level.

```
public void log(Target target, java.lang.String msg, int msgLevel)
```

This method writes the given message to the log for the given target at the given message level.

```
public void setProperty(java.lang.String name, java.lang.String value)
```

This is the setter method for a property in an Ant project given the name and value. For example:

```
<property name="phase3.src.dir" value="../phase3/src"/>
```

sets a property called "phase3.src.dir" to the String value "../phase3/src"".

```
public void setUserProperty(String name, String value)
```

This is the setter method for the UserProperty, given a name and value.

```
public java.lang.String getProperty(java.lang.String name)
```

This is the getter method for a property with the given name.

```
public java.lang.String getUserProperty(java.lang.String name)
```

This is the getter method for a UserProperty with the given name.

```
public java.util.Hashtable getProperties()
```

This method gets a hashtable of the properties belonging to the project.

```
public java.util.Hashtable getUserProperties()
```

This method gets a hashtable of the UserProperties belonging to the project.

```
public void setDefaultTarget(java.lang.String defaultTarget)
```

This method sets the default target for a project.

```
public java.lang.String getDefaultTarget()
```

This method returns a String representation for the default target for a project.

```
public void setDefault(java.lang.String defaultTarget)
```

This method sets the default target for a project.

```
public void setName(java.lang.String name)
```

This method sets the name for a project.

```
public java.lang.String getName()
```

This method gets the name of the project.

```
public void addFilter(java.lang.String token, java.lang.String value)
```

This method adds a filter to the given project.

```
public java.util.Hashtable getFilters()
```

This method returns a hashtable of the filters belonging to the project.

```
public void setBasedir(java.lang.String baseD)
```

This method sets the "baseDir" property of the project to a file resolved to the given String.

```
public void setBaseDir(java.io.File baseDir)
```

This method sets the "baseDir" property of the project to a file resolved to the given file.

```
public java.io.File getBaseDir()
```

This method returns a file representation of the project's "baseDir" property.

```
public static java.lang.String getJavaVersion()
```

This method returns the Java version property of the project.

```
public void setJavaVersionProperty()
```

This method sets the Java version property of the project.

```
public void addTaskDefinition(java.lang.String taskName,
                              java.lang.Class taskClass)
```

This method adds a task to the project based on the "name" and "class" parameters.

```
public java.util.Hashtable getTaskDefinitions()
```

This method returns a hashtable of the TaskDefinitions belonging to the project.

```
public void addDataTypeDefinition(java.lang.String typeName,
                                  java.lang.Class typeClass)
```

This method adds a DataTypeDefinition to the collection belonging to the project.

```
public java.util.Hashtable getDataTypeDefinitions()
```

This method gets a hashtable of the DataTypeDefinitions belonging to the project.

```
public void addTarget(Target target)
```

This method adds a target to the project, matching the parameter.

```
public void addTarget(java.lang.String targetName, Target target)
```

This method adds a target to the project, matching the parameter.

```
public void addOrReplaceTarget(Target target)
```

This method adds a target to the project, matching the parameter, or replaces it if it already exists.

```
public void addOrReplaceTarget(java.lang.String targetName,
                               Target target)
```

This method adds a target to the project, matching the parameters, or replaces it if it already exists.

```
public java.util.Hashtable getTargets()
```

This method returns a hashtable of the Target objects belonging to the project.

```
public Task createTask(java.lang.String taskType)
```

This method returns a new task of the given task type within the scope of the project.

```
public void executeTargets(java.util.Vector targetNames)
```

This method calls execute() on each target within the given collection.

```
public void executeTarget(java.lang.String targetName)
```

This method calls execute() on the given target.

```
public static java.lang.String
translatePath(java.lang.String to_process)
```

This method translates a path into its native (platform-specific) format using a PathTokenizer.

```
public void copyFile(java.lang.String sourceFile,
                     java.lang.String destFile)
```

This is a convenience method to copy a file from a source to a destination without filtering.

```
public void copyFile(java.lang.String sourceFile,
                     java.lang.String destFile, boolean filtering)
```

This is a convenience method to copy a file from a source to a destination given a Boolean to indicate whether token filtering must be used.

```
public void copyFile(java.lang.String sourceFile,
                     java.lang.String destFile,
                         boolean filtering, boolean overwrite)
```

This is a convenience method to copy a file from a source to a destination given Booleans to indicate whether token filtering must be used and whether source files may overwrite newer destination files.

```
public void copyFile(java.lang.String sourceFile,
                     java.lang.String destFile,
                         boolean filtering, boolean overwrite,
                         boolean preserveLastModified)
```

This is a convenience method to copy a file from a source to a destination given Booleans to indicate whether token filtering must be used, whether source files may overwrite newer destination files, and whether the last modified time of destFile file should be made equal to the last modified time of sourceFile.

```
public void copyFile(java.io.File sourceFile,
                     java.io.File destFile)
```

This is a convenience method to copy a file from a source to a destination without filtering.

```
public void copyFile(java.io.File sourceFile,
                     java.io.File destFile,
                        boolean filtering)
```

This is a convenience method to copy a file from a source to a destination given a Boolean to indicate whether token filtering must be used.

```
public void copyFile(java.io.File sourceFile,
                     java.io.File destFile,
                     boolean filtering, boolean overwrite)
```

This is a convenience method to copy a file from a source to a destination given Booleans to indicate whether token filtering must be used and whether source files may overwrite newer destination files.

```
public void copyFile(java.io.File sourceFile,
                     java.io.File destFile,
                        boolean filtering,boolean overwrite,
                        boolean preserveLastModified)
```

This is a convenience method to copy a file from a source to a destination given Booleans to indicate whether token filtering must be used, whether source files may overwrite newer destination files, and whether the last modified time of destFile file should be made equal to the last modified time of sourceFile.

```
public static boolean toBoolean(java.lang.String s)
```

This method returns the Boolean equivalent of a String, which is considered true if “on”, “true”, or “yes” is found, ignoring case.

```
public void runTarget(Target target)

public final java.util.Vector topoSort(java.lang.String root,
                                       java.util.Hashtable targets)
```

This method returns a Vector that is a topologically sorted set of targets given a root (the [String] name of the root target). The sort is created in such a way that the sequence of targets until the root target is the minimum possible such sequence.

```
public void addReference(java.lang.String name,
                         java.lang.Object value)
```

This method adds a reference to the project, given a name and value.

```
public java.util.Hashtable getReferences()
```

This method returns a hashtable of the Reference objects belonging to the project.

Class ProjectHelper

```
public class ProjectHelper
```

Description

ProjectHelper will configure a project (complete with targets and tasks) based on an XML buildfile.

Methods

```
public static void configureProject(Project project,
                                    java.io.File buildFile)
```

This method configures the project with the contents of the given XML file.

```
public static void configure(java.lang.Object target,
              org.xml.sax.AttributeList attrs, Project project)

public static void addText(java.lang.Object target, char[] buf,
                           int start, int end)
```

This method adds the contents of #PCDATA(buf) sections to an element from start to end.

```
public static void addText(java.lang.Object target,
                           java.lang.String text)
```

This method adds the contents of #PCDATA(target) sections to an element.

```
public static String replaceProperties(Project project,
                          String value, Hashtable keys)
```

This method replaces the property at ${NAME} with the given value.

Class RuntimeConfigurable

```
public class RuntimeConfigurable
```

Description

RuntimeConfigurable is a wrapper class that maintains the attributes of a task and configures it at runtime.

Constructor

```
public RuntimeConfigurable(java.lang.Object proxy)
```

This constructor initializes the element to wrap (proxy).

Methods

```
public void setAttributes(org.xml.sax.AttributeList attributes)
```

This is the setter method for the attributes for the wrapped element.

```
public org.xml.sax.AttributeList getAttributes()
```

This is the getter method for the attributes for the wrapped element.

```
public void addChild(RuntimeConfigurable child)
```

This method adds a child element to the wrapped element.

```
public void addText(java.lang.String data)
```

This method adds characters from #PCDATA(data) areas to the wrapped element.

```
public void addText(char[] buf,  int start, int end)
```

This method adds the contents of #PCDATA(buf) sections to an element.

```
public void maybeConfigure(Project p)
```

This method configures the wrapped element and all children within the given project space unless it has already been done.

Class Target

```
public class target
```

Inheritance Information

Extends: `java.lang.Object`

Description

This class implements a collection of work in Ant. A target lives within an Ant project and can contain its own targets and tasks.

Methods

```
public void setProject(Project project)
```

This is the setter method for the parent project.

```
public Project getProject()
```

This is the getter method for the parent project.

```
public void setDepends(java.lang.String depS)
```

This method sets the "depends" property for the target. For example:

```
<target depends="prepare" description="Compile the source tree"
name="compile">
```

sets the "depends" property for the compile target to the entity named Prepare within the project's scope.

```
public void setName(java.lang.String name)
```

This is the setter method for the "name" attribute.

```
public java.lang.String getName()
```

This is the getter method for the "name" attribute.

```
public void addTask(Task task)
```

This method adds the given task to the target's definition. For example:

```
<target name="prepare" depends="set-version">
           <mkdir dir="${build.dir}"/>
       </target>
```

adds a mkdir(type) task to the target named prepare.

```
public Task[] getTasks()
```

This is the getter method for the current set of tasks to be executed by this target.

```
public void addDependency(java.lang.String dependency)
```

This method adds a "dependency" attribute to the task.

```
public java.util.Enumeration getDependencies()
```

This method returns a collection of dependencies associated with the target.

```
public void setIf(java.lang.String property)
```

This is the setter method for the "If" property.

```
public void setUnless(java.lang.String property)
```

This is the setter method for the "Unless" property.

```
public void setDescription(java.lang.String description)
```

This is the setter method for the "Description" property.

```
public java.lang.String getDescription()
```

This is the getter method for the "Description" property.

```
public java.lang.String toString()
```

This method overrides method in String.

```
public void execute() throws BuildException
```

This is the key method when you're using this target. It will call execute() on all tasks within the target.

Class Task

```
public class Task
```

Inheritance Information

Extends: `java.lang.Object`

Description

You know that in Ant, a *task* is defined as a unit of work. A practical example of a task would be to delete a directory or a file, to check the latest version of a class out from a source control system, or to send an email message to your system administrator informing him that a build was successful or that it failed (along with the reasons why). All these tasks are part of the existing Ant framework, but as a developer you may need to create a new task customized to your (or your client's) specific processes and/or needs. For instance, you may want to set up a custom task to make an entry in a database or a spreadsheet, or you may want to restart system services (or restart the Unreal Tournament server that coexists in your production environment). To create a custom task, you create a class that directly or indirectly extends org.apache.tools.ant.Task.

The key method of a given Task object is the execute() method. When you're creating a new task, the execute() method will contain the framework for the job to be performed. When a task is executed, an object of the org.apache.ant.Task class is instantiated and configured and then executes to perform a specific function.

An oversimplified example implementation of a new custom task is listed here:

```
package org.apache.tools.ant.taskdefs;
import org.apache.tools.ant.*;
public class GreetJon extends Task {
        public void execute() throws BuildException{
                System.out.println("Hello Jon!");
        }
}
```

For each property created in a task, there should be public setter and getter methods. The only constructor for Task has no parameters, but for practical purposes it will probably be instantiated and initialized within a project using the createTask() method. It is important to remember that a task usually exists within the scope of both a project and one or more of its child targets.

Methods

```
public Project getProject()
```

This is the getter method for the project to which this task belongs.

```
public void setOwningTarget(Target target)
```

This is the setter method for the owning target object of this task.

```
public Target getOwningTarget()
```

This is the getter method for the owning target object of this task.

```
ublic void setTaskName(java.lang.String name)
```

This is the setter method for the "name" property to use in logging messages.

```
public java.lang.String getTaskName()
```

This is the getter method for the "name" property to use in logging messages.

```
public void log(java.lang.String msg)
```

This method logs a message with the default (INFO) priority.

```
public void log(java.lang.String msg, int msgLevel)
```

This method logs a message with the given priority.

```
public void setDescription(java.lang.String desc)
```

This is the setter method for the description of the current action.

```
public java.lang.String getDescription()
```

This is the getter method for the description of the current action.

```
public void init()
```

This method is called by the project to let the task initialize properly.

```
public void execute()throws BuildException
```

This method is called by the project or target to execute the task.

```
public Location getLocation()
```

This method returns the file location where this task was defined.

```
public void setLocation(Location location)
```

This is the setter method for the file location where this task is defined.

```
public RuntimeConfigurable getRuntimeConfigurableWrapper()
```

This is the getter method for the wrapper class for runtime configuration.

```
public void maybeConfigure()
```

This method configures this task, unless it has already been done.

Class TaskAdapter

```
public class TaskAdapter
```

Inheritance Information

Extends: `Task`

Description

TaskAdapter uses introspection to adapt a bean (using the Bridge design pattern).

Methods

```
public void execute()
```

This method executes the adapted task.

```
public void setProxy(java.lang.Object o)
```

This is the setter method for the target object class.

```
public java.lang.Object getProxy()
```

This is the getter method for the target object class.

Class UnknownElement

```
public class UnknownElement
```

Description

UnknownElement is a class that wraps all information necessary to create a task that did not exist when Ant started.

Constructor

```
public UnknownElement(java.lang.String elementName)
```

Methods

```
public java.lang.String getTag()
```

This is the getter method for the corresponding XML tag.

```
public void maybeConfigure()
```

This method configures this task, unless its been done already.

```
public void execute()
```

This method executes when the real task has been configured for the first time.

```
public void addChild(UnknownElement child)
```

This method adds a child element.

```
protected void handleChildren(java.lang.Object parent,
                RuntimeConfigurable parentWrapper)
```

This method executes children.

Class XmlLogger

```
public class XmlLogger
```

Inheritance Information

Extends: org.apache.tools.ant.XmlLogger

Implements: BuildListener, java.util.EventListener

Description

XmlLogger creates a file (log.xml) in the current directory with an XML description of what happened during a build.

Constructor

```
public XmlLogger()
```

This constructor initializes a new XmlLogger that logs build events to an XML file.

Methods

```
public void buildStarted(BuildEvent event)
```

This method executes before any targets are started.

```
public void buildFinished(BuildEvent event)
```

This method executes after the last target has finished, whether or not errors occurred.

```
public void targetStarted(BuildEvent event)
```

This method executes when a target is started.

```
public void targetFinished(BuildEvent event)
```

This method executes when a target has finished, whether or not errors occurred.

```
public void taskStarted(BuildEvent event)
```

This method executes when a task is started.

```
public void taskFinished(BuildEvent event)
```

This method executes when a task has finished, whether or not errors occurred.

```
public void messageLogged(BuildEvent event)
```

This method executes whenever a message is logged.

Putting It Together

Now, to put all this information together, we will programmatically create a project, give it a single target and task, and call execute() on it. Using our task GreetJon from the description of the Task class, we will build a task that can be executed using its own Main() method.

The project file is as follows:

```
import org.apache.tools.ant.*;

public class ChapterAntProject extends org.apache.tools.ant.Project{

    public ChapterAntProject(){
        super.init();
    }

    public static void main(String[] args){
        try{
            /*
             Create the Project object and add the custom Tag
             */
            Project proj = new ChapterAntProject();
            proj.setName("jonsProject");
            GreetJon task = new GreetJon();
            proj.addTaskDefinition("jonsTask", task.getClass());
            /*
```

```
             Create the Target Object as a child
             of the project and add the Task to
             it
             */
            Target targ = new Target();
            targ.setName("jonsTarget");
            targ.addTask(task);
            proj.addTarget("jonsTarget",targ);
            proj.setDefaultTarget("jonsTarget");
            /*
             Execute the Target
             */
            proj.executeTarget("jonsTarget");
        }
        catch(Exception e){
            e.printStackTrace();
            throw new BuildException("An error occurred while building
                                     and running your custom task",e);

        }
    }

}
```

The task file is as follows:

```
import org.apache.tools.ant.*;
public class GreetJon extends Task {

     public GreetJon(){
        ;}

        public void execute() throws BuildException{
             System.out.println("Hello Zach!");
     }
}
```

Running the project from a Java environment will produce output equivalent to the following Ant build.xml file:

```
<?xml version="1.0"?>

<project name="jonsProject" basedir = "." default = "jonsTarget">
    <target name="jonsTarget">
       <taskdef name="jonsTask" classname="GreetJon"/>
    </target>
</project>
```

This example is meant to be a simplified launching point from which you can build many custom tasks, projects, and targets to perform specific actions within the Ant framework.

CHAPTER 14

JUnit API Reference

This chapter summarizes the JUnit API. Classes used by developers as part of their everyday testing are emphasized.

Package junit.framework

The junit.framework package contains all the classes developers need to begin writing JUnit tests. The TestCase class forms the center of the package, and developers subclass it to create automated unit tests. The rest of the classes in the package support TestCase: collecting its results, aggregating many instances into a test suite, and providing assertion facilities. The Test interface is another crucial package member—it defines a common contract for TestCases and TestSuites, as well as providing a hook into the framework for extensions to use.

Class Assert

```
public class Assert
```

Inheritance Information

Extends: `Object`

Direct known subclasses: `TestCase`, `TestDecorator`

Description

Assert comprises a set of static assert methods that can be used to fail tests. Because TestCase and TestDecorator extend Assert, Assert's methods can be used by their unqualified names in subclasses of these two classes.

If the condition tested by the Assert method evaluates to false, it throws an AssertionFailedError. The framework treats this error as a test failure. Assertion methods are used in TestCases to set up the pass/fail conditions for the test method.

Every Assert method is overloaded to take an additional String parameter as its first argument. This message will be attached to the AssertionFailedError, should it be thrown. The following code sample illustrates ways to use Assert's methods to verify that the code under test has produced the correct results.

```
public void testOpenPortal(){
  Portal hadesPortal = dimensionalGateway.openPortal(new
Plane("Hades"));

  /*verify that a portal object was returned*/
  assertNotNull("null portal returned", hadesPortal);

  /*verify the portal is open*/
  assertTrue(hadesPortal.isOpen());

  /*check that the portal has the correct name*/
  assertEquals("portal name check", "HadesPortal",
               hadesPortal.getName());
  /*try opening a portal to a plane that does not exist*/
  try{
    dimensionalGateway.openPortal(new Plane("xxxfooyyy"));
    fail("should have gotten a PlaneNotFoundException e");
  }
  catch(PlaneNotFoundException e){/*behavior is as expected*/}
}
```

Methods

`assert(boolean condition)` *`Deprecated`*
`public static void assert(boolean condition)`

Use assertTrue(boolean condition).

These are the most basic forms of assertions. If the boolean is not true, the assertion fails. The assert() and assert(String) methods were deprecated in favor of assertTrue() to avoid a conflict with the assert keyword in Java 1.4.

`assert(String message, boolean condition)` *`Deprecated`*
`public static void assert(String message, boolean condition)`

Use assertTrue(String message, boolean condition).

assertTrue(boolean condition)

```
public static void assertTrue(boolean condition)
```

assertTrue(String message, boolean condition)

```
public static void assertTrue(String message, boolean condition)
```

assertEquals(String message, Object expected, Object actual)

```
public static void assertEquals(String message, Object expected,
                                Object actual)
```

assertEquals(Object expected, Object actual)

```
public static void assertEquals(Object expected, Object actual)
```

assertEquals(String message, double expected, double actual, double delta)

```
public static void assertEquals(String message, double expected,
                                double actual, double delta)
```

assertEquals(double expected, double actual, double delta)

```
public static void assertEquals(double expected, double actual,
                                double delta)
```

assertEquals(String message, float expected, float actual, float delta)

```
public static void assertEquals(String message, float expected,
                                float actual, float delta)
```

assertEquals(float expected, float actual, float delta)

```
public static void assertEquals(float expected, float actual,
                                float delta)
```

assertEquals(String message, long expected, long actual)

```
public static void assertEquals(String message, long expected,
                                long actual)
```

assertEquals(long expected, long actual)

```
public static void assertEquals(long expected, long actual)
```

assertEquals(String message, boolean expected, boolean actual)

```
public static void assertEquals(String message, boolean expected,
                                boolean actual)
```

assertEquals(boolean expected, boolean actual)

```
public static void assertEquals(boolean expected, boolean actual)
```

assertEquals(String message, byte expected, byte actual)

```
public static void assertEquals(String message, byte expected,
                                byte actual)
```

```
assertEquals(byte expected, byte actual)
public static void assertEquals(byte expected, byte actual)

assertEquals(String message, char expected, char actual)
public static void assertEquals(String message, char expected,
                                char actual)

assertEquals(char expected, char actual)
public static void assertEquals(char expected, char actual)

assertEquals(String message, short expected, short actual)
public static void assertEquals(String message, short expected,short
                                actual)

assertEquals(short expected, short actual)
public static void assertEquals(short expected, short actual)

assertEquals(String message, int expected, int actual)
public static void assertEquals(String message, int expected, int actual)

assertEquals(int expected, int actual)
public static void assertEquals(int expected, int actual)
```

These methods compare the first (nonmessage) argument to the second and fail if they are not equal. The test for equality is == for primitives and equals() for objects. Floating-point comparisons are made with respect to the delta argument (that is, if the difference between expected and actual is greater than the delta, the test fails).

NOTE:

These comparisons require the delta because floating-point calculations can result in slight precision errors; these errors would cause a test that depended upon exact equality to fail even though the calculated result was as close to the desired result as floating-point calculations could make it.

All the assertEquals methods automatically display the values of the expected and actual parameters as part of their failure message.

```
assertNotNull(Object object)
public static void assertNotNull(Object object)

assertNotNull(String message, Object object)
public static void assertNotNull(String message, Object object)

assertNull(Object object)
public static void assertNull(Object object)

assertNull(String message, Object object)
public static void assertNull(String message, Object object)
```

This method checks whether a given reference is null.

```
assertSame(String message, Object expected, Object actual)
public static void assertSame(String message, Object expected,
                              Object actual)
```

```
assertSame(Object expected, Object actual)
public static void assertSame(Object expected, Object actual)
```

This method verifies that the expected and actual arguments are the same object. (This method uses the == method of comparison, not the .equals() method.

```
fail(String message)
public static void fail(String message)
```

```
fail()
public static void fail()
```

This method fails the test by throwing an AssertionFailedError. It's useful for asserting that a given point in code should not be reached, as with an exception that should have been thrown (see the example at the beginning of this section).

Interface Protectable

```
public interface Protectable
```

Description

The JUnit framework and custom extensions use the Protectable interface to indicate code that requires JUnit-style exception handling. Developers can use an inner class to implement Protectable, defining its protect() method so that it calls relevant code (in the framework, calls to setUp(), the test method, and tearDown() are ultimately located within a protect() method). The Protectable can then be passed to a TestResult object, which will catch and log any exceptions resulting from the call to protect(). See TestResult.runProtected for details and an example. Everyday testing should not require the use of this interface.

Method

```
protect()
public void protect()
```

This method wraps a call to a method requiring protection. (Note: this method throws Throwable.)

Interface Test

```
public interface Test
```

Description

Part of the Composite design pattern, Test represents the common interface for single (TestCase), composite (TestSuite), and special (TestDecorator) tests. The shared interface allows all types of tests to be treated similarly by the framework.

Methods

`countTestCases()`

```
public int countTestCases()
```

This method counts the number of TestCases that will be run by this test (1 for TestCases, or the grand total of contained TestCases for suites).

`run(TestResult result)`

```
public void run(TestResult result)
```

This method runs this test and collects the results in the TestResult parameter.

Class TestCase

```
public abstract class TestCase
```

Inheritance Information

Extends: `Assert`

Implements: `Test`

Known subclasses: `ExceptionTestCase`

Description

TestCase is the central class of the JUnit framework. Subclasses of TestCase form the building blocks of automated test suites in JUnit. A TestCase subclass is usually designed to exercise the public interface of the class under test.

The standard template for a subclass is a String constructor, a setUp() method, a tearDown() method, and any number of (public) test methods named according to the form *test<name of method to be tested>()*. The setUp() method ensures that the test fixture is initialized, and the tearDown() method performs cleanup after a given test. When tests are run, each test method is run as part of a separate instance of the TestCase to which it belongs. The series of steps for test method execution is:

```
setUp()
<testMethod>
tearDown()
```

NOTE

A *test fixture* is loosely defined as all the data and/or objects the test code needs in order to run properly. A TestCase for a sorting method might have a test fixture consisting of several unsorted arrays and a properly instantiated Sorter object.

Constructor

```
TestCase(String name)
public TestCase(String name)
```

TestCase() constructs an instance of the TestCase based on the name argument. TestCase follows the Pluggable Selector design pattern, in which the behavior of an object can be modified externally. In the case of TestCase, this means each TestCase instance will run only *one* of its test methods when a caller invokes run(). Unless the behavior of runTest() is overridden, the name of the TestCase specifies which test method is executed.

Suppose a method testHeatUp() exercises heatUp() on a Weather object. To run this test method in the JUnit framework, we create a new TestCase with the following syntax:

```
TestCase testToRunSoon = new WeatherTest("testHeatUp");
```

When run() is called on testToRunSoon, TestCase uses reflection to find and execute testHeatUp(). Subclasses should provide a String constructor that calls TestCase(String) to maintain this behavior.

NOTE

Initialization code should be located in the setUp() method rather than in the constructor, a method called by the constructor, or an instance initializer block. See setUp() for more information.

Methods

```
countTestCases()
public int countTestCases()
```

This method returns the number of TestCases—in other words, one.

```
createResult()
public TestResult createResult()
```

This method instantiates a new TestResult object.

```
getName()
public String getName()
```

This method returns the name of this TestCase instance. The name usually corresponds to the name of the method under test by this instance.

```
name() Deprecated
public String name()
```

Use getName().

```
run()
public TestResult run()
```

This is a convenience method that runs the test case and returns a new TestResult containing the results.

```
TestResult result = new WeatherTest("testHeatUp").run();
if (!result.wasSuccessful()){
     sendIrateEmailToClassAuthor();
}
run(TestResult result)
public void run(TestResult result)
```

This method runs the whole test, including setUp() and tearDown(), and collects the result in the TestResult argument. See the description of TestResult and Test for more information.

```
runBare()
public void runBare()
```

This method runs the TestCase, including setUp() and tearDown(). It provides no result-gathering functionality. If an exception is thrown during runBare(), the test has failed. This method is used mainly by the framework.

```
runTest()
public void runTest()
```

This method defines the testable behavior (as opposed to setup or result-gathering code) of this instance of the TestCase. The runTest() method is called as part of the run(TestResult) method. The default implementation uses reflection to run the method corresponding to the name of the TestCase.

Instead of using the default implementation, you can also override this method in an anonymous inner class to execute the desired test code. The following two methods of instantiating a WeatherTest that runs the testHeatUp() method are equivalent:

```
TestCase innerClassCase = new WeatherTest("I could use any name here"){
  public void runTest(){
    testHeatUp();
  }
```

```
};

TestCase defaultCase = new WeatherTest("testHeatUp");
```

The anonymous inner class method of specifying TestCase behavior is more type safe and is described in the JUnit documentation. However, it seems to be primarily an artifact from an earlier version of JUnit where the reflection-based implementation did not exist. For most purposes, the reflection implementation is simpler.

setName()

```
public void setName(String name)
```

This method sets the name of the TestCase instance in a manner identical to the String constructor.

setUp()

```
public void setUp()
```

Because setUp() is called by TestCase before the execution of test code, subclasses should override this method to set up the test fixture for test methods to run against. Each test method in the class is executed within a separate instance of the TestCase, so there is no benefit in putting shared setup code in a constructor or an initializer block instead (because these will be run as often as setUp()).

NOTE

In versions of JUnit previous to 3.7, exceptions generated in code that ran as part of TestCase construction yielded confusing stack traces—all the more reason to stick to setUp().

All the test methods in the following subclass would now have access to a catalog with two products in it when executed with run(TestResult):

```
public void setUp(){
  /*initialize an instance variable.*/
  testCatalog = new Catalog();
  testCatalog.addProduct(new Product("Original Koozie"));
  testCatalog.addProduct(new Product("Executive Chubber"));
}
```

suite()

```
public static Test suite()
```

The static suite() method is defined by convention in TestCase subclasses. It provides a convenient way of turning all the test methods in a TestCase into a single TestSuite. The suite() method can also be used by TestCases that define no test methods but instead serve as assemblers of other TestSuites. For Test-Cases with test code in them, suite() methods should probably follow this form:

```
public static Test suite(){
  //shortcut to add all test methods in the class
  return new TestSuite(YourTestCase.class);
}
```

Alternatively, suite() can add the different TestCases to the suite by hand. This technique is convenient when you need more granularity (maybe a test method executes so slowly that you remove it temporarily during development):

```
public static Test suite(){
  //more granular implementation, add each test by hand
  TestSuite suite = new TestSuite();
  suite.addTest(new YourTestCase("testFirstMethod"));
  //suite.addTest(new YourTestCase("testVerySlowMethod"));
  return suite;
}
```

TestCases that serve as assemblers of other tests should use the following form:

```
public static Test suite(){
  TestSuite suite = new TestSuite();
  suite.addTest(FirstClassInPackage.suite());
  suite.addTest(SecondClassInPackage.suite());
  //etc.
  return suite;
}
```

The last implementation shows why it is conventional to define a suite() method for each TestCase()—doing so makes it simpler for assembler Test-Cases to add all the tests in a package to their *own* suite() method.

tearDown()

`public void tearDown()`

This method tears down the test fixture. The tearDown() method is called by TestCase after the test method is finished. Generally, tearDown() should free shared resources such as database connections and perform cleanup. In addition, because a TestSuite may store instantiated and setup TestCases until the test run is complete, it is a good idea to dereference any memory-intensive instance variables:

```
public void tearDown(){
  databaseConnection.close();
  testFile.delete();
  giantArray = null;
}
```

toString()
```
public String toString()
```

This method returns a String representation in the form *<name of instance>(<name of class>)*.

Interface TestListener

```
public interface TestListener
```

Description

The TestListener interface is used by the TestRunners provided by the JUnit framework. Its methods inform the listener object that a test has started, an error or a failure has been encountered, or a test has ended. These notifications allow the TestRunners to build a dynamic view of this information. TestListeners are registered with a TestResult.

Methods

addError(Test test, Throwable t)
```
public void addError(Test test, Throwable t)
```

addFailure(Test test, AssertionFailedError t)
```
public void addFailure(Test test, AssertionFailedError t)
```

endTest(Test test)
```
public void endTest(Test test)
```

startTest(Test test)
```
public void startTest(Test test)
```

Class TestFailure

```
public class TestFailure
```

Inheritance Information

Extends: `Object`

Description

The TestFailure class mates a failed Test with the exception that caused it to fail. It provides a constructor and accessor methods for the Test and the exception. The toString() method returns a short description of the failure.

Constructor

```
TestFailure(Test failedTest, Throwable thrownException)
public TestFailure(Test failedTest, Throwable thrownException)
```

Methods

```
failedTest()
public Test failedTest()

thrownException()
public Throwable thrownException()

toString()
public String toString()
```

Class TestResult

```
public class TestResult
```

Inheritance Information

Extends: `Object`

Description

TestResult is an example of the Collecting Parameter design pattern. The results of an arbitrary number of tests can be collected by passing the same TestResult to each Test's run method.

In addition to aggregating results, TestResult lets you run TestCases and interpret thrown exceptions as test failures. JUnit recognizes two types of negative Test result: failures and errors. *Failures* are the result of assertions that proved untrue at runtime and are represented by AssertionFailedErrors. *Errors* are unanticipated exceptions thrown by the test code (such as ClassCastExceptions). TestResult wraps both types of exceptions in TestFailure objects but stores them differently. In addition to exposing the collections of TestFailures, TestResult also provides a wasSuccessful() method to determine whether all tests passed.

TestResult is used mostly by the JUnit framework, because the provided TestRunners encapsulate code that displays the results of a test run. TestRunners interact with the TestResult through the TestListener interface. TestListeners are registered with the TestResult, which calls the appropriate methods to notify the listener of test lifecycle events (start, end, failure, and error). Here is an example of how we might use TestResult without the framework:

```
TestResult result = new TestResult();
result.addListener(someCustomListener);
```

```
nightlyTestSuite.run(result);
if(!result.wasSuccessful()){
  Enumeration eFailures = result.failures();
  while(eFailures.hasMoreElements()){
    TestFailure failure =(TestFailure)eFailures.nextElement();
    System.out.println(failure.failedTest() + " failed with exception "
+
                       failure.thrownException());
  }
  if(result.failureCount() + result.errorCount() > 10){
    printBigRedWarning();
  }
}
```

Constructor

TestResult()

`public TestResult()`

Methods

addError(Test test, Throwable t)

`public void addError(Test test, Throwable t)`

addFailure(Test test, AssertionFailedError t)

`public void addFailure(Test test, AssertionFailedError t)`

These methods each add an error or failure to the TestResult. The second parameter in each case represents the exception that caused the test to fail.

addListener(TestListener listener)

`public void addListener(TestListener listener)`

This method registers a TestListener with this TestResult.

endTest(Test test)

`public void endTest(Test test)`

This method informs the TestResult (and by extension, its registered listeners) that the specified test is complete.

errorCount()

`public int errorCount()`

This method returns the number of detected errors stored in this TestResult.

errors()

`public Enumeration errors()`

This method returns an Enumeration of the detected errors stored in this TestResult.

failureCount()
```
public int failureCount()
```

This method returns the number of detected failures stored in this TestResult.

failures()
```
public Enumeration failures()
```

This method returns an Enumeration of the detected failures stored in this TestResult.

removeListener(TestListener listener)
```
public void removeListener(TestListener listener)
```

This method unregisters the specified TestListener.

run(TestCase test)
```
protected void run(TestCase test)
```

This method runs the specified TestCase and adds any thrown exceptions to the lists of failures or errors as appropriate.

runCount()
```
public int runCount()
```

This method returns the total number of TestCases whose results are gathered in this TestResult.

runProtected(Test test, Protectable p)
```
public void runProtected(Test test, Protectable p)
```

This method runs the given Protectable under JUnit protection (all caught exceptions, except ThreadDeathException, are added to the error/failure list). The runProtected() method is used internally as part of standard TestCase execution, and it can be used by extensions that execute code in addition to the code directly under test. Any exceptional conditions in the Protectable's protect() method are logged in the TestResult and associated with the Test parameter:

```
//encapsulate database setup inside an anonymous Protectable
Protectable p = new Protectable(){
  public void protect(){
    insertTestDataIntoDB();
  }
};
result.runProtected(testToAssociateFailuresWith, p);
```

runTests() *Deprecated*
```
public int runTests()
```

Use runCount().

shouldStop()
```
public boolean shouldStop()
```

This method checks whether a series of tests being run with this TestResult should stop (usually meaning prematurely). Users of TestResult can signal a premature stop with the stop() method.

```
startTest(Test test)
public void startTest(Test test)
```

This method notifies the TestResult (and its listeners) that the given Test will be started.

```
stop()
public void stop()
```

This method signals that the series of tests being run with this TestResult should stop rather than finishing.

`testErrors()` *Deprecated*
```
public int testErrors()
```

Use errorCount().

`testFailures()` *Deprecated*
```
public int testFailures()
```

Use failureCount().

```
wasSuccessful()
public boolean wasSuccessful()
```

This method returns true if all the Tests run with this TestResult were successful, or false otherwise.

Class TestSuite

```
public class TestSuite
```

Inheritance Information

Extends: `Object`

Implements: `Test`

Direct known subclass: `ActiveTestSuite`

Description

TestSuite represents a composite of Tests. TestSuite implements the Test interface, so TestSuites can contain other TestSuites. Suites are generally used to collect and run all the test methods in a TestCase or all the TestSuites in a package. By nesting TestSuites within TestSuites, you can test portions of a codebase at an arbitrary level of granularity.

TestSuite handles exceptional conditions during Test addition (no valid constructor for the TestCase, exceptions in the constructor, no test methods found in the class during automatic addition, and so on) by adding a new Test to the suite that will fail automatically with an appropriate warning message.

Constructors

`TestSuite()`

```
public TestSuite()
```

`TestSuite(String name)`

```
public TestSuite(String name)
```

This constructor constructs an empty TestSuite. New Tests can be added to the suite by calling the addTest(Test) method.

`TestSuite(Class theClass)`

This constructor constructs a TestSuite containing a TestCase for each test method in the Class argument. *Test methods* are defined as public methods in the class that take no arguments, declare a void return type, and begin with the word *test*:

```
TestSuite suite = new TestSuite(WeatherTest.class);
```

Methods

`addTest(Test test)`

```
public void addTest(Test test)
```

This method adds the specified test to the TestSuite. It's used to hand construct a TestSuite—usually for the purpose of adding other TestSuites to this suite:

```
/*add a single Test*/
theSuite.addTest(new PortalTest("testOpenPortal"));
/*suite() method returns the suite for that class*/
theSuite.addTest(WeatherTest.suite());
```

`addTestSuite(Class testClass)`

```
public void addTestSuite(Class testClass)
```

This method adds all the test methods in the specified class to the suite. It's equivalent to a call to:

```
addTest(new TestSuite(testClass));
```

`countTestCases()`

```
public void countTestCases()
```

This method counts the total number of TestCases in this suite (including TestCases within contained TestSuites).

```
getName()
public void getName()
```

This method returns the name of this TestSuite (as specified by the String constructor or setName()). TestSuites are not required to have a name.

```
run(TestResult result)
public void run(TestResult result)
```

This method runs all the Tests (including TestCases and other TestSuites) contained within the suite. The total results are gathered in the TestResult. The run() method is usually called by one of the framework's TestRunners.

```
runTest(Test test, TestResult result)
public void runTest(Test test, TestResult result)
```

This method runs the given Test with the given TestResult. It's equivalent to test.run(result) in the default implementation. Subclasses can override runTest() to customize how Tests are run by the suite.

```
setName(String name)
public void setName(String name)
```

This method sets the name of the TestSuite.

```
testAt(int index)
public Test testAt(int index)
```

This method returns the Test at the given index. Tests are stored internally in a list, so the index corresponds to the position in the list (the first Test added is index 0, the second is index 1, and so on). The testAt() method is rarely used in everyday testing.

```
testCount()
public int testCount()
```

This method returns the number of Tests immediately contained by this suite (not the grand total number of Tests).

```
tests()
public java.util.Enumeration tests()
```

This method returns the Tests immediately contained by this suite as an Enumeration.

```
toString()
public String toString()
```

This method returns a String representation of the TestSuite. In version 3.7, this is the name of the TestSuite.

Package junit.extensions

The junit.extensions package contains a few useful classes that add functionality to the basics contained within junit.framework. In addition to these, the package contains the TestDecorator class that serves a superclass for third-party extensions to the framework. See Chapter 17 for examples of how JUnitPerf uses the TestDecorator class to add functionality to existing JUnit TestCases.

Class ActiveTestSuite

```
public class ActiveTestSuite
```

Inheritance Information

Extends: `TestSuite`

Description

This is a subclass of TestSuite that runs each of the Tests in the suite in its own thread. The suite does not finish running until the last thread has terminated. ActiveTestSuite does not extend its multi-threaded nature to contained suites. In other words, if an ActiveTestSuite A contains a normal TestSuite B, all of B's tests will execute within the single thread that A assigns to B (unless B specifies some other behavior).

To employ an ActiveTestSuite, simply instantiate it and use it as you would a normal TestSuite. Individual tests can be hand-added to the suite, or all of the test methods in a class can be added. The following code samples illustrate both approaches.

```
//Create an ActiveTestSuite by hand-adding several copies of the same
//Test—perhaps to test performance in a multi-threaded environment:
TestSuite suite = new ActiveTestSuite();
suite.addTest(new YourTestCase("testFirstMethod"));
suite.addTest(new YourTestCase("testFirstMethod"));
suite.addTest(new YourTestCase("testFirstMethod"));

//Replace the standard suite() method so that it uses an ActiveTestSuite
public static Test suite(){
  //shortcut to add all test methods in the class
  return new ActiveTestSuite(YourTestCase.class);
}
```

Methods

`run(TestResult result)`

```
public void run(TestResult result)
```

This method runs each Test contained by the suite in its own thread.

```
runTest(Test test, TestResult result)
public void runTest(Test test, TestResult result)
```

This method spawns a new thread and runs the specified Test within it.

NOTE

Although TestResult synchronizes many of its methods to provide a measure of thread safety, calling runTest(Test, TestResult) on an ActiveTestSuite will result in a new, unsupervised thread. Unless you have a good reason to do so, it is probably not worth calling this method externally.

```
runFinished(Test test)
public void runFinished(Test test)
```

This method notifies the suite that a test thread is about to complete.

WARNING

The runFinished() method may be public by mistake. Calling this method externally could result in premature termination of the suite (before all Tests are run).

Class ExceptionTestCase

```
public class ExceptionTestCase
```

Inheritance Information

Extends: `TestCase`

Description

ExceptionTestCase is a subclass of TestCase that expects a specified exception when run and fails if one is not thrown. This class seems to be of dubious usefulness. If it were subclassed, all instances of the subclass would expect the exception specified in the constructor. As a result, it would be impossible to put test methods that did not throw the exception into such a subclass. If ExceptionTestCase is not subclassed, no convenient way exists to specify which method the TestCase instance should run as the code under test. Anonymous inner classes could solve this problem, but are hardly easier than the alternate syntax for checking an exception:

```
try{
  codeUnderTest();
  fail("expected an ExpectedException");
}
catch(ExpectedException e){/*ignore*/}
```

Constructor

```
ExceptionTestCase(String name, Class exception)
public ExceptionTestCase(String name, Class exception)
```

This constructor constructs the test with the specified name and class of the exception expected to be thrown when the test runs.

Method

```
runTest()
protected void runTest()
```

This method runs this test case. If an exception of the class specified in the constructor is *not* thrown, the test fails.

Class RepeatedTest

```
public class RepeatedTest
```

Inheritance Information

Extends: `TestDecorator`

Description

RepeatedTest is a simple TestDecorator that runs the decorated Test the number of times specified by the constructor. The constructor expects the interface Test (as do most TestDecorators) so that TestCases or TestSuites are all valid targets for repetition (other TestDecorators are also valid targets for repetition—see the code samples for JUnitPerf's use of RepeatedTest in Chapter 17). The run(TestResult) method simply calls run(TestResult) on the decorated Test the specified number of times. Generally, this means that setUp() and tearDown() are called for each repetition on each contained TestCase. However, any fixture set up or dismantling that occurs *outside* of these methods (such as in the constructor of a TestCase) will not be executed multiple times because run() is called multiple times on *the same instance* of the Test.

Constructor

```
RepeatedTest(Test test, int repeat)
public RepeatedTest(Test test, int repeat)
```

This constructor specifies the Test to decorate and the number of repetitions.

Methods

```
countTestCases()
public int countTestCases()
```

As specified in the Test interface, this method counts the total number of TestCases contained in the Test. In the case of RepeatedTest, this count is arrived at by multiplying the number of repetitions by the result of a call to countTestCases() on the decorated test.

```
run(TestResult result)
public void run(TestResult result)
```

```
toString()
public String toString()
```

Class TestDecorator

```
public class TestDecorator
```

Inheritance Information

Extends: `Assert`

Implements: `Test`

Direct known subclasses: `RepeatedTest`, `TestSetup`

Description

TestDecorator is the preferred base class for extensions that decorate (add additional behavior to) Tests. TestDecorator implements Test, so it can be used to decorate suites or TestCases; in addition, decorators can be nested within other decorators. TestDecorator defines the basic structure of a decorator and provides a few convenience functions. Test developers extend TestDecorator and override the run(TestResult) method to provide custom Test decoration.

Constructor

```
TestDecorator(Test test)
public TestDecorator(Test test)
```

This constructor constructs a TestDecorator that wraps the specified Test. Subclasses should provide a constructor that calls this constructor.

Methods

```
basicRun(TestResult result)
public void basicRun(TestResult result)
```

Subclasses can call this method during their own run() method to run the wrapped test without any decoration. See the run() method for an example of use.

```
countTestCases()
public int countTestCases()
```

This method counts the total number of TestCases run by this Test. Subclasses should override this method if the decoration code affects how many TestCases are actually run.

```
getTest()
public Test getTest()
```

This method returns the contained Test that is decorated.

```
run(TestResult result)
public void run(TestResult result)
```

This method runs the contained Test in cooperation with the decoration code. This is the key place for subclasses to define such code:

```
public class RandomTest extends TestDecorator{
  public RandomTest(Test test){
    super(test);
  }

  public void run(TestResult result){
    if(Math.random() > .5){
      basicRun(result);
    }
  }
}
```

Although this decorator violates XP principles (why would you ever *not* run a test?), it shows how decorators can add functionality to a Test.

```
toString()
public String toString()
```

This method simply returns toString() on the enclosed Test in the base implementation. Subclasses should override it to provide additional description of the decoration.

Class TestSetup

```
public class TestSetup
```

Inheritance Information

Extends: `TestDecorator`

Description

TestSetup is a base class for decorators that wish to provide additional fixture setup and teardown. If TestSetup decorates a TestSuite, its setUp() and tear-Down() methods will be executed once for all the tests within the suite. Therefore, subclasses of TestSetup are an ideal place to put expensive set up code (such as the insertion of test data into a database) that does not need to be repeated for each individual test.

Uncaught exceptions resulting from setUp() or tearDown() code are caught and logged in the TestResult as associated with the TestSetup instance. The following subclass sets the specified system properties before the contained test runs:

```
public class PropertiesSetup extends TestSetup{
  java.util.Properties props;
  public PropertiesSetup(Test test, java.util.Properties props){
    super(test);
    this.props = props;
  }

  protected void setUp(){
    System.getProperties().putAll(props);
  }

  protected void tearDown(){
    for(Iterator i= props.keySet().iterator(); i.hasNext();){
        System.getProperties().remove(i.next());
    }
  }
}
```

Methods

`run(TestResult result)`

`public void run(TestResult result)`

This method runs setUp(), then the enclosed Test, and then tearDown().

`setUp()`

`protected void setUp()`

Subclasses should override this method to provide additional one-time fixture code surrounding the decorated Test.

`tearDown()`

`protected void tearDown()`

Subclasses should override this method to dismantle the fixture created by setUp() after the contained Test has run.

CHAPTER 15

Cactus API Reference

This chapter covers the Cactus API, which extends and employs the JUnit API described in Chapters 7 and 14. The Cactus API includes a slew of classes that support the complicated task of getting test cases called *outside* the servlet container to run *inside* it. The classes that test developers use every day are grouped together under the org.apache.cactus package. This chapter accordingly focuses primarily on this package, with a smattering of classes from the other packages thrown in when coverage reveals an important detail about the operation of Cactus.

At the time this book went to press, Cactus 1.2 was just being completed, and Cactus had just been promoted to a top-level project under Jakarta. The package names for Cactus were changed from org.apache.commons.cactus to org.apache.cactus. Please check the Cactus Web site (http://jakarta.apache.org) and the book Web site (www.wiley.com/compbooks/hightower) for additional information.

Package org.apache.cactus

The center of this package is AbstractTestCase, from which the three types of TestCases in Cactus 1.2 derive. Developers will extend these subclasses (ServletTestCase, JspTestCase, and FilterTestCase) to create their own test cases. These TestCases use the WebRequest and WebResponse classes that represent the client-side request to and response from the servlet, respectively. Both of these classes have a variety of convenience methods that make the construction and verification of a test easier. The rest of the classes in the package assist one of these classes or act as "framework machinery."

Class AbstractTest Case

```
public abstract class AbstractTestCase
```

Inheritance Information

Extends: `junit.framework.TestCase`

Implements: `junit.framework.Test`

Direct Known Subclasses: `ServletTestCase, FilterTestCase`

Description

AbstractTestCase is the base class from which Cactus server-side tests are derived. Cactus 1.2 supports three concrete subclasses of AbstractTestCase: ServletTestCase, JspTestCase (which extends ServletTestCase), and FilterTestCase. You should extend these classes instead of AbstractTestCase directly. In general, the principles that apply to one type of TestCase apply to the others as well. The main difference between the types of TestCase from a developer's point of view is the implicit objects available within each.

The JUnit framework already expects that your test cases will define a number of methods with the general name pattern testXXX(). *XXX* usually corresponds to the name of the method under test. Cactus TestCases also expect the (optional) presence of methods with the signature beginXXX(WebRequest) and endXXX(WebResponse). These methods are called by AbstractTestCase in the following order:

1. beginXXX(WebRequest) (client side; specific to testXXX())
2. setUp() (server side; global to the test case)
3. testXXX() (server side)
4. tearDown() (server side; global to the test case)
5. endXXX(WebResponse) (client side; specific to testXXX())

setUp(), testXXX(), and tearDown() are executed in a separate copy of the TestCase instantiated in the servlet container, so they do not share state with beginXXX() and endXXX(). The preferred means of communication between beginXXX()/endXXX() and the server-side methods are the "WebRequest" parameter of beginXXX() and the "WebResponse" parameter of endXXX(). See the method descriptions for further information about the use of these objects and their relationship to the setUp(), testXXX(), tearDown() triad.

The section on ServletTestCase contains an example of how to write Cactus TestCases in general—the section on Cookie contains another example.

Constructor

```
AbstractTestCase(String theName)
public AbstractTestCase(String theName)
```

This constructor constructs a new AbstractTestCase with the name of the method to be tested (testXXX). It has functionality similar to that of the public junit.framework.TestCase constructor of the same signature. Because other methods—beginXXX(), endXXX()—are associated with the test method through the shared *XXX* portion of the name, the only way for instances to specify the test method to be run is through the constructor. For this reason, subclasses should maintain a constructor of this form:

```
public SubclassOfServletTestCase(String name){
  super(name);
}
```

Fields

Although AbstractTestCase does not itself define any fields of interest to test developers, each of its subclasses specifies a number of instance variables that correspond to the objects implicitly available within the context of the server component the TestCase is designed to exercise (a servlet, JSP, or Filter in Cactus 1.2). The variables are initialized just before setUp() is called. Because the redirector handles their initialization, these fields will remain null if executed outside of the container. The following code (taken from a ServletTestCase) would throw a NullPointerException because it executes on the client:

```
public void endDoGet(WebResponse resp)throws Exception{
  /*session was not  initialized on the client!*/
  session.getAttribute("some attribute");
}
```

Methods

```
runBare()
public void runBare() throws Throwable
```

This method is overridden from junit.framework.TestCase to remove calls to setUp() and tearDown() (which are executed separately on the server side by the redirector servlet), leaving what amounts to a call to runTest().

```
runBareServerTest()
public void runBareServerTest() throws Throwable
```

This method is intended to be executed on the server side. It calls the test method specified by the constructor along with the setUp() and tearDown() methods in the following order:

```
setUp()
testXXX()
tearDown()
```

```
runServerTest()
protected void runServerTest() throws Throwable
```

This method runs the method corresponding to the name passed to the constructor. This method plays a similar part to the runTest() method in JUnit, except that it is intended to be executed on the server side.

```
runTest()
protected abstract void runTest() throws Throwable
```

This method is overridden by FilterTestCase, ServletTestCase, and JspTestCase. It serves as a starting point for the execution of the TestCase on the server side. Unlike in basic JUnit, the runTest() method is not meant to be overridden in anonymous inner classes.

Expected Methods

Although not technically defined by AbstractTestCase, the machinery of the class expects a number of methods defined with the following general signature patterns.

```
beginXXX(WebRequest request)
public void beginXXX(WebRequest request)
```

This method is executed on the client side before setUp().You can define this method to construct the client request that will eventually arrive at the code under test (see the section on WebRequest for more information). Cactus 1.1 defined a similar method that expected a ServletTestRequest as its parameter.

```
testXXX()
public void testXXX()
```

This method exercises your code. It's executed on the server by the redirector using reflection.

```
endXXX(WebResponse response)
public void endXXX(org.apache.cactus.WebResponse response)
```

or

```
public void endXXX(com.meterware.httpunit.WebResponse response)
```

AbstractTestCase executes this method on the client side after tearDown(). It serves as the place to assert expected response values like cookies, headers, and the textual body of the response.

There are two possible signatures for an endXXX method in Cactus 1.2 (either of which will be called after server-side execution by the framework). Cactus 1.1 defined a different end signature, expecting a java.net.HttpUrlConnection (this alternate signature remains in deprecated form). The first signature takes a Cactus WebResponse as its parameter, the second takes an HttpUnit WebResponse. These two objects differ mainly in their assertion capabilities. The Cactus version supports limited assertion functionality (such as String comparisons) while the HttpUnit version supports sophisticated analysis of a returned HTML document. See the sections on WebResponse in this chapter as well as in Chapter 16 for more details.

Class Cookie

```
public class Cookie
```

Inheritance Information

Extends: `Object`

Implements: `Serializable`

Description

Cookie represents a client view of an HTTP cookie. This class can be used to add cookies to an HTTP request (in the beginXXX() method of the TestCase) or to verify server-set cookies in an HTTP response (in the endXXX() method).

In order for the Web server to accept a cookie sent in the request it must belong to that server's domain; in this case, the cookie domain must match the one specified for the redirector (as mapped in the cactus.properties file) or the domain of the host set with the setURL() method.

Listing 15.1 contains the code for a "Preferences" servlet that sends all of the request parameters back to the client as cookies (to be used in the future as user preferences. The servlet also prints the names and values of all the existing cookies to the response. The accompanying test demonstrates how to set up and verify cookies in Cactus.

```
package xptoolkit.cactus;

import javax.servlet.http.HttpServlet;
import javax.servlet.http.HttpServletRequest;
import javax.servlet.http.HttpServletResponse;
import javax.servlet.http.Cookie;
import java.util.*;
import java.io.PrintWriter;
import java.io.IOException;

public class PreferencesServlet extends HttpServlet{

  public void doGet(HttpServletRequest request,
                  HttpServletResponse response)throws IOException{

    Map cookieMap =  convertParametersToMap(request);
    addCookiesToResponse(response, cookieMap);

    Cookie[] cookies = request.getCookies();
    addCookiesToMap(cookies, cookieMap);

    PrintWriter writer = response.getWriter();
    printMap(writer, cookieMap);
  }

  public Map convertParametersToMap(HttpServletRequest request){
    Map map = new HashMap();
    Enumeration e = request.getParameterNames();
    while(e.hasMoreElements()){
      String name = (String)e.nextElement();
      String value = request.getParameter(name);
      map.put(name, value);
    }
        return map;
  }

  public void addCookiesToMap(Cookie[] cookies, Map map){
    for(int i =0; i < cookies.length; i++){
      map.put(cookies[i].getName(), cookies[i].getValue());
    }
  }

  public void addCookiesToResponse(HttpServletResponse response, Map map){
    Set mapEntries = map.entrySet();
    for(Iterator iter = mapEntries.iterator(); iter.hasNext();){
      Map.Entry entry = (Map.Entry)iter.next();
      Cookie cookie = new Cookie((String)entry.getKey(),
```

Listing 15.1 Using Cookies (continues)

```
                                (String)entry.getValue());
      cookie.setComment("Set by user through PreferencesServlet");
      response.addCookie(cookie);
    }
  }

  private void printMap(PrintWriter writer, Map map){
        Set mapEntries = map.entrySet();
   for(Iterator iter = mapEntries.iterator(); iter.hasNext();){
      Map.Entry entry = (Map.Entry)iter.next();
      String entryStr = entry.getKey() + "=" + entry.getValue();
      writer.println(entryStr);
    }
  }
}

package xptoolkit.cactus;

import javax.servlet.http.HttpServlet;
import javax.servlet.http.HttpServletRequest;
import javax.servlet.http.HttpServletResponse;
import java.util.*;
import java.io.PrintWriter;
import java.io.IOException;
import junit.framework.*;
import org.apache.cactus.*;

public class PreferencesServletTest extends ServletTestCase {
  PreferencesServlet servlet;

  /* Standard constructor, suite(), and so on, omitted */

  public void setUp() throws Exception{
    servlet = new PreferencesServlet();
    servlet.init(this.config);
  }

  public void beginDoGet(WebRequest request)throws Exception{
    request.addCookie("existingName1", "existingValue1");
    Cookie secondCookie = new Cookie("localhost", "existingName2",
                                 "existingValue2");
    request.addCookie(secondCookie);
    request.addParameter("newName1", "newValue1");
  }

  public void testDoGet()throws Exception {
    servlet.doGet(request, response);
```

Listing 15.1 Using Cookies (continues)

```
    }

    public void endDoGet(WebResponse response){
      String[] lines = response.getTextAsArray();
      List responseList = Arrays.asList(lines);
      assertTrue(responseList.contains("existingName1=existingValue1"));
      assertTrue(responseList.contains("existingName2=existingValue2"));
      assertTrue(responseList.contains("newName1=newValue1"));
      Cookie cookie = response.getCookie("newName1");
      assertEquals("newValue1", cookie.getValue());
    }
  }
```

Listing 15.1 Using Cookies

Constructors

```
Cookie(String theDomain, String theName, String theValue)
public Cookie(String theDomain, String theName, String theValue)
```

This constructor creates a new Cookie with the specified name, value, and domain. See the "Description" section for information about the domain.

Methods

```
equals(Object theObject)
public boolean equals(Object theObject)
```

A Cookie is considered to equal another Cookie if they possess the same name, path, and domain.

```
getComment()
public String getComment()
```

This method returns the comment describing this cookie (if one was set).

```
getDomain()
public String getDomain()
```

This method returns the domain that this cookie belongs to.

```
getExpiryDate()
public Date getExpiryDate()
```

This method returns the Date on which this Cookie will expire.

```
getName()
public String getName()
```

getPath()

```
public String getPath()
```

This method returns the "path" of the cookie. This cookie should only be viewed by resources at URLs conforming to the path.

getValue()

```
public String getValue()
```

isExpired()

```
public boolean isExpired()
```

isSecure()

```
public boolean isSecure()
```

This method returns whether this cookie should only be sent over a secure connection.

isToBeDiscarded()

```
public boolean isToBeDiscarded()
```

This method returns true if the HTTP cookie should not persist any longer than the user's session.

setComment(String theComment)

```
public void setComment(String theComment)
```

This method sets the descriptive comment to go along with this cookie.

setDomain(String theDomain)

```
public void setDomain(String theDomain)
```

This method sets the domain that your cookie is to "come from." See the "Description" section for details on what are acceptable domain values in Cactus.

setExpiryDate(Date theExpiryDate)

```
public void setExpiryDate(Date theExpiryDate)
```

setName(String theName)

```
public void setName(String theName)
```

setPath(String thePath)

```
public void setPath(String thePath)
```

setSecure(boolean isSecure)

```
public void setSecure(boolean isSecure)
```

This method indicates that this cookie should only be sent over a secure connection.

```
setValue(String theValue)
public void setValue(String theValue)
```

FilterTestCase

```
public class FilterTestCase
```

Inheritance Information

Extends: `AbstractTestCase`

Implements: `junit.framework.Test`

Description

FilterTestCase provides access to the implicit objects available in a Filter (defined in Servlets 2.3). See AbstractTestCase for more information about how to use Cactus TestCases in general.

Fields

FilterTestCase defines four instance variables that contain either the actual objects available to the redirector or thinly wrapped versions thereof. In all cases the objects available in FilterTestCase implement the same interfaces as those available in an actual Filter. These fields are available in the setUp(), testXXX(), and tearDown() methods. They will contain null if referenced from a beginXXX() or endXXX() method.

```
config
public FilterConfigWrapper config
```

This variable provides a way to mock up initialization parameters. See the section on FilterConfigWrapper (in the org.apache.cactus.server package) for more details.

```
filterChain
public FilterChain filterChain
```

This variable contains the actual FilterChain object available to the filter redirector. Developers, however, can substitute a different FilterChain object to isolate their unit Tests. Since the FilterChain interface contains a single method, it lends itself to quick test implementations that make assertions easier. The following example illustrates a testXXX and FilterChain implementation that verify that a given filter calls doFilter() as expected. The full example can be found in Chapter 8.

```
/*helper class*/
class RecordingChain implements FilterChain{
  boolean doFilterInvoked = false;
```

```
  public void doFilter(ServletRequest servletRequest,
                       ServletResponse servletResponse) {
    doFilterInvoked = true;
  }

  public boolean verify(){
    return doFilterInvoked;
  }
}

/* testXXX method that uses RecordingChain*/
public void testDoFilter() throws Exception{
  RecordingChain recordingChain = new RecordingChain();
  filter.doFilter(request, response, recordingChain);
  assertTrue(recordingChain.verify());
}
```

```
request
public HttpServletRequestWrapper request
```

This field contains the same wrapper class used in ServletTestRequest.

```
response
public HttpServletResponse response
```

Class JspTestCase

```
public class JspTestCase
```

Inheritance Information

Extends: `ServletTestCase`

Implements: `junit.framework.Test`

Description

JspTestCase provides access to JSP implicit objects (pageContext and out) as member variables in addition to the implicit objects of ServletTestCase (see the sections on ServletTestCase and AbstractTestCase for more information about how to use both these classes). The framework authors intended JspTestCase to be used primarily for the testing of custom tags, which are the main type of code that relies specifically on the context provided by a JSP.

The following might represent a testXXX() method in a subclass of JspTestCase:

```
public void testPrintPageContext (){
  CustomJspDebugger.printPageContext(this.out, this.pageContext);
}
```

Fields

These fields contain the pageContext and out objects available in the JspRedirector. The fields are available in the setUp(), testXXX(), and tearDown() methods. The fields will contain null if referenced from a beginXXX() or endXXX() method. The pageContext object is wrapped by Cactus so as to return the correctly wrapped versions of the implicit objects that are also available in ServletTestCase. See the "Fields" section of AbstractTestCase for details about how this type of instance variable operates in Cactus.

```
pageContext
public org.apache.cactus.server.PageContextWrapper pageContext
```

```
out
public javax.servlet.jsp.JspWriter out
```

Class ServiceDefinition

```
public class ServiceDefinition
```

Description

ServiceDefinition specifies manifest constants used in communication between client-side test code and the redirector (which TestCase to load, which method to call, and so on). It's used primarily by the framework.

Class ServiceEnumeration

```
public class ServiceEnumeration
```

Description

ServiceEnumeration defines a list of valid services that the redirector can perform (such as executing a test or getting the results). It's chiefly a framework class.

Class ServletTestCase

```
public class ServletTestCase
```

Inheritance Information

Extends: `AbstractTestCase`

Implements: `junit.framework.Test`

Direct Known Subclasses: `JspTestCase`

Description

ServletTestCase is a central class of the Cactus API for test developers. It extends JUnit's TestCase class and adds features to support the testing of methods that depend on objects made available in the servlet container. It's behavior serves as a model for the behavior of the other two redirector test cases available in Cactus 1.2.

Listing 15.2 demonstrates how to use ServletTestCase (and by extension, the other redirector test cases). The class under test is Insulter, which contains a static method demonize() that depends upon a servlet request and response. InsulterTest passes its request and response member variables to demonize() in its testDemonize() method. The other methods of the TestCase serve to set up and dismantle the test fixture, as well as to assert the results.

```
package xptoolkit.cactus.reference;
import javax.servlet.http.HttpServletRequest;
import javax.servlet.http.HttpServletResponse;
import javax.servlet.http.HttpSession;

//Class under test
public class Insulter{
  public static void demonize(HttpServletRequest request,
                              HttpServletResponse response,
                              InsultGenerator generator) throws
                                                   java.io.IOException{

    HttpSession sess = request.getSession();
    User user = (User)sess.getAttribute("USER_KEY");
    if(user == null){
      throw new IllegalStateException("no user in session");
    }

    String strengthStr = request.getParameter("INSULT_STRENGTH");
    int strength = Integer.parseInt(strengthStr);
    user.setSelfEsteem(user.getSelfEsteem()-strength);

    generator.setStrength(strength);
    generator.printInsult(response.getWriter());
  }

}


package xptoolkit.cactus.reference;
import org.apache.cactus.*;
```

Listing 15.2 Code sample for ServletTestCase. (continues)

```
import org.apache.cactus.util.*;
import javax.servlet.http.HttpServletRequest;
import java.net.HttpURLConnection;
import junit.framework.*;

public class InsulterTest extends ServletTestCase{
  private InsultGenerator generator;
  private User user;

  public InsulterTest(String name){
      super(name);
  }
  /*
   * Methods are placed in the order of execution.
   */

  /*client side*/
  public void beginDemonize(WebRequest request){
    request.addParameter("INSULT_STRENGTH", "5");
  }

  /*server side*/
  public void setUp(){
    /*instantiate the User and put it into the session*/
    user = new User("TestUserName");
    user.setSelfEsteem(10);
    this.session.setAttribute("USER_KEY", user);

    /*instantiate the InsultGenerator*/
    generator = new InsultGenerator("pederast");
  }

  /*server side*/
  public void testDemonize()throws Exception{
    /*call the method under test*/
    Insulter.demonize(this.request, this.response, this.generator);

    /*test that self esteem equals inital value minus insult strength*/
    assertEquals("self esteem correct", 5, user.getSelfEsteem());
  }

  /*server side*/
  public void tearDown(){
    generator = null;
  }

  /*client side*/
```

Listing 15.2 Code sample for ServletTestCase. (continues)

```
    public void endDemonize(WebResponse response) {

        //assertTrue(user.isCrying());--would throw a NullPointerException,
        //                                because user was never instantiated
        //                                on the client side.

        String clientResponse = response.getText();

        assertTrue("insult strength in response",
                   clientResponse.indexOf("5") > -1);

        assertTrue("insult in response",
                   clientResponse.indexOf("pederast") > -1);
    }

     public static TestSuite suite(){
         TestSuite suite = new TestSuite(InsulterTestCase.class);
         return suite;
     }

     public static void main(String[] args){
         junit.textui.TestRunner.run(suite());
     }
  }

  }
```

Listing 15.2 Code sample for ServletTestCase.

Constructor

```
ServletTestCase(String theName)
public ServletTestCase(String theName)
```

Subclasses should maintain a String constructor that calls this constructor. See the "Constructors" section on AbstractTestCase for details.

Fields

ServletTestCase specifies the instance variables request, response, session, and config, which are initialized to versions of implicit objects available in the redirector servlet. Details on the wrapper classes can be found in the org.apache.cactus.server section.

```
config
public ServletConfigWrapper config
```

request
`public HttpServletRequestWrapper request`

response
`public HttpServletResponse response`

session
`public HttpSession session`

NOTE

If the automaticSession property of the ServletTestRequest in beginXXX() is set to false, this value will not be initialized.

Class ServletTestRequest *Deprecated*

`public class ServletTestRequest`

Inheritance Information

Extends: `Object` (in 1.1) / `WebRequest` (in 1.2)

Description

This class has been deprecated in Cactus 1.2 in favor of the class WebRequest. This section represents the public interface as of 1.1. In general, changes or deletions are few; the new WebRequest class has mainly added functionality.

Methods

addCookie(String theName, String theValue)
`public void addCookie(String theName, String theValue)`

addHeader(String theName, String theValue)
`public void addHeader(String theName, String theValue)`

addParameter(String theName, String theValue)
`public void addParameter(String theName, String theValue)`

getAutomaticSession()
`public boolean getAutomaticSession()`

getCookieNames()
`public Enumeration getCookieNames()`

getCookieValue(String theName)
`public String getCookieValue(String theName)`

getHeader(String theName)
`public String getHeader(String theName)`

getHeaderNames()
`public Enumeration getHeaderNames()`

getHeaderValues(String theName)
`public String[] getHeaderValues(String theName)`

getMethod()
`public String getMethod()`

getParameter(String theName)
`public String getParameter(String theName)`

getParameterNames()
`public Enumeration getParameterNames()`

getParameterValues(String theName)
`public String[] getParameterValues(String theName)`

getURL()
`public ServletURL getURL()`

setAutomaticSession(boolean isAutomaticSession)
`public void setAutomaticSession(boolean isAutomaticSession)`

setMethod(String theMethod)
`public void setMethod(String theMethod)`

public void setURL(...)
```
public void setURL(String theServerName, String theContextPath,
     String theServletPath, String thePathInfo, String theQueryString)
```

Class ServletURL

`public class ServletURL`

Inheritance Information

Extends: `Object`

Description

ServletURL simulates the URL of an HTTP request to a servlet. This class is employed by Cactus to yield values from URL-related function calls in HttpServletRequest that correspond to expected real-world values rather than those of the redirector servlet. The constructor takes five arguments, each of which represents a subsection of the simulated URL.

Constructor

```
public ServletURL(...)
public ServletURL(String theServerName,
                  String theContextPath,
                  String theServletPath,
                  String thePathInfo,
                  String theQueryString)
```

Constructs a simulated URL in this format:

```
"http://" + serverName [includes port] + contextPath + servletPath +
 pathInfo + "?" + queryString
```

Each parameter will be available for retrieval from the test case's request field using the appropriate method from HttpServletRequest. Only "theServerName" cannot be null. The middle three parameters follow the format

```
"/"+name
```

where *name* is the appropriate path (application context, servlet context, path to the resource). "theQueryString" emulates the query string of an HTTP request. In Cactus 1.2 and higher, the parameters in "theQueryString" are automatically added to the actual request, in addition to any set with addParameter(). As a result, the request may contain parameters not present in the query string.

Consult the servlet specification for more details on the parts of a servlet URL.

NOTE

In Cactus 1.1 and earlier, the query string parameter used will affect only the results of HttpServletResquest.getQueryString(); its value will have no effect on the request's parameters and vice versa.

Methods

```
getContextPath()
public String getContextPath()
```

```
getPathInfo()
public String getPathInfo()
```

```
getQueryString()
public String getQueryString()
```

```
getServerName()
public String getServerName()
```

```
getServletPath()
public String getServletPath()
```

```
getURL()
public java.net.URL getURL()
```

This method returns the java.net.URL corresponding to this ServletURL.

```
loadFromRequest(HttpServletRequest theRequest)
public static ServletURL loadFromRequest(HttpServletRequest theRequest)
```

This method instantiates a new ServletURL using parameters saved into the request by saveToRequest.

```
saveToRequest(WebRequest theRequest)
public void saveToRequest(WebRequest theRequest)
```

This method saves the state of this ServletURL to the request as a series of parameters.

Class WebRequest

```
public class WebRequest
```

Inheritance Information

Extends: `Object`

Description

WebRequest encapsulates all the HTTP request data that will be sent from the client-side TestCase to the server-side instance. The data will be available to the setUp(), testXXX(), and tearDown() methods through the test case's request variable (which implements HttpServletRequest). WebRequest contains methods to set request parameters, headers, cookies, and the method of the request (POST or GET). It also lets you create simulated URL data and specify whether a session should automatically be created by the redirector servlet.

NOTE

Some important restrictions exist on the domain of cookies sent to the redirector. See the section on the Cookie class for details.

The following example illustrates how to add setUp information for a specific testXXX method to the request that will be sent to the server.

```
public void beginGoOnVisionQuest(WebRequest request){
  /* The URL being constructed is:
     http://nationalparks.org/organ-pipe-monument/long_walk.do
   */
  request.setURL("nationalparks.org",
                 "/organ-pipe-monument",
                 null,
                 "/long_walk.do",
                 null);

  /*multiple values for same key*/
  request.addParameter("SPIRIT_GUIDES", "Coyote");
  request.addParameter("SPIRIT_GUIDES", "Snake");

  request.addCookie("PREPARED", "true");

}
```

Methods

Most of the accessor methods are used by the framework during the translation of this class into an actual HTTP request. These methods work like the methods specified in HttpServletRequest with the same signatures.

`addCookie(Cookie theCookie)`

```
public void addCookie(Cookie theCookie)
```

This method adds the org.apache.cactus.Cookie instance to the request. See the Cookie class for details on the cookie domains in Cactus.

`addCookie(String theName, String theValue)`

```
public void addCookie(String theName, String theValue)
```

This method adds a cookie consisting of the specified name/value pair to the HTTP request with "localhost" as the cookie domain. See the Cookie class section for details on the cookie domains in Cactus.

`addCookie(String theDomain, String theName, String theValue)`

```
public void addCookie(String theDomain, String theName, String theValue)
```

This method adds a cookie with the specified name, value, and domain to the request. See the Cookie class section for details on the cookie domains in Cactus.

`addHeader(String theName, String theValue)`

```
public void addHeader(String theName, String theValue)
```

This method adds a header consisting of the specified name/value pair to the request. Multiple headers with a given name can be added.

addParameter(String theName, String theValue)

```
public void addParameter(String theName, String theValue)
```

This method adds a request parameter consisting of the specified name/value pair. Multiple parameter values can be added under a given name (to support retrieval with HttpSevletRequest.getParameterValues(String) on the server side).

getAutomaticSession()

```
public boolean getAutomaticSession()
```

This method is the accessor for the automaticSession property. (See the section on setAutomaticSession for more details.)

getCookies()

```
public Vector getCookies()
```

getHeader(String theName)

```
public String getHeader(String theName)
```

getHeaderNames()

```
public Enumeration getHeaderNames()
```

getHeaderValues(String theName)

```
public String[] getHeaderValues(String theName)
```

getMethod()

```
public String getMethod()
```

getParameter(String theName)

```
public String getParameter(String theName)
```

getParameterNames()

```
public Enumeration getParameterNames()
```

getParameterValues(String theName)

```
public String[] getParameterValues(String theName)
```

getURL()

```
public ServletURL getURL()
```

This method returns the simulated URL of this request.

setAutomaticSession(boolean isAutomaticSession)

```
public void setAutomaticSession(boolean isAutomaticSession)
```

This method sets whether a session should be created automatically for this request. The default value is true. If it's set to false, the session variable in the server-side TestCase (if any) called with this request will be null.

```
setMethod(String theMethod)
public void setMethod(String theMethod)
```

This method sets the method of the HTTP request (GET/POST); the default is POST.

```
public void setURL(...)
public void setURL(String theServerName, String theContextPath,
     String theServletPath, String thePathInfo, String theQueryString)
```

This method sets the simulated URL of the HTTP request. It's used so that the URL associated with the TestCase on the server resembles an actual URL instead of the URL used to call the redirector servlet. setURL() essentially calls the ServletURL constructor with the same argument list. See the section on ServletURL for more details.

Class WebResponse

```
public class WebResponse
```

Inheritance Information

Extends: `Object`

Description

WebResponse represents a client-side view of the server's response to a specific request. TestCases interact with this object when the framework passes it into the automatically called endXXX() method. WebResponse supports simple assertions; for more complicated assertions, you should use the alternate endXXX() signature that takes a com.meterware.httpunit.WebResponse.

See the section on the Cookie class for an example of how to use WebResponse in an endXXX() method.

Constructors

```
WebResponse(WebRequest theRequest, HttpURLConnection theConnection)

public WebResponse(WebRequest theRequest,
HttpURLConnection theConnection)
```

This constructor builds a new WebResponse from the original WebRequest used to generate an HTTP request to the server and the HttpURLConnection containing the actual response.

Methods

```
getConnection()
public HttpURLConnection getConnection()
```

This method returns the HttpURLConnection that contains the server's raw response to the request made by the TestCase.

```
getCookie(String theName)
public Cookie getCookie(String theName)
```

This method returns the first Cookie in the response with the specified name (or null if no such Cookie was found).

```
getCookies()
public Cookie[] getCookies()
```

This method returns an array of all of the Cookies sent by the server in this response.

```
getInputStream()
public InputStream getInputStream()
```

This method returns a buffered input stream for reading data out of the underlying response.

```
getText()
public String getText()
```

This method returns the body of the server's response (no headers or Cookies) as a String.

```
getTextAsArray()
public String[] getTextAsArray()
```

This method returns an array of Strings, each corresponding to a single line of the server's response; the headers and cookies are omitted.

```
getWebRequest()
public WebRequest getWebRequest()
```

This method returns the original WebRequest that was configured in the beginXXX() method.

Class WebTestResult

```
public class WebTestResult
```

Inheritance Information

Extends: `Object`

Implements: `Serializable`

Description

WebTestResult stores the result of the TestCase's run on the server. The redirector sends a serialized version of this object back to the client after the test is complete so that the TestCase can provide failure information on the client if necessary.

Constructors

```
WebTestResult(Throwable theException)
public WebTestResult(Throwable theException)
```

This constructor constructs a WebTestResult with the specified Throwable as the reason for failure.

```
WebTestResult()
public WebTestResult()
```

This constructor constructs a WebTestResult that indicates success.

Methods

```
getExceptionClassName()
public String getExceptionClassName()
```

```
getExceptionMessage()
public String getExceptionMessage()
```

```
getExceptionStackTrace()
public String getExceptionStackTrace()
```

```
hasException()
public boolean hasException()
```

This method returns true if the WebTestResult contains an exception (that is, if the test failed).

Package org.apache.cactus.util

Both of the classes in the util package have been deprecated in Cactus 1.2. ClientCookie has been improved to become org.apache.cactus.Cookie and the functionality of AssertUtils has been rolled into WebResponse.

Class AssertUtils *Deprecated*

```
public class AssertUtils
```

Inheritance Information

Extends: `Object`

Description

The functionality of this class has been incorporated into WebResponse as of Cactus 1.2.

AssertUtils is a class of static utility functions that simplify the extraction of information from HttpUrlConnections. Such information can then be used in assertions:

```
/*this is the Cactus 1.1 endXXX() method signature.*/
public void endSomeTestMethod(java.net.HttpURLConnection conn) {

      /*cookie assertions*/
      Hashtable allCookies = AssertUtils.getCookies(conn);

      List chocolateChipCookies = (List)allCookies.get("C_CHIP");
      assertEquals("only one chocolate chip cookie set",
                   1, chocolateChipCookies.size());

      ClientCookie cookie = (ClientCookie)chocolateChipCookies.get(0);
      assertTrue(cookie.getMaxAge() < this.FRESHNESS_DATE);

      /*response assertions*/
      String allResponseText = AssertUtils.getResponseAsString(conn);
      assertTrue("contains descriptive text",
                 allResponseText.indexOf("Cookies 4 U") > -1);

      String[] allTextArray =
               AssertUtils.getResponseAsStringArray(conn);
      int last = allTextArray.length;
      assertTrue("html tag closed",
                 allTextArray[last].endsWith("</html>"));
    }
```

Methods

```
getCookies(HttpURLConnection theConnection)
public static Hashtable getCookies(HttpURLConnection theConnection)
```

This method returns a Hashtable containing cookie names as keys. The associated values are Lists (Vectors) of ClientCookie objects that can be inspected.

```
getResponseAsString(HttpURLConnection theConnection)
public static String getResponseAsString(HttpURLConnection
        theConnection) throws IOException
```

This method returns the output stream contained in the connection as a String.

```
getResponseAsStringArray(HttpURLConnection theConnection)
public static String[] getResponseAsStringArray(HttpURLConnection
        theConnection) throws IOException
```

This method returns the output stream contained in the connection as an array of Strings, where each String corresponds to a line in the output stream.

Class ClientCookie *Deprecated*

```
public class ClientCookie
```

Inheritance Information

Extends: `Object`

Description

The functionality of this class has been expanded and included in the Cookie class of Cactus 1.2.

ClientCookie is a simple class for storing the information about a cookie contained in a set-cookie header. It is usually instantiated by AssertUtils.getCookies(HttpUrlConnection connection).

Constructor

```
public ClientCookie(...)
public ClientCookie(String theName, String theValue, String theComment,
        String theDomain, long theMaxAge, String thePath,
        boolean isSecure, float theVersion)
```

Methods

The following methods are accessors for all the properties specified in the constructor; they correspond to the different parts of the set-cookie response header.

```
getComment()
public String getComment()
```

```
getDomain()
public String getDomain()
```

```
getMaxAge()
public long getMaxAge()
```

```
getName()
public String getName()
```

```
getPath()
public String getPath()
```

```
getValue()
public String getValue()
```

```
getVersion()
public float getVersion()
```

```
isSecure()
public boolean isSecure()
```

Package org.apache.cactus.server

This package contains several framework classes (such as the redirector servlet) that are not covered in this chapter because test developers do not interact with them directly. However, it also contains wrapper classes for several implicit servlet objects with additional or slightly changed behavior. These classes are covered briefly.

Class FilterConfigWrapper

```
public class FilterConfigWrapper
```

Inheritance Information

Extends: `Object`

Implements: `FilterConfig`

Description

Wraps the original FilterConfig passed by the container to the filter redirector. Like ServletConfigWrapper, FilterConfigWrapper returns a wrapped version of ServletContext from getServletContext and provides setter methods for the Filter name and init parameters.

Methods

The methods are as specified in FilterConfig along with the following:

```
getInitParameterNames()
public Enumeration getInitParameterNames()
```

This method returns an enumeration containing both the init parameter names specified in the web.xml as well as those specified by a call to setInitParameter(). The values set by setInitParameter() take precedence.

```
setFilterName(String theFilterName)
public void setFilterName(String theFilterName)
```

This method sets a simulated Filter name that will be returned by getFilterName().

```
setInitParameter(String theName, String theValue)
public void setInitParameter(String theName, String theValue)
```

This method sets an "init" parameter for this FilterConfig as if it had been specified in the web.xml file. Initialization parameters set with this method will "shadow" those actually specified in the web.xml file.

Class HttpServletRequestWrapper

```
public class HttpServletRequestWrapper
```

Inheritance Information

Extends: `Object`

Implements: `javax.servlet.http.HttpServletRequest`

Description

HttpServletRequestWrapper is a thin wrapper around the HttpServletRequest object passed to the redirector servlet by the container.

Constructor

```
HttpServletRequestWrapper(HttpServletRequest theRequest,
                          ServletURL theURL)
public HttpServletRequestWrapper(HttpServletRequest theRequest,
                                 ServletURL theURL)
```

This constructor constructs a wrapper around the given request with the simulated URL contained in the "ServletURL" parameter.

Methods

The methods are generally identical to those specified in HttpServletRequest, except that URL methods such as getQueryString() return the values specified by the ServletURL passed to the constructor rather than those of the actual URL used to invoke the redirector servlet (unless the "ServletURL" parameter was null).

Two other significant changes exist:

```
getOriginalRequest()
public HttpServletRequest getOriginalRequest()
```

This method returns the original request that arrived at the redirector.

```
getRequestDispatcher(String thePath)
public RequestDispatcher getRequestDispatcher(String thePath)
```

This method returns a RequestDispatcherWrapper instead of a Request-Dispatcher. See the section on RequestDispatcherWrapper for details.

Class PageContextWrapper

```
public class PageContextWrapper
```

Inheritance Information

Extends: `AbstractPageContextWrapper` (and thereby `javax.servlet.jsp.PageContext.`)

Description

Wraps a PageContext object so that the implicit objects it returns are the appropriate Cactus-wrapped version of those objects.

Class RequestDispatcherWrapper

```
public class RequestDispatcherWrapper
```

Inheritance Information

Extends: `Object`

Implements: `javax.servlet.RequestDispatcher`

Description

RequestDispatcherWrapper is a thin wrapper for a RequestDispatcher object. The wrapper's purpose is to ensure that forwards and includes are carried out with the original HttpServletRequest instead of the Cactus wrapper (which could cause problems). Any includes or forwards in the tested code will lose the URL simulation capacities of the Cactus request wrapper after the forward. (If A forwards to B, the request received by B will not be a wrapped Cactus request, but the original HttpServletRequest generated by the container.)

NOTE

In Cactus 1.1 and earlier, this wrapper is returned from ServletContextWrapper.getRequestDispatcher(String) but not from HttpServletRequestWrapper.getRequestDispatcher(String). This inconsistency could yield unexpected results.

Constructor

```
RequestDispatcherWrapper(RequestDispatcher theOriginalDispatcher)
public RequestDispatcherWrapper(RequestDispatcher
                                theOriginalDispatcher)
```

Methods

The methods are as specified in RequestDispatcher, except that the include and forward methods will unwrap the "HttpServletRequest" parameter to use the underlying request.

Class ServletConfigWrapper

```
public class ServletConfigWrapper
```

Inheritance Information

Extends: `Object`

Implements: `javax.servlet.ServletConfig`

Description

ServletConfigWrapper wraps a ServletConfig object provided by the container to the redirector servlet. Because this object is the config for the redirector servlet, static initialization parameters expected by test code must be included in the web.xml file used by the redirector servlet or they must be set manually using the setInitParameter() method.

Constructor

```
ServletConfigWrapper(ServletConfig theOriginalConfig)
public ServletConfigWrapper(ServletConfig theOriginalConfig)
```

Methods

Methods are as specified in ServletConfig, except the following:

```
getInitParameterNames()
public Enumeration getInitParameterNames()
```

This method will return an enumeration containing both the init parameter names specified in the web.xml as well as those specified by a call to setInitParameter. The values set by setInitParameter take precedence.

```
setInitParameter(String theName, String theValue)
public void setInitParameter(String theName, String theValue)
```

This method sets an "init" parameter for this ServletConfig as if it had been specified in the web.xml file. Initialization parameters set with this method will "shadow" those actually specified in the web.xml file.

```
setServletName(String theServletName)
public void setServletName(String theServletName)
```

This method sets the servlet's name (retrieved by the getName() method).

Class ServletContextWrapper

```
public class ServletContextWrapper
```

Inheritance Information

Extends: `AbstractServletContextWrapper`

Implements: `javax.servlet.ServletContext`

Description

ServletContextWrapper is a simple wrapper that delegates almost all its calls to the wrapped ServletContext. One notable exception is that all messages passed to the wrapper's log methods are stored in a Vector of Strings (as well as being passed to the original log method) which can be retrieved with getLogs(). Beyond that, the only differences are that getServletContext and getRequestDispatcher return the Cactus wrapper objects, and it supports both getResourcePaths() for Servlet 2.2, and getResourcePaths(String) for Servlet 2.3.

Methods

```
getLogs()
public Vector getLogs()
```

This method returns a Vector of Strings containing each message that was logged with any of the ServletContext's log methods.

CHAPTER 16

HttpUnit API Reference

HttpUnit abstracts elements of an HTTP "conversation" between a server and a client in a way that makes it possible to run JUnit assertions against the result. This chapter details the HttpUnit framework. HttpUnit is designed so that most of the classes that are not directly used by a test developer are hidden from immediate view (as package-level access classes, inner classes, and so on). We used the published Javadoc for HttpUnit as a guide to help us choose which classes to include in this chapter.

HttpUnit automatically parses the HTML contained in a server response into a Document Object Model (DOM) tree. This is one of the key features of the framework as it enables most of the methods that return data about the server response, such as getLinks(). In addition to relying on the DOM tree under the covers, HttpUnit exposes the DOM to allow direct inspection. By interacting directly with the DOM when necessary, TestCases can perform more sophisticated assertions than are available through HttpUnit's convenience methods, but at the price of additional development effort.

Chapter 9 gives a basic example of DOM manipulation with HttpUnit. If you are interested in reading more, see http://www.w3.org/DOM/ for general information, and http://www.w3.org/DOM/2000/12/dom2-javadoc/ for the DOM API in Java.

Package com.meterware.httpunit

This package contains all the classes that comprise the HttpUnit framework. The key classes in the framework are WebConversation (and its parent class

WebClient), WebRequest, and WebResponse. A few classes represent elements of an HTML page (e.g., WebLink and WebTable), others subclass one of the three central players (e.g., PostMethodWebRequest) to provide specific functionality, and a final few act in a supporting role (HttpUnitException, for instance).

Class AuthorizationRequiredException

```
public class AuthorizationRequiredException extends RuntimeException
```

Inheritance Information

Extends: `Object`

Implements: `Serializable`

Description

AuthorizationRequiredException is thrown when the server returns a response that indicates the user must be authorized to view the resource. (See the section on WebClient for an example.)

Methods

```
getAuthenticationParameter(String parameterName)
public String getAuthenticationParameter(String parameterName)
```

This method returns the authentication value for the specified parameter. Under the Basic authentication scheme, there is only one parameter: "realm".

```
getAuthenticationScheme()
public String getAuthenticationScheme()
```

This method returns the authentication scheme used for this resource: Basic or Digest.

```
getMessage()
public String getMessage()
```

Class GetMethodWebRequest

```
public class GetMethodWebRequest
```

Inheritance Information

Extends: `WebRequestDescription`

GetMethodWebRequest is a WebRequest that uses the GET method (see the section on WebRequest for more details).

Constructors

```
GetMethodWebRequest(String urlString)
public GetMethodWebRequest(String urlString)

GetMethodWebRequest(URL urlBase, String urlString)
public GetMethodWebRequest(URL urlBase, String urlString)

GetMethodWebRequest(URL urlBase, String urlString, String target)
public GetMethodWebRequest(URL urlBase, String urlString, String target)
```

See the section on WebRequest for a description of these constructors.

Methods

```
getMethod()
public String getMethod()
```

This method returns the HTTP method of the request (in this case, GET).

```
getURLString()
protected String getURLString()
```

This method returns the full URL of the request, including all the parameters set with setParameter encoded in the query string.

Class HTMLSegment

```
public interface HTMLSegment
```

Inheritance Information

Known implementing classes: `WebResponse`, `TableCellDescription`

HTMLSegment defines the public interface for a chunk of parsed HTML. This interface specifies finder methods for elements of HTML represented in HttpUnit: forms, tables, and links. All the methods in this interface will throw org.xml.sax.SAXExceptions if errors occur when the underlying HTML is parsed.

Many of the examples in this chapter use functionality contained in this interface. See the sections on WebForm, WebLink, and WebTable to see its methods in use.

NOTE

Much of the functionality contained in WebResponse is described in this section.

Methods

```
getForms()
public WebForm[] getForms() throws SAXException;
```

This method returns an array corresponding to the forms found within the HTML segment, in the order in which they occur.

```
getFormWithID(String ID)
public WebForm getFormWithID(String ID) throws SAXException
```

This method gets the form with the specified "id" attribute.

```
getFormWithName(String name)
public WebForm getFormWithName(String name) throws SAXException
```

This method gets the form with the specified "name" attribute.

```
getLinks()
public WebLink[] getLinks() throws SAXException
```

This method returns an array corresponding to the links found within the HTML segment, in the order in which they appear.

```
getLinkWith(String text)
public WebLink getLinkWith(String text) throws SAXException
```

This method gets the first link with the specified user-clickable text in the underlying HTML.

```
getLinkWithImageText(String text)
public WebLink getLinkWithImageText(String text) throws SAXException
```

This method gets the first image link with the specified text as its "alt" attribute in the underlying HTML.

```
getTables()
public WebTable[] getTables() throws SAXException
```

This method returns an array corresponding to the top-level tables found within the HTML segment, in the order in which they appear.

```
getTableStartingWith(String text)
public WebTable getTableStartingWith(final String text) throws
                                                        SAXException
```

This method returns the first table in the HTML segment that has the specified text as the entire contents of its first non-blank row and non-blank column (no partial matches are allowed). See Listing 16.1 for an example.

NOTE

Both getTableStartingWith(final String text) and getTableStartingWithPrefix(String text) will recurse into any nested tables in an attempt to match their search criteria.

```
getTableStartingWithPrefix(String text)
public WebTable getTableStartingWithPrefix(String text) throws
                                                        SAXException
```

This method returns the first table in the HTML segment that has the specified text as the beginning of the contents of its first non-blank row and non-blank column (in other words, partial matches are allowed). See Listing 16.1 for an example.

```
/*
Supposing that the response object was based on the following HTML:
<!--begin-->
<table>
  <tr>
    <td>
      Pizza Hut
    </td>
    <td>
        restaurant
    </td>
  </tr>
</table>
<table>
  <tr>
    <td>
      Pizza
    </td>
    <td>
        Food
    </td>
  </tr>
</table>
<!--end-->
The following test would pass:
*/

public void testTableMatching() throws Exception{
  /*will retrieve the second table because a full match is required*/
  WebTable foodTable = response.getTableStartingWith("Pizza");

  /*will retrieve the first table as the prefix matches*/
  WebTable restaurantTable = response.getTableStartingWithPrefix("Pizza");

  assertEquals("Food", foodTable.getCellAsText(0,1));
  assertEquals("restaurant", restaurantTable.getCellAsText(0,1));
}
```

Listing 16.1 Demonstrating the different table finder methods.

```
getTableWithSummary(String summary)
public WebTable getTableWithSummary(String summary) throws SAXException
```

This method returns the first table with the specified String as its "summary" attribute.

```
getTableWithID(final String ID)
public WebTable getTableWithID(final String ID) throws SAXException
```

This method returns the first table with the specified String as its "id" attribute.

Class HttpException

```
public class HttpException
```

Inheritance Information

Extends: `RuntimeException`

Direct known subclasses: `HttpInternalErrorException`, `HttpNotFoundException`

Description

HttpException is thrown when the Web server under test would return a status code corresponding to a client or server error (4xx or 5xx):

```
public void testIllegalPageAccess() throws Exception{
  WebConversation wc = new WebConversation();
  try{
    wc.getResponse("http://www.junit.org/thispagedoesnotexist.jsp");
  }
  catch (HttpException e){
    System.out.println(e);
    assertEquals(404, e.getResponseCode());
  }
}
```

Methods

```
getResponseCode()
public int getResponseCode()
```

This method returns the HTTP status code of the response that caused the exception.

```
getMessage()
public String getMessage()
```

This method returns a String containing the status code as well as the reason given (if any) for the error.

Class HttpInternalErrorException

```
public class HttpInternalErrorException
```

Inheritance Information

Extends: HttpExceptionDescription

HttpInternalErrorException is thrown when a request results in a response with a status code of 5xx (server error). See the section on HttpException for details.

Class HttpNotFoundException

```
public class HttpNotFoundException
```

Inheritance Information

Extends: HttpException

Description

HttpNotFoundException is thrown when a request results in a response with a status code of 4xx (client error, generally a "not found" error). See the section on HttpException for details.

Class HttpUnitOptions

```
public abstract class HttpUnitOptions
```

Description

This class provides static setters and getters for a variety of properties that parameterize the behavior of HttpUnit. Because the options are stored in static member variables (and will thus affect all HttpUnit tests), we advise you to take care in setting them. The preferred strategy is to use setUp() to set the parameter and tearDown() to reset it to its default value:

```
public void setUp(){
  HttpUnitOptions.setParserWarningsEnabled(true);
}

public void tearDown(){
  HttpUnitOptions.setParserWarningsEnabled(false);
}
```

For options that should be set for entire suites of tests, you can use junit.extensions.TestSetup to make the setting and resetting of the property apply to the suite as a whole.

Methods

This "Methods" section is presented a little differently than others because HttpUnitOptions essentially consists of a set of exposed properties. Therefore, we've grouped the setters and getters instead of presenting them in alphabetical order.

```
autoRefresh
public static boolean getAutoRefresh()
public static void setAutoRefresh(boolean autoRefresh)
```

Default = false. This option specifies whether the WebClient automatically follows page refresh requests (that is, immediately calls getResponse() on the refresh request if latestResponse.getRefreshRequest() does not return null). The default of false allows for the redirect page to be inspected before the next page appears.

WARNING

Setting this property to true could result in an infinite loop if a page refreshes itself.

```
defaultCharacterSet
public static String getDefaultCharacterSet()
public static void setDefaultCharacterSet(String characterSet)
public static void resetDefaultCharacterSet()
```

Default = "iso-8859-1". This option specifies the character encoding that will be used for responses that do not specify encoding in their content-type header. resetDefaultCharacterSet() resets the default character set to iso-8859-1.

```
imagesTreatedAsAltText
public static boolean getImagesTreatedAsAltText()
public static void setImagesTreatedAsAltText(boolean asText)
```

Default = false. If this option is set to true, images will be treated as the value of their "alt" attribute for the purpose of searches (for example, WebResponse.getLinkWith(String)) and displays.

```
loggingHttpHeaders
public static boolean isLoggingHttpHeaders()
public static void setLoggingHttpHeaders(boolean enabled)
```

Default = false. If this option is set to true, both incoming and outgoing HTTP headers are logged to the System.out stream.

```
matchesIgnoreCase
public static boolean getMatchesIgnoreCase()
public static void setMatchesIgnoreCase( boolean ignoreCase )
```

Default = true (matches are case-insensitive). This option controls whether methods such as WebResponse.getTableStartingWith() are case-sensitive in their attempts to match the arguments to the returned HTML.

```
parameterValuesValidated
public static boolean getParameterValuesValidated()
public static void setParameterValuesValidated(boolean validated)
```

Default = true. This option specifies whether the values that are set in a WebRequest are checked against the legal values that the underlying form (if any) would allow.

```
parserWarningsEnabled
public static boolean getParserWarningsEnabled()
public static void setParserWarningsEnabled(boolean enabled)
```

Default = false. If this option is set to true, JTidy (the HTML parser used by HttpUnit) will print warnings to the System.out stream when it encounters HTML that is not structured according to the specification. This option can be useful in debugging unexpected results from HttpUnit. (See the section on WebForm for more information.)

```
redirectDelay
public static int getRedirectDelay()
public static void setRedirectDelay(int delayInMilliseconds)
```

Default = 0 milliseconds. This option controls how long WebClient will wait before following a redirect. It may need to be set higher if the server will not be ready for the redirect request immediately after the redirect is sent (an uncommon occurrence).

Class HttpUnitUtils

```
public class HttpUnitUtils
```

Description

HttpUnitUtils is used internally by WebResponse; it provides a static method to parse a header for content type and encoding information. Content type can also be retrieved from WebResponse.getContentType():

```
public void testContentAndEncoding()throws Exception{
  WebConversation wc = new WebConversation();
  WebResponse response = wc.getResponse("http://www.objectmentor.com/");
  String header = response.getHeaderField("Content-type");
  String[] typeAndEncoding =
HttpUnitUtils.parseContentTypeHeader(header);
  assertEquals("text/html",  typeAndEncoding[0]);
  /*don't expect encoding to be included*/
  assertNull(typeAndEncoding[1]);
}
```

Method

parseContentTypeHeader(String header)

`public static String[] parseContentTypeHeader(String header)`

The returned array contains the content type and the character encoding contained in the header (in that order). If no character encoding information is included, the second entry will be null.

Class IllegalRequestParameterException

`public abstract class IllegalRequestParameterException`

Inheritance Information

Extends: `RuntimeException`

Direct known subclasses: `IllegalFileParameterException, IllegalNonFileParameterException, IllegalParameterValueException, IllegalSubmitButtonException, IllegalUnnamedSubmitButtonException, MultipartFormRequiredException, NoSuchParameterException, SingleValuedParameterException`

Description

IllegalRequestParameterException is thrown when code attempts to set a request parameter that could not be set in a Web browser. See the section on WebForm for a description of how to create a request associated with an HTML form.

Various inner exception classes extend IllegalRequestParameterException to provide more specific information about the exact violation of the form's potential parameters. Most of the exceptions are self-explanatory and include helpful information in their messages (see the "Inheritance Information" section for a list of these exceptions). Following is an example of using IllegalRequestParameterException:

```
public void testIllegalSetting() throws Exception {
  WebConversation wc = new WebConversation();
  WebResponse resp = wc.getResponse("http://www.flimflam.com/order");
  WebForm form = response.getFormWithName("product_choice");
  WebRequest submit = form.getRequest();
  submit.setParameter("product_id", "101");//ok
  try{
    submit.setParameter("shipping_method", "Ultra-quick");
    fail("Ultra-quick shipping only availaible to logged-in users.");
  }
  catch(IllegalRequestParameterException e){}
}
```

Class MessageBodyWebRequest

```
public abstract class MessageBodyWebRequest
```

Inheritance Information

Extends: `WebRequest`

Direct known subclasses: `PostMethodWebRequest`, `PutMethodWebRequest`

Description

This class is used internally to support the stream-handling needs of PostMethodWebRequest and PutMethodWebRequest.

Methods

```
MessageBody newMessageBody();
protected abstract MessageBody newMessageBody();

completeRequest(URLConnection connection)
protected void completeRequest(URLConnection connection)
```

Class PostMethodWebRequest

```
public abstract class PostMethodWebRequest
```

Inheritance Information

Extends: `MessageBodyWebRequest`

Description

PostMethodWebRequest represents a request using the POST method. Tests will usually interact with this object through its superclass WebRequest (see the section on that class for details).

Constructors

```
PostMethodWebRequest(String urlString)
public PostMethodWebRequest(String urlString)

PostMethodWebRequest(String urlString, InputStream source,
                     String contentType)
public PostMethodWebRequest(String urlString, InputStream source,
                            String contentType)
```

This constructor constructs a PostMethodWebRequest that uses the specified InputStream as the message body, overriding any parameters/files set by other means. The "contentType" parameter specifies the content type of the body, including any character set information.

```
PostMethodWebRequest(URL urlBase, String urlString, String target)
public PostMethodWebRequest(URL urlBase, String urlString, String
                            target)
```

Methods

```
MessageBody newMessageBody();
protected MessageBody newMessageBody();
```

This method returns a MessageBody containing the stream specified by the constructor (if any), or an encoded representation of the parameters and files set so far on this request. newMessageBody() is used by the framework to select how the request will be written to the java.net.URLConnection.

```
String getMethod()
public String getMethod()
```

This method returns the method of this request (in this case, POST).

```
selectFile(String parameterName, File file)
public void selectFile( String parameterName, File file )

selectFile(String parameterName, File file, String contentType)
public void selectFile(String parameterName, File file,String
                       contentType)
```

These methods specify a file to be included in the request. They will throw an IllegalRequestParameter if the "parameterName" does not correspond to an expected file parameter.

Class PutMethodWebRequest

```
public class PutMethodWebRequest
```

Inheritance Information

Extends: `MessageBodyWebRequest`

Description

PutMethodWebRequest represents a request using the PUT method.

NOTE

Any parameters or files specified with selectFile() or setParameter() will be ignored. The content of the request is solely specified by the InputStream provided to the constructor.

Constructor

```
PutMethodWebRequest(String url, InputStream source, String contentType)
public PutMethodWebRequest(String url, InputStream source,
                           String contentType)
```

This constructor constructs a request with the specified InputStream forming the body of the request (the request headers are the only other information that will be sent). The "contentType" parameter specifies the content type of the body, including any character set information.

Methods

```
String getMethod()
public String getMethod()
```

This method returns the method of this request (in this case, PUT).

```
MessageBody newMessageBody()
protected MessageBody newMessageBody()
```

This method returns a MessageBody based solely on the InputStream provided in the constructor.

Class SubmitButton

```
public class SubmitButton
```

Inheritance Information

Extends: `Object`

Description

SubmitButton represents a submit button in an HTML form. It's used with Web-Form to create form submissions that simulate the user clicking a particular button. (See the section on WebForm for details and an example.)

Methods

```
getName()
public String getName()
```

This method returns the name of the button.

```
getValue()
public String getValue()
```

This method returns the value of the button.

```
isImageButton()
public boolean isImageButton()
```

This method returns true if the button is an image map.

Class TableCell

```
public class TableCell
```

Inheritance Information

Extends: `ParsedHTML` (package-access-level class)

Implements: `HTMLSegment`

Description

TableCell represents a cell in an HTML table. This class implements the HTMLSegment interface (see the section on that interface for more details), so test developers can interact with it through the methods (getLinks, getForms, getTables, and so on) defined there. In addition, TableCell provides a few methods specific to table cells (see the section on WebTable for an example).

Methods

asText()

```
public String asText()
```

This method returns the contents of the cell as a String.

getColSpan()

```
public int getColSpan()
```

This method returns the value of the "colspan" attribute of this cell in the underlying HTML document.

getDOM()

```
public org.w3c.dom.Node getDOM()
```

This method returns an org.w3c.dom.Node corresponding to the contents of this table cell represented as a DOM.

getRowSpan()

```
public int getRowSpan()
```

This method returns the value of the "rowspan" attribute of this cell in the underlying HTML document.

Class WebClient

```
public abstract class WebClient
```

Inheritance Information

Extends: `ObjectDescription`

WebClient emulates a Web browser for the purpose of maintaining context for a series of HTTP requests. It manages cookies, computes relative URLs, and presents a single object interface for sending requests to and retrieving responses from a server. Generally, every test method in an HttpUnit-based test case will need to access a WebClient.

WebClient is an abstract class with a single concrete subclass (WebConversation) within the HttpUnit framework; the closely related ServletUnit framework defines another one. As such, you will primarily use instances of WebConversation to access the functionality of WebClient.

The following example illustrates the basic use of WebClient/WebConversation:

```
public void testSiteAuthorization(,,,) throws Exception {
  WebConversation wc = new WebConversation();
  String siteUrl = "http://www.eDogFood.com/ordering.jsp";
  boolean caught = false;
  try{
    WebResponse resp = wc.getResponse(siteUrl);
  }
  catch(AuthorizationRequiredException e){
    System.out.println(e);
    caught = true;
  }
  assertTrue(caught);
  wc.setAuthorization("Jane Tester", "TestPassword123");
  WebResponse resp = wc.getResponse(siteUrl);
  assertEquals("Logged In - Welcome", resp.getTitle());
}
```

Methods

addCookie(String name, String value)

`public void addCookie(String name, String value)`

This method adds the specified name/value pair to the list of cookies to be sent with every request to the server. The server may also set such cookies:

```
public void testCookieLogonTransfer() throws Exception{
  WebConversation wc = new WebConversation();
  String siteUrl = "http://www.eDogFood.com/ordering.jsp";
  wc.setAuthorization("Jane Tester", "TestPassword123");
  WebResponse resp = wc.getResponse(siteUrl);

  String sessionIdKey = resp.getNewCookieNames()[0];
  String sessionIdValue = resp.getNewCookieValue(sessionKey);
  WebConversation newBrowser = new WebConversation();
  newBrowser.addCookie(sessionKey, sessionValue);
  newBrowser.getResponse(siteUrl);
  /*--would throw AuthorizationRequiredException if not logged in*/
}
```

```
getCookieHeaderField()
protected String getCookieHeaderField()
```

This method returns the value of the cookie header as a String. It appears to be used internally by WebClient, but it could be used externally for validation purposes.

```
getCookieNames()
public String[] getCookieNames()

getCookieValue(String name)
public String getCookieValue(String name)
```

These methods return the names and values of the active cookies that will be sent to the server with each request. (See addCookie() for an example.)

```
getFrameContents(String frameName)
public WebResponse getFrameContents(String frameName)
```

This method gets the contents of the frame with the specified name as a WebResponse. (See getFrameNames() for an example.)

```
getFrameNames()
public String[] getFrameNames()
```

This method returns a String[] containing the names of all the currently active frames in the virtual Web browser represented by the WebClient. The topmost frame can be retrieved with the keyword _top. As each request is made, the contents of the appropriate frame are replaced with the WebResponse resulting from the request. Assuming the String "fooFrame" is the target of the WebRequest request, resp and frame would refer to the same object after these lines were executed:

```
WebResponse resp = conversation.getResponse(request);
WebResponse frame = conversation.getFrameContents("fooFrame");
```

Listing 16.2 details how you can use frame interaction with HttpUnit. It may help to review the page the example is based on: http://java.sun.com/j2se/1.3/docs/api/index.html (the Javadoc for class URLConnection in java.net).

```
public void testFrameInteraction() throws Exception{
  /*Note: uses collections from java.util*/

  String site = "http://java.sun.com/j2se/1.3/docs/api/index.html";
  WebClient wc = new WebConversation();
  WebResponse response = wc.getResponse(site);

  /*assert that all of the expected frames exist*/
```

Listing 16.2 Use of frames in HttpUnit. (continues)

```
    String[] frameNames = wc.getFrameNames();
    List frameList = Arrays.asList(frameNames);
    assertTrue(frameList.contains("classFrame"));
    assertTrue(frameList.contains("packageListFrame"));
    assertTrue(frameList.contains("packageFrame"));
    assertTrue(frameList.contains("_top"));

    /*get the frame with the name 'packageFrame'*/
    response = wc.getFrameContents("packageFrame");

    /*follow a link which updates the classFrame
    *and assert that we end up in the correct place
    */
    WebLink link = response.getLinkWith("URLConnection");
    assertEquals("classFrame", link.getTarget());
    response = wc.getResponse(link.getRequest());
    String frameString = response.getText();
    assertTrue(frameString.indexOf("URLConnection") > -1);

    /*check that the frame that was updated was actually the classFrame */
    WebResponse frameContents = wc.getFrameContents("classFrame");
    assertSame(response, frameContents);
}
```

Listing 16.2 Use of frames in HttpUnit.

```
getHeaderFields()
protected java.util.Dictionary getHeaderFields()
```

This method returns a Dictionary containing all the active headers that will be sent to the server (including headers set by earlier responses and also those set by calls to setHeaderField).

```
getResponse(java.lang.String urlString)
public WebResponse getResponse(java.lang.String urlString)
                        throws java.net.MalformedURLException,
                               java.io.IOException,
                               org.xml.sax.SAXException
```

This method returns a WebResponse containing the result of a GET method request to the specified URL. It's essentially a convenience method for getResponse(new GetMethodWebRequest(urlString)) (see that method for details).

```
getResponse(WebRequest request)
public WebResponse getResponse(WebRequest request)
                        throws java.net.MalformedURLException,
                               java.io.IOException,
                               org.xml.sax.SAXException
```

One of the key methods in the HttpUnit API, getResponse() embodies a Web-browser request and server response. Functionally, it sends the specified WebRequest to the server using all the state information (cookies, headers, and so on) stored in the WebClient.

The list of exceptions is large but manageable. In most test methods, you'll want to declare that the test method throws Exception and allow JUnit to treat these occurrences as test failures. The java exceptions are simply passed on from classes in the java.net package (representing an illegal URL and IO problem during network connection respectively). The SAXException occurs when an error occurs while parsing the received page as XML.

```
getUserAgent()
public String getUserAgent()
```

This method gets the User-Agent header (the type of browser this WebClient is emulating) that is sent to the server.

```
newResponse(WebRequest request)
protected abstract WebResponse newResponse(WebRequest request)
                                throws java.net.MalformedURLException,
                                            java.io.IOException
```

This method is used internally to talk to the server and create a new WebResponse from the results.

```
setAuthorization(String userName, String password)
public void setAuthorization(String userName, String password)
```

This method sets the Authorization header using the basic authorization scheme. (See the "Description" section of this class for an example.)

```
setHeaderField(String fieldName, String fieldValue)
public void setHeaderField(String fieldName, String fieldValue)
```

This method sets a header that will be sent to the server with every request. If a header is set to null, that header is removed from future requests:

```
conversation.setHeaderField("Cache-Control", "Cache-Control :
                             no-cache");
```

```
setUserAgent(String userAgent)
public void setUserAgent(String userAgent)
```

This method sets the User-Agent header (used to emulate a type of browser).

```
updateClient(WebResponse response)
protected final void updateClient(WebResponse response)
                         throws java.net.MalformedURLException,
                                java.io.IOException,
                                org.xml.sax.SAXException
```

This method is used internally to update the state of the WebClient to reflect the results of the latest transaction.

Class WebConversation

```
public class WebConversation
```

Inheritance Information

Extends: `WebClient`

Description

WebConversation is the concrete implementation of WebClient; it provides no new external behavior. See the section on WebClient for details and examples.

Constructor

`WebConversation()`

```
public WebConversation()
```

Method

`newResponse(WebRequest request)`

```
protected WebResponse newResponse(WebRequest request)
                              throws java.net.MalformedURLException,
                                     java.io.IOException
```

Class WebForm

```
public class WebForm
```

Inheritance Information

Extends: `ObjectDescription`

This class represents an HTML form present in a Web page. It provides a variety of shortcut methods that make examining the form and writing assertions against it easier. It also provides the facility to create a WebRequest that simulates the submission of this form. (See the section on WebRequest for more details.)

NOTE

A common problem that occurs when working with WebForm relates to poorly structured HTML. HttpUnit uses an HTML parser (JTidy) that parses strictly according to the HTML specification. Any improperly nested tags are ignored. For instance, JTidy would not recognize the form tags in the following lines:

```
<table>
  <form>
    <tr>
      <td>form body</td>
    </tr>
  </form>
</table>
```

This behavior can cause inconsistent results in HttpUnit even though the (more forgiving) standard browsers will have no problems with the form. To check if your HTML is improperly formatted, call HttpUnitOptions.setParserWarningsEnabled(true) (see the section on HttpUnitOptions for details) before retrieving the page in question. Doing so will cause any warnings generated by JTidy during parsing to be printed to System.out.

Listing 16.2 (in the section on WebRequest) contains an example of using WebForm and WebRequest to access a form, verify it, and simulate a user's submission to that form.

Methods

```
getCharacterSet()
public String getCharacterSet()
```

This method gets the character set encoding for this form. This information is contained in the Content-type header for the parent page.

```
getDOMSubtree()
public org.w3c.dom.Node getDOMSubtree()
```

This method returns a copy of the DOM Node representing this form in the underlying page.

```
getID()
public String getID()
```

This method gets the "id" attribute of this form from the underlying HTML.

```
getName()
public String getName()
```

This method gets the HTML form name.

```
getOptions(String name)
public String[] getOptions(String name)
```

This method gets an array of Strings corresponding to the displayed options for the specified parameter name.

```
getOptionValues(String name)
public String[] getOptionValues(String name)
```

This method gets an array of Strings corresponding to the option values for the specified parameter name.

```
getParameterNames()
public String[] getParameterNames()
```

This method returns the names of all of the input parameters in the form in order.

```
String getParameterValue(String name)
public String getParameterValue(String name)
```

This method gets the default value associated with the given input parameter, or the first default value if multiple values are possible.

```
getParameterValues(String name)
public String[] getParameterValues(String name)
```

This method gets an array corresponding to the default values of the given input parameter. (If the input parameter supports only one value, the array will contain a single element.)

```
getRequest()
public WebRequest getRequest()
```

This method gets a request that simulates a submission of this form using the default button (see getRequest(SubmitButton button) for more information).

```
getRequest(String submitButtonName, String submitButtonValue)
public WebRequest getRequest(String submitButtonName,
                             String submitButtonValue)
```

This method gets a request that simulates a submission of this form using a submit button with the specified name and value. It will throw an IllegalSubmitButtonException if no such button exists.

```
getRequest(String submitButtonName)
public WebRequest getRequest(String submitButtonName)
```

This method gets a request that simulates a submission of this form using a submit button with the specified name. It will throw an IllegalSubmitButtonException if no such button exists.

```
getRequest(SubmitButton button)
public WebRequest getRequest(SubmitButton button)
```

This method gets a request that simulates a submission of this form using the specified submit button. If the "button" argument is null, getRequest() will attempt to submit using the default button (either the unnamed form button or the only button available in the form).

```
getRequest(SubmitButton button, int x, int y)
public WebRequest getRequest(SubmitButton button, int x, int y)
```

This method acts like getRequest(SubmitButton button) except it also sets the submit position on the button to the specified coordinates. This method will have an effect only if the button is an image button.

```
getSubmitButton(String name)
public SubmitButton getSubmitButton(String name)
```

This method gets the submit button for this form with the specified name (or null if there is no such button).

```
getSubmitButton(String name, String value)
public SubmitButton getSubmitButton(String name, String value)
```

This method gets the submit button for this form with the specified name and value (or null if there is no such button).

```
getSubmitButtons()
public SubmitButton[] getSubmitButtons()
```

This method gets an array of all the buttons declared in this form.

```
getTarget()
public String getTarget()
```

This method returns the "target" attribute of the underlying HTML form, or the parent page's target if no such attribute exists.

```
isFileParameter(String name)
public boolean isFileParameter(String name)
```

This method returns true if the named input parameter is of type "file", or false if not.

```
isMultiValuedParameter(String name)
public boolean isMultiValuedParameter(String name)
```

This method returns true if the named input parameter accepts multiple values, or false if not.

```
isSubmitAsMime()
public boolean isSubmitAsMime()
```

This method returns true if the form should be submitted with MIME encoding (URLEncoding is the default setting).

```
isTextParameter(String name)
public boolean isTextParameter(String name)
```

This method returns true if the named input parameter accepts raw text, false if not.

Class WebLink

```
public class WebLink
```

Inheritance Information

Extends: `ObjectDescription`

This class represents a link in an HTML page. You can retrieve the text of the link, the URL it points to, its target, or its DOM structure. WebLink also provides a method to get a WebRequest version of the link that can be fed back into a WebConversation/WebClient.

The following example gets all the links on a page and follows each one. If no exceptions are thrown, the link is assumed to be good:

```
public void testAllLinks() throws Exception {
  WebConversation wc = new WebConversation();
  WebResponse response = wc.getResponse("http://www.objectmentor.com/");
  WebLink[] links = response.getLinks();
  for(int i =0; i < links.length; i++){
    WebResponse resp = wc.getResponse(links[i].getRequest());
    System.out.println(i+ " followed link " +
           links[i].getRequest().getURL());
            /*no exceptions, page is OK!*/
  }
}
```

Methods

```
asText()
public String asText()
```

This method returns the user-clickable text corresponding to this link.

```
getDOMSubtree()
public org.w3c.dom.Node getDOMSubtree()
```

This method returns a copy of the DOM Node representing this form in the underlying page.

```
getRequest()
public WebRequest getRequest()
```

This method gets a new WebRequest equivalent to a user click on the link.

```
getTarget()
public String getTarget()
```

This method gets the target frame for this link.

```
getURLString()
public String getURLString()
```

This method returns the "href" attribute of the underlying HTML tag.

Class WebRequest

```
public abstract class WebRequest
```

Inheritance Information

Extends: `Object`

Direct known subclasses: `GetMethodWebRequest, MessageBodyWebRequest`

Description

WebRequest represents a generic HTTP request to a Web server. This class is one of the most frequently used in the HttpUnit framework. Several other classes declare methods that return WebRequests representing specific types of requests (such as form submissions and link-clicks). WebRequests can also be constructed from a String representing a URL. In all cases, you can set request parameters and inspect various properties of the request before sending it to the server through a WebClient.

If you use a WebForm to create a WebRequest (and the parameterValuesValidated property of HttpUnitOptions is set to true), then the WebForm will restrict the possible values a given parameter can be set to. The following code snippet would not work unless jojoForm contained a parameter named "mojo" that accepted "zombo" as an input value:

```
WebForm jojoForm = response.getFormWithName("jojoForm");
WebRequest request = jojoForm.getRequest();
request.setParameter("mojo", "zombo");
```

As a result, some of the methods exposed as public in this class will always throw exceptions in certain subclasses (selectFile will never work in a GetMethodWebRequest, which cannot be based on a form).

Listing 16.3 gives an example of using WebRequest and WebForm to simulate a user's form submission.

```
//<form name="dogInfo" enctype="multipart/form-data"  method="post">
//Name of Your Dog:<INPUT type="text" NAME="name" VALUE="Rover">
```

Listing 16.3 Using WebForm and WebRequest to simulate form submission. (continues)

```
//<BR>
//Type Of Dog Food:
//<SELECT NAME="dogFood" multiple>
//<OPTION VALUE="1">1. Kibbles & Bits</OPTION>
//<OPTION VALUE="2">2. Feisty Brand</OPTION>
//<OPTION VALUE="3" SELECTED>3. Chelmore Dog Crunch</OPTION>
//</SELECT>
//<BR>
//Tell us some activities your dog likes:<SELECT NAME="activities">
//<OPTION VALUE="frisbee">frisbee</OPTION>
//<OPTION VALUE="walks">walks</OPTION>
//<OPTION VALUE="dogGolf">Dog Golf!</OPTION>
//</select>
//<BR>
//Upload a Cute Dog Picture!:<input type="file" name="dogPicture"/>
//<p>
//<input type="submit" value="Bark!"/>
//<input type="submit" value="Woof!"/>
//
//</form>
public void testFormSubmission() throws Exception{
  WebConversation wc = new WebConversation();
  WebResponse response = wc.getResponse("http://www.eDogFood.com");
  WebForm form = response.getFormWithName("dogInfo");
  /*check important parameters*/
  assertTrue(form.isFileParameter("dogPicture"));

  String[] activities = form.getParameterValues("activities");
  assertEquals("frisbee", activities[0]);
  /*Note: only gets the *selected* parameter values.*/

  assertTrue(form.isMultiValuedParameter("dogFood"));
  submitForm(form);
}

private void submitForm(WebForm form) throws Exception{
  /*could also use the shortcut methods to get a request*/
  SubmitButton button = form.getSubmitButton("submit", "Bark!");
  WebRequest request  = form.getRequest(button);

  /*would throw an IllegalRequestParameterException- activity is not in
  the list of acceptable values.*/
  //request.setParameter("activities", "canineBowling");

  request.selectFile("dogPicture", new java.io.File("C:\\edgar.jpg"));
  request.setParameter("dogFood", new String[]{"1","3"});
```

Listing 16.3 Using WebForm and WebRequest to simulate form submission. (continues)

```
    /*Test submission without the Dog's name:*/
    request.removeParameter("name");

    WebResponse response = conversation.getResponse(request);
    /*do assertions on the response*/
}
```

Listing 16.3 Using WebForm and WebRequest to simulate form submission.

Constructors

```
WebRequest(String urlString)
protected WebRequest(String urlString)
```

This constructor constructs a new WebRequest to point to the specified URL (represented as a String).

```
WebRequest(URL urlBase, String urlString)
protected WebRequest(URL urlBase, String urlString)
```

This constructor constructs a WebRequest by concatenating the base URL with the relative urlString.

```
WebRequest(URL urlBase, String urlString, String target)
protected WebRequest(URL urlBase, String urlString, String target)
```

This constructor is the same as WebRequest(URL urlBase, String urlString), except it also specifies the target frame of the request.

```
WebRequest(URL urlBase, String urlString, String target,
           WebForm sourceForm, SubmitButton button)
protected WebRequest(URL urlBase, String urlString, String target,
                     WebForm sourceForm, SubmitButton button)

WebRequest(WebRequest baseRequest, String urlString, String target)
protected WebRequest (WebRequest baseRequest, String urlString,
                      String target) throws MalformedURLException
```

These two protected constructors are used internally by the framework to build requests out of forms and other requests.

Methods

```
completeRequestURLConnection connection)
protected void completeRequest(URLConnection connection)
                                                    throws IOException
```

This method is meant to be overridden to provide the actual machinery for sending the request to the server using different methods (POST, GET, PUT, and so on).

getCharacterSet()
```
protected final String getCharacterSet()
```

getMethod()
```
public abstract String getMethod()
```

This method returns the method of the HTTP request (POST, GET, PUT, and so on).

getParameter(String name)
```
public String getParameter(String name)
```

This method returns the value of the named parameter in the request, or null if one has not been set.

getParameterNames()
```
public java.util.Enumeration getParameterNames()
```

This method returns an Enumeration containing the names of all the parameters set in the request so far (either using the methods of WebRequest or specified as defaults in the form on which this request is based).

getParameterString()
```
protected final String getParameterString()
```

See getQueryString().

getParameterValues(String name)
```
public String[] getParameterValues(String name)
```

This method returns all the values set so far for the named parameter as a String array.

getQueryString()
```
public String getQueryString()
```

This method returns the query string for this request. It will work even if the request would not generate a visible query string in real life. The number of characters in the query string is limited only by the capacity of the java String.

getTarget()
```
public String getTarget()
```

This method returns the target frame for this request.

getURL()
```
public java.net.URL getURL() throws MalformedURLException
```

This method returns a new URL corresponding to the URL that will be used to submit this request.

getURLBase()
```
protected final URL getURLBase()
```

```
getURLString()
protected String getURLString()

hasNoParameters()
protected final boolean hasNoParameters()

isFileParameter(String name)
protected boolean isFileParameter(String name)

isMimeEncoded()
protected final boolean isMimeEncoded()
```

These methods are all used internally by WebRequest and its subclasses.

```
removeParameter(String name)
public void removeParameter(String name)
```

This method removes a previously set parameter from the request.

```
selectFile(String parameterName, File file)
public void selectFile(String parameterName, File file)

selectFile(String parameterName, File file, String contentType)
public void selectFile(String parameterName, File file,
                       String contentType)
```

These methods select a file for upload if the form this WebRequest is based on supports the named parameter as a file upload parameter.

```
setParameter(String name, String value)
public void setParameter(String name, String value)

setParameter(String name, String[] values)
public void setParameter(String name, String[] values)
```

These methods set the named parameter either to the single value or the String array, depending on which method is called. If the underlying form (if any) would not allow such a value to be set, an IllegalRequestParameterException will be thrown.

```
toString()
public String toString()
```

This method returns the method type and URL string for this request.

Class WebResponse

```
public abstract class WebResponse
```

Inheritance Information

Extends: `Object`

Implements: `HTMLSegment`

Description

WebResponse represents the response from the Web server to a request. It is one of the core abstractions of the HttpUnit framework. This class provides a variety of methods that expose properties of the underlying response for inspection. Users of the class can get a DOM tree representing the HTML document, get newly set cookie names and values, inspect header fields, and so on. A variety of examples of WebResponse use appear throughout this chapter. Because WebResponse is abstract, WebResponse objects that appear in HttpUnit tests will likely be of type HttpWebResponse (a package-level access class).

NOTE

WebResponse implements the HTML segment interface. For the sake of brevity, methods belonging to that interface are defined and described there. WebResponse also declares several methods as protected. Because WebResponse is not meant to be subclassed as part of ordinary development, these methods are listed but not described.

Constructor

```
WebResponse(String target, URL url)
protected WebResponse(String target, URL url)
```

Methods

```
defineRawInputStream(InputStream inputStream)
protected final void defineRawInputStream(InputStream inputStream)
```

```
getCharacterSet()
public String getCharacterSet()
```

This method returns the charset portion (if any) of the HTTP Content-type header for this response.

```
getContentType()
public String getContentType()
```

This method returns the content type portion (as distinct from the character set portion) of the HTTP Content-type header for this response.

```
getDOM()
public org.w3c.dom.Document getDOM() throws org.xml.SAXException
```

This method attempts to return the DOM tree associated with this response. If the response is determined to be HTML, a special HTML-savvy parser (JTidy) will be used. If not, a regular SAX parser will be used on the response text. If errors are encountered during parsing (for instance, if the response contains neither HTML nor XML), a SAXException will be thrown.

```
getFrameNames()
public String[] getFrameNames() throws SAXException
```

This method returns an array containing the names of all the frames contained in this page. You can retrieve the contents of individual frames by these names from the WebClient (see that section for details).

```
getHeaderField(String fieldName)
public String getHeaderField(String fieldName)
```

This method gets the contents of the header field specified by the given name:

```
public void testContentLength() throws Exception{
  WebConversation conversation = new WebConversation();
  WebResponse response =
conversation.getResponse("http://www.junit.org");
  assertEquals("6575", response.getHeaderField("CONTENT-LENGTH"));
}
```

```
getInputStream()
public InputStream getInputStream()
```

This method returns the textual contents of this response as an input stream.

```
getNewCookieNames()
public String[] getNewCookieNames()
```

This method returns all the cookie names defined as part of this response. (See the section on WebClient.addCookie for an example of this method in action.)

```
getNewCookieValue(String name)
public String getNewCookieValue(String name)
```

This method returns the value associated with the given new cookie name (see getNewCookieNames()).

```
getRefreshDelay()
public int getRefreshDelay()
```

This method returns the delay specified by the refresh metatag contained in the header (or 0 if none is found). This delay corresponds the waiting period before a standard browser would follow the refresh request.

```
getRefreshRequest()
public WebRequest getRefreshRequest()
```

This method gets the WebRequest embodying the refresh URL contained in the refresh metatag in the header (or null if none exists).

```
getResponseCode()
public abstract int getResponseCode()
```

This method returns the HTTP response code for this request.

```
getTarget()
public String getTarget()
```

This method gets the frame in which the WebResponse resides (the default frame for any WebRequests originating from this response).

```
getTitle()
public String getTitle() throws SAXException
```

This method returns the title element of the underlying HTML page.

```
getText()
public String getText() throws IOException
```

This method returns a String representation of the underlying HTML page (roughly equivalent to calling "view source" in a traditional browser). This method is preferred over toString() for the retrieval of page contents.

```
getURL()
public java.net.URL getURL()
```

This method returns the URL of the request that generated this response.

```
isHTML()
public boolean isHTML()
```

This method returns true if the content-type for the underlying page is specified as "text/html".

```
loadResponseText()
protected void loadResponseText() throws IOException

newResponse(URLConnection connection)
public static WebResponse newResponse(URLConnection connection)
                                       throws IOException

readRefreshRequest(String contentTypeHeader)
protected final void readRefreshRequest(String contentTypeHeader)

setContentTypeHeaderString value)
protected void setContentTypeHeaderString value)

toString()
public String toString()
```

In the default implementation, this method returns the response text. In Http-WebResponse (the only concrete subclass in the HttpUnit API), it returns only the response headers.

Class WebTable

```
public class WebTable
```

Inheritance Information

Extends: `ObjectDescription`

WebTable represents an HTML table. It provides methods to get various attributes of a table (row count, column count, id, and summary) and methods to get single table cells (as TableCells or as text), and also lets you convert the entire table into a array-based representation.

Methods

asText()

```
public String[][] asText()
```

This method returns the entire table as a two-dimensional String array. The first dimension contains the rows, and the second dimension contains the cells.

getCell(int row, int column) *Deprecated*

```
public String getCell(int row, int column)
```

Use getCellAsText(int row, int column).

getCellAsText(int row, int column)

```
public String getCellAsText(int row, int column)
```

This method returns the contents of the cell in the given position as text. The row and column numbers are zero based, and this method will throw an IndexOutOfBoundsException if the parameters are not within the table's range.

getColumnCount()

```
public int getColumnCount()
```

getID()

```
public String getID()
```

getRowCount()

```
public int getRowCount()
```

getSummary()

```
public String getSummary()
```

getTableCell(int row, int column)

```
public TableCell getTableCell(int row, int column)
```

This method returns the contents of the cell in the given position as a TableCell. The row and column numbers are zero based, and this method will throw an IndexOutOfBoundsException if the parameters are not within the table's range.

purgeEmptyCells()

```
public void purgeEmptyCells()
```

This method removes from this table all rows and columns in that do not contain anything.

CHAPTER 17

JUnitPerf API Reference

JUnitPerf is a small set of test decorators and related classes that extend the JUnit API. In order to use JUnitPerf, you will need to be familiar with the functionality and use of basic JUnit tests as well as junit.extensions.TestDecorator.

Package com.clarkware.junitperf

This package contains all of the classes that make up JUnitPerf. The key classes in this package are LoadTest and TimedTest (as well as TimedTest's associated Timer interface). ConstantTimer and RandomTimer provide implementations of the Timer interface. The remaining classes are used mainly by the framework.

Class ConstantTimer

```
public class ConstantTimer
```

Inheritance Information

Extends: `Object`

Implements: `Timer`

Description

ConstantTimer is a Timer that always returns a constant delay. (See the sections on Timer and LoadTest for more information.)

Constructor

```
ConstantTimer(long delay)
public ConstantTimer(long delay)
```

This constructor constructs a Timer with the specified delay in milliseconds.

Method

```
getDelay()
public long getDelay()
```

This method returns the delay specified by the constructor.

Class LoadTest

```
public class LoadTest
```

Inheritance Information

Extends: `Object`

Implements: `junit.framework.Test`

Description

LoadTest runs a Test with a specified number of concurrent users and/or a specified number of iterations for each user. Each Test is run in a separate thread, and LoadTest waits until all these threads have completed before ending the test. To create a Test with 20 simulated users, you would use the following code:

```
Test targetTest = new ServerTest("testProcessPage");
LoadTest loadTest = new LoadTest(targetTest, 20);
```

To create a LoadTest that simulates users who run a test multiple times, first wrap the test in a junit.framework.RepeatedTest and decorate it, or use the convenience constructor provided by LoadTest to do the same thing (see Listing 17.1 and the "Constructors" section for examples).

You can combine LoadTests with Timers to provide ramping behavior. Adding a Timer instance provides a delay between the addition of each new user to the pool of active users. The timer's getDelay() method specifies the amount of time between additions.

NOTE

The Timer specifies the delay between the addition of users, not the delay between successive runs of the same decorated Test, which is controlled by a Timer-unaware junit.extensions.RepeatedTest. However, it would be trivial to extend RepeatedTest to add Timer functionality to it. See Listing 17.1 for an example.

You can combine LoadTest with a TimedTest to provide performance criteria for the load test. Either a TimedTest can be used to decorate the LoadTest (to ensure that execution of the whole test does not exceed a certain period of time) or the LoadTest can decorate a TimedTest (so that no individual Test exceeds the specified time, even when the system is under load).

LoadTest lets users specify the atomicity of the test under decoration. There are two modes: atomic and non-atomic. A LoadTest that does not enforce atomicity waits only for the threads simulating users to terminate before terminating itself—the Test is assumed to police its own threads. If atomicity is enforced, the LoadTest waits on all threads spawned by the decorated Test. In addition, an uncaught exception thrown during atomic LoadTest execution will interrupt all the threads spawned by the test.

Listing 17.1 demonstrates the use of LoadTest with other test decorators to create complex performance expectations.

```
import junit.framework.*;
import junit.extensions.RepeatedTest;
import com.clarkware.junitperf.*;
import test.com.company.ServerTest;

public class ServerLoadTest{

  public static Test suite(){

    /*create a basic JUnit test*/
    Test basicTest = new ServerTest("testProcessPage");

    /*
      Wrap basicTest in a TimedTest—a page load should
      never exceed 5 seconds.
     */
    Test timedTest = new TimedTest(basicTest, 5000L);

    /*
      Wrap timedTest in a RepeatedTimerTest (defined below) to simulate
      multiple page hits with time between repeat page views.
     */

     /*average 3.5 s. between views, with a variation of 2.5 s.*/
     Timer timer = new RandomTimer(3500L, 2.50);
     /*25 page views per user*/
     Test repeatedTest = new RepeatedTimerTest(timedTest, 25, timer);

     /*
```

Listing 17.1 LoadTest used with other decorators. (continues)

```
        Now make the repeated page viewing part of a load test: 10
        concurrent users, added at constant 5s intervals.
       */
       timer = new ConstantTimer(5000);
       Test loadTest = new LoadTest(repeatedTest, 10, timer);

       /*
         Finally set a maximum time out for the load test with another
         TimedTest: time should not exceed 350 s.
        */
       Test loadTestWithTimeOut = new TimedTest(loadTest, 350000);

       return loadTestWithTimeOut;
   }//end suite()

     public static void main(String[] args){
         junit.textui.TestRunner.run(suite());
     }
}

/**
 * Adds a delay specified by a Timer between iterations of
 * the test.
 */
class RepeatedTimerTest extends RepeatedTest{
  Timer timer;
  private int repeats;
  public RepeatedTimerTest(Test test, int repeats, Timer timer){
    super(test, repeats);
    this.repeats = repeats;
    this.timer = timer;
  }

  public void run(TestResult result) {

    for (int i= 0; i < repeats; i++) {

       /*verifies that the test should continue*/
       if (result.shouldStop()){
         break;
       }

       /*wait for delay given by timer*/
       try {
         Thread.sleep(timer.getDelay());
       }
       catch(InterruptedException ignored) {
```

Listing 17.1 LoadTest used with other decorators. (continues)

```
        }

        /* run the Test*/
        basicRun(result);

      }
    }

}//class
```

Listing 17.1 LoadTest used with other decorators.

Constructors

`LoadTest(Test test, int users)`

`public LoadTest(Test test, int users)`

This constructor decorates the specified Test as a LoadTest with the specified number of concurrent users and a user-addition delay of zero milliseconds (all threads start at once).

`LoadTest(Test test, int users, int iterations)`

`public LoadTest(Test test, int users, int iterations)`

This constructor decorates the specified Test as a LoadTest with the specified number of concurrent users, the number of iterations per user (that is, the number of times the Test is repeated), and a user-addition delay of zero milliseconds (all threads start at once).

`LoadTest(Test test, int users, int iterations, Timer timer)`

`public LoadTest(Test test, int users, int iterations, Timer timer)`

This constructor decorates the specified Test as a LoadTest with the specified number of concurrent users, the number of iterations per user, and a user-addition delay drawn from the Timer argument.

`LoadTest(Test test, int users, Timer timer)`

`public LoadTest(Test test, int users, Timer timer)`

This constructor decorates the specified Test as a LoadTest with the specified number of concurrent users and a user-addition delay drawn from the Timer argument.

Methods

`countTestCases()`

`public int countTestCases()`

This method returns the total number of TestCases run by this LoadTest (essentially decoratedTest.countTestCases() multiplied by the number of users).

run()
```
public int countTestCases()
```

setEnforceTestAtomicity(boolean isAtomic)
```
public void setEnforceTestAtomicity(boolean isAtomic)
```

This method sets the enforcement policy of the LoadTest with respect to test atomicity. The policy should be set to true when the completion of threads spawned by the decorated Test is essential to the completion of the Test but the decorated Test does not wait on its own spawned threads.

Class RandomTimer

```
public class RandomTimer
```

Inheritance Information

Extends: `Object`

Implements: `Timer`

Description

RandomTimer is a Timer (see the sections on Timer and LoadTest) that returns random delays based on the average delay and variation specified in the constructor.

Constructor

RandomTimer(long delay, double variation)
```
public RandomTimer(long delay, double variation)
```

Both the base delay and the potential variation are in milliseconds (despite the difference in types). getDelay() will return a number between delay and delay + variation. (In other words, the variation will never be negative.)

Method

getDelay()
```
public long getDelay()
```

Class ThreadBarrier

```
public class ThreadBarrier
```

Inheritance Information

Extends: `Object`

Description

ThreadBarrier waits for a constructor-defined number of threads to complete execution and reports on whether the number has been reached. LoadTest uses it in non-atomic mode to keep track of the status of the threads used for test-running.

Constructor

```
ThreadBarrier(int numDispatched)
public ThreadBarrier(int numDispatched)
```

This constructor constructs a ThreadBarrier with the given number of threads to wait for.

Methods

```
onCompletion(Thread t)
public synchronized void onCompletion(Thread t)
```

This method is called when the "Thread" argument has finished execution.

```
isReached()
public boolean isReached()
```

This method returns true if the thread barrier has been reached—that is, if the number of Threads specified in the constructor equals the number of times onCompletion() has been called.

NOTE

If onCompletion() is called *more* times than the number of threads waited for, the isReached() method will return false. Because the ThreadBarrier class is intended for internal use, this result should not present a problem for test developers.

Class ThreadedTest

```
public class ThreadedTest
```

Inheritance Information

Extends: `Object`

Implements: `junit.framework.Test`

Description

ThreadedTest is a decorator that runs a Test in a separate thread. LoadTest uses this class internally to manage the creation of multiple users running a Test simultaneously.

Constructors

ThreadedTest(Test test)

```
public ThreadedTest(Test test)
```

This constructor creates a Test that will run in its own thread. The new thread belongs to the current thread group.

ThreadedTest(Test test, ThreadGroup group, ThreadBarrier barrier)

```
public ThreadedTest(Test test)
```

This constructor creates a Test that will run in its own thread. The new thread belongs to the specified thread group and will register its completion with the ThreadBarrier.

Methods

countTestCases()

```
public int countTestCases()
```

run(TestResult result)

```
public void run(TestResult result)
```

toString()

```
public String toString()
```

Class ThreadedTestGroup

```
public class ThreadedTestGroup
```

Inheritance Information

Extends: `ThreadGroup`

Description

ThreadedTestGroup is a subclass of ThreadGroup used by the framework for exception handling while using ThreadedTests. Uncaught exceptions in a ThreadedTestGroup are added as failures or errors to the TestResult passed into setTestResult(). This class is used by LoadTest to keep track of and manage threads that simulate users.

Constructor

ThreadedTestGroup(Test test)

```
public ThreadedTestGroup(Test test)
```

This constructor constructs a new ThreadGroup associated with the given Test (the association is maintained so that accurate failures will result from testing).

Method

```
setTestResult(TestResult result)
public void setTestResult(TestResult result)
```

This method sets the TestResult object that failures should be registered with.

```
uncaughtException(Thread t, Throwable e)
public void uncaughtException(Thread t, Throwable e)
```

This method is overridden from ThreadGroup to catch uncaught, non-ThreadDeath throwables and record them as test failures. It interrupts all the threads in the group if such a throwable is caught.

Class TimedTest

```
public class TimedTest
```

Inheritance Information

Extends: `junit.framework.extensions.TestDecorator`

Implements: `junit.framework.Test`

Description

TimedTest is a TestDecorator that fails the decorated Test if the specified time limit is exceeded. You could use this class on individual TestCases for fine-grained results, or on TestSuites/TestDecorators (such as RepeatedTests or LoadTests) for aggregate results. (See the section on LoadTest for information about how to combine the two decorators.)

NOTE

The time a JUnit test takes to run includes the time consumed by the setUp() and tearDown() methods as well as the running of the actual test. Users of TimedTest should factor the effect of setUp() and tearDown() into their specified performance criteria.

You can construct two types of TimedTests. The first waits until the Test has completed and then checks the elapsed time against the specified maximum. The second fails immediately if the elapsed time exceeds the maximum.

This second kind of TimedTest carries a few caveats; you should weigh these drawbacks against the advantages of faster test runs, should the maximum time be exceeded. First, TimedTest spawns a thread to run the decorated test that is not externally terminated, even if the time runs out. Second, because of implementation details, a slim chance exists that a TimedTest using this method will not fail even if the maximum time has been exceeded. The likelihood of this occurrence increases as the number of threads running as peers of the thread that called run() on the TimedTest increases. Because of this possibility, it is bad idea to wrap a TimedTest using the second method in a LoadTest (where the number of threads running as peers of the TimedTest can be high).

Constructors

```
TimedTest(Test test, long maxElapsedTime)
public TimedTest(Test test, long maxElapsedTime)
```

This constructor decorates the specified Test with the given time in milliseconds. The TimedTest will wait for the completion of the test and then measure the elapsed time against the specified maximum. If the elapsed time exceeds the maximum, the test will fail. TimedTests that fail in this manner include the information on the expected versus actual time in their failure messages. The following code creates a new ServerTest instance that executes the testProcessPage method, and then decorates it so it will fail (after the fact) if the test takes longer than half a second to complete:

```
long maximumTime = 500;
Test targetTest = new ServerTest("testProcessPage");
TimedTest test = new TimedTest(targetTest, maximumTime);
```

```
TimedTest(Test test, long maxElapsedTime, boolean waitForCompletion)
public TimedTest(Test test, long maxElapsedTime, boolean
                                           waitForCompletion)
```

This constructor decorates the specified Test with the given time in milliseconds. Depending on the value of waitForCompletion, the TimedTest will either wait for the completion of the test and then measure the elapsed time against the specified maximum (true, see the previous constructor) or fail the test immediately if the specified time is exceeded (false).

This TimedTest will fail after 2.5 seconds if the ServerTest has not finished its execution by that point:

```
long maximumTime = 2500;
Test targetTest = new ServerTest("testPotentially30SecondMethod");
TimedTest test = new TimedTest(targetTest, 2500, false);
```

Methods

```
countTestCases()
public int countTestCases()
```

See junit.framework.TestDecorator.

```
outOfTime()
public boolean outOfTime()
```

This method returns whether the TimedTest exceeded the specified maximum time. This method is intended to be called after run() as a reporting tool.

`run(junit.framework.TestResult result)`

```
public void run(junit.framework.TestResult result)
```

This method runs the test in one of the two ways specified by the constructor.

`runUntilTestCompletion(junit.framework.TestResult result)`

```
protected void runUntilTestCompletion(TestResult result)
```

`runUntilTimeExpires(junit.framework.TestResult result)`

```
protected void runUntilTimeExpires(final junit.framework.TestResult
                                                        result)
```

These methods provide the two types of timed execution. They're used internally.

`toString()`

```
public String toString()
```

This method informs you whether the test is waiting or non-waiting, but it does not give information about the maximum time specified for this TimedTest instance.

Interface Timer

```
public interface Timer
```

Description

This interface defines a timer that can be used with LoadTest to regulate the addition of new users to the LoadTest. This interface can be implemented by developers who wish to customize the simulation of user loads.

Method

`getDelay()`

```
public long getDelay()
```

This method returns a number of milliseconds representing the delay between two events regulated by this Timer.

Index

A

B

C

D

I

J

K

L

Q

R

S

T

U

V

W